Lecture Notes in Computer Science 8203

Commenced Publication in 1973
Founding and Former Series Editors:
Gerhard Goos, Juris Hartmanis, and Jan van Leeuwen

Rafael Accorsi   Silvio Ranise (Eds.)

Security and Trust Management

9th International Workshop, STM 2013
Egham, UK, September 12-13, 2013
Proceedings

 Springer

Volume Editors

Rafael Accorsi
University of Freiburg
Department of Telematics
Friedrichstraße 50
79098 Freiburg, Germany
E-mail: rafael.accorsi@iig.uni-freiburg.de

Silvio Ranise
Fondazione Bruno Kessler (FBK)
Centre for Information Technology
Via Sommarive 18
38123 Trento, Italy
E-mail: ranise@fbk.eu

ISSN 0302-9743　　　　　　　　　　　　e-ISSN 1611-3349
ISBN 978-3-642-41097-0　　　　　　　　e-ISBN 978-3-642-41098-7
DOI 10.1007/978-3-642-41098-7
Springer Heidelberg New York Dordrecht London

Library of Congress Control Number: 2013948239

CR Subject Classification (1998): K.6.5, K.4.4, E.3, D.4.6, C.2, J.1

LNCS Sublibrary: SL 4 – Security and Cryptology

Typesetting: Camera-ready by author, data conversion by Scientific Publishing Services, Chennai, India

Printed on acid-free paper

Springer is part of Springer Science+Business Media (www.springer.com)

Preface

The Security and Trust Management (STM) group is a Working Group (WG) of the European Research Consortium in Informatics and Mathematics (ERCIM) established in 2005 to provide a platform for researchers to present and discuss their ideas and foster cooperation. One of the means to achieve these goals is the organization of a yearly workshop. These proceedings contain the papers selected for presentation at the 9th International Workshop on Security and Trust Management (STM 2013) held September 12–13, 2013 in conjunction with the 18th European Symposium on Research in Computer Security (ESORICS 2013) in Egham, U.K.

The STM 2013 workshop received 47 submissions that were evaluated on the basis of their significance, novelty, technical quality, and appropriateness to the STM audience. After intensive reviewing and electronic discussions, 15 papers were selected for presentation at the workshop, giving an acceptance rate of less than 32%. The workshop program includes two invited talks by

- Michael Huth (Imperial College, London, UK) entitled "Verifiable Numerical Aggregation of Trust Evidence for Policy-Based Access Control" and
- Claire Vishik (Intel Corporation, UK) entitled "Building Trusted Systems: Lessons of the First Generation of Trusted Computing."

As in previous editions, the program of the STM'13 workshop also features the talk by Pouyan Sepehrdad (École Polytechnique Fédérale de Lausanne, Switzerland), recipient of the 2013 ERCIM WG STM Best PhD Award for the thesis entitled "*Statistical and Algebraic Cryptanalysis of Lightweight and Ultra-Lightweight Symmetric Primitives.*"

We would like to thank all the people who volunteered their time and energy to make this year's workshop happen. In particular, we thank the authors for submitting their manuscripts to the workshop and all the attendees for contributing to the workshop discussions. We are also grateful to the members of the Program Committee and the external reviewers for their work in reviewing and discussing the submissions, and their commitment to meeting the strict deadlines.

Last but not least, our thanks also go to all the people who played a role in the organization of the event: Pierangela Samarati (chair of the STM working group) for her energy, support, and the many useful pieces of advice; Keith Mayes (general chair of ESORICS 2013) together with Jason Crampton and Sushil Jajodia (program chairs of ESORICS 2013) for their support; and Giovanni Livraga for taking care of the publicity of the workshop.

We hope that the papers collected in these proceedings will be a source of inspiration for your work.

September 2013   Rafael Accorsi
                                                           Silvio Ranise

Organization

Program Committee

Program Chairs

Rafael Accorsi	University of Freiburg, Germany
Silvio Ranise	Fondazione Bruno Kessler, Trento, Italy

Publicity Chair

Giovanni Livraga	Università degli Studi di Milano, Italy

Members

Benjamin Aziz	University of Portsmouth, UK
Liqun Chen	Hewlett Packard Labs, UK
Mauro Conti	University of Padua, Italy
Jorge Cuellar	Siemens, Germany
Frédéric Cuppens	Télécom Bretagne, France
Nora Cuppens-Boulahia	Télécom Bretagne, France
Roberto Di Pietro	Università di Roma Tre, Italy
Wenliang Du	Syracuse University, USA
Isao Echizen	National Institute of Informatics, Japan
Carmen Fernández-Gago	University of Malaga, Spain
Sara Foresti	Università degli Studi di Milano, Italy
Joaquin Garcia-Alfaro	Télécom SudParis, France
Xinyi Huang	Fujian Normal University, China
Meiko Jensen	Independent Centre for Privacy and Data Protection Schleswig-Holstein, Germany
Jan Jürjens	TU Dortmund and Fraunhofer ISST, Germany
Dimitris Karagiannis	University of Vienna, Austria
Florian Kerschbaum	SAP Research, Germany
Doğan Kesdoğan	Universität Regensburg, Germany
Felix Klaedtke	ETH Zurich, Switzerland
Adam J. Lee	University of Pittsburgh, USA
Giovanni Livraga	Università degli Studi di Milano, Italy
Patricia Longstaff	Syracuse Universtiy, USA
Javier Lopez	University of Malaga, Spain
Fabio Martinelli	IIT-CNR, Italy
Raimundas Matulevicius	University of Tartu, Estonia
Catherine Meadows	NRL, USA
Charles Morisset	Newcastle University, UK
Indrakshi Ray	Colorado State University, USA

Pierangela Samarati   Università degli Studi di Milano, Italy
George Spanoudakis   City University London, UK
Mark Strembeck   Vienna University of Economics and BA,
                                 Austria
Willy Susilo   University of Wollongong, Australia
Mahesh Tripunitara   The University of Waterloo, Canada
Michael Waidner   Fraunhofer SIT, Germany
Nicola Zannone   Eindhoven University of Technology,
                                 The Netherlands

Additional Reviewers

Yousra Aafer   Huajian Liu
Wafa Ben Jaballah   Tongbo Luo
Phillipa Bennett   John Mace
Eyüp Canlar   Srdjan Marinovic
Jannik Dreier   Hoang-Quoc Nguyen-Son
Ezzaldeen Edwan   Federica Paci
Nicholas Farnan   Paul Ratazzi
William Garrison   Ruben Rios
Fuchun Guo   Andrea Saracino
Nabil Hachem   Sigrid Schefer-Wenzl
Jinguang Han   Axel Schroepfer
Isabelle Hang   Martin Stopczynski
Hao Hao   Meilof Veeningen
Marcel Heupel   Antonio Villani
Anh-Tu Hoang   Waldemar Berchtold
Marek Jawurek   Wei Wu
Lukas Kalabis   Artsiom Yautsiukhin
Fatih Karatas   Xiao Zhang
Aliaksandr Lazouski   Yuexin Zhang

STM Steering Committee

Theo Dimitrakos   British Telecom, UK
Sjouke Mauw   University of Luxembourg, Luxembourg
Stig F. Mjølsnes   Norwegian University of Science and
                                 Technology, Norway
Babak Sadighi   SICS, Sweden
Pierangela Samarati (Chair) Università degli Studi di Milano, Italy
Ulrich Ultes-Nitsche   University of Fribourg, Switzerland

Table of Contents

Business Process Security

Watermarking for Security

On Enhancement of 'Share The Secret' Scheme for Location Privacy

Costas Delakouridis[1] and Christos Anagnostopoulos[2]

[1] Athens University of Economics and Business,
Department of Informatics, Athens 10434, Greece
kodelak@aueb.gr
[2] Ionian University, Department of Informatics, Corfu 49100, Greece
christos@ionio.gr

Abstract. Since location information is considered as personal information, location privacy has been emerged as one of the most important security concerns. In this paper, we enhance the 'Share The Secret' (STS) scheme, a privacy mechanism that segments location information into pieces (shares), distributes the shares to multiple untrustworthy location servers, and reconstructs the original location on authorized entities. We introduce certain policies based on the theory of optimal stopping in order to achieve time-optimized decisions for different levels of privacy. Moreover, we evaluate the performance of STS in terms of communication and computation load, and energy consumption. Experimental results quantify the benefits stemming for STS adoption.

Keywords: Location privacy, secret sharing, optimal stopping theory.

1   Introduction

The recent smartphone applications, intelligent Location-based Services (LBS), and modern gadgets come with a penalty. Legitimate service providers exploit location information of mobile users but either without the previous consent of end–users or revelation of location information to unauthorized third parties. Moreover, location information is subject to inference or target by malicious attackers, traders, or marketers. The location information privacy scheme, hereinafter refereed to as 'Share The Secret' (STS), originally proposed in [1], supports location privacy over non-trusted servers. In this work, (i) we enhance the functionality of STS by introducing and evaluating a time-optimized location information distribution scheme, and (ii) we evaluate STS using real mobile devices and an Infrastructure as a Service (IaaS) cloud.

STS provides location privacy without relying on the existence of trusted third parties. The idea presented in [1] is to segment the location information into pieces and distribute them to multiple untrustworthy locations, referred to as STS Servers (STS-S). An authorized entity, such as a LBS, accesses the STS-Ss, retrieves the corresponding pieces of location information and reconstructs the location information of a mobile user. This method is achieved by the segmentation of the location information through the use of Shamir's perfect Sharing

R. Accorsi and S. Ranise (Eds.): STM 2013, LNCS 8203, pp. 1–16, 2013.

threshold Algorithm [2] and a lightweight protocol for data exchange between the STS-S.

The deployment of STS and the decentralized approach of location dissemination diminish the possibility of a successful collusion between the STS-S, since each of them retains partial knowledge of the location of the user. Furthermore, users interact with each STS-S through pseudonyms. The aforementioned pseudonyms are different per STS-S. Hence, even if the STS-S are compromised, the corresponding pieces of location information cannot be correlated, since there is no direct relationship with each other. Hence, the location privacy level is significantly enforced.

From a user point of view, the user has control over her location information. The location retrieval and segmentation is performed on her mobile device, while the reconstruction of the location is conducted only by authorized entities. Hence, there is no intermediate location server storing this information (single point of trust, single point of failure). In addition, user has the ability to select the specific STS-S that she prefers to distribute her location information based on some policy rules (e.g., proximity). STS manages to minimize the eavesdropping affect, since a possible attacker has to monitor more than one entity to reveal the *secret*, i.e., the location of the user.

The structure of the paper has as follows: Section 2 reports certain rationale on the concept of STS. Section 3 introduces the time-optimized STS update scheme. Section 4 reports on experimental evaluation of STS, while Section 5 discusses relevant work. Finally, Section 6 concludes the paper.

2   Rationale

2.1   Secret Sharing Concept

In our previous approach [1], we consider as *secret* the time-stamped location information $\mathbf{p}[t]$ of a moving object, identified by ID, at time t, i.e.,

$$\mathbf{p}[t] = \langle x, y, ID, t \rangle$$

where the position (x, y) of user with unique identifier ID is estimated at t with respect to a coordinate system.

The aim in [1] is to split the secret into segments with an efficient way, and distribute such segments to multiple locations (STS-S), in such a way, that only authorized entities are able to retrieve them and, thus, reconstructing the secret. In order to accomplish this goal, the model in [1] adopted the Shamir's perfect Sharing threshold Algorithm (SSA) introduced in [2]. The SSA assumes that the secret is shared among the n out of m available entities ($n < m$) and any set of at most $n - 1$ entities cannot rebuild the secret. Shamir's algorithm is based on the fact that in order to compute the equation of a polynomial of degree n, one must know at least $n + 1$ points that it lies on. For instance, in order to determine the equation of a line (i.e., $n = 1$) it is essential to know at least two points that it lies on. Let assume that the secret is some data p, which is (or can be easily made) a number. According to Shamir's (n, m) scheme, to divide p into pieces p_i one can pick a random $n - 1$ degree polynomial f, which $f(0) = p$ and evaluate $p_1 = f(1), \ldots, p_n = f(n)$. Given any subset of n of these p_i values, we can determine the coefficients of f, and rebuild p, since $p = f(0)$. On the other hand, knowledge of at most $n - 1$ of these values is not sufficient to determine p. In STS architecture, p refers to $\mathbf{p}[t]$ at time t.

2.2   Procedures of STS

Register to STS. Users have to register to the STS service. This procedure requires a handshake between user and each STS-S as described in [1]. For registration to a STS-S, a unique identifier ID is required to distinguish a user and, in parallel, allows LBS to retrieve the appropriate share for the corresponding user. Each STS-S keeps a Location Information Table, where each record refers to the tuple

$$\langle g(\mathbf{p}[t]), UID \rangle$$

where $g(\mathbf{p}[t])$ is a random share of $\mathbf{p}[t]$ produced by SSA and UID is a selected pseudonym. STS incorporates multiple user profiles to provide different precision of $\mathbf{p}[t]$. A user can use different pseudonyms per service and choose a profile that denotes the required level of the precision on $\mathbf{p}[t]$. The pseudonyms production mechanism is described in [1].

Register to LBS. Through a registration procedure, user provides to LBS the required information (i.e., certain STS-Ss hold the location shares and the corresponding pseudonyms used by a user during registration) in order to retrieve the shares from the STS-Ss and, thus, being able to reconstruct the user's location.

Location Retrieval. When the LBS requires the location for a user, it sends a request to each corresponding STS-S. STS-S retrieves the corresponding LIT record and replies to LBS. Hence, LBS, is able to reconstruct the location of the user by using the minimum required segments. More information about all the procedures is discussed in [1].

3   Time-Optimized STS-S Update Mechanism

When a secret sharing technique is used for shares distribution, users distribute the shares among either trustworthy or/and untrusted entities. In the former case, an adversary will try to compromise these entities in order to get access to shares, and, eventually, infer the location information. In the latter case, there is always a potential threat to employ entities that might collude in order to reveal to secret. The time period required for an attack to reveal the location information is subject to several factors that are difficult to measure.

In this section we focus on possible threats and analyse when users should update their STS scheme in order to defend against potential attacks. The update of STS is actually the procedure in which the STS-Ss that a user employs to store location shares are changed to a completely different set. In such case, upon selection of a new set of STS-Ss, user informs LBS for that update and sends the location shares to the new STS-Ss. Apart from selecting new STS-Ss, the user might alter the parameters of the SSA algorithm (i.e., m and n).

Since the probability of a successful attack depends on system vulnerabilities, the attacker knowledge, skills and the adopted methods, it is difficult to estimate a probability function for successful attack. On the other hand, it is preferable to know in advance when the risk of attack is high enough in order to update a priori the STS-Ss. In other words, instead of estimating the absolute time for STS-S update, we could force an update when the risk of an attack is relatively high. For the rest of the paper, we assume that an attack is successful when the attacker compromises the STS-Ss, thus, grant access to location information shares, and reconstructs the location information.

3.1   Problem Formulation

Consider an established STS scheme and several LBSs which are used by various mobile users. When users store their location information to STS-Ss, they should be ensured that their location information is accessible only by authorized LBSs for a particular time horizon. Additionally, opponents are attempting to compromise STS-Ss and reveal the location of users during the same horizon. If we take a snapshot of the system during runtime, we notice that the number of location shares that each STS-S stores for a particular user increases with time. Intuitively, the probability of reconstructing location information from shares increases as the number of location updates from user to LBS back-end system increases. Hence, once the number of LIT records for specific pseudonym increases, the risk of location information revelation by an eavesdropper increases.

The STS-S update procedure introduces additional cost, i.e., transmission of information to LBSs, communication overhead, or even a small interruption of the offered LBS. Such communication overload is getting more significant as STS-S update procedure is performed frequently. Ideally we would like to perform just one STS-S update, the initial one and no any other. One objective in order to minimize the overhead is to intentionally delay the interval between successive STS-S updates. Specifically, we would like to decrease the frequency of distributing shares per user among STS-Ss, thus, minimize the rate of initiating STS-S updates.

We run the risk of shares revelation once we continue the process of using the same STS-Ss for long periods since, at each stage of the process plethora of location information shares is circulated among STS-Ss. This is risky since eavesdropper inferences information and analyzes all disseminated information in order to extract knowledge on how to reveal the secret. We are about to stop the process once our belief that the eavesdropper is capable to extract knowledge from the disseminated information is high. Such degree of belief certainty comes along with the decision on when to stop the process, initiate a STS-S update, at the expense of computational cost and network overhead. The open issue, though, is to find when to decide on a STS-S update in order to balance the risk of shares revelation and the system overhead.

A possible solution is to periodically invoke the STS-S update procedure. However, this is arbitrarily decided and there is no information on how to estimate a possibly effective period of the update. A more sophisticated decision is to observe:

- volume of the disseminated pieces of information, i.e., a set of shares $g_i(\mathbf{p}[t])$, $i = 1, \ldots$ among STS-Ss at time t, say X_t,
- cumulative information up to time t, i.e., $S_t = X_1 + \cdots + X_t$, and
- amount of time period from the antecedent STS-S update procedure.

The volume of the disseminated pieces of information X_t cannot be predicted at time t since it depends on the mobility pattern of the mobile user, the number of current registered LBSs at time t, and the requirement of any LBS for using recent and fresh location information. Moreover, a reasonable hypothesis is that probability that an entity reveals the location information from the disseminated shares can increase with:

- time passed from previous initiation of the STS-S update procedure, and
- volume of information assembled up to time t.

Hence, we attempt to delay the share dissemination process as much as possible in order to disseminate a significant amount of information among the STS-Ss, however, in fear of location revelation by a possible eavesdropper.

The problem is to find a *stopping time* in order to stop the process of disseminating shares among STS-Ss and initiate the STS-S update procedure. This problem can be treated as an Optimal Stopping Time (OST) problem with infinite horizon. In the remainder, we propose three optimal stopping policies which calculate the condition (a.k.a. *optimal stopping rule*) that determines when a STS-S update should take place.

3.2 Optimal Stopping Policies for STS-S Update

Optimal Stopping Theory. The Optimal Stopping Theory (OST) is related to choosing the best time instance to take a decision of performing an action [3]. This decision is based on sequentially observed random variables $X_1, X_2, \ldots$ whose joint distribution is assumed to be known. For each stage $t = 1, 2, \ldots$ after observing $x_1, x_2, \ldots$ values one may stop and receive cost y_t or continue and observe X_{t+1}. The *optimal stopping rule* is to stop at some stage t^* (*optimal stopping time*) to minimize the expected cost. An OST problem with unknown upper bound of stages is an infinite-horizon problem.

Optimal Stopping Policies. Consider at discrete time $t = 1, 2, \ldots$ that STS-S receives X_t pieces of information (shares). We assume that X_t random variable has finite mean $E[X] < \infty$. Let $Z_1, \ldots, Z_t$ be the random variables that indicate whether the eavesdropper reveals all pieces of information up to t with $Z_t = 0$

denoting that at time t the eavesdropper reveals the location shares and $Z_t = 1$ indicating that the eavesdropper is not able to reveal the shares at t having all pieces of information up to t. We assume that Z_t are i.i.d. The three policies for time-optimized STS-S update are:

1. *Static optimal Stopping Policy* (SSP) in which we consider the probability that eavesdropper reveals the location shares remains constant for all t with

$$P(Z_t = 1) = \beta \quad To \quad P(Z_t = 0) = \beta$$

   and $P(Z_t = 1) = 1 - \beta$, where $0 < \beta < 1$.
2. *Dynamic optimal Stopping Policy* (DSP) in which we consider the probability that the eavesdropper reveals the location shares increases with time. This is reasonable since the more information the eavesdropper compiles, i.e., observing the $X_1, X_2, \ldots, X_t$ process, the more capable is the eavesdropper in order to reveal the location shares. In this case we consider

$$P(Z_t = 1) = \beta^{t-1} \quad To \quad P(Z_t = 0) = \beta^{t-1}$$

   with $P(Z_1 = 0) = 1$; we assume that at $t = 1$ the eavesdropper observing only X_1 has a little knowledge for revealing the location shares and the system is considered almost surely robust.
3. *Cumulative Dynamic optimal Stopping Policy* (CDSP) in which we consider the probability that eavesdropper reveals the location shares at time t depends on the information that she might gather up to $t - 1$, i.e.,

$$P(Z_t = 0) = \beta^{S_{t-1}}$$

where $S_t = \sum_{k=1}^{t} X_k$ and $S_0 = 0$.

The aim of the system is to delay the process in order to transfer as much pieces of information as possible in fear of an eavesdropper capable of revealing the location shares. That is, the system by adopting SSP, DSP, or CDSP should stop the process at *optimal stopping time* t^* to maximize the sum $X_1 + X_2 + \cdots + X_{t^*}$ with respect to probability of revealing the location shares: β, β^{t_*-1}, and $\beta^{S_{t^*}}$, respectively.

We define the payoff (reward) at time t for the optimal policies through the random variable

$$Y_t = \prod_{k=1}^{t} Z_k \sum_{k=1}^{t} X_k \qquad (1)$$

for $t = 1, 2, \ldots$, and we obtain $Y_\infty = 0$. The stopping time t^* at which Y_{t^*} in Eq(1) is maximized is referred to as optimal stopping time. Let $\mathcal{F}_t$ denote the σ-algebra generated by both $X_1, X_2, \ldots, X_t$ and $Z_1, Z_2, \ldots, Z_t$. Based on the *principle of optimality*, the system should stop the process at t once

$$Y_t \geq E[Y_{t+1}|\mathcal{F}_t]$$

with respect to one–stage look-ahead optimal stopping rule. We are interested in finding t^* provided that at t the eavesdropper has not revealed the location shares, that is, we compute $E[Y_{t+1}|\mathcal{F}_t]$ on $\prod_{k=1}^{t} Z_k = 1$. Hence, we obtain that

$$E[Y_{t+1}|\mathcal{F}_t] = E[Z_{t+1}\sum_{k=1}^{t+1}X_k|\mathcal{F}_t]$$

Since, $S_t = \sum_{k=1}^{t} X_k$ then we obtain that $Y_t = S_t$.

1. In case of SSP we obtain that:

$$E[Y_{t+1}|\mathcal{F}_t] = P(Z_{t+1} = 1) \cdot (\sum_{k=1}^{t}X_k + E[X]) = \beta(S_t + E[X])$$

Hence the optimal stopping rule for SSP is

$$t^* = \inf\{t \geq 1|S_t \geq \frac{\beta}{1-\beta}E[X]\}$$

The optimal stopping rule for SSP refers to stopping the process at the first time t at which the accumulated pieces of information $X_1 + X_2 + \cdots + X_t$ is at least $\frac{\beta}{1-\beta}$. That is, at this time t, the STS-S update phase takes place. After STS-S update, the process starts–off with new observations of the X_t process.

2. In a similar way, we obtain the optimal stopping rule for DSP:

$$t^* = \inf\{t \geq 1|S_t \geq \frac{\beta^t}{1-\beta^t}E[X]\}$$

It is worth noting that the stopping threshold for SSP remains constant for all time t. In DSP, the stopping threshold decreases with t thus enforcing the system not to delay the process since the probability of revealing the location shares increases.

3. In the case of CDSP, we obtain that $E[Z_{t+1}] = P(Z_{t+1}) = \beta^{S_t}$, thus,

$$E[Y_{t+1}|\mathcal{F}_t] = \beta^{S_t}(S_t + E[X])$$

and the corresponding optimal stopping time is given by

$$t^* = \inf\{t \geq 1|\frac{1-\beta^{S_t}}{\beta^{S_t}}S_t \geq E[X]\}$$

The β factor indicates the sensitivity / self-confidence of the system in light of taking a risk to delay the process. High β indicates that the system renders secure enough. This results to longer periods between STS-S replacement. Low β denotes a less risky system in delaying the process, thus, resulting in high frequency of STS-S updates.

Figure 1 shows the optimality achieved by the proposed policies. Specifically, for each policy we evaluate the expected reward Y if the system stops at the optimal stopping time t^* assuming the $X_t \sim U(0, 1)$, i.e., normalized in the unit interval. We also compared the achieved reward with a system which change the STS-Ss in a random fashion. As depicted by the histograms in Figure 1, the proposed policies guarantee optimality which maximizes the expected reward with respect to a system which randomly chooses a decision to update the STS-Ss. In addition, Figure 2 shows the impact of β factor for all optimal policies and the random policy. Obviously, optimal policies achieve extremely higher expected reward with respect to the random policy. Moreover, one can observe that DSP scales well for low β values, that is, with low probability of eavesdropping, the system optimally delays the X_t process, thus, avoiding needless frequent STS-S updates. On the other hand, for high β value SSP is deemed appropriate for adopting assuming the highest reward from all policies. CDSP attempts to balance the trade–off between relatively high frequency of STS-S update and prolongation of the X_t process in light of saving communication and computational resources.

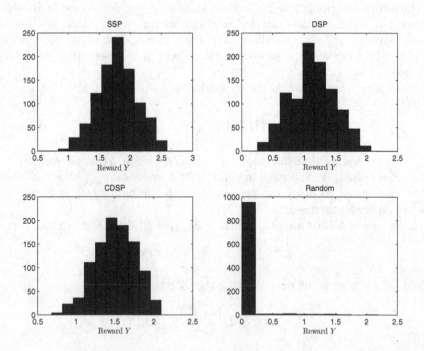

Fig. 1. The histogram of expected reward Y for SSP, DSP, CDSP, and Random policies with $\beta = 0.9$

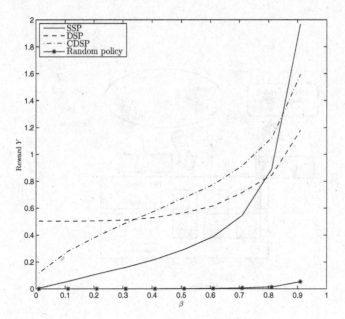

Fig. 2. The expected reward Y for SSP, DSP, CDSP, and Random policies against β

4   Performance Evaluation

4.1   Simulation Environment

While STS-Ss are deployed on resilient infrastructures with sufficient resources, in terms of storage and capacity, the STS Clients (STS-Cs), which perform complicate tasks (e.g., generate shares, encrypt data) are mainly deployed on handsets with limited capabilities. Hence, our main concern is to evaluate the performance of STS-C on mobile devices.

Network Infrastructure. Figure 3 depicts the architecture used for evaluation of STS. Regarding deployment of STS-Ss, we have to ensure that the STS-Ss be deployed on several locations over the network and have sufficient storage and processing capabilities. Another critical factor was that STS-Ss should be accessible at any time. Therefore, we address this specification by establishing STS over an 'Infrastructure as a Service' (IaaS) cloud network model. Iaas provides the most appropriate underlying infrastructure, since it is transparent to the user, provides all aforementioned capabilities, and enables user to run custom processes. We utilized the open source IaaS Nimbus[1] cloud provided by the Future Grid[2] as network infrastructure. Based on Nimbus, we established a virtual

---

[1] www.nimbusproject.org
[2] portal.futuregrid.org

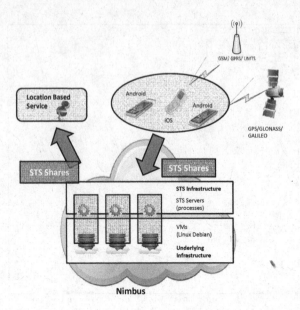

Fig. 3. Network infrastructure

network by deploying multiply Virtual Machines (VM), running Linux Dedian[3] version 5.

STS Architecture Deployment. STS-Cs were developed for iOS and Google Android mobile operating systems. Table 1 summarizes the SDK for the application deployment as well as the technology and tools used to retrieve position information. For STS-S, all required modules were developed through (Java) Web Services. For reasons of completeness, the LBS was developed in Java and deployed on an external PC able to communicate with the Nimbus cloud.

Table 1. Deployment Environments

Characteristics	iOS	Google Android
SDK	4.1 Apple iPhone SDK	Android version 2.2 (Froyo)
Position Information	GPS API	GPS API
CPU / Energy consumption	Apple Instruments application	PowerTutor
Memory consumption	mach build–in library	TOP command (Android OS)

Simulation Setup. Table 2 depicts the simulation details. During the experiments, one STS-S was deployed on each running VM. Furthermore, the STS-C was deployed on real mobile devices and the users where on the University surroundings, receiving GPS location updates based on their individual mobility

---

[3] www.debian.org/index.en.html

Table 2. Simulation Parameters

Parameters	Value/Range
Number of VMs	30
Number of STS Servers	30 (each one per VM)
Number of LBS	2
Number of STS Clients	2–8
Mobile devises running iOS	1–5
Mobile devises running Android	1–5

patterns. The position information was used as input for the STS-C, the STS algorithm was applied and the created position shares were sent to the STS-Ss deployed on Nimbus. Furthermore, for each LBS, the required refresh rate of location information $\mathbf{p}[t]$ was modified, based on the type of the service (e.g. navigation service, Point-Of-Interest service).

4.2 Experimental Results

Computational Overhead & CPU. Our first goal is to evaluate the processing overhead and the CPU usage of STS-Cs required to prepare the STS shares. According to SSA, the complexity for producing shares is related to n and m values, i.e., the degree of Shamir's polynomial and the total number of shares, respectively. Based on this, we deployed two different STS *configurations*:

1. STS-C distributes the location shares among a fix number of STS-Ss whilst the number of servers required to reconstruct the secret varies.
2. For the same number of n STS-Ss, we altered the total number of STS-Ss where the secret was distributed.

Additionally, in order to further enhance the privacy mechanisms, we introduced and evaluated the Encrypted STS (E-STS). The main difference from the typical STS is that, prior to distribution of the segments to STS-Ss, we applied to them AES encryption using a symmetric 128 bit key. For the experiments, the OAKLEY extension of the Diffie–Hellman key agreement protocol was used once for the establishment of an AES 128 bit key. AES was chosen as the current NIST FIPS standard for symmetric encryption. The key was agreed in advance between STS-C and LBS. With this modification, the attacker should have to decrypt STS segments, before try to reconstruct the location information. Figure 4 shows the results of the aforementioned experiments form an Apple iPhone 4S and an HTC Bravo running iOS and Android v2.2 respectively. Table 3 states the hardware specifications of the handsets.

For the first configuration, we altered the number of n on each experiment. Regarding the processing, Figure 4 depicts the average processing time for both STS and E-STS schemes where $m = 10$ and $n \in \{2, 5, 7, 10\}$. Note that, for STS the processing time reflects to the time required to segment the $\mathbf{p}[t]$ based on the current m, n configuration while for E-STS the processing time includes

Table 3. Handset Hardware Specifications

Mobile device	Apple iPhone 4S	HTC Bravo
Memory	16G Storage, 512MB RAM	4G Storage, 576MB RAM
Operating System	iOS 5.0	Android v2.3
Battery	Li-Po 1432 mAh battery	Li-Ion 1400 mAh battery
CPU	Dual-core 1 GHz Cortex-A9	1 GHz Scorpion

additionally the time required to apply the encryption. Figure 4(a) shows that even in complex SSA schemes the processing time for STS segmentation is significant small. Furthermore, as n increases the corresponding time to compute the shares is not significantly increased. From a CPU point of view, we measured the average CPU usage for the aforementioned scenarios. During these experiments we were sampling the percentage of CPU usage over time with frequency 1Hz. Figures 4(c) and (d) show the usage on an Apple iPhone 4S and an HTC Bravo respectively. We noted that, as expected the CPU usage is higher when E-STS is used, however remains in acceptable levels.

In the second configuration, we measured the average processing time to compute the STS shares for fixed n i.e. $n = 2$, and variable $m \in \{2, 5, 7, 10\}$ (Figure 4(b)). We noted that the average processing time for share generation is small and increased on average by 0.2 msecs/per additional m server. Additionally, when E-STS was applied to both configurations, even though the processing time increased the overall processing overhead was not significantly altered even in more complex Shamir schemes.

Overall, from the aforementioned sets of experiments, we can conclude that both STS and E-STS schemes can provide multiple levels of privacy by altering m, n parameters according to user needs and at the same time, keep the overall processing overhead and the CPU usage in acceptable levels.

Memory Usage & Energy Consumption. Regarding the memory usage, we measured the average memory (in KBs) required from handset while performing the most demanding STS procedure, i.e. segmentation of $\mathbf{p}[t]$, encryption of the segments (in case of E–STS) and their distribution to STS-Ss. We evaluated the memory usage for the scenarios using the same hardware configuration. The STS-Cs updated their positions every 1 sec. Figures 4(e) and (f) depict the average memory usage in KBs for different STS and E-STS scenarios. As expected the memory usage is slightly higher when E–STS is applied. However even in complex SSA scheme the average memory required to perform the STS segmentation, encryption and distribution tasks does not exceed the 85 KBs. Hence, STS Scheme for location privacy could be easily adopted on today's handsets.

In order to measure the energy consumption, we conducted experiments where various SSA schemes were used in either STS or E–STS. The goal of these measurements was to calculate the power consumption, in Joule, in order to evaluate both the overall performance of STS and the performance of individual SSA schemes. In Figure 5 scenarios S3, S4 and S10, S11 correspond to $(n, m) = (7, 10)$

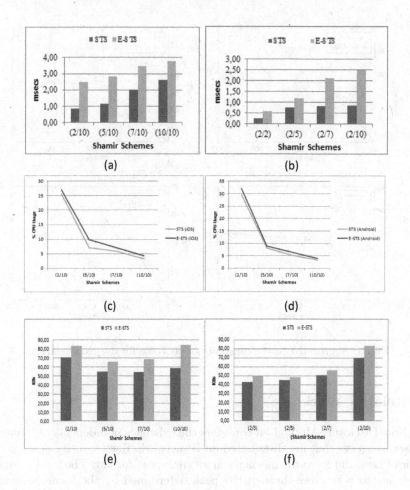

Fig. 4. Experimental Results

and $(n, m) = (10, 10)$ when STS and E–STS is used, respectively. Furthermore, scenarios S1, S8 and S7, S14 corresponds to $(n, m) = (2, 10)$ and $(n, m) = (2, 7)$ when STS and E–STS is used, respectively. As expected, the energy consumption when encryption is used is higher than the encryption of plain texts. Note that in absolute numbers, the power consumption even in encryption mode is tolerable, and applicable in modern mobile handsets. In addition, the results show that, in terms of energy consumption, when n is changing, the aggregated power consumption is higher than the scenarios where the parameter m is changing. Experiments were performed on an HTC Desire Bravo smartphone, running Android 2.3 (Table 3), which is considered as an average capability device with 3.7 Volt battery (1800mAh), and consumes 23976 Joules without charging. Hence, excluding the energy consumption due to the Android OS, a mobile device can run STS module for more than 15 hours (i.e, scenario S4 with $(10, 10)$).

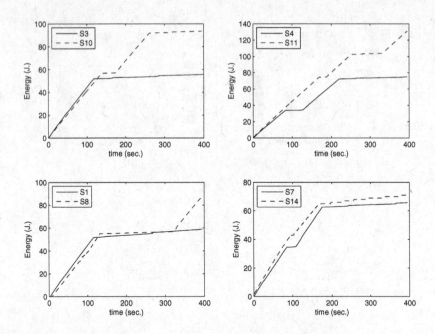

Fig. 5. Aggregated power consumption in Joule for diverse scenarios

5   Related Work

The Non–Disclosure Method [4] considers the existence of independent, security
(software) agents that are distributed on IP network. Each security agent holds
a pair of keys and forwards messages in an encrypted format. The sender routes
a message to a receiver through the path determined by the security agents.
The Mist system [5] handles the problem of routing a message though a mobile network by keeping the sender's location private from intermediate routers,
the receiver and possible eavesdroppers. The Mist system [5] consists of several routers ordered in a hierarchical structure. Portal routers are aware of the
location of the mobile user without knowing the identity of the user, while the
lighthouse routers are aware of the user's identity without knowing her/his exact
location. The aforementioned approaches enforce location privacy in IP–layer.

Beyond these solutions, anonymity-based approaches have been proposed to
address the location privacy issue on the application layer. Through anonymity,
location information is unlinked from the subject prior to the information collection process. This means that subjects are reporting their location, but the use
of nicknames or pseudonyms, such that anybody that gain access to the location
information will not be able to determine the owner of this information. The
idea of using pseudonyms instead of the identities of the users is used by the
authors in [6]. They propose the replacement of the identity with a sequence of
chained idempotent filters governed by a specific policy language. The authors in

[7] proposed the idea of mixed-zones where the user position is protected within these zones. In [7], this is realized within a zone by not sending any location updates. Additionally, in spatial obfuscation approaches privacy in enhanced by intentionally reducing the precision of the location information. In the model in [8], the user uses circular areas as location info instead of his exact positions. The model in [9] also considers spatio-temporal obfuscation to protect movement trajectories of users.

STS enables location privacy without relying on the existence of third trusted parties. The main idea behind STS is to divide the location information into shares and distribute it to multiple STS-Ss. These are no-trustworthy entities, assigned to store, erase, and provide segments of location data that anonymous users register. Third party services, such as LBS, personal assisting or pervasive applications, access multiple STS-Ss to determine the location of the user through the combination of the distributed shares.

6   Conclusions

We report on the enhanced STS, which segments and distributes location information to certain, non-trusted, entities from where it will be reachable for reconstruction by authorized LBS. STS does not require any third trusted party. We also introduce a time-optimized mechanism for updating the STS-Ss based on the Optimal Stopping Theory. Furthermore, we evaluate STS in terms of computational and energy efficiency. Evaluation results show that STS does not overload the mobile operations.

References

1. Marias, G.F., Delakouridis, C., Kazatzopoulos, L., Georgiadis, P.: Location Privacy Through Secret Sharing Techniques. In: 1st IEEE International Workshop on Trust, Security and Privacy for Ubiquitous Computing, TSPUC 2005, Taormina, Italy, pp. 614–620 (June 2005)
2. Ben-Or, M., Goldwasser, S., Wigderson, A.: 'Completeness theorems for non-cryptographic fault-tolerant distributed computations'. In: Proc. of the 20th ACM Symp. on the Theory of Computing, pp. 1–10 (1988)
3. Peskir, G., Shiryaev, A.: Optimal Stopping and Free Boundary Problems (ETH Zuerich). Birkhäuser (2006)
4. Fasbender, A., Kesdogan, D., Kubitz, O.: Analysis of Security and Privacy in Mobile IP. In: Proc. 4th International Conf. on Telecommunication Systems, Modeling and Analysis (1996)
5. Al-Muhtadi, J., Campbell, R., Kapadia, A., Mickunas, D., Yi, S.: Routing Through the Mist: Privacy Preserving Communication in Ubiquitous Computing Environments. In: Proc. International Conf. of Distributed Computing Systems (2002)
6. Friday, A., Muller, H., Rodden, T., Dix, A.: A Lightweight Approach to Managing Privacy in Location-Based Services. In: Proc. Equator Annual Conference (October 2002)

7. Beresford, A.R., Stajano, F.: Mix zones: User privacy in location-aware services. In: PerCom Workshops 2004, pp. 127–131 (2004)
8. Ardagna, C.A., Cremonini, M., Damiani, E., De Capitani di Vimercati, S., Samarati, P.: Location privacy protection through obfuscation-based techniques. In: Barker, S., Ahn, G.-J. (eds.) Data and Applications Security 2007. LNCS, vol. 4602, pp. 47–60. Springer, Heidelberg (2007)
9. Gruteser, M., Grunwald, D.: Anonymous usage of location-based services through spatial and temporal cloaking. In: Proc. of MobiSys 2003, pp. 31–42 (2003)

New Attacks against Transformation-Based Privacy-Preserving Linear Programming

Peeter Laud[1] and Alisa Pankova[1,2,3]

[1] Cybernetica AS
[2] Software Technology and Applications Competence Centre (STACC)
[3] University of Tartu, Institute of Computer Science

Abstract. In this paper we demonstrate a number of attacks against proposed protocols for privacy-preserving linear programming, based on publishing and solving a transformed version of the problem instance. Our attacks exploit the geometric structure of the problem, which has mostly been overlooked in the previous analyses and is largely preserved by the proposed transformations. The attacks are efficient in practice and cast serious doubt to the viability of transformation-based approaches in general.

Keywords: Cryptanalysis, Secure multiparty computation, Linear programming.

1 Introduction

Linear programming (LP) is one of the most versatile polynomial-time solvable optimization problems. It is usually straightforward to express various production planning and transportation problems as linear programs. There exist LP solving algorithms that are efficient both in theory and in practice. If the instances of these problems are built from data belonging to several mutually distrustful parties, the solving procedure must preserve the privacy of the parties. Thus it would be very useful to have an efficient privacy-preserving protocol that the data owners (and possibly also some other parties that help with computation) could execute for computing the optimal solution to a linear program that is obtained by combining the data of different owners. It is likely that such protocol would directly give us efficient privacy-preserving protocols for many other optimization tasks.

Several such protocols have indeed been proposed, following one of two main approaches. In the *secure multiparty computation (SMC) approach*, composable protocols for privacy-preserving arithmetic and relational operations are used to build a privacy-preserving implementation of some LP solving algorithm, typically the simplex algorithm. In the *transformation-based approach*, the algebraic structure of systems of linear inequalities and equations is used to apply a linear transformation to the description of the original problem, thus disguising it and allowing it to be solved publicly.

R. Accorsi and S. Ranise (Eds.): STM 2013, LNCS 8203, pp. 17–32, 2013.

The security properties of the protocols of SMC approach can be derived from the properties of the protocols for primitive arithmetic and relational operations through composability. The privacy guarantees these protocols offer are thus pretty well understood. The transformation-based methods have so far lacked the understanding of their privacy properties at a comparable level. The current paper demonstrates that such unavailability of security definitions is dangerous.

2   Privacy-Preserving Linear Programming

Throughout this paper, the upright upper case letters A denote matrices, and the bold lower case letters **b** denote column vectors. Writing two matrices/vectors together without an operator A**b** denotes multiplication, while separating them with a whitespace and putting into parentheses (A **b**) denotes augmentation. By augmentation we mean attaching a column **b** to the matrix A from the right. This can be generalized to matrices: (A B) denotes a matrix that contains all the columns of A followed by all the columns of B. Row augmentation is defined analogously.

The *canonical form* for a linear programming task is the following:

$$\text{minimize } \mathbf{c}^{\mathrm{T}} \cdot \mathbf{x}, \text{ subject to } A\mathbf{x} \le \mathbf{b}, \mathbf{x} \ge \mathbf{0} . \tag{1}$$

Here A is an $m \times n$ matrix, **b** is a vector of length m and **c** is a vector of length n. There are n variables in the vector **x**. The inequality of vectors is defined pointwise.

The LP solving algorithms, as well as protocols for privacy-preserving solution commonly expect the task to be in the *standard form*:

$$\text{minimize } \mathbf{c}^{\mathrm{T}} \cdot \mathbf{x}, \text{ subject to } A\mathbf{x} = \mathbf{b}, \mathbf{x} \ge \mathbf{0} . \tag{2}$$

The inequality constraints of the canonical form can be transformed to equality constraints by introducing *slack variables*. The system of constraints $A\mathbf{x} \le \mathbf{b}$, $\mathbf{x} \ge \mathbf{0}$ is equivalent to the system $A\mathbf{x} + I\mathbf{x}_{\mathrm{s}} = \mathbf{b}$, $\mathbf{x}, \mathbf{x}_{\mathrm{s}} \ge 0$, where I is $m \times m$ identity matrix and $\mathbf{x}_{\mathrm{s}}$ is a vector of m new variables.

A *feasible solution* of a linear program is any vector $x_0 \in \mathbb{R}^n$ that satisfies its constraints. An *optimal solution* of a linear program is any feasible solution that maximizes the value of its cost function. The *feasible region* of a linear program is the set of all its feasible solutions. It is a polyhedron — the intersection of a finite number of hyperplanes and half-spaces. A feasible solution is *basic* if it is located in one of the vertices of that polyhedron.

In the privacy-preserving setting, the elements of the matrix A and the vectors **b**, **c** are somehow contributed by several different parties. The cost vector **c** may be either held entirely by some party, or its entries may belong to different parties. Two standard ways of partitioning the constraints $A\mathbf{x} \le \mathbf{b}$ are the horizontal partitioning (each party contributes some of the constraints) and the vertical partitioning (each party knows certain columns of the matrix A). More general ways of data partitioning are possible, but these are not considered by the transformation methods that we are attacking.

In general, there are two main approaches to privacy-preserving linear programming. One approach is the straightforward cryptographic implementation of a privacy-preserving version of some LP solving algorithm [14,9]. Its main problem is efficiency since the entire optimization process must be performed in a manner that protects all intermediate values and comparison results. Another approach is transforming the program such a way that it could be given to a solver for offline computation. The optimal solution to the initial program has to be recoverable from the optimal solution to the transformed program.

In this work we present new attacks against some of the existing transformation methods. Without lessening the generality, we assume the number of parties to be 2, called Alice and Bob.

2.1 Transformation Methods

Transformation-based methods have been proposed in [4,3,15,11,12,16,8,2,10,7]. A set of "standard" transformations, applicable to the initial program, have been proposed over the years. Depending on the partitioning of constraints and the objective function, the application of a transformation may require cryptographic protocols of varying complexity. Each of the methods proposed in the literature typically uses several of these standard transformations.

Multiplying from the left. The idea of multiplying A and b in (2) by a random $m \times m$ invertible matrix P from the left was first introduced by Du [4]. This transformation conceals the outer appearance of A and b, but the feasible region remains unchanged.

Multiplying from the right. The idea of multiplying A and b in (2) by a random invertible matrix Q from the right was also proposed by Du [4]. This hides also the cost vector $\mathbf{c}$. Unfortunately, it changes the optimal solution if some external constraints (e.g. the non-negativity constraints) of the form $B\mathbf{x} \geq \mathbf{b}'$ are present, as it has been shown in [2]. In this case, the vector $\mathbf{b}'$ should also be modified according to the transformation, but that in fact reveals all the information about Q.

Scaling and Permutation. Bednarz et al. [2] have shown that, in order to preserve the inequality $\mathbf{x} \geq \mathbf{0}$, the most general type of Q is a positive generalized permutation matrix (a square matrix where each row and each column contains exactly one non-zero element). This results in scaling and permuting the columns of A. This transformation may also be applied to a problem in the canonical form (1).

Shifting. The shifting of variables has first been proposed in [3], and it has been also used in [16]. This transformation is achieved by replacing the constraints $A\mathbf{x} \leq \mathbf{b}$ with $A\mathbf{y} \leq \mathbf{b} + A\mathbf{r}$, where $\mathbf{r}$ is a random non-negative vector of length n and $\mathbf{y}$ are new variables, related to the variables $\mathbf{x}$ through the equality $\mathbf{y} = \mathbf{x} + \mathbf{r}$. To preserve the set of feasible solutions, the inequalities $\mathbf{y} \geq \mathbf{r}$ have to be added to the system. A different transformation must then be used to hide $\mathbf{r}$.

2.2   Security Definition

There are no formal security definitions used in the transformation-based approach. The definition that has been used in the previous works is the *acceptable security*. This notion was first used in [5].

Definition 1. *A protocol achieves acceptable security if the only thing that the adversary can do is to reduce all the possible values of the secret data to some domain with the following properties:*

1. *The number of values in this domain is infinite, or the number of values in this domain is so large that a brute-force attack is computationally infeasible.*
2. *The range of the domain (the difference between the upper and lower bounds) is acceptable for the application.*

More detailed analysis [1,3] estimates the probability that the adversary guesses some secret value. The leakage quantification analysis [3] is a compositional method for estimating the adversary's ability to make the correct guess when assisted by certain public information.

Although acceptable security could make the analysis simpler, it is not very well applicable in practice. Attacks on schemes that are secure by this definition have been found [2,1]. The security of different transformation methods is very dependent on the initial settings of the problem — the partitioning of initial data, as well as on the type of used constraints (inequalities or equations).

2.3   Classification of Initial Settings

For each of the proposed transformation methods, the applicability and security strongly depend on the initial settings of the problem. For that reason, Bednarz [1] has introduced a classification of initial settings, provided with corresponding notation. She proposes to consider the following parameters:

Objective Function Partitioning. How is the vector c initially shared? Is it known to Alice, to Bob, or to both of them? Are some entries known to Alice and others to Bob? Or does $c = c_{Alice} + c_{Bob}$ hold, where c_{Alice} is "completely" unknown to Bob and vice versa?

Constraint Partitioning. How is the matrix A initially shared? Is it public, known to one party, partitioned horizontally or vertically, or additively shared?

RHS Vector Partitioning. How is the vector b initially shared?

Allowable Constraint Types. Does the method admit only equality constraints, only inequalities, or both of them? Note that admitting only equality constraints means that the "natural" representation of the optimization problem is in terms of equalities. The use of slack variables to turn inequalities to equalities is not allowed.

Allowable Variable Types. May the variables be assumed non-negative? Or may they be assumed free? Or can both types be handled?

Additionally, the classification considers which party or parties learn the optimal solution. This aspect does not play a role for our attacks.

The attacks described in this paper mostly target the transformation methods for LP tasks where the constraints are in the form of inequalities (1), and the set of constraints has been horizontally partitioned between Alice and Bob. The optimization direction $\mathbf{c}$ and its sharing does not play a big role in the main attacks, although some proposed transformation methods leave into it information that makes the attacks simpler. In our treatment, we assume all variables to be non-negative.

2.4   Overview of Proposed Methods

For exactly the setting described in the previous paragraph, Bednarz [1, Chap. 6] has proposed the following transformation. The set of constraints in (1) is transformed to

$$\hat{A}\mathbf{y} = \hat{\mathbf{b}}, \mathbf{y} \geq \mathbf{0}, \tag{3}$$

where $\hat{A} = P\left(A\ I\right)Q$, $\hat{\mathbf{b}} = P\mathbf{b}$, I is the $m \times m$ identity matrix, P is a random invertible $m \times m$ matrix and Q is a random positive $(m+n) \times (m+n)$ generalized permutation matrix. New variables $\mathbf{y}$ are related to the original variables $\mathbf{x}$ and the slack variables $\mathbf{x}_s$ by the equation $\left(\begin{smallmatrix} \mathbf{x} \\ \mathbf{x}_s \end{smallmatrix}\right) = Q\mathbf{y}$. The objective function is disguised as $\hat{\mathbf{c}}^{\mathrm{T}} = (\mathbf{c}^{\mathrm{T}}\ \mathbf{0}^{\mathrm{T}})Q$, where $\mathbf{0}$ is a vector of m zeroes.

Other proposed transformations for horizontally partitioned constraints can be easily compared with Bednarz's. Du [4] applied the multiplication with both P and Q (where Q was more general) directly to the system of inequalities (1). Unfortunately, this transformation did not preserve the feasible region (and possibly the optimal solution) as shown by Bednarz et al. [2]. Vaidya [15] uses only the matrix Q, with similar correctness problems. Mangasarian [12] uses only the multiplication with P for a system with only equality constraints (2). Hong et al. [8] propose a complex set of protocols for a certain kind of distributed linear programming problems. Regarding the security, they prove that these protocols leak no more than what is made public by Bednarz's transformation. Li et al. [10] propose a transformation very similar to Bednarz's, only the matrix Q is selected from a more restricted set. This transformation is analyzed by Hong and Vaidya [7] and shown to provide no security (their attack has slight similarities with the one we present in Sec. 3.2). They propose a number of methods to make the transformation more secure and to also hide the number of inequalities in (1), including the addition of superfluous constraints and the use of more than one slack variable per inequality to turn them to equalities. We will further discuss the use of more slack variables in Sec. 3.1. The transformation by Dreier and Kerschbaum [3], when applied to (1), basically shifts the variables (Sec. 2.1), followed by Bednarz's transformation. We discuss the details and attacks specific to this transformation in Sec. 3.3.

3   Attacks

The system of constraints (1) consists of m inequalities of the form $\sum_{i=1}^{n} a_{ji}x_i \leq b_j$ for $j \in \{1, \ldots, m\}$, in addition to the non-negativity constraints. We assume that Alice knows the first r of these inequalities.

When Alice attempts to recover (1) from the result of Bednarz's transformation (3), she will first try to locate the slack variables, as described in Sec. 3.1. When she has located the slack variables, she can remove these, turning the equalities back to inequalities of the form $A'x' \leq b'$. These constraints are related to (1) by $A' = P'AQ'$, $b' = P'b$, where both P' and Q' are generalized permutation matrices (of size $m \times m$ and $n \times n$, respectively; Q' is also positive). Multiplication with P' from the left does not actually change the constraints, so the goal of Alice is to find Q'. The correspondence of the variables in x and x' can be found by looking at scale-invariant quantities related to constraints. Once the correspondence is found, the scaling factors can be easily recovered. All this is described in Sec. 3.2.

3.1   Identifying the Slack Variables

Looking at the Objective Function. When we add the slack variables to the system of inequalities in order to turn them to equations, then the coefficients of these slack variables in the cost vector c will be 0. In the existing transformation methods, the cost vector c is hidden by also multiplying it with a monomial matrix Q (product of a positive diagonal matrix and a permutation matrix) from the right. In this way, the zero entries in c are not changed. If all original variables had non-zero coefficients in the objective function, then the location of zeroes in the transformed vector c tells us the location of slack variables.

This issue can be solved by applying the transformation to the *augmented form* of linear program that includes the cost vector into the constraint matrix, and the cost value is expressed by a single variable:

$$\text{minimize } w, \text{ subject to } \begin{pmatrix} 1 & -c^T & 0 \\ 0 & A & I \end{pmatrix} \begin{pmatrix} w \\ x \\ x_s \end{pmatrix} = \begin{pmatrix} 0 \\ b \end{pmatrix}, \begin{pmatrix} w \\ x \\ x_s \end{pmatrix} \geq 0 . \quad (4)$$

The slack variables may be now hidden amongst the real variables by permutation. The location of the variable w should be known to the solver, although he may also solve all the n instances of linear programming tasks: for each variable in the task, try to minimize it.

There may be possibly other means of hiding c. Hence we introduce more attacks that are not related to c.

Looking at Sizes of Entries. If the positions of slack variables have been hidden in the cost vector, they may be located by exploiting the structure of A. Namely, after the slack variables are introduced, they form an identity matrix that is attached to A from the right. Thus each slack column contains exactly one non-zero entry. The columns of A are very unlikely to contain just one non-zero entry. We have found that the columns of $P\left(A\ I\right)$ can be distinguished by performing statistical analysis on the sizes of their entries. Even if using both positive and negative entries in A makes the mean more or less the same, the variance is smaller for the slack variables. The following scaling of the columns with the entries of Q does not provide any more protection.

We have discovered this problem occasionally, just because the columns appeared too different after applying the existing transformation methods. The previous works do not state precisely the distribution from which the entries of P (and Q) should be sampled. We have made experiments where we have sampled these entries independently of each other, according to the uniform distribution, or the normal distribution (the parameters of the distribution are currently unimportant, they only affect the scale of the resulting matrix, as well as the variance of its entries relative to each other). It turns out that selecting the entries of P randomly according to either one of these distributions keeps the variables distinguishable.

We performed a series of experiments, described below in detail. The instances of linear programming tasks were generated from a certain distribution that may differ from the distributions typical to some particular real-life problems, but nevertheless covers a large class of linear programs.

First, let us define the following probability distribution:

Definition 2. *If a random variable X is distributed according to the normal distribution $\mathcal{N}(\mu, \sigma^2)$, then the distribution of the absolute value $|X|$ is called the folded normal distribution and is denoted $\mathcal{N}_f(\mu, \sigma^2)$.*

Our experiments were parametrized by the following quantities:

- the number of variables n and the number of inequality constraints m in (1);
- the fraction $p \in [0, 1]$ of zero entries in A;
- the fraction $a \in [0, 1]$ of constraints with non-negative coefficients;
- the fraction $q \in [0, 1]$ of zero entries outside the main diagonal of P.

We performed two sets of experiments. In one of them we sampled the entries of P, Q from a uniform distribution, and in the other one from a normal distribution.

An experiment proceeded as follows.

1. Generate a random point $v = (v_1, \ldots, v_n) \in \mathbb{R}^n$ where v_i is chosen uniformly from $(0, 100]$. This point will be contained in the polyhedron defined by the constraints in (1), thereby ensuring its non-emptiness.
2. Generate a random $m \times n$ matrix $A = (a_{ij})_{i,j=1,1}^{m,n}$ whose entries are assigned in the following way:
    - The value 0 is taken with the probability p.
    - A random value is sampled uniformly from $[-100, 100] \subseteq \mathbb{R}$ (or from a normal distribution $\mathcal{N}(0, 100)$) with probability $1 - p$.
    - After a row of A is generated, with probability a all entries in this row are replaced with their absolute values.

3. Generate the entries of the vector **b** of length m in such a way that the polyhedron defined by $\mathbf{Ax} \leq \mathbf{b}$ definitely contains the point v. That is, for each $i \in \{1, \ldots, m\}$, compute $b_i = a_{i1}v_1 + \ldots + a_{in}v_n + s$, where s is a random positive number. In our experiments, s was chosen uniformly from $[1000, 2000]$.

4. Let P be a $m \times m$ random matrix, the entries of which are assigned in the following way:
   - The value 0 is taken with the probability q (except the main diagonal, which stays non-zero in any case).
   - A random value is sampled uniformly from $[-100, 100]$ (or from a normal distribution $\mathcal{N}(0, 100)$) with probability $1 - q$.

   Note that P is invertible with probability 1.

5. Let Q be a $(m + n) \times (m + n)$ random positive generalized permutation matrix. The permutation defined by Q was picked uniformly from S_{m+n} and the non-zero entries of Q were uniformly sampled from $[1, 100]$ (or sampled from a folded normal distribution $\mathcal{N}_f(0, 100)$).

6. Construct $\hat{A}$ and $\hat{\mathbf{b}}$ according to Bednarz's transformation.

7. For each column of $\hat{A}$ compute the mean and the variance of its entries. Find the sets of m columns where (a) the means are the largest, (b) the means are the smallest, (c) the variances are the largest, or (d) the variances are the smallest.

8. The experiment was considered *successful* if one of the four sets of m columns found in the previous step exactly corresponded to the slack variables in **y** introduced by Bednarz's transformation.

When sampling the entries of P, Q from the uniform distribution, we ran 5 experiments for all possible values of the parameters, where $m+n \in \{100, 250, 500\}$, $m/(m + n) \in \{25\%, 50\%, 75\%\}$, $p, q \in \{0\%, 25\%, 50\%, 75\%, 90\%\}$, and $a \in \{0\%, 25\%, 50\%, 100\%\}$. For almost all settings, there was at least one experiment that was successful. The experiments were less successful only if m was small and p was large. When sampling the entries of P, Q from the normal distribution, we ran the same number of experiments with the same parameters. Again, for most settings, at least one of the experiments was successful. Again, we had less success if many entries in A were 0 (i.e. p was large) and there were less constraints than variables (i.e. $m/(m + n)$ was small). As we assumed, the best metrics was the variance, larger for the initial variables and smaller for the slack variables. For the largest parameters ($m+n = 500$), an attack took just a couple of seconds on a server with two Intel X5670 processors with 12 MB cache running at 2.93 GHz, and with 48 GB of main memory. The linear algebra operations were imported from *sage* [13]. Since sage does not round floating point numbers in the process of matrix multiplication, the transformation itself turned out to be too inefficient for choosing the initial parameters with high precision. For example, while the attack still takes several seconds for 64-bit initial numbers, the transformation takes half an hour. However, this issue affects significantly the transformation, but not the attack timing. The attack timing grows less than linearly with the number of bits. We also did not notice that choosing more precise numbers would affect the outcome of the attack.

This problem can be potentially resolved by scaling the columns by a value that comes from a sufficiently large distribution to hide these differences. Although this makes the columns approximately the same size, it makes the values of the slack variables in the optimal solution to the transformed LP task much smaller than the values of the original variables, still keeping them distinguishable. Also, this modification does not affect the variances of the variables.

Another way is to add extra constraints whose entries that are large enough to provide noise for all the variables. The problem is that introducing more constraints requires introducing more slack variables for correctness. These slack variables cannot be protected by the same method. Once they have been revealed, they may be removed from the system by Gaussian elimination.

We would also like to note that the adversary may always bring the transformed matrix to its reduced row echelon form. This means that this transformation provides the best possible hiding, and the security analysis should be performed on this form. Unfortunately, it cannot be used for hiding instead of P since it is expensive to compute it while preserving the privacy.

Sampling the Vertices of the Polyhedron. If the previous attack does not work well because the random values used during the transformation have been sampled in such a way that the entries of the resulting matrix have similar distributions, then there are still more ways of locating the slack variables. Consider (3), where each of the new variables $y_i \in \mathbf{x}$ is either a scaled copy of some original variable $x_{i'} \in \mathbf{x}$ or a (scaled) slack variable. The constraints (3) define an n-dimensional polyhedron in the space $\mathbb{R}^{m+n}$ (due to its construction, the matrix $\hat{A}$ has full rank). In each vertex of this polyhedron, at least n of the variables in $\mathbf{y}$ are equal to zero. We have hypothesized that for at least a significant fraction of linear programs, it is possible to sample the vertices of this polyhedron in such manner, that slack variables will be 0 more often than the original variables.

To verify our hypothesis, we performed a series of experiments, described below in detail. Our experiments were parametrized by the quantities m, n, p, a described at the previous experiment. Additionally, the number $k \in \mathbb{N}$ determines the number of vertex samples done in an experiment, and the fraction $e \in [0, 1]$ affects the polyhedron that we use to look for variables that most often take the value 0 in vertices.

An experiment proceeded as follows.

1–6. Generate A, b, $\hat{A}$, $\hat{b}$ as in the previous experiment, using the current values of m, n, p, a, and taking $q = 0$. The entries of all matrices are sampled from the uniform distribution.
7. Modify $\hat{A}$ [resp. $\hat{b}$] by removing their first $e \cdot m$ rows [resp. elements]. This corresponds to discarding a fraction of e equations from the system $\hat{A}\mathbf{y} = \hat{b}$. We have found that such removal increases the success rate of the experiments for certain parameters.
8. Initialize the counters $z_1, \ldots, z_{m+n}$ to 0.
9. Repeat the following k times.

(a) Generate the optimization direction $\mathbf{c} \in \mathbb{R}^{m+n}$ sampling each entry from the distribution $\mathcal{N}_f(0, 1)$.

(b) Find an optimal *basic* solution (a solution located in a vertex of the polyhedron) to the linear program

$$\text{minimize } \mathbf{c}^T \cdot \mathbf{y}, \text{ subject to } \hat{A}\mathbf{y} = \hat{\mathbf{b}}, \mathbf{y} \geq \mathbf{0} \ .$$

(c) If the optimal solution $\mathbf{y}_{\text{opt}}$ exists, then increase by one each z_i where the i-th element of $\mathbf{y}_{\text{opt}}$ equals 0.

10. The experiment was considered *successful* if the counters with n largest values exactly corresponded to the slack variables in $\mathbf{y}$ introduced by Bednarz's transformation.

We have performed our experiments with different settings. In all experiments, k was fixed to 100 (larger values did not seem to give any significant difference). For each set of values for the parameters (m, n, p, a, e), we performed 20 experiments. The results for all sets of experiments are reported in Table 1. For given (m, n, p, a), the symbol $*$ in the corresponding cell of the table indicates that none of 20 experiments performed for all values of e we considered were successful. If at least one experiment was successful for some value of e, given the parameters (m, n, p, a), then this value of e is given in the corresponding cell of the table.

Each attack took a couple of minutes. The largest matrices were obtained for $\frac{m}{m+n} = 0.75$; for $m + n = 250$ it took less than one minute, and for $m + n = 500$ about five minutes.

We also performed some initial experiments where the entries of the optimization direction $\mathbf{c}$ were sampled from $\mathcal{N}(0, 1)$. This choice did not perform better (and sometimes performed much worse) than the sampling from $\mathcal{N}_f(0, 1)$.

We see that the worst case for our algorithm is when m is much smaller than n and the fraction of zero entries in A is large. The problem is that there are too few inequalities already in the beginning, and the zeroes make the initial matrix A even sparser and less constraining. The initial variables thus do not differ too much from the slack variables. However, if A is sparse, there may possibly exist other attacks based looking for certain affine relationships between the variables, similarly to the attacks from Sec. 3.3.

For $m > n$ it may happen that even the slack variables will not be allowed to take the value 0 at all because of too tight bounds. In this case, some equations have been just eliminated from the transformed program. This is not equivalent to removing bounds from the initial polyhedron, and it is not quite clear what exactly happens to it. However, there are definitely less constraints than before, and the slack variables again have higher probabilities of becoming 0.

The results also show something interesting about the effect of the structure of A on the outcome of the attack. It can be seen than the attack performs better when all the entries of A are non-negative. The success rate is in general higher for smaller fraction of zero elements in A, especially for the smaller number of constraints.

Table 1. Results of the vertex-sampling experiments

m	n	p	a 0.0	0.25	0.5	1.0	m	n	p	a 0.0	0.25	0.5	1.0
25	75	0	*	0	0	0	125	375	0	*	*	*	*
		0.25	*	*	0	0			0.25	*	*	*	*
		0.5	0	0	0	0			0.5	*	*	*	*
		0.75	0	0	0	0			0.75	*	*	*	*
		0.9	*	*	*	*			0.9	*	*	*	*
50	50	0	0	0	0	0	187	63	0	0.75	0.75	0.75	0.5
		0.25	0	0	0	0			0.25	0.75	0.5	0.75	0.5
		0.5	0	0	0	0			0.5	0.75	0.75	0.75	*
		0.75	*	0	0	0			0.75	*	0.75	0.75	0.5
		0.9	*	*	*	*			0.9	*	*	*	0.9
62	188	0	*	*	*	*	250	250	0	*	0	*	0
		0.25	*	*	*	*			0.25	*	0	*	0
		0.5	*	*	*	0			0.5	*	*	*	0
		0.75	*	*	*	0			0.75	*	*	*	0
		0.9	*	*	*	*			0.9	*	*	*	*
75	25	0	0.75	0.5	0.75	0.5	375	125	0	*	0.75	0.75	0.5
		0.25	0.75	0.5	0.75	0.5			0.25	0.75	0.75	0.75	0.75
		0.5	0.75	0.5	0.75	0.5			0.5	0.75	*	*	0.5
		0.75	0.75	0.5	0.75	0.5			0.75	*	0.75	*	0.5
		0.9	*	*	0.75	0.5			0.9	*	0.75	*	0.75
125	125	0	0	0	0	0	475	25	0	0.9	0.9	0.9	0.9
		0.25	0	*	0	0			0.25	0.9	0.9	0.9	0.9
		0.5	0	0	0	0			0.5	0.9	0.9	0.9	0.9
		0.75	*	0	0	0			0.75	0.9	0.9	0.9	0.9
		0.9	*	*	*	*			0.9	0.9	0.9	0.9	0.9

Our experimental results show that for many linear programs in canonical form (1), it is possible to identify the slack variables after Bednarz's transformation. The validity of our hypothesis has been verified.

Several Slack Variables per Inequality. The authors of [7] proposed introducing multiple slack variables for the same inequality. We have tried experimentally that in this case there is even higher probability that the slack variables are those that most often take the value 0 in a vertex sampled as described previously; this can also be explained in theory. Also, in this case, the columns in $\hat{A}$, corresponding to slack variables added to the same inequality, are multiples of each other. This makes them easily locatable.

Removing the Slack Variables. Once we have located the slack variables, we will reorder the variables in the constraints $\hat{A}y = \hat{b}$ so, that the non-slack variables are the first n variables and the slack variables are the last m variables in y. This corresponds to the first n columns of $\hat{A}$ containing the coefficients of non-slack variables in the system of equations, and the last m columns containing the coefficients of slack variables. We will now use row operations to bring the system to the form $(A' \ I) \, \mathbf{y} = \mathbf{b}'$, where I is $m \times m$ identity matrix. This system, together with the non-negativity constraints, is equivalent to the system of inequalities $A' \mathbf{x}' \le \mathbf{b}'$, where $\mathbf{x}'$ are the first n elements of $\mathbf{y}$.

3.2 Finding the Permutation of Variables

We will now describe the attack that allows to remove the scaling and the permutation of variables. An attack based on exploiting the slack variables has been proposed in [3]. If the system contains only inequalities, then they completely reveal a scaled permutation of P that may be afterwards used to recover a scaled permutation of M whose scaling may be afterwards removed by searching for common factors. The factoring attack can be avoided by using real entries in Q. Our attack does not use factoring, but exploits the geometrical structure of the transformed program.

Recall that the initial linear program is partitioned horizontally, so each party holds some number of constraints. Suppose Alice knows r inequalities $\sum_{i=1}^{n} a_{ji} x_i \le b_j$ (where $j \in \{1, \ldots, r\}$) of the original system of constraints, from a total of m. We assume that r is at least 2. Alice also knows all scaled and permuted constraints $\sum_{i=1}^{n} a'_{ji} x'_i \le b'_j$ (where $j \in \{1, \ldots, m\}$). If we could undo the scaling and permuting, then this set of m inequalities would contain all original r inequalities known by Alice. Next we show how Alice can recover the permutation of the variables. Once this has been recovered, the scaling is trivial to undo.

Alice picks two of the original inequalities she knows (e.g. k-th and l-th, where $1 \le k, l \le r$) and two inequalities from the scaled and permuted system (e.g. k'-th and l'-th, where $1 \le k', l' \le m$). She makes the guess that k-th [resp. l-th] original inequality is the k'-th [resp. l'-th] scaled and permuted inequality. This guess can be verified as follows. If the guess turns out to be correct, then the verification procedure also reveals the permutation (or at least parts of it).

For the inequality $\sum_{i=1}^{n} a_{ji} x_i \le b_j$ in the original system let H_j be the corresponding hyperplane where "$\le$" has been replaced by "$=$". Similarly, let H'_j be the hyperplane corresponding to the j-th inequality in the scaled and permuted system. The hyperplane H_j intersects with the i-th coordinate axis in the point $(0, \ldots, 0, z_{ji}, 0, \ldots, 0)$, where $z_{ji} = b_j / a_{ji}$ (here z_{ji} is the i-th component in the tuple). Also, let $(0, \ldots, 0, z'_{ji}, 0, \ldots, 0)$ be the point where H'_j and the i-th coordinate axis intersect.

Note that scaling the (initial) polyhedron s times along the i-th axis would increase z_{ji} by s times, too, for all j. Scaling it along other axes would not change z_{ji}. Hence the quantities z_{ki} / z_{li} (for $i \in \{1, \ldots, n\}$) are scale-invariant.

To verify her guess, Alice computes the (multi)sets $\{ z_{ki} / z_{li} \mid 1 \le i \le n \}$ and $\{ z'_{k'i} / z'_{l'i} \mid 1 \le i \le n \}$. If her guess was correct, then these multisets are equal. Also, if they are equal, then the i-th coordinate in the original system can only correspond to the i'-th coordinate in the scaled and permuted system if $z_{ki} / z_{li} = z'_{k'i'} / z'_{l'i'}$. This allows her to recover the permutation. If there are repeating values in the multisets, or if division by 0 occurs somewhere, then she cannot recover the complete permutation. In this case she repeats with other k, l, k', l'.

But note that the presence of zeroes in the coefficients also gives information about the permutation.

This attack does not allow to discover precise permutations if the known inequalities are symmetric with respect to some variables, and the scaling cannot be derived for the variables whose coefficients in all the known inequalities are 0. It is also impossible if the right sides of all the known inequalities are 0. However, it would reduce the number of secure linear programming tasks significantly. Also, if two variables in the system look the same for Alice (they participate in the same way in all inequalities she knows) then it should not matter to her how they end up in the recovered permutation.

We have followed up our experiments reported in the previous section, and verified that the attack works in practice.

3.3   Attacks Specific to [3]

Dreier and Kerschbaum [3] propose a transformation that is applicable to LP tasks containing both equality and inequality constraints. In this paper, we only consider its application to tasks with inequality constraints only (although the operations presented in this section are also applicable to equations). In their transformation, the variables are first shifted by a positive vector (as described in Sec. 2.1), and then Bednarz's transformation is applied to the resulting system. In [3], the construction is described somewhat differently and the resulting positive generalized permutation matrix Q used to scale and permute the columns of the constraint system is not the most general matrix possible. The attacks described below work for any possible Q.

Shifting Back. The shifting of variables that has been used in [3] (and also in the transformation presented by Wang et al. [16], which only applies to LP tasks with equality constraints, and is thus outside the scope of this paper) reduces to scaling. The inequalities $\mathbf{y} \geq \mathbf{r}$ for the variables $\mathbf{y}$ are transformed to equalities by the introduction of new slack variables $\mathbf{s}$. For the variable $y_i \in \mathbf{y}$, related to the original variable x_i through the equality $y_i = x_i + r_i$, we have the equality $y_i - s_i = r_i$, where s_i is a new slack variable. After applying Bednarz's transformation, the variables are scaled and this equality becomes $q_i \hat{y}_i - q'_i \hat{s}_i = r_i$. The new variables $\hat{y}_i$ and $\hat{s}_i$ are related to the previous ones by $y_i = q_i \hat{y}_i$ and $s_i = q'_i \hat{s}_i$, where q_i and q'_i are certain non-zero entries in the matrix Q. Thus $\hat{s}_i = (q_i \hat{y}_i - r_i)/q'_i = (y_i - r_i)/q'_i = x_i/q'_i$. I.e. the slack variable $\hat{s}_i$ is a scaled copy of the original variable x_i.

We could now eliminate the variables $\mathbf{y}$ (the shifted versions of the original variables $\mathbf{x}$) from the system of constraints and the objective function. We will then be left with the system that involves only the slack variables $\mathbf{s}$ from the inequalities $\mathbf{y} \geq \mathbf{r}$ and the slack variables $\mathbf{x_s}$ from the inequalities in the original system. The resulting LP task could have been obtained from the original task through Bednarz's transformation and the attacks described above can be applied to it.

To eliminate the variables $\mathbf{y}$, we need to know their location. Dreier's and Kerschbaum's transformation [3] does not actually hide these variables, due to their choice of Q. But even if the permutation encoded in Q were more general, we could still recover the locations of the variables $\mathbf{y}$ as described below. The procedure described below also recovers the pairs $(\hat{y}_i, \hat{s}_i)$ of variables and corresponding slack variables, the difficulty of which is postulated in the cryptanalysis performed in [3].

Affine Relationships in Small Sets of Variables. Each variable from $\mathbf{y} = \mathbf{x} + \mathbf{r}$ is associated with exactly one slack variable from $\mathbf{s}$. To find the pairs $(\hat{y}_i, \hat{s}_i)$, the adversary can just pick pairs of variables and then verify that they correspond to each other. The correspondence that the adversary can verify is the affine relationship $q_i \hat{y}_i - q_i' \hat{s}_i = r_i$ between these variables.

This problem can be stated more generally. Suppose that we have a linear equation system $\mathbf{A}\mathbf{x} = \mathbf{b}$. Consider the solution space of this system. If the space contains small sets of t variables that are in affine relationship $\alpha_1 x_{i_1} + \ldots + \alpha_t x_{i_t} = \beta$ for some $\alpha_i, \beta \in \mathbb{R}$ (that may be not obvious from the outer appearance A), then these equations may be recovered by looking through all the sets of variables of size t. To expose the affine relationship between $x_{i_1}, \ldots, x_{i_t}$, we will just use Gaussian elimination to get rid of all other variables. The procedure can be described as follows:

1. Repeat the following, until only variables $x_{i_1}, \ldots, x_{i_t}$ remain in the system.
   (a) Pick any other variable x_j that has not been removed yet.
   (b) Take an equation where x_j has non-zero coefficient. Through this equation, express the variable x_j in terms of the other variables. Substitute it into all the other equations. Remove the equation and the variable x_j. If there are no equations where x_j has non-zero coefficient, then remove only x_j, without touching any remaining equations.
2. The previous operations do not change the solution set of the system (for the remaining variables). Therefore, if there are any equations left, then there exist $\alpha_i, \beta \in \mathbb{R}$ (not all $\alpha_i = 0$) such that $\alpha_1 x_{i_1} + \ldots + \alpha_t x_{i_t} = \beta$.

In this manner, the adversary is able to find all unordered pairs $\{\hat{y}_i, \hat{s}_i\}$ related to each other through $q_i \hat{y}_i + q_i' \hat{s}_i = r_i$. The signs of q_i, q_i', r_i in this relationship determine, which one is the original variable ($q_i r_i > 0$), and which one the slack variable ($q_i' r_i < 0$).

4 Conclusions

We have presented attacks against transformation-based methods for solving LP tasks in privacy-preserving manner. The attacks are not merely theoretical constructions, but work with reasonable likelihood on problems of practical size. The aim of this paper was to show that the attacks work in practice. It was not intended to estimate their theoretical complexity.

We have presented our attacks against methods that handle LP tasks where the constraints are specified as inequalities. May the methods for differently-represented LP tasks, e.g. as systems of equations [12,16], still be considered secure? Our attacks are not directly applicable against this setting because the set of equations representing the subspace of feasible solutions is not unique and the hyperplanes in the original and transformed systems of constraints cannot be directly matched against each other like in Sec. 3.2. In our opinion, one still has to be careful because there is no sharp line delimiting systems of constraints represented as equations, and systems of constraints represented as inequalities. The canonical form (1) and the standard form (2) can be transformed to each other and the actual nature of the constraints may be hidden in the specified LP task.

The lack of precise definitions of confidentiality for transformation-based methods makes it harder to argue about the (in)security of a particular method. Further advances in this field would benefit from an indistinguishability-based definition of security, similar to [6]. In such a definition, the adversary would be allowed to pick two LP tasks, one of which would then be transformed by the environment. The adversary's goal is to find out, which of the two tasks was transformed. In this definition, it would also be possible to precisely state which parts of the task the transformation will not attempt to protect: the environment would check that these parts are equal for the two tasks selected by the adversary.

Acknowledgements. This work has been supported by the European Regional Development Fund through the Estonian Center of Excellence in Computer Science, EXCS, and the Software Technologies and Applications Competence Centre, STACC. This research was also supported by the European Union Seventh Framework Programme (FP7/2007-2013) under grant agreement no. 284731 "Usable and Efficient Secure Multiparty Computation (UaESMC)".

References

1. Bednarz, A.: Methods for two-party privacy-preserving linear programming. PhD thesis, University of Adelaide (2012)
2. Bednarz, A., Bean, N., Roughan, M.: Hiccups on the road to privacy-preserving linear programming. In: Proceedings of the 8th ACM workshop on Privacy in the Electronic Society, WPES 2009, pp. 117–120. ACM, New York (2009)
3. Dreier, J., Kerschbaum, F.: Practical privacy-preserving multiparty linear programming based on problem transformation. In: SocialCom/PASSAT, pp. 916–924. IEEE (2011)
4. Du., W.: A Study Of Several Specific Secure Two-Party Computation Problems. PhD thesis, Purdue University (2001)
5. Du, W., Zhan, Z.: A practical approach to solve secure multi-party computation problems. In: New Security Paradigms Workshop, pp. 127–135. ACM Press (2002)
6. Goldwasser, S., Micali, S.: Probabilistic encryption. J. Comput. Syst. Sci. 28(2), 270–299 (1984)

7. Hong, Y., Vaidya, J.: An inference-proof approach to privacy-preserving horizontally partitioned linear programs. In: Optimization Letters (to appear, 2013) (published online October 05, 2012)
8. Hong, Y., Vaidya, J., Lu, H.: Secure and efficient distributed linear programming. Journal of Computer Security 20(5), 583–634 (2012)
9. Li, J., Atallah, M.J.: Secure and private collaborative linear programming. In: International Conference on Collaborative Computing, pp. 1–8 (2006)
10. Li, W., Li, H., Deng, C.: Privacy-preserving horizontally partitioned linear programs with inequality constraints. Optimization Letters 7(1), 137–144 (2013)
11. Mangasarian, O.L.: Privacy-preserving linear programming. Optimization Letters 5(1), 165–172 (2011)
12. Mangasarian, O.L.: Privacy-preserving horizontally partitioned linear programs. Optimization Letters 6(3), 431–436 (2012)
13. Stein, W.A., et al.: Sage Mathematics Software (Version 5.10). The Sage Development Team (2013), http://www.sagemath.org
14. Toft, T.: Solving linear programs using multiparty computation. In: Dingledine, R., Golle, P. (eds.) FC 2009. LNCS, vol. 5628, pp. 90–107. Springer, Heidelberg (2009)
15. Vaidya, J.: Privacy-preserving linear programming. In: Shin, S.Y., Ossowski, S. (eds.) SAC, pp. 2002–2007. ACM (2009)
16. Wang, C., Ren, K., Wang, J.: Secure and practical outsourcing of linear programming in cloud computing. In: 2011 Proceedings IEEE INFOCOM, pp. 820–828 (2011)

Maintaining Database Anonymity
in the Presence of Queries

Ryan Riley[1], Chris Clifton[2], and Qutaibah Malluhi[1]

[1] Department of Computer Science and Engineering
Qatar University
{ryan.riley,qmalluhi}@qu.edu.qa
[2] Department of Computer Science
Purdue University
clifton@cs.purdue.edu

Abstract. With the advent of cloud computing there is an increased interest in outsourcing an organization's data to a remote provider in order to reduce the costs associated with self-hosting. If that database contains information about individuals (such as medical information), it is increasingly important to also protect the privacy of the individuals contained in the database. Existing work in this area has focused on preventing the hosting provider from ascertaining individually identifiable sensitive data from the database, through database encryption or manipulating the data to provide privacy guarantees based on privacy models such as k-anonymity. Little work has been done to ensure that information contained in queries on the data, in conjunction with the data, does not result in a privacy violation. In this work we present a hash based method which provably allows the privacy constraint of an unencrypted database to be extended to the queries performed on the database. In addition, we identify a privacy limitation of such an approach, describe how it could be exploited using a known-query attack, and propose a counter-measure based on oblivious storage.

1   Introduction

With the advent of cloud computing, the desire to outsource databases continues to grow. Database as a service is a quickly growing industry, attracting companies looking to reduce costs by maintaining fewer servers and IT personnel. However, as the usage of database outsourcing grows, so does the risk of privacy violations. In some cases this outsourcing may even conflict with privacy laws that are designed to safeguard the identities and the individuals the data is about. An outsourced database has a new threat to consider: the hosting provider itself.

Existing work has explored a variety of privacy constraints such as k-anonymity [1, 2], l-diversity [3], and t-closeness [4]. These works aim to provide metrics for the privacy protection of data stored in a database. Little work has been done to safeguard privacy in the queries themselves, beyond the extreme model of Private Information Retrieval [5] and related works that involved

R. Accorsi and S. Ranise (Eds.): STM 2013, LNCS 8203, pp. 33–48, 2013.

encrypting the entire database. In our model, we assume that the data is intentionally stored unencrypted so that the hosting provider can provide value added services such as address correction and analysis of the (anonymized) data.

Previous work involving unencrypted, anonymized databases ignores the impact of information contained in queries and essentially models queries as having been drawn randomly from the global pool of all possible queries, meaning they would not leak any sensitive information. Even the authors' prior work on querying anonymized data requires this assumption [6, 7]. This is rarely a reasonable assumption. The very existence of a query or set of queries can easily leak information about individuals in a database.

Consider the scenario that John is found collapsed on the street. The reason for his collapse is unknown. When he arrives at the ER, the doctors notice that John's arms contain punctures indicative of illegal drug use. In order to better determine John's situation, the doctor queries his medical records to determine if he has any of the diseases that may come from shared needles. The queries would look something like:

```
SELECT * FROM DB WHERE PATIENT = "John" AND (Disease = "HIV" OR
Disease = "hepatitis" OR Disease = "tuberculosis");
```

Given that those three diseases are considered high risk for illegal drug users but not for the general population, someone with a knowledge of those queries may be able to reasonably assume that John is an illegal drug user. (Why else would a doctor issue this particular set of queries?) Private information about John has been leaked, even if the database itself is stored in a privacy-preserving fashion. The queries themselves leak the information.

We model query privacy leakage based on the probability of a link between identifying information and sensitive information. For no leakage to occur, a query should not convey any private information that is not already revealed by the database itself. In the example above, queries for those three diseases increases the probability that John is at a high risk for diseases transmitted from blood. This knowledge, in turn, increases the probability that he has one or more of the diseases. A leak can be described as follows:

Given:

t = An individual (or identifying information for that individual)

v = A sensitive value

D = A database

Q = A sequence of queries

Private information is leaked if:

$Pr(t \text{ is linked to } v|D) < Pr(t \text{ is linked to } v|D, Q)$

In this work we propose a technique to build an anatomized database designed to safeguard the privacy of individuals whose data is being queried. We base our models on the principle of k-anonymity. The technique functions by separating individually identifiable users into buckets of size $\geq k$ and ensuring that queries to the database always involve at least an entire bucket. While our database model, described in more detail in [6, 7], allows INSERTs and UPDATEs, this paper only discusses SELECT queries. INSERTs and UPDATEs inherently pose

SSN	Name	Disease
000-07-7083	Luis	HIV
000-26-9073	Donna	Diabetes
000-03-3060	Zachary	Hepatitis A
000-04-4396	Kenneth	Cancer
000-09-4349	Michelle	Tuberculosis
000-22-6531	Thomas	Hepatitis B

Fig. 1. Sample Database

different privacy risks because an attacker can analyze the before and after states of the database. Managing these risks imposes limitations on the statements and requires a certain amount of encryption [7]. The result is that INSERTs and UPDATEs that do not violate privacy based on the host comparing before and after states of the database inherently avoid the type of privacy violation described in this work.

The contributions of this work are as follows:

1. We identify and define the problem of private data leakage from the query in anonymized databases,
2. We provide a proof that can be used to demonstrate whether leakage can occur for many group-based privacy protection schemes,
3. We propose a hash based technique to prevent private data leakage through the query in a k-anonymized database,
4. We identify a type of privacy leak based on a known-query attack that would allow an attacker to violate query privacy, and
5. We propose the usage of oblivious storage as a mechanism to protect against known-query attacks.

1.1 Database Model

The basis for our database model is anatomization [8] with an encrypted join key [6, 7]. For the sake of simplicity of presentation we assume that the groupings provide only k-anonymity; however, similar privacy models may be also used without adjustments to our model.

In the anatomy model, the identifying information and the sensitive information are split into two separate tables, and a group number is used to link groups of items from both tables together. An attacker who is able to analyze the database cannot link a sensitive value to a particular identifying value, instead each can only be linked to the group it is a part of. An encrypted sequence number allows a client who knows the secret key to perform a query and then filter the results to determine the exact answer. Fig. 1 shows a simple database storing patient disease information. Now, suppose that we want to release this database while still maintaining the privacy of the individuals in it. We decide that we want to release the database to meet k-anonymity requirements with $k = 2$, and so we ensure that each group contains at least two individuals in it.

SSN	Name	GID	SEQ
000-07-7083	Luis	1	1
000-26-9073	Donna	1	2
000-03-3060	Zachary	2	3
000-04-4396	Kenneth	2	4
000-09-4349	Michelle	3	5
000-22-6531	Thomas	3	6

(a) Identifier Table (IT)

HSEQ	GID	Disease
$H_{k_1}(1)$	1	HIV
$H_{k_1}(2)$	1	Diabetes
$H_{k_1}(3)$	2	Hepatitis A
$H_{k_1}(4)$	2	Cancer
$H_{k_1}(5)$	3	Tuberculosis
$H_{k_1}(6)$	3	Hepatitis B

(b) Sensitive Table (ST)

Fig. 2. Anatomized Database

Fig. 2 shows the same database anatomized in this way. An attacker analyzing the database can only link a particular piece of sensitive information to a specific group, not to an individual within the group. The groups can be chosen using any group-based privacy criteria (such as l-diversity) in much the same way.

When a query is performed (either on the identifying information or the sensitive information) then all results from the corresponding group are returned. The client then uses the secret key to match the sequence number from the identifying information with the sequence number in the sensitive information in order to determine which elements of the group were actually queried. The details of query processing for such a database can be found in [6, 7].

We assume that one of the fields (in this case social security number) is used as the unique identifier for indexing the tables. We call this field the lookup key.

We explicitly assume an unencrypted database. While one might think that encryption should be used for data sent to a cloud provider, there are a number of good reasons not to do this:

- Databases commonly experience issues related to the accuracy and completeness of their data. Address information, phone numbers, zip codes, etc. may be incomplete. A cloud provider with an unencrypted database can provide "information fixing as service" to help fill in some of these gaps.
- Large, demographic queries that don't involve mixing identifiers and sensitive data (such as "How many customers do I have in Chicago?") do not require privacy protection, and can be performed on the unencrypted DB without a performance penalty. This could not occur in an encrypted DB.
- Data stored on the cloud can be offered to a third party for performing data analytics in order to extract useful information.

1.2 Threat Model

The owner of the database (the client) wishes to outsource their database to an outsourcing provider (the server). Before sending data to the server, the client anatomizes it. The client then queries the server requesting information about specific users, identifying them by their lookup key, as in this query:

```
SELECT * from DB WHERE SSN="000-03-3060" AND
    Disease ="Hepatitis A";
```

The client should not issue queries that use any other field as the identifier. We assume the client has permission to access any record in the database.

Our attacker is the server and has full access to all data in the database as well as all queries issued. Given a query, the goal of the attacker is to determine which user a specific query is about. The server is honest-but-curious, meaning that it does not interfere with the correct operation of the database. Our assumption is that an active attacker (who alters queries, their results, or the database) would eventually be detected and the client would stop using their services. Therefore, it is in the best interest of the server to operate correctly while it attempts to learn private information.

2   Data Privacy of the Query

As a straightforward solution to this problem we propose that instead of performing queries based on individually identifying information, queries are performed on entire groups.

Returning again to the database from Fig. 2, instead of performing a query such as:

```
SELECT * from DB where SSN="000-03-3060" and Disease = "Hepatitis A";
```
The client would instead send the following:
```
SELECT * from DB where GID=2 and Disease = "Hepatitis A";
```

This assumes that the individual identified by 000-03-3060 is in group 2; ways the client can efficiently learn this without violating privacy will be described in Sections 3.2 and 4.2. The client will receive back database entries where Disease = Hepatitis A for all users in group 2. The client then simply filters out entries for all users except the one it intended to query. This process does not need to be done manually. A simple query processing tool that runs at the client can make this process transparent. In order to perform this query the client must already know which group the SSN is in. How the client can learn this without causing a privacy violation will be discussed in Section 3.

We will now prove that performing group based queries can have the same privacy guarantees as the underlying grouping methodology.

2.1   Definitions and Notations

Throughout the paper, a table T has d identifier attributes, $A_1, \ldots, A_d$, and a sensitive attribute A_s. (This could easily be extended to multiple sensitive attributes, we use a single one for clarity.) We will use dot notation to refer to some attribute of a tuple (e.g., for a tuple $t \in T$, $t.A_i$ denotes t's value for the corresponding attribute where $1 \leq i \leq d$ or $i = s$).

Our work is based on the k-anonymity family of privacy definitions, which group individuals such that each individual is indistinguishable from others in the group with respect to the sensitive value that goes with each individual.

Definition 1 (Group/Equivalence class). *A group (also known as equivalence class) G_j is a subset of tuples in table T such that $T = \bigcup_{j=1}^{m} G_j$, and for any pair (G_{j_1}, G_{j_2}), where $1 \le j_1 \ne j_2 \le m$, $G_{j_1} \cap G_{j_2} = \emptyset$.*

Definition 2 (k-anonymity). *A set of groups is said to satisfy k-**anonymity**, iff $\forall$ groups G_j,*

$$|G_j| \ge k$$

where $|G_j|$ is the number of tuples in G_j.

While much of this work (particularly in this section) applies to any k-anonymity based model, our examples are based on the anatomy definition used in [6], which is a variation of that given in [8].

Definition 3 (Anatomy). *Given a table T partitioned into m groups using k-anonymity without generalization, anatomy produces an identifier table (IT) and a sensitive table (ST) as follows. IT has schema*

$$(A_1, \ldots, A_d, GID, SEQ)$$

where $A_i \in Q_T$ for $1 \le i \le d = |Q_T|$, Q_T is the set of identifying attributes in T, GID is the group id and SEQ is the unique sequence number for a tuple. For each $G_j \in T$ and each tuple $t \in G_j$, IT has a tuple of the form:

$$(t.A_1, \ldots, t.A_d, j, seq)$$

The ST has schema

$$(HSEQ, GID, A_s)$$

where A_s is the sensitive attribute in T, GID is the group id and HSEQ contains the output of a keyed cryptographic hash function denoted by $H_{\bar{k}}(seq)$ where seq is the corresponding unique sequence number in IT for a tuple. For each $G_j \in T$ and each tuple $t \in G_j$, ST contains a sensitive value v in a tuple of the form:

$$(H_{\bar{k}}(seq), j, v)$$

The key issue with the Anatomy model is that actual data values are preserved; the anonymization occurs by generalizing the link between identifying and sensitive values to the group level. Thus we expect user queries to be based on specific (rather than group level) values. This could communicate user knowledge about relationships between individuals and sensitive data to the server; a query that could convey such knowledge is deemed *sensitive*. Our goal is to preserve the privacy guarantees enforced on the underlying data even after a sequence of queries from a user with knowledge about the data that would violate privacy if revealed to the server.

Definition 4 (Query Privacy). *Any sequence of queries, $Q = <q_1, ..., q_j>$, preserves privacy of individuals if for every tuple $t \in IT$ and for every $v \in ST$ where $v.GID = t.GID$*

$$Pr(t \to v|T^*) = Pr(t \to v|T^*, Q)$$

where T^* is an $\{IT, ST\}$ anatomized table pair as in Definition 3 and $t \to v$ means that v is the sensitive value corresponding to t.

This definition states that a sequence of queries does not change the server's knowledge of the mapping between any individual and a sensitive value. While we do not formally prove it here, we claim that this is sufficient (although perhaps not necessary) to maintain the privacy guarantees of the k-anonymity family of measures. (While there are some special cases where this is not true, e.g., data meeting k-anonymity with all sensitive values in the group being the same $(Pr = 1)$ could meet definition 4 by maintaining the same probability while disclosing information that reduces the group size, we feel such cases reflect failure of the privacy metric to adequately protect sensitive information rather than a failure of query privacy.)

2.2   Query Privacy Preservation

Query streams that contain only information about the identifying attributes, or only about the sensitive attribute, clearly do not change the probability of the mapping and thus satisfy Definition 4. The problem is with queries that affect both:

Definition 5 (Sensitive Query). *A sensitive query, denoted by q, is a selection query in the form*
    SELECT * FROM $\langle$IT,ST$\rangle^1$ WHERE P$_{IT}$ and P$_{ST}$;

where P_{IT} is a predicate uniquely identifying one or more individuals in IT and P_{ST} restricts the range of sensitive values from ST.

To avoid revealing information, we require that at least one side of the sensitive query (either the identifying or sensitive information) not distinguish between any items in the group:

Definition 6 (k-anonymized Query). *Given a sensitive query, q, as in Definition 5, a k-anonymized sensitive query, denoted by q^*, is a selection query in either the form*
    SELECT * FROM $\langle$IT,ST$\rangle$ WHERE P$^*_{IT}$ and P$_{ST}$;
or the form
    SELECT * FROM $\langle$IT,ST$\rangle$ WHERE P$_{IT}$ and P$^*_{ST}$;
where P^*_{IT} is a predicate identifying a group in IT, P^*_{ST} is a predicate identifying a group in ST, (i.e., each $t' \in G_{t.GID}$ satisfies P^*_{IT} or each $v' \in G_{v.GID}$ satisfies P^*_{ST})

We now show that a stream of k-anonymized queries satisfies Definition 4. We show that if each single query satisfies Definition 4, any pair of queries that the

---

[1] This is not a join operation, it is the selection query described in [6] which is semantically equal to
SELECT * FROM IT*, ST WHERE P$_{IT}$ and P$_{ST}$ and involves client-server interaction.

groups queried are disjoint or the same, and if the sequence of queries groups either entirely in IT or entirely in ST, then the sequence of queries satisfies Definition 4.

Lemma 1. *Given a sequence of queries $Q = < q_1, ..., q_n >$ where $\forall i$, q_i satisfies Definition 4 and either*
$$\forall i, j: P_{i\,IT}^* = P_{j\,IT}^* \text{ or } P_{i\,IT}^* \cap P_{j\,IT}^* = \emptyset \text{ or}$$
$$\forall i, j: P_{i\,ST}^* = P_{j\,ST}^* \text{ or } P_{i\,ST}^* \cap P_{j\,ST}^* = \emptyset,$$
Q satisfies Definition 4.

Proof (By Induction). Base case: With only one query, by the preconditions of the lemma the query satisfies Definition 4.

Inductive case: Assume $Q' = < q_1, ..., q_{n-1} >$ satisfies Definition 4. Then $\forall$ individuals I, $Pr(t \rightarrow v|T^*) = Pr(t \rightarrow v|T^*, Q')$. Divide Q into two sets Q_d and Q_m, where Q_d consists of queries that have an empty intersection with q_n ($P_{i\,IT}^* \cap P_{n\,IT}^* = \emptyset$), and Q_m consists of queries that exactly match q_n ($P_{i\,IT}^* = P_{n\,IT}^*$). Definition 4 must hold for both Q_d and Q_m.

First, Q_d and Q_m each satisfy Definition 4, since we could have a query sequence consisting only of disjoint or only of matching queries (which by the inductive hypothesis we assume would satisfy the lemma.) Now we show that adding q_n still satisfies Definition 4.

For Q_m: For every individual $t \notin P_{n\,IT}^*$, then neither Q_m or q_n gives any information about t, and $Pr(t \rightarrow v|T^*) = Pr(t \rightarrow v|T^*, Q_m + q_n)$. For every $t \in P_{n\,IT}^*$, the information obtained from Q_m and q_n is exactly the same for all t, and $Pr(t \rightarrow v|T^*, Q_m + q_n) = Pr(t \rightarrow v|T^*, Q_m) = Pr(t \rightarrow v|T^*, q_n) = Pr(t \rightarrow v|T^*)$.

For Q_d: For an individual $t \in P_{n\,IT}^*$, no information is obtained from Q_d, and $Pr(t \rightarrow v|T^*, Q_d + q_n) = Pr(t \rightarrow v|T^*, q_n) = Pr(t \rightarrow v|T^*)$. Likewise, for $t \notin P_{n\,IT}^*$, $Pr(t \rightarrow v|T^*, Q_d + q_n) = Pr(t \rightarrow v|T^*, Q_d) = Pr(t \rightarrow v|T^*)$.

Extending this argument to Q_d and Q_m allows us to combine them, giving $Pr(t \rightarrow v|T^*, Q_d + Q_m) = Pr(t \rightarrow v|T^*, Q_d) = Pr(t \rightarrow v|T^*, Q_m) = Pr(t \rightarrow v|T^*)$.

The same argument holds if the group-level information is about the sensitive rather than identifying information (P_{ST}^*).

Theorem 1. *Transforming a sequence of sensitive queries, $Q = q_1, ..., q_n$, into a sequence of k-anonymized queries, $Q^* = q_1^*, ..., q_n^*$, protects the privacy of individuals based on k-anonymity and Definition 4.*

Proof. Let q be a k-anonymized query, (P_{IT}^*) be the group-level identifying information for q, and $v = P_{ST}$ be the sensitive value in the query. Let S be the multiset of sensitive values for the group P_{IT}^* in T^*.

First, if $t \notin P_{IT}^*$, then the query discloses no information about t, and $Pr(t \rightarrow v|T^*, q) = Pr(t \rightarrow v|T^*)$.

If $v \notin S$, then $Pr(t \rightarrow v|T^*, q) = 0 = Pr(t \rightarrow v|T^*)$.

Finally, assume $v \in S$. We assume that the server/adversary has no reason to assume a particular $t \in P_{IT}^*$ is being queried, and that any mapping is equally likely. Therefore $Pr(t \to v|q) = 1/|\mathbf{P}_{\mathtt{IT}}^*|$, the same as $Pr(t \to v|T^*)$ (note that we are interpreting v as the particular instance of a value in a multiset; if there are multiple occurrences of $v \in S$, then we need to multiply both sides by the number of instances.)

Thus Definition 4 holds for q. By Lemma 1, the Theorem holds.

(Note that this theorem does not hold if the adversary has knowledge of the probability that $t \to v$ beyond that contained in the query stream and the dataset. Such background information raises problems with the underlying static data under many anonymization models, and is not considered here.)

3   A Basic Solution

At a high-level, simply querying entire groups is a straightforward and simple solution. There is a complication with it, however, that must be addressed: It is not clear how the client can determine which group a given user is in. The client may know the lookup key for the user, but there is not a straightforward way to translate that into a group. In addition, the client cannot request the group number for a given lookup key from the server, as this would leak which user the client is going to later request. It is also not reasonable for the client to store (or request) the entire mapping of lookup keys to groups, as part of the purpose of outsourcing a database is that you no longer need to maintain a local database.

3.1   Group Membership Constraint

There is an important constraint that must be discussed with respect to group membership in this model: Once a group is formed, the membership of that group cannot be changed without potentially leaking private information to a server that is performing a statistical analysis of which groups are queried. For example, assume that group 5 is being frequently accessed, and as such is somewhat of a hotspot. If a member of that group is removed, and the frequent queries stop, then the server can ascertain that the removed entity was the target of most of those queries. The same argument can be used in reverse to describe why a member can never be added to a group. (For further discussion of these issues in the context of INSERTs and UPDATEs, see [7].)

3.2   Solution Overview

We propose adding a separate translation table at the server that can be queried to determine the bucket for a specific lookup key. It is crucial, however, that this operation does not reveal which lookup key is being queried. In order to accomplish this, the lookup table will store a keyed hash of the lookup key as well as the bucket that lookup key is in. The value of the key for the keyed hash is not known to the server, but is known to all clients that access the data.

SSN	Name	GID	SEQ
000-07-7083	Luis	1	1
000-26-9073	Donna	1	2
000-03-3060	Zachary	2	3
000-04-4396	Kenneth	2	4
000-09-4349	Michelle	3	5
000-22-6531	Thomas	3	6

(a) Identifier Table (IT)

HSEQ	GID	Disease
$H_{k_1}(1)$	1	HIV
$H_{k_1}(2)$	1	Diabetes
$H_{k_1}(3)$	2	Hepatitis A
$H_{k_1}(4)$	2	Cancer
$H_{k_1}(5)$	3	Tuberculosis
$H_{k_1}(6)$	3	Hepatitis B

(b) Sensitive Table (ST)

Hash	GID
$H_{K_L}(000\text{-}07\text{-}7083)$	1
$H_{K_L}(000\text{-}26\text{-}9073)$	1
$H_{K_L}(000\text{-}03\text{-}3060)$	2
$H_{K_L}(000\text{-}04\text{-}4396)$	2
$H_{K_L}(000\text{-}09\text{-}4349)$	3
$H_{K_L}(000\text{-}22\text{-}6531)$	3

(c) Lookup Table (LT)

Fig. 3. Sample Anatomized Database With a Lookup Table

The database needs to be initialized before sending it to the cloud provider:

1. Distribute entries into groups as is done in anatomization. The groupings should provide the group privacy protection (k-anonymity, l-diversity, etc.) that is desired. For the purpose of presentation, we assume that the groupings chosen are identical to the anatomization groupings, but they are not required to be.
2. Choose a random cryptographic key K_L.
3. Create a new table that maps H_{K_L}(Lookup Key) to the corresponding group for that entry. (With $H()$ being a keyed, cryptographic hash function.) See Fig. 3 for an example.

3.3   Operations

The following basic database operations can be supported as follows:

- *Select:* The client queries based on the hash of the lookup key instead of on the lookup key itself:
  SELECT * from DB where idhash=H_{K_L}("000-03-3060") and glucose > 250;
  The server then uses the value of idhash to determine the correct bucket from the lookup table and return all relevant results from that group.
- *Insert:* In terms of the data itself, inserts must be batched in groups and inserted with care to ensure the group based privacy guarantees are maintained. In short, tuples to be inserted are not inserted immediately, but are instead temporarily stored in an encrypted cache. Once enough new tuples

in are the cache that they can be safely grouped together and added to the database without violating the privacy constraints, then they are inserted into both the anatomized database and the lookup table as an entire batch.

- *Delete:* As we have already described, removing an item from a bucket can potentially leak information. As such, data is not deleted from the tables; instead the (encrypted) join key is modified to show deletion.
- *Update:* Updates involving information other than the lookup key can simply be processed as is. However, it is important to note that during an update the server knows the identity of the user or users being updated. (As long as the server does not know the old or new value of the sensitive data, privacy is not violated.) Updating the lookup key requires generating a new K_L and completely refreshing the lookup table, which requires downloading and then re-uploading it. Due to the overhead of this approach, it is recommended these types of updates be batched or simply not permitted.

Further information on insert/delete/update can be found in Nergiz *et al.* [7]. While that paper does not discuss private queries or the hashing approach presented here, an extension of the solutions presented for regenerating the hash table are straightforward.

4   Known-Query Attack

Under this model, the identity of the user being queried is protected by the keyed hash. However, some information is still indirectly leaked. If the same user is constantly queried, then the same entry in the bucket lookup table will be referenced. The server won't know which lookup key is being accessed, but it will know that the same lookup key is being referenced repeatedly. Under the standard privacy definitions used thus far, *this is not considered a privacy leak.* However, with a small amount of outside information, an attacker could completely compromise all past and present queries for a given user.

Assume that our attacker, in addition to monitoring the database at the cloud provider, also has the ability to learn the original form of one query. We call this a *known-query attack.* For example, if we are storing medical information the attacker might observe someone visiting the hospital and correlate the timing of their visit with a database query made. From this information, the attacker could know which user a specific $H_{K_L}(\text{SSN})$ is associated with. This means that any future (or past, if they were logged) queries about this user can be individually identified by the attacker.

4.1   Oblivious Lookups

In order to prevent this information leakage, it must be ensured that different queries to the lookup table for the same individual are indistinguishable from lookups to other individuals in the same group. (We are only concerned with making it indistinguishable at the group level because the result of the query will ultimately reveal the group anyway.)

The classic approach to hiding the pattern of access to data is the oblivious RAM simulation [9–11]. Under oblivious RAM, a client performs a series of accesses to a RAM that is monitored by an attacker, but the client does not reveal which data she was interested in. A related concept is oblivious storage [12, 13], which is an adaptation of oblivious RAM techniques to make use of the primitives provided by cloud database providers.

As an inefficient solution to this problem, one could apply the simplest oblivious transfer technique and simply download the entire lookup table and query it locally. In this scenario, the server doesn't know which entry a client queried because the entire lookup table is downloaded every time. The problem, of course, is that every lookup to the table requires downloading it in its entirety. This would make the efficiency for a single lookup $O(N)$, where N is the number of individuals in the lookup table. This is unacceptable.

This overhead can be greatly reduced by making use of oblivious storage techniques. In [13], a method of oblivious storage is provided for the Amazon S3 [14] API. Their work is applicable to a variety of database models. Below we describe a method drawn from their work that satisfies our requirements.

4.2   Oblivious Storage Solution

As a solution to the known-query attack described above, we propose making use of the simple, square-root, miss-intolerant oblivious storage solution found in Goodrich et. al. [13]. In order to make use of this solution we must make the following assumptions:

1. There are N individuals to be stored in the lookup table.
2. The lookup table will contain $N + \sqrt{N}$ items.
3. The client performing the lookup has $2\sqrt{N}$ local storage space.
4. The client and server can exchange $\sqrt{N}$ items in one lookup. (For example, by the client issuing a range query.)
5. The client will only lookup an item that exists in the database. (The database lookups are miss-intolerant.)

While the details of the construction can be found in the original work, a brief summary is provided here. First, the lookup keys themselves (here the SSNs) are hashed using a key and a random nonce chosen by the client. Next, the values associated with the lookup keys (in this case the GIDs) are encrypted with a probabilistic encryption scheme which also includes a random nonce chosen by the client. (Such as $E(r||GID)$.) Note this usage of encryption does not violate our original goal of storing unencrypted data, as only the lookup table is encrypted while the original, anatomized data is not. The client also maintains a local cache of size $\sqrt{N}$ that stores items it has recently accessed. Initially, this cache is empty.

To perform a general lookup for a specific identifier S, the client:

1. Looks for S in its local cache. If it fails to find it there, it queries for S in the encrypted lookup table by searching for the keyed-hash value of it. The server returns the entry.

Table 1. Real Values for Oblivious Storage Applied to the Lookup Table

Items in Lookup Table	Server Storage	Client Storage	Amortized Accesses per Lookup
10,000 items	10,014 items	27 items	13 accesses
100,000 items	100,017 items	34 items	13 accesses
1,000,000 items	1,000,020 items	40 items	13 accesses

2. Requests that the server delete S from the lookup table.
3. Adds S to the local cache.
4. Once $\sqrt{N}$ items have been retrieved from the server, then the cache will be full. The client then obliviously shuffles all items in the cache and the lookup table, and also re-encrypts every item with a new random nonce. In this way the entire table can be shuffled without the server being able to tell which items are which.

As can be seen from this description, most lookups will require $O(1)$ database accesses. However, after the local cache is full then the client must reshuffle the entire lookup table, which requires $O(N/\sqrt{N})$ databases accesses. If we amortize these accesses, then it turns out that the amortized lookup time is $O(1)$.

There are some details missing from this description regarding what to do when a lookup is found in the cache, exactly how to perform the oblivious lookup using the client's limited memory, and a proof of the performance just described. This information can be found in the original paper.

In order to give an idea of what this performance would look like in practice, in Table 1 we present some real numbers based on this technique.

5 Related Work

The problem of query privacy has been most deeply studied with research on Private Information Retrieval (PIR) [5]. The goal with PIR is perfect confidentiality - no information is revealed about the query or what it returns. This results in high computational complexity (order of the size of the database for a single server, although there are some better results assuming non-colluding servers [5] or with quadratic preprocessing [15]). Our setting has somewhat different privacy constraints - it is not the privacy of the query that concerns us, but the privacy of the subjects in the data. Information disclosure from the query is only an issue if it leaks information violating the privacy of the data subjects. This allows us to avoid the impractical computational constraints imposed by PIR.

Closer to our model is Paulet et al. [16], where oblivious transfer is used to provide a limited form of k-anonymity for a query as well as to prevent the client from accessing records it should not. Oblivious transfer is used to guarantee the client only accesses 1 record out of k. Their technique, however, relies on the client requesting the record of interest as well as $k - 1$ other *random* records.

This provides k-anonymity for a single query, but a statistical attack performed by the server over multiple queries will be able to infer information.

Another related area is encrypted database. The seminal work in this area by Hacıgümüş et al. [17] follows an approach in that queries contain only a hashed value at the granularity of an entire block. Theorem 1 shows that this is sufficient to maintain the privacy constraints guaranteed by the underlying data model (in the case of [17], connecting any information at the block level only.) It is an interesting question how this model relates to the anonymization-based models we target – what capabilities and background knowledge (e.g., identity of a querier) would an adversary need to go from obtaining an encrypted block to being able to discern something about the values in that block? However, such a comparison is beyond the scope of this paper. Popa et al. [18] allow querying a fully encrypted database. Their work is focused on protecting the confidentiality of the data in the database, but the queries may be susceptible to a weaker version of the known-query attack described in Section 4. Future work in encrypted database, however, could focus on protecting the query as well and may be able to achieve many of the same goals as this work.

While we make use of research in the area of oblivious RAM and oblivious storage to hide which entry in our lookup table is being accessed, one could ask why oblivious RAM (o-ram) is not applied for all queries to begin with. While these techniques seem like an obvious solution to original problem in this work, there are a few reasons it is infeasible. First, o-ram requires the data being protected to be encrypted. As discussed in Section 1, in our scenario we assume an unencrypted database so that a cloud provider can provide a variety of services or allow unrestricted queries on non-sensitive data. (There do exist some o-ram schemes that do not rely on cryptography [9]; however, the efficiency is significantly worse than their cryptographic counterparts.) Another issue with applying o-ram to this scenario is the performance of such systems is still very low. Even the most efficient form of the algorithm currently known [11] has an $O((\log N)^2)$ amortized cost of with a $O((\log N)^3)$ worst-case cost.

Farnan et al. [19] addresses the issue of sensitive queries in a decentralized database by providing a way to specify privacy constraints as part of the SQL query. Their work is primarily concerned with ensuring that the various, decentralized databases involved in servicing a query not be aware of what information is being queried from each other. This differs from our centralized model, but still illustrates the importance of focusing on privacy leakage related to queries.

Most anonymization work sidesteps the issue of query privacy entirely. The use case of anonymization is traditionally privacy-preserving data publishing; the client will obtain a copy of the anonymized data, and thus queries will not be revealed to the server. In practice, Public Use Microdata Sets [20, 21] are often accessed through a query interface, but the server is presumed to be controlled by the agency holding the original data, so queries that enable the server to infer private information are only disclosing data already known to the server. With the rise in data outsourcing, it will be interesting to study if techniques such as the one presented in this paper will be necessary for other anonymization use cases where the agency holding the original data outsources the hosting and query processing to an external entity.

6 Conclusion

We have shown that given an anatomized database that meets a privacy constraint, the same constraint can still hold in the face of queries as long as those queries are performed at the group level. The complication in applying this result is to ensure that the client can determine the group a specific user is in without querying the server to ask. To solve this problem, we include a keyed hash based lookup table which can be used to determine which group an individual is located in. To provide even further privacy protection in the face of a known-query attack, oblivious storage is used to further protect the lookup table.

Future work should explore using a more robust oblivious storage technique that better supports multiple clients, applying these techniques to a more general data protection model such as fragmentation[22], investigating supporting any column as a potential lookup key, and expanding support to include both update and delete operations.

Acknowledgments. Special thanks to Erhan Nergiz for his assistance with the proofs in this paper. This publication was made possible by the support of the NPRP grant 09-256-1-046 from the Qatar National Research Fund. The statements made herein are solely the responsibility of the authors.

References

1. Samarati, P.: Protecting respondents identities in microdata release. IEEE Transactions on Knowledge and Data Engineering 13(6), 1010–1027 (2001)
2. Sweeney, L.: k-anonymity: A model for protecting privacy. International Journal of Uncertainty Fuzziness and Knowledge Based Systems 10(5), 557–570 (2002)
3. Machanavajjhala, A., Kifer, D., Gehrke, J., Venkitasubramaniam, M.: l-diversity: Privacy beyond k-anonymity. ACM Transactions on Knowledge Discovery from Data (TKDD) 1(1), 3 (2007)
4. Li, N., Li, T., Venkatasubramanian, S.: t-closeness: Privacy beyond k-anonymity and l-diversity. In: IEEE 23rd International Conference on Data Engineering, ICDE 2007, pp. 106–115. IEEE (2007)
5. Chor, B., Kushilevitz, E., Goldreich, O., Sudan, M.: Private information retrieval. Journal of the ACM 45(6), 965–981 (1998)
6. Nergiz, A.E., Clifton, C.: Query processing in private data outsourcing using anonymization. In: Li, Y. (ed.) Data and Applications Security and Privacy XXV. LNCS, vol. 6818, pp. 138–153. Springer, Heidelberg (2011)
7. Nergiz, A.E., Clifton, C., Malluhi, Q.M.: Updating outsourced anatomized private databases. In: Proceedings of the 16th International Conference on Extending Database Technology, EDBT 2013, pp. 179–190. ACM, New York (2013)
8. Xiao, X., Tao, Y.: Anatomy: simple and effective privacy preservation. In: Proceedings of the 32nd International Conf. on Very Large Data Bases, pp. 139–150 (2006)

9. Ajtai, M.: Oblivious rams without cryptogrpahic assumptions. In: Proceedings of the 42nd ACM Symposium on Theory of Computing, STOC 2010, pp. 181–190. ACM, New York (2010)

10. Pinkas, B., Reinman, T.: Oblivious RAM revisited. In: Rabin, T. (ed.) CRYPTO 2010. LNCS, vol. 6223, pp. 502–519. Springer, Heidelberg (2010)

11. Shi, E., Chan, T.-H.H., Stefanov, E., Li, M.: Oblivious RAM with $o((\log n)^3)$ worst-case cost. In: Lee, D.H., Wang, X. (eds.) ASIACRYPT 2011. LNCS, vol. 7073, pp. 197–214. Springer, Heidelberg (2011)

12. Boneh, D., Mazieres, D., Popa, R.A.: Remote Oblivious Storage: Making Oblivious RAM Practical. Technical Report MIT-CSAIL-TR-2011-018, Computer Science and Aritificial Intelligence Laboratory (March 2011)

13. Goodrich, M.T., Mitzenmacher, M., Ohrimenko, O., Tamassia, R.: Practical oblivious storage. In: Proceedings of the Second ACM Conference on Data and Application Security and Privacy, pp. 13–24 (2012)

14. Amazon: Amazon Simple Storage Service (S3),
http://aws.amazon.com/documentation/s3/

15. Asonov, D., Freytag, J.-C.: Almost optimal private information retrieval. In: Dingledine, R., Syverson, P.F. (eds.) PET 2002. LNCS, vol. 2482, pp. 209–223. Springer, Heidelberg (2003)

16. Paulet, R., Kaosar, M.G., Yi, X.: K-anonymous private query based on blind signature and oblivious transfer. In: 2nd International Cyber Resilience Conference, pp. 55–62 (2011)

17. Hacigümüş, H., Iyer, B., Li, C., Mehrotra, S.: Executing sql over encrypted data in the database-service-provider model. In: Proceedings of the 2002 ACM SIGMOD International Conference on Management of Data, SIGMOD 2002, pp. 216–227. ACM, New York (2002)

18. Popa, R.A., Redfield, C., Zeldovich, N., Balakrishnan, H.: Cryptdb: protecting confidentiality with encrypted query processing. In: Proceedings of the Twenty-Third ACM Symposium on Operating Systems Principles, pp. 85–100. ACM (2011)

19. Farnan, N.L., Lee, A.J., Chrysanthis, P.K., Yu, T.: Don't reveal my intension: Protecting user privacy using declarative preferences during distributed query processing. In: Atluri, V., Diaz, C. (eds.) ESORICS 2011. LNCS, vol. 6879, pp. 628–647. Springer, Heidelberg (2011)

20. Moore Jr., R.A.: Controlled data-swapping techniques for masking public use microdata sets. In: Statistical Research Division Report Series RR 96-04, U.S. Bureau of the Census, Washington, DC (1996)

21. Subcommittee on Disclosure Limitation Methodology, Federal Committee on Statistical Methodology: Report on statistical disclosure limitation methodology. Statistical Policy Working Paper 22 (NTIS PB94-16530), Statistical Policy Office, Office of Information and Regulatory Affairs, Office of Management and Budget, Washington, DC (May 1994)

22. Ciriani, V., di Vimercati, S.D.C., Foresti, S., Jajodia, S., Paraboschi, S., Samarati, P.: Combining fragmentation and encryption to protect privacy in data storage. ACM Transactions on Information and System Security (TISSEC) 13(3), 22:1–22:33 (2010)

A Probabilistic Framework for Distributed Localization of Attackers in MANETs*

Alessandra De Benedictis[2], Behzad Koosha[1], Massimiliano Albanese[1], and Valentina Casola[2]

[1] Center for Secure Information Systems
George Mason University, Fairfax, VA, USA
{bkoosha,malbanes}@gmu.edu
[2] Department of Electrical Engineering and Information Technology
University of Naples "Federico II", Naples, Italy
{alessandra.debenedictis,casolav}@unina.it

Abstract. Mobile Ad-hoc Networks (MANETs) are frequently exposed to a wide range of cyber threats due to their unique characteristics. The lack of a centralized monitoring and management infrastructure and the dynamic nature of their topology pose new and interesting challenges for the design of effective security mechanisms. While conventional methods primarily focus on detecting attacks, in this work we focus on estimating the attackers' physical location in the network, and propose a probabilistic framework for aggregating information gathered from nodes reporting malicious activity in their vicinity. In order to overcome the limitations of the decentralized nature of MANETs, we present a distributed approach to attacker localization based on dynamically partitioning the network into clusters. These self-organizing clusters can (i) independently find the approximate location of the attackers in real time, and (ii) deploy trusted resources to capture attackers. We show, through experiments in a simulated environment, that our approach is effective and efficient.

Keywords: Attacker Localization, Mobile Ad-hoc Networks, Distributed Computing, Clustering.

1 Introduction

Mobile Ad-hoc Networks (MANETs) consist of mobile nodes able to communicate without a fixed infrastructure. Due to their flexibility, they have been widely adopted in a variety of applications, such as military battlefield monitoring and control, civilian sensor networks, humanitarian disaster relief operations, etc.

MANETs are characterized by several unique features that differentiate them from other wireless networks, such as the lack of a centralized management, the absence of rigid boundaries, power constraints, bandwidth limitations, dynamic topology, scalability and cooperativeness. These features expose MANETs to a

---

* The work presented in this paper is supported in part by the Office of Naval Research under award number N00014-12-1-0461.

R. Accorsi and S. Ranise (Eds.): STM 2013, LNCS 8203, pp. 49–64, 2013.

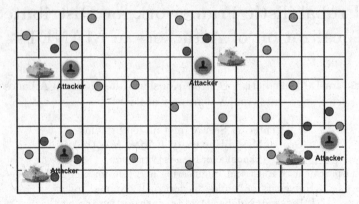

Fig. 1. A MANET scenario where attackers are captured by trusted resources

wide range of cyber threats and pose new challenges for the design of effective security mechanisms. As Fig. 1 illustrates, network nodes may be threatened by attackers physically located within their transmission range. Therefore, it would be highly desirable for nodes to cooperate locally – without relying on a centralized monitoring function – and locate the attacker as soon as possible. Moreover, once localized, attackers may be physically captured by dispatching trusted resources so that they cannot cause additional damage.

Extensive research efforts have been devoted to the problem of detecting various types of attacks, while the problem of physically localizing attackers has not been sufficiently studied, and in most cases it has been studied only with respect to specific types of attacks. Existing approaches are mostly based on measuring and processing parameters related to node communication, such as connections with neighboring nodes, time of arrival (TOA), angle of arrival (AOA) and received signal strength (RSS), but they could be easily manipulated by attackers, thus reducing the effectiveness of such solutions.

In our previous work [1], we proposed a more general solution to the problem of attackers' localization, based on a probabilistic framework for processing the alerts generated in the network. Estimation of the attacker's location was based on information collected from nodes raising alerts, assuming that malicious nodes are located in the vicinity of those nodes. As stated in [1], this assumption is reasonable – due to the wireless nature of MANETs – and has been adopted by several intrusion detection systems, such as [7].

The main limitation of our previous solution is the way alerts are processed, as we assumed the existence of a centralized entity able to gather information about all alerts generated in the network and deploy proper resources to capture localized attackers. In this paper, we overcome this limitation and propose a distributed localization framework, in which information about alerts is processed locally within dynamically established clusters of nodes. Moreover, unlike its centralized version, the proposed distributed framework aggregates and processes alerts as soon as they are triggered, rather than offline. This is critical to capture attackers before they can cause extensive damage.

The reminder of the paper is organized as follows. Section 2 discusses related work. Section 3 states the goals of this paper with respect to the state of the art. In Section 4, we present a detailed description of the proposed framework, whereas Section 5 provides a description of the clustering strategy we adopted to run the localization algorithm in a distributed fashion. Experimental results are presented in Section 6. Finally, concluding remarks are given in Section 7.

2   Related Work

Considerable research efforts have been recently devoted to the problem of detecting various types of attacks against wireless networks, and there is an increasing interest in attacker localization, in both wireless sensor networks and ad-hoc mobile networks.

The work presented by Zeng et al. [9] discusses and categorizes current solutions to both secure localization and location verification for wireless sensor networks. However, when the network is deployed in hostile environments, attackers might easily interfere with the localization process, so as to generate incorrect location estimates. In addition, since sensor nodes might be compromised, the base station cannot rely on the locations disclosed by sensor nodes.

In this regard, the work by Zhan and Li [10] tackles the problem of locating a static malicious source that deliberately conceals or forges its position with the help of a directional antenna in sensor networks. The main idea is to use coordination of multiple sensors to locate the adversary and optimize the process with a finite horizon discrete Markov decision process. The result of this work is a localization mechanism for sensor networks – called Active Cross-Layer Location Identification (ACLI). Unlike other localization schemes, this mechanism is not influenced by an attacker that falsifies its location by methods such as smart antennas and software defined radio equipments.

Yang et al. [8] proposed the use of spatial information to localize multiple adversaries performing spoofing attacks. They analyzed the spatial correlation of received signal strengths of the wireless nodes. The received signal strength-based spatial correlation, as a physical property related to every wireless node, is difficult to forge, and is independent of cryptographic schemes. The proposed approach can detect the existence of attacks in addition to determining the number of adversaries.

Liu et al. [6] addressed the problem of localizing multiple jammers in wireless networks by analyzing the network topology changes caused by jamming activities. The proposed framework groups network nodes into clusters, and estimates the position of jammers by analyzing situations where jamming areas have common intersections.

Most of the existing approaches that provide ad-hoc solutions to the problem of localizing attackers depend on the specific nature of attacks. In order to define a more general approach to attacker localization in MANETs, we proposed a framework [1] based on a probabilistic model of the attacker's location, and presented two polynomial time heuristic algorithms to estimate the position of attackers. The proposed framework relies on the nodes' capability to detect malicious activity in their vicinity. This can be accomplished by having IDSs running on each node. The localization algorithm is run by a centralized entity that collects information about alerts that have been triggered throughout the network during a given observation period.

The main goal of the localization algorithm is to find the minimum set of candidate locations that could explain, if actually hosting attackers, all the alerts generated in the network. After modeling the observation field as a grid, we compute a probability value $Pr(attacker(p))$ for each point p in the grid, representing the probability that p is hosting an attacker, based on its proximity to alerts. $Pr(attacker(p))$ is obtained by aggregating the values of $Pr(causes(p, a))$ for each alert a, that is the probability that p has caused alert a. This provides a set of candidate locations that are likely to host attackers.

Although our previous solution is able to obtain good results in practice, it presents some drawbacks that we aim to overcome in this paper. First, it relies upon the existence of a centralized entity, that is usually not practical in a MANET due to the lack of a fixed infrastructure and its typical self-organizing nature. Second, it only processes alerts at the end of a relatively long observation interval instead of trying to identify and capture attackers as soon as possible.

Unlike cellular networks where the nodes (users) can gather information about other nodes via a control unit (base station), ad-hoc networks lack this feature due to their infrastructure-less nature. Communications in cellular networks are mainly point to point, whereas, in ad-hoc networks, communications are mostly between groups of nodes which are likely to harmonize their mobility patterns within the network. In order to increase the life cycle of routes and reduce the routing control overhead, clustering of nodes into groups is considered.

Using the concept of clusters in an ad-hoc network has several benefits. Current routing protocols can be immediately applied to the clusters. Additionally, communication overhead can be reduced by reducing the amount of control and signaling data needed to achieve consistent data transmission in the network. This will have a substantial effect on reducing routing overhead particularly in large dense networks where finding a solution to the scalability problem is of great importance.

Several approaches have been proposed to form clusters and elect cluster-heads in ad-hoc networks. In the *Lowest ID cluster algorithm* (LIC) [3], every node is assigned a unique *id*. At regular intervals, each node broadcasts a list of nodes that it can hear in its vicinity. The node with the minimum *id* is selected as a cluster-head. The downside of this algorithm is the fact that some selected nodes are likely to operate as cluster-heads for a longer period of time and this causes them to loose their battery power quickly.

In the *Highest Connectivity Clustering algorithm* (HCC) [2], the selection of the cluster-heads is executed such that the node having the highest number of neighbors (maximum degree) in its transmission range is elected as a cluster-head. This network is very stable in terms of cluster-head change despite the low throughput.

The basic idea behind the *mobility based metric* [4] for clustering algorithms is to take into account the relative mobility of a node compared to its neighbors. Nodes with lower speed (relative to their adjacent neighbors) have better chances to be elected as cluster-heads. Using the variance of a node's speed relative to each neighbor, the cumulative local speed of a mobile node is estimated.

Finally, the main idea behind *Weighted Clustering Algorithm* (WCA) [5] is to assign a weight to each node in the network according to its mobility, degree of freedom, cumulative time of acting, and the remaining battery level. In our framework, we adopt an enhanced version of such algorithm, that we will present in Section 5.

3   Problem Statement

In this paper, we propose a framework for attackers' localization, based on a completely distributed localization algorithm, directly deriving from the centralized algorithm presented in [1]. In this new and enhanced version of the localization framework, we eliminate the need for a centralized entity and distribute the localization process among nodes. Moreover, we perform an early processing of alerts, in such a way that countermeasures can be taken to reduce further damage to the system. The main contributions of this paper are the following:

1. we introduce a distributed strategy to process alerts as they are triggered,
2. we define a protocol to exchange messages related to the localization strategy, defining specific message types,
3. we evaluate the performance of the distributed framework with respect to the centralized version.

Before going into details about our proposal, we present some preliminary definitions that will be used throughout this paper.

Definition 1 (Neighbors). *Two nodes i and j are considered neighbors if they are within the transmission range of each other. If considering a free space propagation model, it means that $d(i,j) \leq r$, where d denotes the Euclidean distance and r is the transmission range.*

Definition 2 (k-Neighbors). *Two nodes i and j are considered k-neighbors if there exists a path between them of at most k hops.*

Definition 3 (Cluster). *Given a network $\mathcal{N}$, and a node $n \in \mathcal{N}$, a cluster for n is a set $C \subseteq \mathcal{N}$ including all nodes $q \in \mathcal{N}$ such that q and n are k-neighbors. Throughout the paper, we will refer to the parameter k as the* cluster depth, *and we will use $\mathcal{C}$ to denote the set of all clusters.*

Definition 4 (Cluster-heads). *Given a cluster $C \subseteq \mathcal{N}$, the cluster-head of C is a node $c_h \in C$ selected such that it maximizes an objective function f (e.g., battery level, degree, etc.). The cluster-head functions as a local coordinator and supervises the cluster's overall activity.*

Definition 5 (Compatible Alerts). *Alerts that are potentially triggered by the same attacker are said to be compatible. Two alerts a_1 and a_2 are compatible if $d(a_1, a_2) \leq 2 \cdot r$.*

The general idea behind the proposed framework is the following: when a node detects an attack and generates an alert, it starts a clustering procedure that involves its k-neighbors. A cluster-head is then elected based on significant parameters such as the current battery level, computational power, average speed or the number of neighbors. The cluster-head collects information about the newly generated alert, along with information about other possible alerts known by nodes belonging to the cluster, and runs the localization algorithm.

In this approach, the process of deploying resources to capture attackers – as introduced in [1] – can still be applied, assuming that deployed resources can communicate with cluster-heads. Even in this case, to increase precision, deployment should be performed iteratively, by checking the suspected regions and updating the attackers' probability distribution accordingly. However, as new alerts could be triggered later on by attackers located in regions that were checked in a previous run of the algorithm, we cannot always assume that a cleared location will remain such for an extended period of time.

In the next section, a detailed description of the localization framework is presented, followed by a graphical example of its behavior. Further on, we illustrate the clustering strategy adopted by our framework for the actual execution of the localization algorithm.

4   Distributed Attackers Localization Framework

The core of our approach is the strategy adopted to group and process alerts as they are generated, in order to ensure early localization of attackers and stop them before they can cause further damage to the network. The adopted strategy is characterized by:

- the events that activate the localization process,
- the information used by the localization process, and
- the actual executor of the localization algorithm.

The precision of the localization algorithm proposed in [1] depends on the distribution of alerts: when the alerts to process are closer, it is easier to identify regions with higher probability of hosting attackers. These regions can be inspected and possibly cleared by proper deployed resources. This suggests that the localization algorithm should be run on a significant subset of relatively close alerts, while on the other side we are interested in processing them as soon as possible. Therefore, in order to obtain more precise results, the algorithm should be run after acquiring information about a possibly small group of compatible alerts.

These considerations led us to define a trigger for the localization process based on the availability of other alerts previously triggered in the same region.

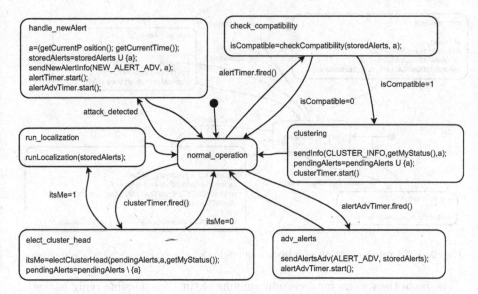

Fig. 2. FSM representation of a node's behavior when detecting an attack

In this way, the set of candidate locations that may contain attackers, according to the localization algorithm, can be minimized. At the detection of an attack, the victim node advertises the local alert to its neighbors, that in turn send information about stored alerts. If there exist two or more *compatible* alerts, the node will launch the localization process on this set of alerts.

In order to maximize the dissemination of information about alerts that are physically localized in different regions, nodes periodically broadcast information about known alerts while moving. Such information is stored by their neighbors and used later when needed. To limit the overhead, alert information is not disseminated over the whole network, but only sent to a subset of nodes that are physically located in the vicinity of the attacked node.

As stated, the localization process involves not only the node raising the alert, but also all the nodes in its vicinity at that time. The execution of the localization algorithm requires a certain computational capability and could influence the node's normal operation. For this reason, we devised the election of a cluster-head, that actually runs the algorithm on behalf of all the nodes belonging to the cluster.

Based on the described strategy, an alert may be processed multiple times by different clusters, as the related information is carried by different nodes moving through the network, helping increase the localization precision.

The behavior of the framework is illustrated by the state machine diagrams depicted in Fig. 2 and Fig. 3. More specifically, Fig. 2 reports the behavior of a node when it detects a malicious activity: information about the physical location of the node at the time of detection and the timestamp itself are inserted into a packet, and sent to its k-neighbors.

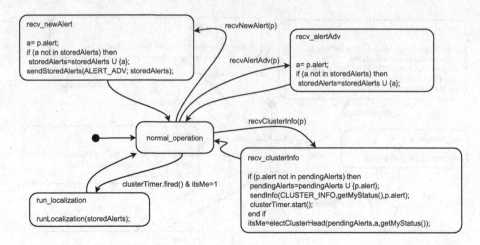

Fig. 3. FSM representation of a node's behavior when receiving protocol messages

The node then waits for a certain amount of time for possible reply packets, containing information about other alerts. Upon receipt of those replies, the node will update its local list of stored alerts and check if the clustering procedure can be launched, based on the availability of a sufficient number of compatible alerts. In this case, the node sends a packet containing information about its current status to its k-neighbors, in order to participate to the clustering procedure.

Fig. 3 shows the behavior of a node when it receives a packet related to the localization protocol. The protocol adopts 3 different types of packets:

- *NEW_ALERT_ADV*: contains information about new alerts triggered in the network. Nodes receiving such packet must respond with their list of stored alerts.
- *ALERT_ADV*: contains information about stored old alerts that are being re-advertised by mobile nodes.
- *CLUSTER_INFO*: contains information on the current status of a node, useful to elect the cluster-head that will execute the localization algorithm. Such information is related to a specific alert event, as clustering is launched by a node raising an alert. Actually, a single node could be involved in different clustering procedures at the same time, launched by different nodes. For this reason, as shown in Fig. 3, a node receiving such kind of packet will first check whether it is a duplicate of a previous packet, and then will add this request to a local list of pending alerts. Afterwards, it will send information about its current status to its k-neighbors, in order to participate to the clustering procedure for the involved alert. For each received *CLUSTER_INFO* packet, the node will compare its own status with the received ones, in order to determine whether it should be elected as the cluster-head. After a predefined amount of time, if the variable *itsMe* for that alert is set to 1, the node will assume it is the cluster-head and will run the localization algorithm on alerts in its *storedAlert* list.

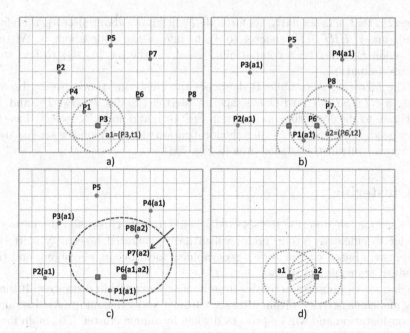

Fig. 4. A simple example of execution of the distributed localization algorithm: a) alert a_1 is triggered by P_3, no clustering launched; b) alert a_2 is triggered by P_6, which starts clustering; c) the cluster is formed and P_7 is elected as the cluster-head; d)P_7 runs the localization algorithm on the set of alerts $\{a_1,a_2\}$

The behavior of the proposed framework is graphically visualized in Fig. 4. Fig. 4(a) illustrates the initial configuration of an 8-node network $\mathcal{N}$. These nodes with identical transmission ranges are capable of broadcasting signals to their neighbors and transmit or receive data within their predefined transmission range.

In the network configuration depicted in Fig. 4, P_3 triggers an alert a_1 at time t_1, and sends a *NEW_ALERT_ADV* packet to its neighbors, setting a Time-To-Live (k) equal to 2. Node P_1 first receives the packet and, after updating its list of stored alerts, re-broadcasts it to node P_4, without sending anything to P_3, as its initial list is empty. The packet reaches P_4 with a TTL = 0; node P_4's *storedAlert* list is empty too, therefore, it simply updates it by adding alert a_1. From this moment on, nodes P_1, P_4 and P_3 have information about alert a_1 stored in their local lists. This condition is denoted with $P_1(a_1)$, $P_4(a_1)$ and $P_3(a_1)$ respectively in the figure. No clustering is launched, as there are no alerts compatible with a_1.

Fig. 4(b) shows a new alert a_2 triggered by P_6 at time t_2. Assume that in the meantime, node P_3 moved in the neighborhood of node P_2 and re-advertised information about alert a_1: this condition is depicted by denoting $P_2(a_1)$ in Fig. 4(b). At time t_2, node P_6 sends a *NEW_ALERT_ADV* packet with TTL = 2 to its neighbors. The packet is first received by P_1, P_7 and P_8: node P_7 only updates its list of stored alerts, and then re-broadcasts the packet. The packet reaches P_8, that acts similarly. As for node P_1, it knows about alert a_1, therefore it sends an *ALERT_ADV* packet to P_6 to inform the node about it. At this point, node P_6 will runs a compatibility check on the set $\{a_1, a_2\}$ to find that they are compatible.

In the following step, node P_6 launches the clustering procedure by broadcasting a *CLUSTER_INFO* message for alert a_2. nodes P_1, P_6, P_7, and P_8 participate to the clustering, as shown in Fig. 4(c), and node P_7 is elected as the cluster head. Finally, node P_7 runs the localization algorithm on the set $\{a_1, a_2\}$, returning as output the shaded area in Fig. 4(d).

5   Clustering

In this section, we describe the selected scheme to form clusters in the network. In order to efficiently group nodes which have generated a security alert, we form clusters based on the node's geographical location, its neighbors, and the predefined transmission range r.

Each node can observe activities from its neighbors within distance r. If there is any malicious activity within distance r from a node, this information is taken into consideration and will be processed when forming a cluster. The main focus for clustering is to group the nodes which have detected some malicious activity in the same region. As previously pointed out, in order to make the best use of alert information, a cluster is built starting from an alert and including all the k-neighbors of such alert.

Thus, the nodes which have formed a cluster might not be all neighbors with one another, but there are nodes in between which can form a chain. Indeed, nodes in a cluster must be pairwise neighbors (see Fig. 5). In other words, the following property holds (for clusters with more than two nodes):

$$(\forall C \in \mathcal{C}) \, (\forall n_i, n_j \in C) \, (d(n_i, n_j) \leq 2 \cdot r \ \lor \ (\exists n_1, \ldots, n_k) \, (d(n_i, n_1) \leq 2 \cdot r \ \land$$
$$(\forall l \in [2, k-1]) \, (d(n_l, n_{l+1}) \leq 2 \cdot r) \ \land \ d(n_k, n_j) \leq 2 \cdot r)) \quad (1)$$

Intuitively, for clusters with one or two nodes there are no additional constraints as the notion of *neighboring nodes* defines the cluster.

The established clusters can individually and independently execute the localization algorithms proposed in [1] without any exchange of information between clusters. The reason behind this is that we consider the transmission range of

Fig. 5. Chain of nodes forming a cluster

the attackers to be the same as the legitimate nodes and we assume the attackers to be static. In other words, the approximate location of attackers can be determined by processing alert information belonging to a particular cluster. The nodes that have generated an alert gather the information listed below and exchange it with their k-neighbors.

Node Degree $(Deg(n))$: in graph theory, the *order* (*degree*) of a node is the number of attached nodes. In our scenario, nodes within the transmission range are counted towards a node's degree. Intuitively, hub nodes have a higher order compared to ordinary nodes. The difference between in-degree and out-degree in a directed graph could be calculated at unique depths: adjacent nodes (depth 1), adjacent nodes of adjacent nodes (depth 2), etc. The following equation holds for adjacent nodes (depth 1):

$$Deg(n_i) = \mid Neighbors(n_i) \mid = \sum_{n_j \in \mathcal{N}} (d(n_i, n_j) \leq r) \qquad (2)$$

This parameter can determine the number of interconnected nodes which are in the transmission range (depth 1) and can be used later on as a factor in determining the priority for the node to become a cluster-head.

Mobility$(M(n))$: for each node, we calculate its average speed over a time interval T as follows:

$$M(n_i) = \frac{1}{T} \cdot \sum_{t=1}^{T} \sqrt{(X_t(n_i) - X_{t-1}(n_i))^2 + (Y_t(n_i) - Y_{t-1}(n_i))^2} \qquad (3)$$

In the equation above, $(X_t(n_i), Y_t(n_i))$ and $(X_{t-1}(n_i), Y_{t-1}(n_i))$ are the Cartesian coordinates for the node at time t and $t-1$, respectively. The nodes with less mobility are more likely to be selected as cluster-heads as they will be potentially more immune to sudden changes, assuring more stability.

Residual Power $(P(n))$: each transmitted packet includes a value that represents the residual power of the transmitting node. This estimate might not be precise as nodes consume power while receiving packets. Nevertheless, it can be used as an acceptable estimate for the purpose of cluster-head election. This vital information aids in determining if a node has enough power to perform the tasks related to a cluster-head. Nodes with longer battery life have a better chance to be selected as cluster-heads, as they have the required resources to operate for a sufficient amount of time.

In summary, an ideal cluster-head should maintain high node degree and residual power in addition to low mobility, compared to other candidates. This ensures best performance as a dominant node which supervises the cluster activities during the network operation.

The above mentioned parameters represent quality factors assigned to each node over time. In order to select the cluster-head, they must be combined according to a quality function to achieve a final weight. As shown in [5], the weight to be assigned to each node n which has generated an alert can be computed using the following formula:

$$W(n) = k_1 \cdot Deg(n) + k_2 \cdot M(n) + k_3 \cdot P(n) \tag{4}$$

Parameters k_1, k_1, and k_3 are weighting factors which all add up to a constant value K. When a node receives a $CLUSTER\_INFO$ message, the included weight is compared with its own weight. The node which has the smallest weight among all the neighboring nodes is selected as the cluster-head.

In addition, when the process of selecting a cluster-head begins, depending on the geographical location of legitimate nodes and the nodes raising an alert, it might be prudent to elect a legitimate node in the close vicinity as a cluster-head to avoid any future possible failure of the cluster-head. Nevertheless, the proposed attributes need to be considered in the election process.

Once the clusters have been established and cluster-heads have been elected, we can execute the heuristic algorithms proposed in [1] on each cluster in order to estimate the attackers' approximate location.

6   Experimental Results

We implemented a prototype of the proposed framework in the NS-2 network simulator, and developed a Java application for processing the alerts in the cluster heads. As previously illustrated, nodes exchange information on alerts triggered in the network, and nodes that have detected an attack autonomously decide whether to launch the clustering procedure in order to process known alerts. We used NS-2 to simulate different scenarios in which nodes move according to a Random Way Point model[1] and attackers randomly choose one of more of their neighbors as their targets. We recorded the time of each attack, along with the position of the victim at the time of the attack, and run the localization algorithm on the set of alerts known by a cluster at the time when localization was launched.

For our experiments, we adopted the MIN-K deployment algorithm presented in [1], and analyzed the behavior of the distributed localization framework in different scenarios and operational conditions.

In the first set of experiments, we considered a $1km \times 1km$ field, and deployed 40 network nodes and 6 attackers, both uniformly distributed. We considered an observation interval of 60 ms, enabling attacks in the first 50 ms of simulation, and set the cluster depth to 2. All nodes are assumed to be compatible with the free space radio propagation model and to have a transmission range of 100 meters. To calculate the attacker's probability distribution, we assumed that, given an alert a, the attacker's probability for a is uniformly distributed in the circle having its center in a and radius equal to the transmission range.

---

[1] However, our approach allows us to use any mobility model as well as any radio propagation model in the simulation.

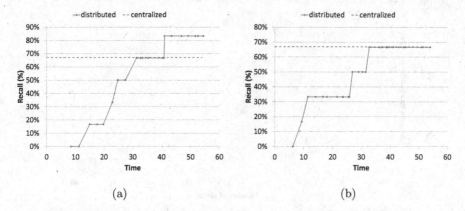

(a)   (b)

Fig. 6. Centralized vs. distributed localization in different scenarios

We considered several random scenarios and run both versions of the framework (centralized and decentralized) on each scenario to compare the number of attackers that they were able to capture within a single deployment cycle. Contrary to one's expectations, the centralized version of the localization framework does not always perform better than the distributed one, even if the knowledge about existing alerts is more complete. This is due to the way alerts are combined by the localization algorithm, that aims at minimizing the number of expected attackers in the network, trying to combine as many compatible alerts as possible. Fig. 6 shows the fraction of attackers "captured" within the first and only deployment cycle – also referred to as *recall* – in two different cases: in the case shown in Figure 6(a), the distributed framework is able to capture more attackers than its counterpart before the end of the observation interval, while in the case of Figure 6(b) the centralized framework works better.

In order to analyze the impact of the number of alerts on the localization accuracy, we considered a particular attack scenario, consisting of a single attacker that launches an attack against all the nodes in its transmission range (e.g. a jammer). In this scenario, the above discussed influence of alert distribution on localization accuracy is reduced, as the goal of minimizing the number of attackers responsible for all alerts is consistent with the existence of a single attacker. In [1], we already showed that our approach is able to localize jammers with higher precision than other existing approaches based on geometrical considerations, and is less dependent on network density. With the introduction of the distributed version of the framework, we are able to obtain even better results, as the attacker can be localized earlier, by locally processing a limited number of alerts. Fig. 7 reports the average localization error as the number of alerts increases, showing that it significantly reduces even with small increments in the alerts' number.

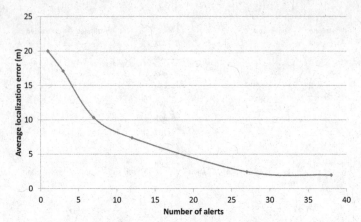

Fig. 7. Impact of the number of alerts on the localization accuracy

As discussed in Section 4, in order to cope with mobility and temporary network partitioning, nodes advertise both locally generated alerts and old stored alerts to their k-neighbors. The choice of the k parameter, also called *cluster depth*, impacts both the protocol overhead and the localization precision: as the size of the set of alerts to process in a localization step increases, the probability that such set contains overlapping alerts, which are useful for a successful localization, increases. Fig. 8 shows the trend of recall when choosing two different values of cluster depth, namely 1 and 3, for the same simulation scenario. As shown, the framework achieves better results when the depth is set to 3, even if in this case the total number of alert advertisement packets sent by nodes during the simulation time is much higher compared to the other case (139 vs. 57).

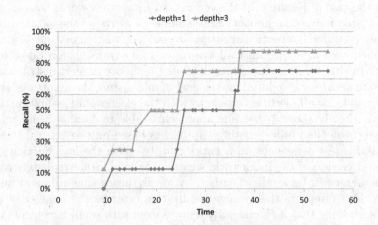

Fig. 8. Recall values for different cluster depths

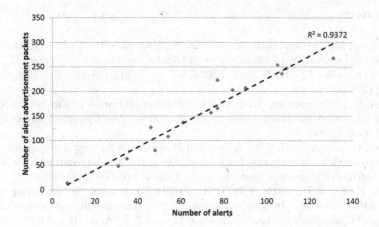

Fig. 9. Communication overhead

Clearly, as the introduced alert advertisement protocol adopts a controlled-flooding strategy, the localization framework is subject to a communication overhead due to the forwarding of packets containing information about generated alerts. Nevertheless, such overhead is limited and has a linear trend, as shown in Fig. 9, which reports the number of NEW_ALERT_ADV packets generated and forwarded to k-neighbors (with $k = 2$).

7   Conclusions

In this paper, we addressed the problem of localizing attackers in MANETs. In particular, we developed a distributed framework based on dynamically partitioning the network in order to process subsets of alerts. The proposed distributed framework aggregates and processes alerts as soon as they are reported. The protocol can independently estimate the approximate position of attackers in a distributed manner through cooperation of neighboring nodes.

In order to enable distributed localization, we implemented the following two tasks. First, we grouped alerts to form clusters for local processing. Second, we introduced a strategy to elect a cluster-head for the actual execution of the localization algorithm. Polynomial heuristic algorithms have been used to localize the attackers in each cluster.

We evaluated the performance of our distributed framework in the NS-2 network simulator and experiments indicated that our scheme achieves better results compared to the centralized localization approach. Our future plans include extending our distributed localization framework to consider mobile attackers. In this case, the goal will be that of *chasing* the attackers rather than simply estimating their location.

References

1. Albanese, M., De Benedictis, A., Jajodia, S., Shakarian, P.: A probabilistic framework for localization of attackers in mANETs. In: Foresti, S., Yung, M., Martinelli, F. (eds.) ESORICS 2012. LNCS, vol. 7459, pp. 145–162. Springer, Heidelberg (2012)
2. Baker, D.J., Ephremides, A.: The architectural organization of a mobile radio network via a distributed algorithm. IEEE Transactions on Communications 29(11), 1694–1701 (1981)
3. Baker, D.J., Ephremides, A.: A distributed algorithm for organizing mobile radio telecommunication networks. In: Proceedings of the 2nd International Conference on Distributed Computer Systems, Paris, France, pp. 476–483 (1981)
4. Basu, P., Khan, N., Little, T.D.C.: A mobility based metric for clustering in mobile ad hoc networks. In: Proceedings of the 21st International Conference on Distributed Computing Systems Workshops, Mesa, AZ, USA, pp. 413–418 (April 2001)
5. Chatterjee, M., Das, S.K., Turgut, D.: WCA: A weighted clustering algorithm for mobile ad hoc networks. Cluster Computing 5(2), 193–204 (2002)
6. Liu, H., Liu, Z., Chen, Y., Xu, W.: Localizing multiple jamming attackers in wireless networks. In: Proceedings of the 31st International Conference on Distributed Computing Systems (ICDCS 2011), Minneapolis, MN, USA, pp. 517–528 (June 2011)
7. Marti, S., Giuli, T.J., Lai, K., Baker, M.: Mitigating routing misbehavior in mobile ad hoc networks. In: Proceedings of the 6th Annual International Conference on Mobile Computing and Networking (MobiCom 2000), Boston, MA, USA, pp. 255–265 (August 2000)
8. Yang, J., Chen, Y., Trappe, W., Cheng, J.: Detection and localization of multiple spoofing attackers in wireless networks. IEEE Transactions on Parallel and Distributed Systems 24(1), 44–58 (2013)
9. Zeng, Y., Cao, J., Hong, J., Xie, L.: Secure localization and location verification in wireless sensor networks. In: IEEE 6th International Conference on Mobile Adhoc and Sensor Systems (MASS 2009), Macao, China, pp. 864–869 (October 2009)
10. Zhan, S., Li, J.: Active cross-layer location identification of attackers in wireless sensor networks. In: Proceedings of the 2nd International Conference on Computer Engineering and Technology (ICCET 2010), Chengdu, China, vol. 3, pp. 240–244 (2010)

MITHYS: Mind The Hand You Shake - Protecting Mobile Devices from SSL Usage Vulnerabilities

Mauro Conti[1,*], Nicola Dragoni[2], and Sebastiano Gottardo[1,2]

[1] University of Padua, IT
conti@math.unipd.it, sgottard@studenti.math.unipd.it
[2] Technical University of Denmark, DK
ndra@dtu.dk, s124645@student.dtu.dk

Abstract. Recent studies have shown that a significant number of mobile applications, often handling sensitive data such as bank accounts and login credentials, suffers from SSL vulnerabilities. Most of the time, these vulnerabilities are due to improper use of the SSL protocol (in particular, in its *handshake* phase), resulting in applications exposed to man-in-the-middle attacks. In this paper, we present MITHYS, a system able to: (i) detect applications vulnerable to man-in-the-middle attacks, and (ii) protect them against these attacks. We demonstrate the feasibility of our proposal by means of a prototype implementation in Android, named MITHYSApp. A thorough set of experiments assesses the validity of our solution in detecting and protecting mobile applications from man-in-the-middle attacks, without introducing significant overheads. Finally, MITHYSApp does not require any special permissions nor OS modifications, as it operates at the application level. These features make MITHYSApp immediately deployable on a large user base.

1 Introduction

The spread of mobile smartphones have led web service providers to pay attention to how the users could benefit from their services, while users are on the move. To this end, two main approaches have been adopted. At first, providers chose to offer a mobile-shaped version of their web service, which the users could access through a mobile web browser (acting as a "thin" client). As an alternative, providers started to offer their services by means of native applications for each specific mobile platform (also called "fat client" approach). This second approach rapidly became the most popular (interested readers can refer to [7] for a thorough comparison between the two approaches). Indeed, as the number of daily activated devices grows at a relentless rate, so does the number of applications which are downloaded and available to a huge end-user base.

An application that relies on a web service requires an active Internet connection. To gain this connection, a mobile device is typically equipped with two types

* Mauro Conti is supported by a Marie Curie Fellowship funded by the European Commission under the agreement n. PCIG11-GA-2012-321980. This work has been partially supported by the TENACE PRIN Project 20103P34XC funded by the Italian MIUR.

R. Accorsi and S. Ranise (Eds.): STM 2013, LNCS 8203, pp. 65–81, 2013.
© Springer-Verlag Berlin Heidelberg 2013

of network interfaces: a 3G/4G module and a Wi-Fi module. The Wi-Fi module gives the user the opportunity of connecting a device to a wireless network created through a wireless access point. The Wi-Fi connection became more and more important, as many companies started offering free Internet access points, as an additional service for their customers. We can also find this scenario in many public infrastructures, such as libraries and universities. Unfortunately, this increasing popularity of free access points has led to new malicious attacks, based on the Man-In-The-Middle principle (from now, MITM attack). The *rogue access point attack* is a typical example of how dangerous the use of a free public access point might be [17]. As a consequence, protecting the communication in these open environments is crucial to keep user data private. This means that a mobile device must establish a secure connection with the remote server offering the needed web service. In a desktop environment, this connection lies between the web browser and the remote server. On the other hand, a mobile application is directly responsible of establishing the secure connection with the remote server, without relying on a web browser.

Technically speaking, the most common way of establishing a secure connection is by using Secure Sockets Layer (SSL) [1] and Transport Layer Security (TLS) [18], two cryptographic protocols that grant endpoint authentication and network data confidentiality over a TCP connection. These protocols were also designed to prevent malicious MITM attacks against two communicating entities. The problem is that, as recently pointed out [10], a significant number of mobile applications often do not perform the required steps to ensure a secure communication between the communicating parties. The flowing data between the application and the server, which is supposedly private, can be intercepted by a malicious third party by performing a MITM attack. This is a known problem that affects a huge number of mobile applications, mainly due to the respective developers that underestimate the importance of a proper use of the SSL/TLS protocols. Even if the problem has been raised more than one year ago, our recent test revealed that several applications (including widely used ones, such as PayPal and Facebook) are still vulnerable.

Example 1. *Let us assume a scenario where an attacker performs a rogue access point attack, with Starbucks' free Wi-Fi service as a target. The original Starbucks' access point (AP from now on) name is "Starbucks", while the attacker's AP name is "Starbucks Free". Let us suppose Alice visits Starbucks and notices the free Wi-Fi opportunity. She sees two open access points on her Android smartphone, so she chooses a random one, the attacker's "Starbucks Free" in this case. Alice wants to check her PayPal account, therefore she opens the PayPal Android application, which she had used before. Since the PayPal application suffer from the above SSL usage problem, the attacker is able to intercept Alice's PayPal account data, including her personal login information. What is more, she is not aware that she is a victim of a MITM attack.*

Again, given the huge number of vulnerable applications, the "wait-and-hope" approach is not appropriate, since it exposes the users to malicious MITM attacks until the developers release a security update. Instead, there is the need for an application-independent solution that: (i) detects the vulnerable applications; (ii) warns the user about the potential leak of sensitive data; and (iii) eventually compensates the lack of security by performing the adequate checks. Such a solution would not only secure the application-web server communication, it would also act as a security tool for mobile developers — who want to test the security level of their applications against SSL-based MITM attacks.

Contribution. In this paper we present MITHYS (Mind The Hand You Shake), a platform independent system architecture that:

- Detects mobile applications vulnerable to SSL-based MITM attacks, automatizing the detection of vulnerabilities pointed out in [10],[11])
- Protects mobile applications (especially, vulnerable ones) from SSL-based MITM attacks, by taking care of SSL certificate validation
- Gives the user full control on the vulnerable applications' behavior (e.g. the application can be blocked if vulnerable)

The MITHYS architecture is, to the best of our knowledge, the first solution that tackles the vulnerability of mobile applications to SSL-based MITM attacks [10],[11]. A fully-working, end-user-ready implementation of MITHYS, namely MITHYSApp, has been developed for the Android mobile platform, which represents one of the most flexible and popular mobile OS at the time being.

Being implemented at the application level, MITHYSApp does not require mobile OS alterations nor special permissions (i.e., root access). MITHYSApp just relies on a single manual configuration performed by the user. According to the selected configuration, MITHYSApp can operate in three modes:

- Automatic - detection of vulnerable applications and protection for all the installed applications, without requiring any user interaction;
- Selective - detection of vulnerable applications is automatic, but the user can decide whether to allow their execution or not;
- Manual - the user can manually select which applications must be analysed and which must be protected.

Finally, a set of experiments show the feasibility of our solution. In particular, we show that the current (non-optimized) version of MITHYSApp does not introduce a significant delay in network communication nor in the ordinary applications/OS behavior, while it effectively protects users from MITM attacks that can steal personal and sensible information.

Roadmap. Section 2 discusses related work. Section 3 introduces the details of the security problem we solve. Section 4 presents MITHYS, our solution for protecting mobile applications vulnerable to MITM attacks. Section 5 focuses on the implementation of MITHYSApp. Section 6 evaluates our solution in terms of effectiveness and network delay. Finally, Section 7 concludes the paper.

2   Related Work

Today's smartphones are capable of handling different types of personal data, which most of the times can be considered sensible. As a result, smartphones security is becoming more and more a key topic in the security research community, generating a lot of studies about dangerous threats and possible solutions (as shown by the proceedings of recent top conferences on security, such as ESORICS, POLICY and CCS). Considering only the Android case and to mention only a few papers, Davi et al. [9] presented an analysis of the privilege escalation attacks, together with some possible approaches to the problem [5], [6]. Becher et al. [3] gave a more general security overview about the mobile smartphones environment, whereas Shabtai et al. [16] focused more deeply in an Android security assessment. Other works focused on the direction of extending Android security features: e.g. considering Context-based access control [8] and enforcing different modes of uses based on security profiles [15]. To mention all the papers aiming at securing Android is out of the scope of this paper. What we consider instead important to point out is that, although this increasing research effort, a significant work has still to be done in order to secure smartphone platforms. This is proved by the huge vulnerability recently discovered regarding the use of the SSL cryptographic protocol.

Various misuses of the SSL protocol are spread both in the desktop environment and in the mobile environment, exposing private data (potentially sensible) to malicious attacks. In particular, Georgiev et al. [11] analysed the SSL usage across various environments, only to find out that this protocol's implementation is "completely broken in many security-critical applications and libraries". Meanwhile, Fahl et al. [10] analysed the SSL usage on 13,500 Android applications, and found out that a large percentage of them suffer from SSL vulnerabilities, which expose them to dangerous man-in-the-middle attacks. To add it up, some of these applications (such as PayPal and Facebook) are very popular, covering up to 185 million users. Both studies just gave some advices to developers, but did not mention any solution to the SSL usage problem.

SSL misuse vulnerabilities have been also considered in the literature. For example, the work in [4] shows an approach to detect SSL-based man-in-the-middle-attacks. However, this approach is designed for desktop web browsers, so it is not suitable for the setting of mobile applications that we are considering in this work. Furthermore, a simple MITM attack towards the third-party server proposed in [4] completely invalidates their protection mechanism. This problem is also acknowledged by the authors in their work.

Despite the size of the problem, the SSL usage vulnerability problem for mobile applications is still out there, threatening millions of users and their private data. We will focus on this problem in the next Section.

3   The Problem: Validating SSL Certificates

Nowadays Internet browsers, electronic mail clients, instant messaging clients, and nearly every entity that needs a secure communication to a remote service are using SSL and TLS, two standard cryptographic protocols that perform network data encryption and endpoint authentication over a TCP connection. An SSL secure communication begins with an operation called *handshake*, in which the server is authenticated by the client (and viceversa, eventually). After that, these two entities agree on a common cryptographic material, used to begin the encrypted communication. This flow can be roughly summarised as follows (we are not considering the client authentication steps, which are optional):

1. The client contacts the server, and they exchange some preliminary parameters, among which the certificates (the client's certificate is optional, therefore often missing); the exchanged parameters are called context of a SSL session.
2. The client authenticates the server by using the information obtained in the previous step, especially the server's certificate; for a secure session to be established, the server must be successfully authenticated by the client (either implicitly or explicitly).
3. The client, thanks to the previous information exchange, creates a pre-master secret, encrypted with the server's public key obtained from the server's certificate, and sends it to the server.
4. The server decrypts the message and uses the pre-master secret to compute the master secret while the client does the same.
5. Using the master secret, both the client and the server generate the so called session keys, that will be used to communicate securely.
6. The communication starts as the client sends the first encrypted message.

There is a slight problem on the second point of the above flow. The client must authenticate the server in order to be sure that it is communicating with the right server and not with, for instance, a malicious one which is faking its identity (a typical MITM situation). This is mostly done by thoroughly checking the server's SSL certificate fields (e.g., expiration date, issuer, signature).

Example 2. *Continuing the scenario described in Example 1, let us suppose Alice is using PayPal's Android application (PayPalApp), which needs to communicate with PayPal's remote server (PayPalServer). However, the attacker (MITM) is able to intercept the ingoing and outgoing traffic of PayPalApp. The following steps are performed as part of the SSL handshaking process:*

1. *PayPalApp queries PayPalServer for its X.509 certificate (which contains PayPalServers's public key).*
2. *MITM intercepts PayPalApp's request and asks PayPalServer for its certificate pretending she is PayPalApp; PayPalServer sends its certificate to MITM.*
3. *MITM now generates a fake X.509 certificate containing MITM's public key instead of the PayPalServer's one; MITM also makes this fake certificate look like PayPalServer's one, then sending it back to PayPalApp.*
4. *Depending on how strict are PayPalApp's checks against MITM's certificate, PayPalApp will eventually think that she's talking to PayPalServer.*
5. *At this point, MITM can intercept the plain text of every message (i.e., MITM can easily decrypt the messages) PayPalApp sends to PayPalServer and viceversa, but she is undetected.*

In Example 2, *PayPalApp* performs very poor checks against MITM's certificate (e.g., it might not check the issuer name of the certificate, therefore not recognizing a MITM attack). As a result, Alice is not able to detect that the communication with *PayPalServer* is not secure at all, allowing MITM to intercept all the available data. It is important to stress that this is not just a toy example, we have actually developed a demo implementing this specific attack.

It is clear by now that the key point of this procedure consists in validating the server's certificate in a proper way. Since many mobile applications do not perform this step correctly, exposing the end-user to dangerous MITM attacks, our solution focuses on solving this specific problem.

4   MITHYS: Mind The Hand You Shake

In this section, we present MITHYS (Mind The Hand You Shake), a system designed to detect potentially MITM-vulnerable applications, and to compensate the lack of security by protecting applications from MITM attacks. To the best of our knowledge, MITHYS represents the first solution that tackles the MITM vulnerability of mobile applications by taking on the security checks required to establish a proper secure connection. For space limitation, we omit details on MITHYS user interface and configuration. Instead, we focus on the core of MITHYS and we describe it from a system point of view, focusing on its architecture, its implementation (Section 5) and its evaluation (Section 6).

The main idea behind MITHYS is to act as a friendly MITM on the mobile device. Every time a "new" application (an application which has not been tested yet) requests a resource via the HTTP over the SSL protocol (from now on, HTTPS requests), the MITHYS system tries to act as a man-in-the-middle, forging a fake ad-hoc SSL certificate for the application. If the application is not vulnerable, it will immediately block the communication; otherwise (the application is vulnerable), the communication will proceed normally, as if there is no third party between the application and the remote server. In both scenarios, MITHYS is able to protect the application from potentially malicious MITM attacks by performing additional checks on the SSL connection (Section 4.3).

An high-level overview of the MITHYS architecture is shown in Figure 1. At a macroscopic level, there are two main components, highlighted in the figure by thicker borders. The first one is called *MITHYS Proxy*, a proxy-based mobile application that runs on the mobile device. The second one is called *MITHYS WebServer*, a remote web server hosted and reachable through the Internet.

We now describe the two key components of MITHYS: MITHYS WebServer (Section 4.1) and MITHYS Proxy (Section 4.2). Then, in Section 4.3 we describe how the overall system works.

4.1   MITHYS WebServer

This component acts as a trusted party for the solution. It features only one servlet, whose purpose is to retrieve the SSL certificates chain (typically in the

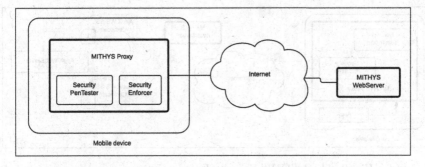

Fig. 1. The MITHYS high-level architecture

X.509 standard) of the URL passed as an argument; then, it serializes the chain in a proper way and returns it as a result. This servlet is only reachable via HTTPS, meaning that it has a SSL certificate associated to it. This is a key point of the whole architecture. This SSL certificate is self-signed, i.e. generated from the root certificate of our private Certification Authority (i.e., *MITHYS CA*). Since we have access to the original certificate, we can use its information to add an extra layer of security against MITM attacks, as we discuss in Section 4.2. Finally, we underline that we do not consider this component as a possible target for attacks, mainly because (i) it can be hosted on highly secure cloud services (e.g., Google Compute Engine) and (ii) it is easier to protect this single component rather than protecting millions of user devices with an highly variable set of installed applications. However, in order to prevent Denial-of-Service (DoS) attacks, we recommend the redundancy approach, by means of a MITHYS WebServer pool.

4.2 MITHYS Proxy

This represents the main component of the architecture. Its main purpose is to receive all the HTTPS requests coming from the applications installed on the mobile device, and to pass the information back and forth between the application and its associated web server. It can also strengthen the applications' security by performing additional checks (as detailed later in this section) on the SSL connection. In order to fulfill its tasks, it features two independent modules (see Figure 1): *Security PenTester* and *Security Enforcer*.

Security PenTester. This module is the component which represents the actual MITM. It impersonates the original remote server by forging a fake SSL certificate for the mobile application. It also contacts the original remote server, pretending to be the application itself. If Security PenTester is able to establish a secure connection with the application (that is to say, the application accepts the fake SSL certificate), it acknowledges that the application is vulnerable. Otherwise, we can only have some degree of confidence that the application is not vulnerable, while it could be actually vulnerable in other circumstances. This module runs continuously, so every application is basically tested every time it

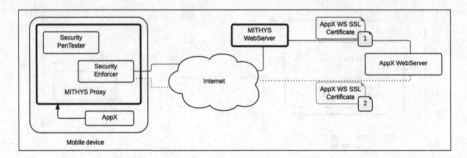

Fig. 2. The MITHYS Security Enforcer interaction scheme

issues an HTTPS request. Since we want *"PenProof"* applications (i.e., applications that are not vulnerable to the PenTester) to be excluded from further security tests, an effective approach consists in adding them to a whitelist: every application on that list avoids the Security PenTester module, but may still be strengthened by the Security Enforcer module.

We want to point out that the use of a whitelist is actually mandatory. A PenProof application that receives a fake SSL certificate for an HTTPS request will terminate the connection immediately, therefore not working correctly. As a consequence, the MITHYS system needs to be aware of the already (successfully) tested applications, so that we do not hinder their normal operations.

Security Enforcer. This module performs additional checks on the SSL connection to the remote server in place of the mobile application. More specifically, given the HTTPS request issued by AppX (an installed application), this module performs the following operations (illustrated in Figure 2):

- Issues an HTTPS request to the MITHYS WebServer, in order to retrieve the SSL certificates chain associated to the URL of the application's HTTPS request (Step 1 in the figure);
- Retrieves the SSL certificates chain associated to the URL of the HTTPS request (Step 2 in the figure);
- Compares the two certificates chains. Each certificate of one chain is compared to the respective certificate of the other chain. This is done by checking if the signatures of the two certificates correspond.

If the certificates contained in the two chains do not match, it means that a MITM attack might be in place. On the other hand, if the two chains have a 1:1 match, we can be sure that no SSL-based MITM attack is being held at that time. This assumption is based on the fact that the HTTPS request to the MITHYS WebServer is MITM-proof. To achieve such requirement, since the SSL certificate of our MITHYS WebServer is known a priori, we can store it on a keystore and embed it in our MITHYS Proxy mobile application. So, when the HTTPS request to the MITHYS WebServer is issued, the obtained SSL certificate is matched against our keystore: any failure will invalidate the certificates chains comparison, indicating an ongoing MITM attack of some kind. It is worth pointing out that an application which has passed the Security PenTester's controls might still be monitored by the Security Enforcer (e.g., as an extra security measure for the user). What is more, Security Enforcer only sends to MITHYS WebServer the URL of the original HTTPS request, without transmitting any sensitive information of the user.

4.3   MITHYS Workflow

In order to better understand how the overall MITHYS system works, Figure 3 shows a simplified workflow of a generic scenario where the mobile application AppX issues an HTTPS request (e.g., to *https://www.appx.com/api/login*). The request is intercepted by our MITHYS Proxy, that checks whether the application has ever been whitelisted. If not, Security PenTester tries to act as a MITM and determines if AppX is aware of a third entity between AppX's remote server and itself. If the application is aware of the MITM, it is whitelisted: each subsequent HTTPS request coming from that application will be executed as is, without any interception. Otherwise, Security Enforcer is activated in order to prevent any malicious MITM attacks. Again, note that even a whitelisted application might take advantage of the latter module, if specified by the user.

Example 3. *Back to our running example, let us consider Example 2 to show the workflow of MITHYS with PayPal's Android application. The key assumption is that Alice is using a MITHYS implementation on her smartphone. Alice starts the PayPalApp, which in turn issues HTTPS requests to the PayPalServer. These requests are intercepted by MITHYS' Security PenTester (PenTester from now on). PenTester retrieves the list of whitelisted applications to check if PayPalApp is among those. The whitelist is initially empty, so PenTester acts as a SSL MITM and forges a fake SSL certificate. PayPalApp, as we show in Section 6.1, is vulnerable to this attack, so it accepts the certificate. Now that PenTester has acknowledged that PayPalApp is vulnerable, it reports this information to the MITHYS' Security Enforcer module (Enforcer from now on). Enforcer must now protect PayPalApp from actual MITM attacks by performing the steps described in Section 4.2. What is more, Enforcer will protect all the future PayPalApp's HTTPS requests.*

Example 4. *We reconsider Example 3, but we assume that this time Alice wants to use the Twitter application, which is not vulnerable to SSL MITM attacks (Section 6.1). Again, Alice is using a MITHYS implementation. Alice starts TwitterApp, PenTester intercepts the HTTPS requests to TwitterServer and tries to act as a SSL MITM for TwitterApp. The latter is not vulnerable, so it will reject the fake SSL certificate and abort the current operation. Now PenTester knows that the application is secure, so it adds TwitterApp as a new whitelist entry. TwitterApp can operate without the Enforce protection, but the user might want to be protected anyway. If this is the case, Enforcer will protect all the future TwitterApp's HTTPS requests. Otherwise, it will simply forward the HTTPS requests/responses between TwitterApp and TwitterServer.*

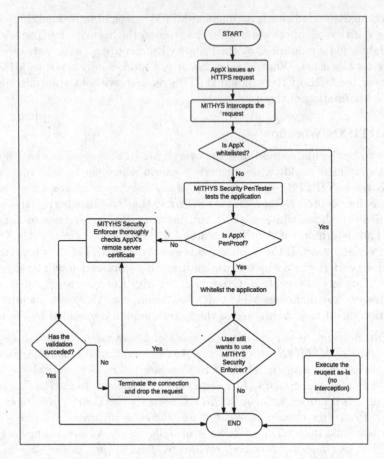

Fig. 3. Workflow of the MITHYS architecture with the AppX mobile application

5   Implementation of MITHYS: MITHYSApp

This section discusses our implementation of MITHYS, namely the MITHYSApp Android application which acts as the MITHYS Proxy component. The MITHYS WebServer consists in a Micro Instance of Amazon's Elastic Compute Cloud Web Services (AWS EC2) [2]: a continuously running Apache Tomcat instance serves an HTTPS-only Java servlet called `GetSSLCertificate`.

5.1   The MITHYSApp WebServer

MITHYSApp WebServer implements the MITHYS WebServer component. It is hosted on Amazon Elastic Compute Cloud (Amazon EC2) [2] as part of the Amazon Web Services. A Micro Instance of the EC2 cloud, which we can consider as a proper Virtual Private Server (VPS), runs the Apache Tomcat web server and servlet container. There is only one servlet, called `GetSSLCertificateServlet` that takes in input two arguments: the first one is the target URL, the second one is the HTTP method that should be used to invoke that URL. This servlet simply issues an HTTPS request to the target URL (accordingly to the HTTP method) and retrieves the SSL certificates chain associated to that URL. The Base64 serialization of the chain is returned as a JSON-formatted result. Please note that this servlet is only available via HTTPS, and it uses an SSL certificate generated from our MITHYS Certification Authority (MITHYS CA) in order to prevent MITM attacks against our MITHYSApp application.

5.2   The MITHYSApp Android Application

MITHYSApp is an Android app that implements the MITHYS Proxy component. It relies on the open source Android library SandroProxyLib[1], which is based in turn on the OWASP WebScarab project, that offers a working-out-of-the-box proxy for Android. What is more, it behaves as the MITHYS Security PenTester by default due to the fact that, every time it receives a new HTTPS request, it acts as a MITM and forges ad-hoc fake certificates. These certificates are generated from the MITHYS CA, and their hostname matches the hostname of the target server, looking similar to the original ones. From now on we will use also the term "proxy" to refer to the proxy part of this library. While not requiring any special permission or OS modifications, MITHYSApp requires the installation of the MITHYS CA certificate and the setup of the proxy address for the current Wi-Fi connection. MITHYS guides the user in both these steps, both performed only once at installation time.

Security PenTester. We had to modify and to extend the SandroProxyLib library in order to implement the above component correctly. First of all, given an intercepted HTTPS request, we need to know which application generated it: in terms of Java objects, we only have a `Socket` instance that represents the connection between the application and the proxy, of which we only know the port. But, since Android is a Linux-based OS, we can read the content of the */proc/net/tcp* (or */proc/net/tcp6* if an IPv6 address is available) file that maps all the active sockets to their Unix processes: in this way we know which port is being used, so we can obtain the UID of the process which is using that port. This information, together with the `PackageManager.getPackagesForUid(uid)` method provided by Android, offers us the possibility of knowing which application issued the HTTPS request given just the port of its `Socket` object. To the best of our knowledge, this is the only technique available at the time being, so we created a small and useful Android library[2] which eases this process for the developer. Another modification to the proxy library consisted in introducing the whitelisting mechanism, so that each time an installed application refuses to establish a secure connection with the proxy (that is, the SSL handshake phase between our proxy and the application cannot be completed) it communicates

---

[1] https://github.com/SandroB/sandrop/tree/master/projects/SandroProxyLib
[2] https://github.com/dextorer/AndroidTCPSourceApp

the non-vulnerable application to MITHYSApp. To do so, an `AppDescriptor` object containing package name, application version and requested URL is created and sent to the running instance of MITHYSApp. The latter receives the `AppDescriptor` object and inserts its values on a local SQLite database. This database must be encrypted in order to prevent manual tampering, so we used a custom Android library called SQLCipher[3] to provide "transparent 256-bit AES encryption of database files". In addition, for each new HTTPS request the proxy checks if the application who issued it has been whitelisted before, by querying the SQLite database: if so, no interception is made and the proxy simply passes the data back and forth between the whitelisted application and the remote server. In addition, in order to prevent alterations to the local MITHYS keystore, we invoke a JNI-compiled library that checks the current Java package name and the keystore size. Thanks to this approach, any attempt to (i) replace the native library, to (ii) modify the Java code of MITHYSApp or even to (iii) replace the keystore will lead to a non working application.

Security Enforcer. In order to implement the Security Enforcer module, we had to extend the SandroProxyLib library so that, every time a vulnerable application issues an HTTPS request, the proxy performs the following steps:

1. Retrieves the SSL certificates chain associated to the URL of the HTTPS request.
2. Issues an HTTPS request to the MITHYSApp WebServer, in order to retrieve the SSL certificates chain associated to the URL of the application's HTTPS request.
3. Compares the two certificates chains, as described in Section 4.2.

If no MITM attack is in place, the comparison will succeed and the HTTPS request will be issued without further ado. If a MITM attack is in place, the HTTPS request issued towards the MITHYSApp WebServer will simply fail (as we explained in Section 4.2). A smarter attacker might decide not to intercept the HTTPS requests addressed to our MITHYSApp WebServer: but this won't prevent our Security Enforcer module from detecting a MITM attack, since the two certificates chains are still compared one against the other.

6   System Evaluation

In this section, we present a set of tests that assess the performance impact of the MITHYS approach and determine its ability to successfully detect vulnerable applications. More specifically, we want to show that, although MITHYS requires additional HTTPS requests in order to protect the mobile device from MITM attacks, the user is not dramatically affected by this overhead. First, we will analyse the effectiveness of MITHYSApp's vulnerability detection in Section 6.1. Then, in order to determine the additional overhead, we will discuss our test method in Section 6.2 and the results in Section 6.3.

---

[3] https://guardianproject.info/code/sqlcipher/

6.1   Vulnerability Detection

In their analysis, Fahl et al. [10] manually audited some of the most popular Android applications, in order to test their vulnerability to SSL-based MITM attacks. We manually tested the same set of applications (that, in the meantime, could have been updated, fixing this MITM vulnerability) against MITHYSApp, therefore evaluating the capability and the accuracy of detecting vulnerable applications. We show our results in Table 1. The results show that MITHYSApp is able to successfully detect vulnerable applications (according to Fahl et al.'s findings). MITHYSApp is also consistent with the results in [10] in detecting *Twitter* and *Voxie Walkie Talkie* as non vulnerable.

Table 1. MITHYSApp results in detecting apps safe from SSL-based MITM attacks. (✓) indicates that the app is safe; (×) means that the app is vulnerable.

Application	Test result	Application	Test result
Amazon MP3	×	Google Play Store	×
Chrome	×	Google+	×
Dolphin Browser HD	×	Hotmail	×
Dropbox	×	Instagram	×
Ebay	×	OfficeSuite Pro 6	×
Expedia Bookings	×	PayPal	×
Facebook Messenger	×	Twitter	✓
Facebook	×	Voxie Walkie Talkie	✓
Foursquare	×	Yahoo! Messenger	×
GMail	×	Yahoo! Mail	×

6.2   Experimental Setting

We have tested MITHYSApp with three of the most popular Android applications. These application belong to different categories of Google's Play Store, and represent three different important aspects that a typical mobile user is interested to: social networking, finance checking, cloud storage access. In particular, the applications we considered are: Facebook[4] (social networking service), PayPal[5] (global e-commerce business allowing online payments and money transfers), and Dropbox[6] (web-based file hosting service).

In our tests we considered two operations common to all the applications listed above: *login* and *logout*. These operations are very network-intensive, hence representing a perfect test scenario for MITHYSApp. As main tool for testing, we used `monkeyrunner` [13]. This tool allows interacting (e.g., pressing buttons, typing text) with an Android device by writing a simple Python script and

---

[4] https://play.google.com/store/apps/details?id=com.facebook.katana

[5] https://play.google.com/store/apps/details?id=com.paypal.android.
p2pmobile

[6] https://play.google.com/store/apps/details?id=com.dropbox.android

running it via Android Debug Bridge (adb[7]). We wrote three scripts, one for each considered application. Each script basically performs these operations:

1. Connects to the Android device;
2. Opens the Android logcat in a subprocess (more on this later);
3. Starts the application's login activity;
4. Enters the credentials for a valid account;
5. Presses the login button and saves the current time on a variable called LoginStartTime;
6. Monitors the logcat in order to see when the main activity of the application is displayed - as soon as this happens, it saves the current time on the LoginEndTime variable;
7. Calculates the login time as (LoginEndTime - LoginStartTime);
8. Executes a number of actions in order to start the logout procedure; as soon as the logout button is pressed, it saves the current time on LogoutStartTime;
9. Monitors the logcat in order to see when the login activity of the application is displayed - as soon as this happens, it saves the current time on LogoutEndTime;
10. Calculates the logout time as (LogoutEndTime - LogoutStartTime);
11. Prints the two results.

We want to focus for a moment on the use of the logcat [12]. This tool allows the developer to collect and view the log messages, both coming from the Android OS and from the installed applications. We used specific logcat messages to determine the end of each operation (login and logout). Every time that the system displays a particular activity of the application (i.e., the main activity after the login, the login activity after the logout), we are sure that the considered operation has ended. This approach leads to reliable and repeatable tests, whereas it does not pollute the tests results at all.

6.3   Network Overhead

The results of our experiments are reported in Figure 4. In particular, Figure 4(a) and Figure 4(b) represent the overhead for the login and logout operation, respectively. We can observe that the average delay added by using MITHYSApp is approximately five seconds. Since this value is almost constant for each of the considered situations, the delay is more likely to be noticed by the user for shorter operations. The two figures show a higher delay in using MITHYSApp for both the login and the logout operations. This overhead is not surprising though, because MITHYSApp needs to issue additional network requests in order to protect mobile applications from MITM attacks. If we consider Facebook, the introduced delay for the login operation is about 55%, whereas for the logout operation it is about 33%.

There is an important point here we want to stress. While the current version of MITHYSApp is a fully-working implementation, we need to consider that it

---

[7] http://developer.android.com/tools/help/adb.html

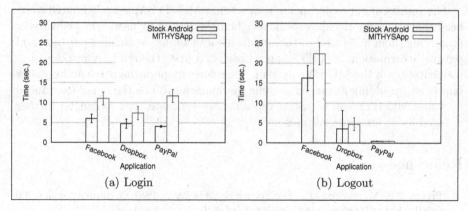

Fig. 4. MITHYS: time overhead for representative applications

has not yet been optimised, both in terms of certificate caching and in terms of network performances. As a consequence, the values that emerged from the tests can be considered as an upper bound for the additional delay, which in some situations may be indeed noticeable by the user. We believe that, by properly optimising our implementation, we can reduce the five seconds average delay to a value of three or even two seconds. Another aspect that we have to take into account is that MITHYSApp is able to prevent MITM attacks that usually are performed nearby free Internet access points. Therefore, the user should take advantage of it while she is connected to a wireless access point, whereas it could be deactivated in other less attack-prone circumstances.

7 Conclusion

In this paper we have addressed a SSL vulnerability that has been recently shown affecting a base of many millions of users of mobile devices. To solve this problem, we have proposed MITHYS, a system for mobile devices which is able to protect mobile applications from SSL vulnerabilities. The architecture of MITHYS is light and feasible for several mobile platforms. To support this claim, we implemented MITHYSApp, i.e., MITHYS for Android. In particular, we implemented MITHYSApp at the application level, thus facilitating the spread of our solution and its installation on Android-powered mobile devices. We decided to focus on the Android platform mostly due to its popularity and flexibility. However, we have reasons to believe that mobile applications for Apple devices (e.g., iPhone, iPad) are just as vulnerable as the ones available for Android. For example, Thampi [19] was able to perform an SSL-based MITM attack to analyse the Path iOS application, discovering an illegitimate upload of the user's contacts to Path's servers. As a consequence, Path released a security update to its application, acknowledging the problem [14].

The results of our experiments showed that MITHYSApp has a limited over-head that even if noticeable, we believe being accepted by users when effectively protecting them from man-in-the-middle attacks aiming at stealing personal and sensible information. MITHYSApp represents a first (though fully working) implementation of the MITHYS system. Therefore, its performances can be vastly improved by adding advanced caching mechanisms. While the delay introduced by using MITHYSApp is still acceptable, we estimate that it can be further reduced by at least two seconds.

References

1. Freier, P.K.A., Karlton, P.: The Secure Sockets Layer (SSL) Protocol Version 3.0 (2001), http://tools.ietf.org/html/rfc6101
2. Amazon.com, Inc. Amazon Elastic Compute Cloud (Amazon EC2), http://aws.amazon.com/ec2/
3. Becher, M., Freiling, F., Hoffmann, J., Holz, T., Uellenbeck, S., Wolf, C.: Mobile security catching up? revealing the nuts and bolts of the security of mobile devices. In: 2011 IEEE Symposium on Security and Privacy (SP), pp. 96–111 (2011)
4. Benton, K., Jo, J., Kim, Y.: Signaturecheck: a protocol to detect man-in-the-middle attack in ssl. In: Proceedings of CSIIRW 2011. ACM (2011)
5. Bugiel, S., Davi, L., Dmitrienko, A., Fischer, T., Sadeghi, A.-R.: Xmandroid: A new android evolution to mitigate privilege escalation attacks. Technische Universität Darmstadt, Technical Report TR-2011-04 (2011)
6. Bugiel, S., Davi, L., Dmitrienko, A., Fischer, T., Sadeghi, A.-R., Shastry, B.: Towards taming privilege-escalation attacks on android. In: Proceedings of NDSS 2012 (2012)
7. Charland, A., Leroux, B.: Mobile application development: web vs. native. Commun. ACM 54(5), 49–53 (2011)
8. Conti, M., Nguyen, V.T.N., Crispo, B.: CRePE: Context-related policy enforcement for android. In: Burmester, M., Tsudik, G., Magliveras, S., Ilić, I. (eds.) ISC 2010. LNCS, vol. 6531, pp. 331–345. Springer, Heidelberg (2011)
9. Davi, L., Dmitrienko, A., Sadeghi, A.-R., Winandy, M.: Privilege escalation attacks on android. In: Burmester, M., Tsudik, G., Magliveras, S., Ilić, I. (eds.) ISC 2010. LNCS, vol. 6531, pp. 346–360. Springer, Heidelberg (2011)
10. Fahl, S., Harbach, M., Muders, T., Baumgärtner, L., Freisleben, B., Smith, M.: Why eve and mallory love android: an analysis of android ssl (in)security. In: Proceedings of CCS 2012, pp. 50–61. ACM, New York (2012)
11. Georgiev, M., Iyengar, S., Jana, S., Anubhai, R., Boneh, D., Shmatikov, V.: The most dangerous code in the world: validating ssl certificates in non-browser software. In: Proceedings of CCS 2012, pp. 38–49. ACM, New York (2012)
12. Google Inc. logcat, http://developer.android.com/tools/help/logcat.html
13. Google Inc. monkeyrunner, http://developer.android.com/tools/help/monkeyrunner_concepts.html
14. Path Inc. Path - We are sorry, http://blog.path.com/post/17274932484/we-are-sorry

15. Russello, G., Conti, M., Crispo, B., Fernandes, E.: Moses: supporting operation modes on smartphones. In: Proceedings of SACMAT 2012, pp. 3–12. ACM (2012)

16. Shabtai, A., Fledel, Y., Kanonov, U., Elovici, Y., Dolev, S., Glezer, C.: Google android: A comprehensive security assessment. IEEE Security Privacy 8(2), 35–44 (2010)

17. Shetty, S., Song, M., Ma, L.: Rogue access point detection by analyzing network traffic characteristics. In: MILCOM 2007, pp. 1–7. IEEE (2007)

18. Dierks, C.A.T.: The TLS Protocol Version 1.0 (1999), http://www.ietf.org/rfc/rfc2246.txt

19. Thampi, A.: Path uploads your entire iPhone address book to its servers, http://mclov.in/2012/02/08/path-uploads-your-entire-address-book-to-their-servers.html

Evaluating the Manageability of Web Browsers Controls

Alexios Mylonas, Nikolaos Tsalis, and Dimitris Gritzalis

Information Security & Critical Infrastructure Protection Research Laboratory
Dept. of Informatics, Athens University of Economics & Business (AUEB)
76 Patission Ave., GR-10434, Athens, Greece
{amylonas,ntsalis,dgrit}@aueb.gr

Abstract. The proliferation of smartphones has introduced new challenges in web browsing security. These devices often have limited resources and small size, which may limit the security 'arsenal' of their user. This, however, does not seem to deter smartphone users from accessing the Web via their devices. On the same time, the popularity of browser-based exploits among attackers is also on the rise, especially in the form of Blackhole exploit kit, i.e. frameworks that attack browsers using 0-day exploits (e.g., in Java, Flash). In this context, the paper contributes by comparing the availability and manageability of security controls that are offered by popular smartphone and desktop browsers. It also provides insights about their preconfigured protection against web threats.

Keywords: Web browser security, Smartphone, Privacy, Exploit, Control.

1   Introduction

The proliferation of smartphones has introduced new challenges in secure web browsing. These devices often have limited resources, as well as small size, which limits the security 'arsenal' of their users. Such lack of protection controls, however, does not seem to hinder users from browsing the web via smartphones. On the contrary, according to a recent report, by the year 2017 smartphone mobile data traffic will increase 81%, comparing to 2012 [11].

Average users are not familiar with the details of security controls used while browsing the web. For instance, a user may understand that SSL offers a level of protection to online transactions. It is rather unlikely, though, that she is aware of the relevant security details and threats she is exposed to. Nowadays, users come across to different threats while browsing the web. These range from traditional client-side attacks (e.g. Cross-Site-Scripting) to zero-day exploits that target Java plugins[1]. Contrary to what one would expect, CISCO [10] reports that browser malware are not only present in 'bad' webpages (e.g. ones hosting pirated software, etc.), but also in benign ones (e.g. social media sites, etc.). The latter may unwittingly serve malware embedded in their active content, typically after a server compromise or with the inclusion of malicious advertisements. Furthermore, progressively more attackers use in their client-side attacks, browser exploitation frameworks (e.g. Blackhole exploit kit) [33].

---

[1] http://www.reuters.com/article/2013/01/11/
us-java-security-idUSBRE90A0S320130111

R. Accorsi and S. Ranise (Eds.): STM 2013, LNCS 8203, pp. 82–98, 2013.
© Springer-Verlag Berlin Heidelberg 2013

Web browsers (hereinafter referred to as browsers) communicate security events to users through their graphical user interfaces. For instance, the padlock icon appears every time a user visits a website with a valid digital certificate. Moreover, they include window gadgets (widgets), such as checkboxes, buttons, etc., for the configuration of their security controls. Users are expected to configure the browser's security controls as they see fit (by interacting with its menu), so as to protect their security and privacy. To aid users in this task, every web browser contains a menu option focused on the configuration of security and/or privacy controls. Even though ordinary users generally tend to ignore security events [14,22,24,36,38], some have been trained to interact with the interfaces in desktop browsers towards a safe web browsing.

In this context, this paper contributes by providing a systematic and comprehensive analysis of browser security controls. In particular, we focus on popular browsers in smartphones and desktops, enumerate their security controls, and collect and compare their default settings as well as their manageability options. Then, we provide a comparative evaluation of the offered protection against web threats. Our goal is to examine: (a) the protection of preconfigured security settings against web threats, and (b) the manageability of security controls that protect from certain web threats. The former provides indications of the offered protection to average users. The latter reveals the manageability of countermeasures for each threat, i.e. the flexibility to adjust the offered protection according to the users' "risk appetite" (e.g. a user may be willing to receive targeted advertising). Our work summarizes the differences in the availability and manageability of browsers' security controls. Overall, as expected, desktop browsers provide an increased manageability and availability. Regarding protection against web threats, our analysis revealed that browsers by default focus mostly on a subset of the examined threats (e.g. malware, privacy breach, phishing), while offering poor protection against the rest (e.g. third-party tracking, browser fingerprinting).

The rest of the paper is organized as follows. Section 2 presents related work. Section 3 includes the methodology of our research. Section 4 includes our observations. Finally, Section 5 includes a discussion of the results and our conclusions.

2   Related Work

Our work relates to [3], which provides a simple comparison of the availability of security options in Internet Explorer 7 and Internet Explorer Mobile (Windows Mobile 6 Professional Ed.). Our work contributes by providing up to date results, which include both the availability of security controls in current web browsers, as well as their manageability and preconfigured protection against web threats. Part of our work relates to [1], which focuses on the visibility of security indicators in smartphones. Our work confirmed the findings of this publication, regarding how smartphone browsers handle invalid digital certificates.

Recent literature on web security has focused on the visibility of security indicators in desktop browsers, indicating that the majority of users ignore them [1,14,27]. Moreover, novel browser security architectures have been proposed, which add new components that offer more security [6,9]. Finally, static and/or dynamic analysis for JavaScript malware has been studied in [5,12,20,21].

Table 1. Availability of smartphones browsers in test devices

Platform	Version	Device	Chrome Mobile (v. 26)	Firefox Mobile (v.21)	Opera Mobile (v. 14)	Opera Mini (v. 10)	Stock Browser†
Android	2.3.5	HTC Explorer			X		X
	2.3.6	LG-E400			X		X
	4.0.3	LG - P700	X	X	X		X
	4.0.4	Sony Xperia	X	X	X	X	X
	4.1.2	Samsung Galaxy S3	X	X	X		X
		Samsung Nexus S	X	X	X		X
iOS	5.1.1	iPhone 4	X			X	X
	6.1.2	iPhone 4S	X			X	X
Windows Phone	7.5	HTC Trophy7					X

† Browser for Android, Safari for iOS, and IE Mobile for Windows Phone.

3   Methodology

Our analysis' scope includes the current popular browsers for Windows desktops [34], i.e. Chrome (v. 27), Firefox (v. 21), Internet Explorer 10, Opera (v. 12.15), and Safari (v. 5.1.7), as well as their smartphone counterparts. Windows was selected due to its popularity among desktops [35]. Contrary to desktops, browsers are not available in all smartphones (see Table 1). The analysis includes Android, iOS and Windows Phone, which constitute the 93.6% of the smartphone market share [19]. Furthermore, the examined Android versions, i.e.: Gingerbread (v. 2.3), Ice Cream Sandwich (ICS, v. 4.0.*), and Jelly Bean (JB, v. 4.1.2), constitute the 91% of the in use Android devices [17]. Thus, our results are representative both in the desktop and smartphone platforms. Finally, for readability and space reasons, Table 1 refers to stock browsers of Android, iOS, Windows Phone (i.e. Browser, Safari, IE Mobile) as 'stock browser'.

Initially, the browsers' support pages that are dedicated in security controls were enumerated, as a user is expected to use them to be trained to configure browser controls. Then, their graphical interfaces were also enumerated and all the configurable security controls, as well as their default values, were collected. Any confusing text labels were marked, as well as any widgets that had obvious usability problems.

4   Manageability of Security Controls

Overall, thirty two (32) security controls appear in the browsers' interfaces, which are listed herein. The majority of the controls' labels are self-explanatory (e.g. block JavaScript). The rest of them are briefly described here, namely: (a) *external plugin check* refers to the existence of a web service that analyses the browser's plugins for vulnerabilities (e.g. [24]), (b) *local blacklist* enables users to enforce controls on a per-site basis via local blacklist/whitelist (e.g. per-site cookie blocking), (c) under *master password* the browser requests the entry of a master password every time it restarts, before accessing any stored passwords, and (d) *website checking* enables a user to manually initiate analysis (for malware/phishing) on the website she visits.

4.1 Availability and Manageability of Security Controls

Tables 2-6 summarize the availability and manageability status of all the security controls that are available via the browsers' interfaces. Their availability and manageability differs between each browser, as well as between two types, i.e. desktop and smartphone, of same browser. The findings are grouped together into five categories, according to the controls intended use from the support pages, namely: (a) content controls, (b) privacy controls, (c) browser manageability, (d) third-party software controls, and (e) web browsing controls.

Tables 2-6 use the following notation: (i) ⊠ is used when the mechanism *is not supported*, (ii) □ is used when the mechanism *is supported but not configurable*, (iii) ▣ is used when the mechanism *is supported but is not easily configurable*, and (iv) ■ is used when the mechanism *is supported and easily configurable*. A security control is marked as 'not easily configurable' when it can only be configured from a hidden menu (e.g. *about:config*, see Appendix), or when there is a usability problem in the configuration of the control (e.g. confusing wording of the widget's label). In such cases, it is rather unlikely that users will be able to find and/or correctly configure it.

Regarding the default values of security controls, ● and ○ stand for default enabled and default disabled control, respectively. The notation used is: {GC=Chrome, MF =Firefox, IE=Internet Explorer, OP=Opera, AS=Safari; AB= Android's stock browser, CM=Chrome Mobile, FM= Firefox Mobile, IM=IE Mobile, OM=Opera Mobile, Om=Opera Mini, SM=Safari Mobile}. Finally, the stock browser of Android is referred to as 'ABrowser'.

Content Controls. Table 2 summarizes the manageability of the content controls, i.e. controls that enable users to block cookies, images, and pop-ups. Desktop browsers provide similar availability and configurability for content controls, which is especially true for cookies and pop-ups. Even though images are essential for the correct functionality of websites, a user may wish to block images for various reasons, such as to protect privacy [39], to speed up browsing, etc. Contrary to desktop browsers, where users can block images in all browsers, this option is not available in most smartphone browsers. In Firefox Mobile such blocking images and pop-ups is only available via hidden menus (c.f. Appendix).

Table 2. Manageability of content controls

Controls	GC	MF	IE	OP	AS	AB	CM	FM	IM	OM	Om	SM
Block cookies	■○	■○	■○	■○	■○	■○	■○	■○	■○	■○	■○	■○
Block images	■○	■○	■○	■○	■○	■○	⊠	▣○	⊠	⊠	■○	⊠
Block pop-ups	■●	■●	■●	■●	■●	■●	■●	▣●	□●	■●	□●	■●

Furthermore, although pop-ups are often used by attackers (e.g. phishing, malware, etc.), their default blocking without the manageability of the control, as in IE Mobile and Opera Mini, may break the functionality of web applications that use benign pop-ups (e.g. uploading files).

Privacy Controls. Table 3 presents the heterogeneity in the availability and configurability of privacy controls, even between browsers in the same platform. Overall, in desktops the greatest heterogeneity is in location data and the referrer, whereas in smartphones it exists in all privacy controls. A lot of them are unavailable in smartphones. More specifically, only Chrome and Safari block location data by default by prompting users. Safari Mobile follows a similar approach, but this control is not configurable until such a request is made by the browser for the first time. In this case, the user is prompted and access to data is subsequently manageable from the settings of the location data, not from those of the browser. Thus, this may confuse average users. This control is configured in both of the two Firefox versions only from a hidden menu. Finally, it is supported differently in iOS and Android, being unavailable and available but disabled by default, respectively. The referrer is a value in HTTP headers (it is misspelled as 'referer' in the header), that can be collected for user tracking [16]. Referrer blocking is unavailable in most smartphone browsers and Internet Explorer and Safari. In both versions of Firefox this control is enabled only via a hidden menu. In Chrome it involves starting its executable with a shell parameter (see Appendix).

Table 3. Manageability of privacy controls

Controls	GC	MF	IE	OP	AS	AB	CM	FM	IM	OM	Om	SM
Block location data	■●	▣○	■○	■○	■●	■○	⊠|■○†	▣○	■○	⊠	⊠	▣●
Block referrer	▣○	▣○	⊠	■○	⊠	⊠	⊠	▣○	⊠	⊠	⊠	⊠
Block third- party cookies	■○	■○	■○	■○	■●	⊠	⊠	■○	⊠	⊠	⊠	■●
Enable DNT	■○	■○	■●	■○	▣○	⊠	■○	■○	⊠	⊠	⊠	⊠|▣○†
History Manager	■	■	■	■	▣	▣	■	■	□	■	▣	▣
Private browsing	■	■	■	■	■	⊠|▣	■†	■	⊠	⊠	⊠	■

† heterogeneity in different platforms.

The manageability of third-party cookies, DNT (do-not-track HTTP header value [39]), history manager, and private browsing –i.e. a session where browsing data (cookies, downloads) are not stored locally- is similar in desktop browsers. On the other hand, most smartphone browsers accept all cookies in an all-or-nothing approach, thus failing to protect user's privacy. This holds true, since they either block both first-party and third-party cookies, or allow them (c.f. Table 3). One could argue that enabling tracking by default is acceptable, since in the majority of the examined browsers the user is allowed to block it. However, during browser installation a user is not explicitly asked if she wishes to receive personalized advertisements. It is unclear whether users can understand the impact of tracking [23], which, in its ultimate form (e.g. via user identification [13]) may constitute an intrusion of her fundamental right to privacy. On the other hand, blocking all cookies, even first-party cookies, i.e. those that are not created from a third-party domain, can cause disruptions in website functionality, as they are normally used for user authentication. Finally, in Safari, the manageability of DNT is available only in iOS 6 and the wording near the widget is confusing, i.e. "Limit ad tracking". Thus, a user may accidentally enable web tracking by selecting the option "off", believing that she is disabling ad tracking in this way.

ABrowser, Opera mini, and Safari Mobile allow history deletion, but their widgets are scattered in the browsers' interfaces. Safari provides the control under a widget with a confusing title "Reset Safari...". Also, (a) ABrowser does not offer private browsing in Android Gingerbread - while the newest versions offer this mechanism only from a hidden menu (see Appendix) and (b) Chrome Mobile offers this control, but its effectiveness is hampered by the platform's limitations in iOS[2].

Browser Manageability. As depicted in Table 4, the manageability and availability of controls via which users manage the browser is similar in most desktop browsers, except for SSL\TLS version selection and task manager (can aid control over web browsing by inspecting resource consumption). On the contrary, smartphone browsers either do not support or offer poor manageability of these controls. Most desktop browsers offer automatic browser updates, but Safari (for Windows and Mac OS Leopard) does not. Thus, its users are exposed to more than 100 vulnerabilities, which were patched in Safari 6 [2], without being explicitly informed about it in the browser's download page or during/after its installation. Contrary to desktop browsers, most smartphone browser updates are semi-automatic and require user initiation. Stock browsers update along with platform updates and most third-party browsers update via the app repository (e.g. Google Play). Also, smartphone browser updates often suffer from delays. Updates for third-party browsers may be delayed by the app analysis process of the app repository. Also, updates of Android may be either delayed or even be unavailable by the device vendor. Thus, ABrowser may not get updates even if Google makes them available.

Table 4. Mechanisms for browser management

Controls	GC	MF	IE	OP	AS	AB	CM	FM	IM	OM	Om	SM
Browser update	■●	■●	■●	■●	⊠	□●	▣●	■●	□●	▣●	▣●	□●
Certificate manager	■	■	■	■	□	□/■²	■/□²	□	□	□	⊠	□
Master Password	⊠	■○	⊠	■○	⊠	⊠	⊠	■○	⊠	⊠	⊠	⊠
Proxy server	■	■	■	■	■	▣¹	▣¹	▣¹	▣¹	⊠	▣¹	▣¹
Search engine manager	■	■	■	■	□¹	□¹	□¹	⊠	⊠	⊠	□¹	□¹
SSL/TLS version selection	⊠	⊠	■	■	⊠	⊠	⊠	⊠	⊠	⊠	⊠	⊠
Task manager	■	⊠	⊠	⊠	⊠	⊠	⊠	⊠	⊠	⊠	⊠	⊠

[1] the control has a limitation, [2] heterogeneity in different platforms

Among desktop browsers, only Safari does not offer a configurable (a) certificate manager,[3] i.e. an interface to add certificates or remove compromised ones [30], and (b) search engine manager allowing the addition of an engine that does not track users (e.g. DuckDuckGo, Startpage).[4] In contrast, in smartphones only ABrowser, Opera

---

[2] http://support.google.com/chrome/bin/answer.py?hl=en&answer=95464
[3] Safari uses Internet Explorer's certificate manager without providing a link to its interface.
[4] https://duckduckgo.com/, https://startpage.com/

Mobile and Chrome for Android use the certificate manager that is provided by Android (i.e. new versions of Gingerbread). Regarding, the manageability of search engines, most smartphone browsers allow only the selection from a static list (e.g. Google, Yahoo, etc.).

Only Firefox, Opera, and Firefox Mobile offer a master password, therefore an attacker with physical access to the browser can login to websites having stored passwords. Chrome and Firefox also enable password unmasking; hence an attacker can access them. The risk of the two scenarios is greater in smartphones, due to their small size, mobility, and because smartphone users may not password-protect their devices [27]. Similarly, only Internet Explorer and Opera provide manageability of SSL\TLS protocols. Their interfaces allow users to disable or select an older version of SSL\TLS protocol, as any other non-security related setting in the browser's menu, thus, potentially reducing the offered security. All browsers provide proxy server manageability.[5] In smartphones, proxy manageability requires navigation to the Wi-Fi settings (c.f. Appendix), which is confusing since it clearly violates the three-click rule. The proxy server is not available when the smartphone uses cellular Internet (e.g. UMTS, etc.).

Third-Party Software Control. Desktop browsers provide similar[6] manageability for third-party software (i.e. JavaScript, Java, extensions, plugins) and are preconfigured to enable it. Thus, since webpages may contain malicious active content [10], by default the offered security is lowered for the sake of functionality. On the contrary, smartphone browsers provide poor manageability of third-party software, which are enabled by default (where applicable).[7] In particular: (a) JavaScript is manageable only by ABrowser, Chrome Mobile (only for Android), Firefox Mobile (only from a hidden menu), and Safari Mobile, and (b) only ABrower (versions ICS and JB) and Firefox Mobile provide an 'all-or-nothing' control over plugins via 'tap to play', i.e. each time users explicitly enable individual plugins. Also, smartphones do not provide manageability of other apps which are invoked to present content (e.g. video players).

Desktop browsers and Firefox Mobile auto-update extensions, but users may disable them (e.g. while roaming) only in Firefox and Safari. Moreover, Internet Explorer, Opera and Firefox Mobile do not support their manually update. On the contrary, browsers do not automatically update plugins. Thus, an interface is required, for spotting and manually updating vulnerable and/or buggy plugins. To this end, Chrome and Firefox highlight and provide update links for such plugins. Chrome's highlighting (the plugin's version is colored red) is rather easy to ignore, among the various plugin details. Moreover, Firefox provides a web based plugin check [25], but its use is confusing, since: (a) as a link on top of the plugins it is difficult to spot, and (b) users may accidentally interact with the widget for extension updates, which resides in the corner of the same interface.

Web Browsing Controls. Desktop browsers provide comparable manageability in web browsing controls, whereas these controls are mostly unavailable in their smartphone counterparts. Specifically, desktop browsers enable by default malware and

---

[5] Chrome and Safari use a link to the interface implemented by Internet Explorer.

[6] Safari does not disable plugins. Plugins can only be removed from their installation folder.

[7] Smartphone browsers do not support Java and only Firefox Mobile supports extensions.

Table 5. Mechanisms for third-party software control

Controls	GC	MF	IE	OP	AS	AB	CM	FM	IM	OM	Om	SM
Auto update extensions	□●	■●	□●	□●	■○	N/A	N/A	□●	N/A	N/A	N/A	N/A
Auto update plugins	⊠	⊠	⊠	⊠	⊠	⊠	⊠	⊠	⊠	⊠	⊠	⊠
Disable extension	■○	■○	■○	■○	■○	N/A	N/A	■○	N/A	N/A	N/A	N/A
Disable Java	■○	■○	■○	■○	■○	N/A	N/A	N/A	N/A	N/A	N/A	N/A
Disable JavaScript	■○	■○	■○	■○	■○	■○	□∣■[1]○	⊡○	⊠	⊠	⊠	■○
Disable plugin	■○	■○	■○	■○	⊠	■○∣●[1]	⊠	■●	⊠	⊠	⊠	⊠
External plugin check	⊠	⊡	⊠	⊠	⊠	⊠	⊠	⊠	⊠	⊠	⊠	⊠
Manually update extensions	■	■	⊠	⊠	■	N/A	N/A	⊠	N/A	N/A	N/A	N/A
Manually update plugins	⊡	■	⊠	⊠	⊠	⊠	⊠	⊠	⊠	⊠	⊠	⊠

[1] heterogeneity in different platforms

phishing protection, which includes a system's wide blacklist and/or page analysis [31,32,34]. Such detection controls exist only in a minority of smartphone browsers (Table 5). Among them, only Safari Mobile provides manageability of the phishing protection control. Regarding the manageability of malware and phishing protection control of desktop browsers, the deactivation of the offered security happens as easy as altering any other browser's setting without displaying any warning to the user. Furthermore, Internet Explorer and Opera offer manual analysis of a current webpage and Firefox, Internet Explorer, and Opera permit a user to report a rogue site directly from their interface. Finally, only Chrome, Firefox, Opera, and Internet Explorer provide local blacklists/whitelist for per-site assignment of controls. Among them, only Internet Explorer provides a fine grained assignment of controls to the list, i.e. the majority of controls can be assigned to trusted/restricted lists (referred as zones).

Most smartphone browsers allow modification of the user-agent (i.e. an HTTP variable including browser's software details), to navigate to the desktop version of a site with her smartphone. In desktop browsers the manageability of this control takes place from a hidden menu or via a menu navigation that violates the three-click rule (see Appendix). Finally, Opera Mini is the only browser that does not display a security warning for rogue digital certificates, i.e. invalid certificate (e.g., domain mismatch, expired) and/or untrusted one (i.e. not signed by a trusted CA).

Table 6. Web browsing controls

Controls	GC	MF	IE	OP	AS	AB	CM	FM	IM	OM	Om	SM
Certificate Warning	□●	□●	□●	□●	□●	■●	□●	□●	□●	□●	⊠	□●
Local blacklist	■	■	■	■	⊠	⊠	⊠	⊠	⊠	⊠	⊠	⊠
Malware protection	■●	■●	■●	■●	■●	⊠	⊠	□●	⊠	□●	⊠	⊠
Modify user-agent	⊡	⊡	⊡	■	⊡	■	■	■	■	■	⊠	⊠
Phishing protection	■●	■●	■●	■●	■●	⊠	⊠	□●	⊠	□●	⊠	■●
Report rogue Website	⊠	■	■	■	⊠	⊠	⊠	⊠	⊠	⊠	⊠	⊠
Website checking	⊠	⊠	■	■	⊠	⊠	⊠	⊠	⊠	⊠	⊠	⊠

4.2   Overall Availability of Controls

Fig. 1 outlines the percentage of security controls provided by each browser. The descriptive statistics omit controls, where applicable, for instance "Disable Extensions" in Chrome Mobile. As the figure illustrates, smartphone browsers form three groups, regarding the availability of controls. The first group includes Firefox Mobile that offers the majority of security controls in smartphones (67.14%). The second includes browsers with control availability around 50%, i.e. ABrowser, Chrome Mobile and Safari Mobile. The browsers in the last group, i.e. Internet Explorer Mobile, Opera Mobile, and Opera Mini, provide around 30% control availability. Similarly, desktop browsers form three groups. Firefox and Opera form the group of browsers that offers the majority of security controls (87.5%, 84.38% respectively). Google Chrome and Internet Explorer provide control availability around 80%. Finally, Apple Safari browser provides only 62.5% of the security controls.

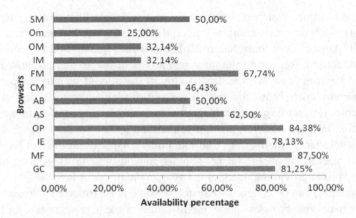

Fig. 1. Availability of security controls in web browsers. The figure holds the percentage for AB (later than Gingerbread), CM (Android) and SM (iOS 6). The percentage for AB (Gingerbread), CM (iOS) and SM (iOS 5) is 46.43%, 42.86%, 46.43% respectively.

As expected, smartphone browsers implement a subset of security controls that are available in their desktop counterparts (c.f. Tables 2-6). One could argue that the unavailability of controls is due to the restrictions that are imposed by the smartphone sandbox profiles to all applications [26]. To test the validity of this argument we filtered the security controls that are implemented by at least one smartphone browser, while being not implemented by other smartphone browsers in the same smartphone OS. Such controls exist both in iOS and Android. More specifically, the controls in {Block images, Block location data, Block third-party cookies, Certificate manager, Certificate Warning, Disable JavaScript, Private browsing} are counterexamples of this argument both in Android and iOS, as well as {Block referrer, Master Password, Search engine manager} in Android (c.f. Tables 2-6). Thus, any browser that does not support any of these controls (where applicable) is not restricted by the OS's sandbox.

Table 7. Taxonomy of browser controls and web threats [28]

Threat (T$_i$)	Security Controls
Annoyance (T1)	C4, C6, C11, C12, C13, C14, C15, C19, C24
Browser fingerprinting (T2)	C14, C19, C24, C27
Exploits/Malware (T3)	C1, C2, C6, C9, C12, C13, C14, C15, C17, C19, C20, C21, C22, C24, C27, C28, C32
Identity theft (T4)	C14, C18, C19, C23, C25, C26, C28, C32
Data interception (T5)	C10, C11, C19, C30
Phishing (T6)	C6, C10, C11, C14, C19, C25, C27, C28, C32
Privacy breach (T7)	C3, C4, C5, C7, C8, C11, C12, C13, C14, C15, C16, C18, C19, C20, C23, C24, C25, C26, C27, C28, C29, C32
Resource abuse (T8)	C12, C13, C14, C15, C17, C19, C20, C28, C31, C32
Rogue certificates (T9)	C10, C11, C19
Spam advertisements (T10)	C4, C6, C19, C27, C29
Technical failure (T11)	C1, C2, C9, C12, C13, C14, C15, C17, C20, C21, C22, C31

When a browser implements the majority of security controls, it does not de facto mean that this is the most secure browser. This holds true, as browsers are preconfigured to disable security controls for the sake of functionality. Our analysis continues with the default values of security controls.

4.3   Protection from Web Threats

This section examines: (a) the protection of preconfigured security settings against web threats, and (b) the manageability of security controls that protect from certain web threats. Initially, we created a taxonomy of the security controls and web threats. The threats, which combine ICT threats [15] and smartphone threats [37], are listed in Table 7 along with their mapping to security controls (the table uses the same notation for controls as in [28]). The mapping was created in line with the controls' descriptions in the browser help pages, as well as the recommendations from [4,7,8]. Then, two heat maps were introduced summarizing the number of security controls that are enabled by-default in each browser, and the manageability of security controls that browsers provide, according to Tables 2-6.

Fig. 2a presents the heat map of the security controls that are enabled by-default in each browser. Our analysis revealed that desktop browsers (except for Safari) and Firefox Mobile have the majority of pre-enabled controls (c.f. Fig. 1). Opera Mini provides no protection for the majority of the threats. Overall, the majority of pre-enabled security controls protect users from phishing, privacy and malware/exploits. Specifically: (a) desktop browsers (except from Safari) and Firefox Mobile enable by default the most controls against malware/exploits, (b) Chrome, Internet Explorer, Safari, Firefox Mobile, and Safari Mobile provide similar privacy protection, while ABrowser, Internet Explorer Mobile, and Chrome Mobile weak privacy protection, and (c) preconfigured settings in all browsers offer a comparable protection level against phishing (except for ABrowser, Chrome Mobile, IE Mobile, and Opera Mini).

Regarding the threat of technical failure (browser crashing), desktop browsers (except for Safari) and Firefox Mobile pre-enable the most relevant controls. The results indicate that all browsers provide similar protection from annoyance, interception of network data, rogue certificates, and spam/advertisements. The preconfigured browser settings provide similar protection against identity theft - except for ABrowser, Chrome Mobile, IE Mobile, and Opera Mini, which do not enable any relevant security control. Similarly, they provide comparable protection against resource abuse (except for Chrome Mobile, IE Mobile, and Opera Mini). Finally, the results suggest that none of the browsers is preconfigured to avoid browser fingerprinting.

Fig. 2b summarizes the number of security controls that protect users from each web threat and are manageable. As expected, desktop browsers provide greater manageability of security controls than their smartphone counterparts. Overall, Opera and ABrowser provide the greatest manageability among desktop browsers and smartphone browsers, respectively. Chrome, Firefox and Internet Explorer offer comparable manageability and this also holds true among Chrome Mobile and Firefox Mobile and Opera Mobile and Safari Mobile. In addition, Safari provides the least manageability of security controls in desktop browsers. Similarly in smartphones, this holds true for IE Mobile and Opera Mini. In both platforms, privacy controls are the most manageable, whereas data interception and rogue certificates are the least manageable ones. In desktops the threat of malware/exploits follow privacy controls w.r.t. control manageability, which in turn is followed by annoyance, identity theft, phishing, and resource abuse. Likewise, in smartphones the controls for annoyance and malware/exploits follow privacy controls w.r.t. control manageability. On the other hand, browser fingerprinting, data interception, rogue certificates and technical failure are the threats in desktops having the less manageable controls. In smartphones the least configurable ones are: data interception, recourse abuse, rogue certificates, and spam/-advertisements. Finally, browser crashing, browser fingerprinting, identity theft and phishing are threats that smartphone browsers do not offer manageable controls.

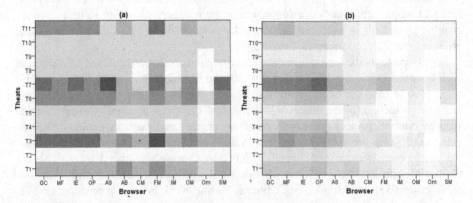

Fig. 2. (a) Preconfigured enabled security controls. (b) Manageability of security controls. For space and readability reasons the heat maps include only CM for Android and SM for iOS 6.

Table 8. Comparison of security-oriented settings vs. preconfigured desktop security settings. The suggestions[1,2] do not apply to vendor settings (c.f. Tables 2-6).

Status	Security-oriented settings	Vendor settings	Common settings
■●	C1[1], C2[1], C5[2], C7, C8[2], C12, C13, C14, C15, C16[2], C23[2]	C20, C25	C6, C9[1]
■○		C5, C7, C8, C12, C13, C14, C15, C16	C3[2], C4
□●	C20[1], C25[1]	C1	C11[1]
■	C17, C22, C30[1], C31, C32		C10[1], C18, C19, C21, C24, C26, C27, C28, C29
☒		C2, C17, C22, C23, C30, C31, C32	

[1] configuration from an advanced interface, [2] user preference before/upon installation.

5   Recommendations

Security-Oriented Settings. Table 8 (columns 3 and 4) presents the preconfigured security settings in the examined desktop browsers (it uses the same notation for controls as in [28] and their status as in Tables 2-6). These settings were collected by noting the default value and/or configurability option that appeared more often in them. Only the settings of desktops were examined, since (a) they offer a superset of security controls comparing to smartphone browsers (c.f. Fig. 1) and (b) their longer presence in the field has made them more mature than their smartphone counterparts. As depicted in Table 8, this default configuration is functionality-oriented, i.e. provides reduced security for the sake of functionality (e.g. support of active content).

Average users are less likely to change the default values of security controls. For this reason, we propose a (default) configuration, which is security-oriented, i.e. aims to maximize the protection of the user's security and privacy (cf. Table 8, columns 2 and 4). This set extends the configuration that is proposed in [4,7,8]. We consider that all security controls should be, where applicable, implemented and enabled by default to maximize the offered protection. We also consider that a user should be able to configure them as she feels fit to adjust the level of her protection, except for (C11,C20,C23). Users should be discouraged from disabling malware and phishing protection (C20,C23) and warnings for invalid certificates (C11), or should be able to do so from an interface where only advanced users can reach, such as a hidden menu (e.g. about:config). Also, we propose that the controls C1, C2, C9, should reside also in an advanced interface, e.g. one that asks for user confirmation before changes are applied. This will protect average users from accidentally disabling the controls.

We propose that the browser before/upon its installation should provide an interface which guides the user to configure the settings of C3, C5, C8, C16, and C23. This interface should be reasonably comprehensive by a normal user, e.g. "Would you like to receive targeted advertising" instead of "Enable third-party cookies" (the proposition of such an interface falls outside of the paper's scope). Finally, one should note that the configuration of the above controls by the user avoids any conflict with other stakeholders on the web (e.g. ad companies [18]).

Table 8 summarizes the differences between the security-oriented settings and the preconfigured settings of desktop browsers. Almost half of controls (14/32) have the same status (i.e. configurability, default enabled/disabled). We propose a 22% (7/32) to be added in browsers as configurable and/or enabled by default and 25% (8/32) of existing controls to be enabled by default. Comparing to vendor settings, 9% (i.e. C1, C20, C25) are proposed to change configurability status. Our security configuration is rather restrictive, i.e. functionality is disabled for the sake of security (e.g. cookies, location data, etc.). To ensure user experience, the browser should allow the user to enable such controls via local whitelists, similarly to the NoScript extension.

Rogue Sites. Smartphones include sandboxes that place restrictions in functionality of third-party (security) apps [26]. As a result, while desktops' antivirus or other security software may be able to filter rogue webpages (i.e. those hosting malware and/or phishing scams), this is currently not feasible in smartphones. In this context, it appears that the browser itself must detect and/or block rogue sites. We regard that this can be achieved either with a frequent acquisition of a blacklist, or with ad-hoc queries in an online blacklist (e.g. Safe Browsing [31]). Alternatively, the smartphone may connect to a secure proxy, i.e. one that filters rogue sites. Current smartphone browsers do not permit the connection to a proxy, when mobile Internet is used.

Third-Party Software Management. As discussed earlier, smartphone browsers must provide an interface where users can inspect the plugins and other applications that are being used by them. Browsers must also allow them to selectively disable this software, as they see fit. Furthermore, both desktop and smartphone browsers must efficiently and timely inform users regarding third-party software vulnerabilities.

User Awareness. As discussed earlier, browsers offer support pages dedicated to security and privacy. These pages must provide adequate background, as well as links to material (e.g. [29]), focusing on the current threats on the web and the available countermeasures. This will help users understand the relevant threats and effectively adjust the browser's protection level, according to their security and privacy needs.

6   Discussion and Conclusions

This paper provided a systematic and comprehensive analysis of the availability and manageability of security controls in popular smartphone and desktop browsers. It also provided a comparative evaluation of the: (a) preconfigured security settings against web threats, and (b) manageability of security controls that protect from certain web threats. The former provides indications of the 'out of the box' offered protection to average users. The latter reveals the flexibility to adjust the offered protection according to the users' "risk appetite" (e.g. a user may be willing to receive targeted advertising). Our results can be used from browser users to adjust their protection level, as well as from browser vendors to cross-compare their security offerings.

We proved that the controls that are available in desktop browsers are a superset of the ones found in smartphones. Currently in smartphones, a user has to use multiple browsers in order to use certain security controls - e.g., in iOS she has to use Chrome Mobile for a robust control of security warnings, and Safari Mobile for both private browsing and phishing detection. This unavailability of browser controls can be partially explained by the restrictions of the smartphones' security models (e.g. private browsing in Chrome Mobile for iOS). However, our evaluation reveals occasions where a security control is available in a subset of browsers of a smartphone platform. This suggests that the restrictions from the sandbox were not the reason that the control was 0not implemented in the rest smartphone browsers in this platform.

Our analysis revealed that two browsers (Safari and Opera Mini) had a number of security issues, which are serious (i.e. unpatched vulnerabilities, no protection from invalid digital certificates). Furthermore, our analysis of the preconfigured security settings in browsers revealed that Firefox Mobile provides comparable protection against web threats to desktop browsers (c.f. Fig. 2). The evaluation also revealed that third-party advertising is enabled by default in most desktop browsers. In addition, in their smartphone counterparts it is not easily manageable, since they adopt all-or-nothing approach in cookie management. Therefore a user has to either accept all cookies including tracking cookies, or disable all of them, which will break the functionality of several benign sites. Also, DNT is disabled by default - or unavailable as a control in smartphone browsers. We propose that privacy controls should be configured during browser installation or post installation (i.e. first time the browser executes), where the user should be reasonably aided to make an informed decision. Finally, private browsing is not supported in a subset of smartphone browsers.

Users are unprotected from rogue sites, which serve malware and/or perform phishing scams, while browsing with their smartphone. This holds true, as smartphone browsers fail to detect rogue sites. Users can be protected by disabling all dynamic content (i.e. the plugins, JavaScript) - a control that is not offered in all smartphone browsers. This, however, will not protect them from a Blackhole exploit framework that targets vulnerabilities in the browser's software (e.g. in plugins). It also hinders their browsing experience, since most web applications require JavaScript to function correctly. For this reason, we proposed that smartphone browsers either use a local blacklist or ad-hoc query an online blacklist with reported rogue sites, such as Google's Safe Browsing. This, however, will introduce delays, as well as additional bandwidth consumption, which in the case of mobile Internet may not be acceptable (due to cost and bandwidth quota limitations). Moreover, online queries introduce privacy issues. Alternatively, a proxy server may be used that provides detection of rogue sites. This proxy may also be used for UA spoofing, which protects users from system disclosure attacks. In this case, the proxy - apart from altering the device's UA - must filter out JavaScript code that may leak the UA string. Our analysis revealed that security controls can be disabled as easy as disabling controls that are not security oriented. Also, security controls often reside together with non security related options, (e.g. zoom, font size etc). As discussed earlier, the interface of security controls must be reorganized to assist users correctly configure the browser's security level.

Our evaluation focused on smartphone and Windows desktop and it omits differences in the availability of controls in other platforms in the former (e.g. BlackBerry, Symbian), or latter (e.g. Mac-OS) device type. However, since the evaluation includes the most popular devices, we regard that security findings are adequately representative in the two platforms. Another limitation is that security controls may be added to browsers - especially to smartphone browsers - when they update. However, updates for smartphone browsers are less frequent, semi-automatic, suffer from delays (from the app market or device vendor), and an update may also be unavailable if the device is not supported anymore. Also, the comparative evaluation of protection against web threats that was conducted is quantitative and not qualitative. In future work we plan to measure and compare the performance and efficiency of security controls.

Acknowledgments. This research has been co-funded by the European Union (ESF) and Greek national funds, through the Operational Program "Education and Lifelong Learning" of the National Strategic Reference Framework (Program HERACLEITUS II: Investing in knowledge society through the ESF).

Appendix

Hidden Menus. The navigation to hidden menus are given in Table A.1.

Table 9. Hidden functionality in browsers

Browser	Element	Element location
Safari	developers tools	hidden menu item configurable from the advanced menu settings.
Safari	alter user-agent	develop (must be enabled see above) -> user agent-> other
Android (v. ICS, JB)	private browsing	tabs icons-> menu device key -> new incognito tab
Firefox all, Chrome all	private menu	about: about
ABrowser	private menu	about:debug
Chrome	block referrer	Execute Chrome with the parameter "-no-referrers"
Chrome	User agent	Menu->Developer Tools->Settings-Overrides
Internet Explorer	User agent	Menu-Developer Tools->Tools-Change user agent string

Navigation to Proxy. Starting from the browser's configuration interface, i.e. browser's menu (e.g. Chrome Mobile), device menu (e.g. iPhone Safari), the navigation clearly violates the three-click rule.

Table 10. Navigation to proxy configuration widget

Browser	Path
Safari Mobile	tap back (settings) -> scroll up -> wifi -> connected wifi network (hit blue icon) -> scroll down -> http proxy manual -> setting server & port
Android Gingerbread	home button-> options button from device ->settings->wireless and networks->wi-fi settings->options button from device ->advanced->wi-fi proxy->fill in proxy details
Android ICS/ JB	home button-> device's options button -> settings-> wifi->on->hold network id* -> modify network-> scroll down-> check show advanced options-> scroll down-> proxy setting -> manual -> scroll down-> fill in proxy details -> tap save *unless the user holds the network id for a few seconds the hidden menu will not appear
Windows Phone 7.5	Settings (General) -> Scroll down to Wi-Fi Option -> Toggle Wi-Fi networking -> tap the desired WiFi Network from the list -> toggle Proxy option -> specify any additional proxy options needed

References

1. Amrutkar, C., Traynor, P., van Oorschot, P.C.: Measuring SSL Indicators on mobile browsers: Extended life, or end of the road? In: Gollmann, D., Freiling, F.C. (eds.) ISC 2012. LNCS, vol. 7483, pp. 86–103. Springer, Heidelberg (2012)
2. About the security content of Safari 6, http://support.apple.com/kb/HT5400
3. Botha, R., Furnell, S., Clarke, N.: From desktop to mobile: Examining the security experience. J. Computers & Security 28(3-4), 130–137 (2009)
4. Browser Security Settings for Chrome, Firefox and Internet Explorer: Cybersecurity 101, http://www.veracode.com/blog/2013/03/browser-security-settings-for-chrome-firefox-and-internet-explorer/
5. Canali, D., Cova, M., Vigna, G., Kruegel, C.: Prophiler: A fast filter for the large-scale detection of malicious web pages. In: 20th International Conference on World Wide Web, pp. 197–206. ACM, India (2011)
6. Carlini, N., Felt, A., Wagner, D.: An evaluation of the google chrome extension security architecture. In: 21st USENIX Conference on Security, USA (2012)
7. CERT, Browsing Safely: Understanding active content and cookies, http://www.us-cert.gov/ncas/tips/st04-012
8. CERT, Securing Your Web Browser, http://www.cert.org/tech_tips/securing_browser/
9. Chen, E., Bau, J., Reis, C., Barth, A., Jackson, C.: App isolation: Get the security of multiple browsers with just one. In: 18th ACM Conference on Computer and Communications Security, pp. 227–238. ACM, USA (2011)
10. Cisco, 2013 Cisco Annual Security Report. Technical Report (2013)
11. Cisco, Visual Networking Index: Global Mobile Data Traffic Forecast Update. Technical Report (2013)
12. Curtsinger, C., Livshits, B., Zorn, B., Seifert, C.: Zozzle: Fast and precise in browser JavaScript malware detection. In: 20th USENIX Security Symposium, USENIX, USA, pp. 33–48 (2011)
13. Eckersley, P.: How unique is your web browser? In: Atallah, M.J., Hopper, N.J. (eds.) PETS 2010. LNCS, vol. 6205, pp. 1–18. Springer, Heidelberg (2010)
14. Egelman, S., Cranor, L., Hong, J.: You've been warned: An empirical study of the effectiveness of web browser phishing warnings. In: 26th Conference on Human Factors in Computing Systems, pp. 1065–1074. ACM, USA (2008)
15. ENISA, ENISA threat landscape - Responding to the evolving threat environment. Technical Report (2012)
16. Fielding, R., Gettys, J., Mogul, J., Frystyk, H., Masinter, L., Leach, P., Berners-Lee, T.: Hypertext Transfer Protocol–HTTP/1.1. Technical Report (1999)
17. Google Dashboards, http://developer.android.com/about/dashboards/index.html
18. IE 10's 'Do-Not-Track' Default Dies Quick Death, http://www.wired.com/threatlevel/2012/06/default-do-not-track/
19. Gupta, A., Cozza, R., Milanesi, C., Lu, C.: Market Share Analysis: Mobile Phones, Worldwide, 4Q12 and 2012. Technical Report (2013)
20. Jang, D., Jhala, R., Lerner, S., Shacham, H.: An empirical study of privacy-violating information flows in javascript web applications. In: 17th ACM Conference on Computer and Communications Security, pp. 270–283. ACM, USA (2010)
21. Kolbitsch, C., Livshits, B., Zorn, B., Seifert, C.: Rozzle: De-cloaking internet malware. In: 33rd IEEE Symposium on Security and Privacy, pp. 443–457. IEEE, USA (2012)

22. Lekkas, D., Gritzalis, D.: Long-term verifiability of healthcare records authenticity. International Journal of Medical Informatics 76(5-6), 442–448 (2006)
23. Madrigal, I'm being followed: How Google - and 104 other companies - are tracking me on the Web, http://www.theatlantic.com/technology/archive/2012/02/im-being-followed-how-google-151-and-104-other-companies-151-are-tracking-me-on-the-web/253758/
24. Motiee, S., Hawkey, K., Beznosov, K.: Do windows users follow the principle of least privilege?: Investigating user account control practices. In: 6th Symposium on Usable Privacy and Security, pp. 1–13. ACM, USA (2010)
25. Mozilla: Check Your Plugins, http://www.mozilla.org/en-US/plugincheck/
26. Mylonas, A., Dritsas, S., Tsoumas, B., Gritzalis, D.: Smartphone security evaluation: The malware attack case. In: 8th International Conference on Security and Cryptography, pp. 25–36. SciTePress, Spain (2011)
27. Mylonas, A., Kastania, A., Gritzalis, D.: Delegate the smartphone user? Security awareness in smartphone platforms. Computers & Security 34, 47–66 (2013)
28. Mylonas, A., Tsalis, N., Gritzalis, D.: Poster: Hide and seek: On the disparity of browser security settings. In: 9th Symposium on Usable Privacy and Security, UK (2013)
29. National Cyber Security Alliance: StaySafeOnline.org, http://www.staysafeonline.org/
30. Network Computing: Certificate authority compromises are global in reach, http://www.networkcomputing.com/security/certificate-authority-compromises-are-gl/231601123
31. Opera: Fraud and Malware Protection, http://www.opera.com/help/tutorials/security/fraud/
32. Safe Browsing API, https://developers.google.com/safe-browsing
33. SERT: Quarterly Threat Intelligence Report Q4 2012. Technical Report (2013)
34. SmartScreen Filter: frequently asked questions, http://windows.microsoft.com/en-us/windows7/smartscreen-filter-frequently-asked-questions-ie9
35. StatCounter: StatCounter Global Stats, http://gs.statcounter.com
36. Sunshine, J., Egelman, S., Almuhimedi, H., Atri, N., Cranor, L.: Crying wolf: An empirical study of SSL warning effectiveness. In: 18th Conference on USENIX Security Symposium, pp. 399–416. USENIX Association, USA (2009)
37. Theoharidou, M., Mylonas, A., Gritzalis, D.: A risk assessment method for smartphones. In: Gritzalis, D., Furnell, S., Theoharidou, M. (eds.) SEC 2012. IFIP AICT, vol. 376, pp. 443–456. Springer, Heidelberg (2012)
38. Tryfonas, T., Kokolakis, S., Gritzalis, D.: A qualitative approach to information availability. In: 15th Conference on Information Security for Global Information Infrastructures, pp. 37–48. Kluwer, China (2000)
39. Zeigler, A., Bateman, A., Graff, E.: Web Tracking Protection, http://www.w3.org/Submission/web-tracking-protection/

Using Interpolation for the Verification of Security Protocols*

Marco Rocchetto, Luca Viganò, Marco Volpe, and Giacomo Dalle Vedove

Dipartimento di Informatica, Università di Verona, Italy

Abstract. Interpolation has been successfully applied in formal methods for model checking and test-case generation for sequential programs. Security protocols, however, exhibit such idiosyncrasies that make them unsuitable to the direct application of such methods. In this paper, we address this problem and present an interpolation-based method for security protocol verification. Our method starts from a formal protocol specification and combines Craig interpolation, symbolic execution and the standard Dolev-Yao intruder model to search for possible attacks on the protocol. Interpolants are generated as a response to search failure in order to prune possible useless traces and speed up the exploration. We illustrate our method by means of a concrete example and discuss the results obtained by using a prototype implementation.

Keywords: Security protocols, Symbolic execution, Craig's interpolation, Formal methods, Verification.

1   Introduction

Context and Motivation. Devising security protocols that indeed guarantee the security properties that they have been conceived for is an inherently difficult problem and experience has shown that the development of such protocols is a highly error-prone activity. A number of tools have thus been developed for the analysis of security protocols at *design time*: starting from a formal specification of a protocol and of a property it should achieve, these tools typically carry out model checking or automated reasoning to either *falsify* the protocol (i.e., find an attack with respect to that property) or, when possible, *verify* it (i.e., prove that it does indeed guarantee that property, perhaps under some assumptions such as a bounded number of interleaved protocol sessions [17]). While verification is, of course, the optimal result, falsification is also extremely useful as one can often employ the discovered attack trace to directly carry out an attack on the protocol implementation (e.g., [3]) or exploit the trace to devise a suite of test cases so as to be able to analyze the implementation at *run-time* (e.g., [4,6]).

Such an endeavor has already been undertaken in the programming languages community, where, for instance, *interpolation* has been successfully applied in

---

* Work partially supported by the FP7-ICT-2009-5 Project no. 257876, "SPaCIoS: Secure Provision and Consumption in the Internet of Services".

R. Accorsi and S. Ranise (Eds.): STM 2013, LNCS 8203, pp. 99–114, 2013.

formal methods for model checking and test-case generation for sequential programs, e.g., [12,13], with the aim of reducing the dimensions of the search space. Since a state space explosion often occurs in security protocol verification, we expect interpolation to be useful also in this context. Security protocols, however, exhibit such idiosyncrasies that make them unsuitable to the direct application of the standard interpolation-based methods, most notably, the fact that, in the presence of a Dolev-Yao intruder [8], a security protocol is not a sequential program (since the intruder, who is in complete control of the network, can freely interleave his actions with the normal protocol execution).

Contributions. In this paper, we address this problem and present an interpolation-based method for security protocol verification. Our method starts from the formal specification of a protocol and of a security property and combines Craig interpolation [7], symbolic execution [10] and the standard Dolev-Yao intruder model [8] to search for goals (representing attacks on the protocol). Interpolation is used to prune possible useless traces and speed up the exploration.

More specifically, our method proceeds as follows: starting (Sect. 3.1) from a specification of the input system, including protocol, property to be checked and a finite number of session instances (possibly generated automatically by using a preprocessor), it first creates a corresponding sequential non-deterministic program, in the form of a *control flow graph* (Sect. 3.2), according to a procedure that we have devised, and then defines a set of goals and searches for them by symbolically executing the program (Sect. 3.3). When a goal is reached, an attack trace is extracted from the constraints that the execution of the path has produced; such constraints represent conditions over parameters that allow one to reconstruct the attack trace found. When the search fails to reach a goal, a backtrack phase starts, during which the nodes of the graph are annotated (according to an adaptation of the algorithm defined in [13] for sequential programs) with formulas obtained by using Craig interpolation. Such formulas express conditions over the program variables, which, when implied from the program state of a given execution, ensure that no goal will be reached by going forward and thus that we can discard the current branch. The output of the method is a proof of (bounded) correctness in the case when no goal location can be reached starting from a finite-state specification; otherwise one or more attack traces are produced. We illustrate our method by means of a concrete example.

In Sect. 4, we briefly report on some experiments performed by using a prototype implementation. We summarize other characteristics of our method in the concluding remarks (Sect. 5), where we also discuss future work.

2   Background

Security protocols describe how agents exchange messages, built using cryptographic primitives, in order to obtain security guarantees. The algebra of messages tells us how messages are constructed. Following [5], we consider a countable *signature* Σ and a countable set *Var* of *variable symbols* disjoint from Σ, and then write Σ^n for the symbols of Σ with arity n; thus Σ^0 is the set of *constants*, which we assume to have distinct subsets that we refer to as *agent names* (or simply just *agents*), *public keys*, *private keys* and *nonces* (we omit symmetric keys from our treatment since we do not use them in our running example, but of course our method can fully support them). The variables are, however, untyped (unless denoted otherwise) and can be instantiated with arbitrary types, yielding an *untyped* model. We will use upper-case letters to denote variables (e.g., $A, B, \ldots$ to denote agents, N for nonces, etc.) and lower-case letters to denote the corresponding constants (concrete agents names, concrete nonces, etc.) All these may be possibly annotated with subscripts and superscripts.

The symbols of Σ with arity greater than zero are partitioned into the set Σ_p of *(public) operations* and the set Σ_m of *mappings*. The public operations represent all those operations that every agent (including the intruder) can perform on messages they know. In this paper, we consider the following operations: $\{M_1\}_{M_2}$ represents the *asymmetric encryption* of M_1 with public key M_2; $\{M_1\}_{inv(M_2)}$ represents the *asymmetric encryption* of M_1 with private key $inv(M_2)$ (the mapping $inv(\cdot)$ is discussed below); $[M_1, M_2]$ represents the concatenation of M_1 and M_2. For simplicity, we will often simply write M_1, M_2 instead of $[M_1, M_2]$.

In contrast to the public operations, the mappings of Σ_m do not correspond to operations that agents can perform on messages, but are rather mappings between constants. In this paper, we use the following ones: (i) $inv(M)$ gives the private key that corresponds to public key M; (ii) for long-term key infrastructures, we assume that every agent A has a public key $pk(A)$ and corresponding private key $inv(pk(A))$; thus $pk(\cdots)$ is a mapping from agents to public keys.

Since we will below also deal with terms that contain variables, let us call *atomic* all terms that are built from constants in Σ^0, variables in *Var*, and the mappings of Σ_m. The set $\mathcal{T}_\Sigma(Var)$ of all *terms* is the closure of the atomic terms under the operations of Σ_p. A *ground term* is a term without variables, where we denote the set of ground terms with $\mathcal{T}_\Sigma$. It is standard in formal verification of security protocols to interpret terms in the *free algebra*, i.e., every term is interpreted by itself and thus two terms are equal iff they are syntactically equal.

Our approach is independent of the actual strength of the intruder; here we consider the Dolev and Yao [8] model of an active intruder, denoted i, who controls the network but cannot break cryptography. In particular, i can intercept messages and analyze them if he knows the proper keys for decryption, and he can generate messages from his knowledge and send them under any agent name.

3 A Security Protocol Interpolation Method

The method we propose takes as input a protocol specification, together with a finite scenario of the protocol and one or more properties to be verified in that scenario. In the following, we give a recipe for producing a sequential program for the protocol scenario that we are considering, in the form of a control flow graph. The graph is enriched with locations required for handling the goals; in particular, for each property to be verified, a *goal location* is defined, and the

$$A \to B : \{N_A, A\}_{pk(B)} \qquad A \to B : \{N_A, A\}_{pk(B)} \qquad A \to i : \{N_A, A\}_{pk(i)}$$
$$B \to A : \{N_A, N_B, B\}_{pk(A)} \qquad B \to A : \{N_A, N_B\}_{pk(A)} \qquad i(A) \to B : \{N_A, A\}_{pk(B)}$$
$$A \to B : \{N_B\}_{pk(B)} \qquad A \to B : \{N_B\}_{pk(B)} \qquad B \to i(A) : \{N_A, N_B\}_{pk(A)}$$
$$i \to A : \{N_A, N_B\}_{pk(A)}$$
$$A \to i : \{N_B\}_{pk(i)}$$
$$i(A) \to B : \{N_B\}_{pk(B)}$$

Fig. 1. NSL message exchange (left), NSPK message exchange (middle) and Man-in-the-middle attack on NSPK (right)

verification task consists in checking whether any execution of the protocol can reach one or more of such locations. The exploration is performed by using the algorithm of [13], which proceeds by executing symbolically the program and exploits Craig interpolation in order to prune the search over the graph. In the case when a goal location is reached, an attack trace is extracted.

3.1 Input

Given a protocol $\mathcal{P}$ involving a set $\mathcal{R}$ of *roles* (*Alice*, *Bob*, ..., a.k.a. *entities*), a *session (instance) of* $\mathcal{P}$ is a function si assigning an agent (honest agent or the intruder i) to each element of $\mathcal{R}$. A *scenario of a protocol* $\mathcal{P}$ is a finite number of session instances of $\mathcal{P}$. The input of our method is then: (1) a specification of a protocol $\mathcal{P}$, (2) a scenario $\mathcal{S}$ of $\mathcal{P}$, (3) a set of goals (i.e., properties to be verified) in $\mathcal{S}$. For what concerns the definition of a scenario, we remark that when a role is assigned the agent i, it is intended to be played by the intruder, either under his real name i or pretending to be some other agent.

Example 1. As a running example, we will use NSL (Fig. 1, left), the Needham-Schroeder Public Key (NSPK) protocol with Lowe's fix [11], which aims at mutual authentication between A and B. The presence of B in the second message prevents the man-in-the-middle attack that NSPK suffers from (see Fig. 1, right, where $i(A)$ denotes that the intruder is impersonating the honest agent A).

As a formal specification language, we will use a subset of ASLan++ [1, 18]. In the following extract of the specifications for NSL, the two roles are *Alice*, who is the *initiator* of the protocol, and *Bob*, the *responder*.

```
1   entity Alice(Actor, B: agent) {     11   entity Bob(A, Actor: agent) {
2     symbols                           12     symbols
3       Na, Nb: text;                   13       Na, Nb: text;
4     body{                             14     body{
5       Na := fresh();                  15       ? -> Actor: {?Na,?A}_pk(Actor);
6       Actor -> B: {Na,Actor}_pk(B);   16       Nb := fresh();
7       B -> Actor: {Na,?Nb,B}_pk(Actor); 17     Actor -> A: {Na,Nb,Actor}_pk(A);
8       Actor -> B: {Nb}_pk(B);         18       A -> Actor: {Nb}_pk(Actor);
9     }                                 19     }
10  }                                   20   }
```

The elements between parentheses in line 1 declare which variables are used to denote the agents playing the different roles along the specification of the role *Alice*: `Actor` refers to the agent playing the role of *Alice* itself, while B is the variable referring to the agent who plays the role of *Bob*. Similarly, the section

$Alice_1.Actor \rightarrow Alice_1.B : \{Alice_1.Na, Alice_1.Actor\}_{pk(Alice_1.B)}$ $a \rightarrow i : \{c_1, a\}_{pk(i)}$

$? \rightarrow Bob_2.Actor : \{Bob_2.Na, Bob_2.A\}_{pk(Bob_2.Actor)}$ $i(a) \rightarrow b : \{c_1, a\}_{pk(b)}$

$Bob_2.Actor \rightarrow Bob_2.A : \{Bob_2.Na, Bob_2.Nb\}_{pk(Bob_2.A)}$ $b \rightarrow i(a) : \{c_1, c_2\}_{pk(i(a))}$

$Alice_1.B \rightarrow Alice_1.Actor : \{Alice_1.Na, Alice_1.Nb\}_{pk(Alice_1.Actor)}$ $i \rightarrow a : \{c_1, c_2\}_{pk(a)}$

$Alice_1.Actor \rightarrow Alice_1.B : \{Alice_1.Nb\}_{pk(Alice_1.B)}$ $a \rightarrow i : \{c_2\}_{pk(i)}$

$Bob_2.A \rightarrow Bob_2.Actor : \{Bob_2.Nb\}_{pk(Bob_2.Actor)}$ $i(a) \rightarrow b : \{c_2\}_{pk(b)}$

Fig. 2. Symbolic attack trace of man-in-the-middle-attack on NSPK (left) and instantiated attack trace (right) obtained with our method

symbols declares that Na and Nb are variables of type *text*. The section body specifies the behavior of the role. First, the operation fresh() assigns to the nonce Na a value that is different from the value assigned to any other nonce. Then *Alice* sends the nonce, together with her name, to the agent B, encrypted with B's public key. In line 7, *Alice* receives her nonce back together with a further variable (expected to represent B's nonce along a regular session of the protocol) and the name of B, all encrypted with her own public key. The "?" in ?Nb is used to represent an assignment of the value received to the variable Nb. As a last step, *Alice* sends to B the nonce Nb encrypted with B's public key.

The variable declarations and the behavior of *Bob* are specified by lines 12-21. We omit a full description of the code and only remark that the "?" in the beginning of line 16 denotes the fact that the sender of such a message can be any agent, though no assignment is made for ? in that case.   □

3.2   From a Protocol Specification to a Sequential Program

The algorithm of [13] is designed for sequential programs. In order to apply it to security protocols, we define a translation from the specification of a protocol $\mathcal{P}$ for a given scenario into a corresponding sequential non-deterministic program. Such a program will be encoded in a pseudo-language admitting the standard constructs for assignments and conditional statements, as well as a type Message.

3.2.1   Translating a Session Specification into a Sequential Program

We now describe how to obtain a program for a single session instance *si*; we will then consider more session instances in Sect. 3.2.3. First of all, note that the exchange of messages in a session follows a given flow of execution that can be used to determine an order between the instructions contained in the different roles. Such a sequence of instructions will constitute the skeleton of our program. However, we will omit from the sequence those instructions contained in a role that is played by the agent *i*, whose behavior will be treated differently.

We use as program variables the same names used in the specification. However, in order to distinguish between variables with the same name occurring in the specification of different roles, program variables have the form E.V where E denotes the role and V the variable name in the specification. An additional variable IK, of a type *MessageSet*, is used in the program to represent the intruder knowledge. Similarly, constants of the specification become program constants.

Whenever a session is played only by honest agents, the execution of the corresponding sequential program is univocally determined. The behavior of the intruder introduces a form of non-determinism, which we capture by representing the program, in the case when the intruder plays a role, as a procedure depending on a number of parameters, denoted by variables Y, possibly subscripted.

3.2.1.1 Initialization of the Variables. A first section of the program initializes the variables. For each role *Alice* such that $si(Alice) \neq i$, we have an instruction Alice.Actor := a, where a is an agent name such that $si(Alice) = a$. Whenever *Alice* is an initiator, for each responder *Bob* with B being the variable referring to the role *Bob* between the agent variables of *Alice*: if $si(Bob) \neq i$, then we have the assignment Alice.B := b, where b is such that $si(Bob) = b$, else we have Alice.B := Y, for Y an input variable not introduced elsewhere in the program.

Finally, we need to initialize the intruder knowledge. A typical IK initialization has the form: IK := {a_1,...,a_n,i,pk(a_1),...,pk(a_n),pk(i),inv(pk(i))}. That is, i knows the agents a_j involved in the scenario and their public keys pk(a_j), as well as his own public and private keys pk(i) and inv(pk(i)). Specific protocols might require a specific initial IK or the initialization of further variables, depending on the context, such as symmetric keys. In our programs, we also allow a construct of the form IK |- M to denote that the intruder is able to construct the message M from its current intruder knowledge IK (i.e., derive it using its inference rules for generating and analyzing messages).

3.2.1.2 Sending and Receipt of a Message. The sending of a message Actor -> B: M defined in a role *Alice* is translated into the instruction IK := IK + M, where the symbol + denotes the addition of the message M to IK.

In order to define the receipt of a message R -> Actor: M in a role *Alice* from some *Bob* we distinguish two cases. If the message is sent by the intruder, i.e., $si(Bob) = i$, then the instruction is translated into the following code:

```
1  If (IK |- Alice.M)
2    then Alice.Q_1 := Y_1; ... ; Alice.Q_n := Y_n;
3  else end
```

where Q_1, ..., Q_n are the variables occurring preceded by ? in R -> Actor : M and Y_1, ..., Y_n are distinct input variables not introduced elsewhere.

If $si(Bob) \neq i$, then the receipt R -> Actor: M corresponds to, and within the flow of execution is immediately preceded by, a sending Actor -> R': M' in the specification of *Bob*, which matches R -> Actor: M. In this case, we translate the instruction into: Alice.Q_1 := q_1; ...; Alice.Q_n := q_n where Q_1, ..., Q_n are all the variables occurring preceded by ? in R -> Actor: M and q_1, ..., q_n the expressions matching with Q_1, ..., Q_n, respectively, in Actor -> R': M'. For instance, the receipt ? -> Actor:{?Na,?A}_pk(Actor) at line 15 in the specification of *Bob* in Example 1 corresponds to the sending Actor -> B: {Na,Actor}_pk(B) at line 6 in the specification of *Alice*. We can translate such a receipt into: Bob.Na := Alice.Na; Bob.A := Alice.Actor.

3.2.1.3   Generation of Fresh Values. An instruction of the form `N := fresh`
`()` in *Alice*, which assigns a fresh value to a nonce, can be translated into the
instruction `Alice.N := c_1`, where `c_1` is a constant not introduced elsewhere.

Example 2. Fig. 3 shows the programs obtained for the two session instances of
the NSL scenario we are interested in: in session 1, *Alice* and *Bob* are played by
a and i respectively; in session 2, they are played by i and b, respectively.   □

3.2.2   Introducing Goal Locations. The next step consists in decorating
the program with a goal location for each security property to be verified. As it
is common when performing symbolic execution [10], we express such properties
as correctness assertions, typically placed at the end of a program. Once we have
represented a protocol session as a program, and defined the properties we are
interested in as correctness assertions in such a program, the problem of verifying
security properties over (a session of) the protocol is reduced to verifying the
correctness of the program with respect to those assertions.

We consider here three common security properties (authentication, confidentiality and integrity) and show how to represent them inside the program in
terms of assertions. They are expressed by means of the statement `prove`, which
in symbolic execution is commonly used to represent an output assertion required
to evaluate to *true* in order to have the correctness of the program. Semantically,
the instruction `prove(expr)` is equivalent to `if (not(expr))then error`.

3.2.2.1   Authentication. Assume we want to verify that *Alice* authenticates *Bob*
with respect to a message `M` in the specification of the protocol, in a given session
instance si. We can restrict our attention to the case when $si(Bob) = i$, since if
Bob is played by an honest agent, then the authentication property is trivially
satisfied. The problem thus reduces to verifying whether the agent i is playing
under his real name (in which case authentication is again trivially satisfied) or
whether i is pretending to be someone else, i.e., whether the agent playing *Alice*
believes she is speaking to someone who is not i. Hence, we can simply add the
assertion `prove(Alice.B = i)`, where `B` is the agent variable referring to the
role *Bob* inside *Alice*, immediately after the receipt of the message `M`.

Example 3. In NSL, we are interested in verifying a property of authentication
in the session that assigns i to *Alice* and b to *Bob*: we want *Bob* to authenticate
Alice with respect to the nonce `Bob.Nb` in the receipt of line `2.14` (Fig. 3).
Since the statement corresponding to such a receipt is the last instruction of the
program, we can just add the instruction `prove (Bob.A = i)` at the end.   □

3.2.2.2   Confidentiality. Assume that we want to verify that the message corresponding to a variable `M`, in the specification of a role *Alice* of the protocol, is
confidential between a given set of roles $\mathcal{R}$ in a session si. As we did for authentication, since we are in an instantiated scenario, we ignore the case when the
session is played only by honest agents, in which case confidentiality is preserved.
In general, we can restrict to checking whether the agent i got to know the confidential message `M` even though i is not included in $\mathcal{R}$. Inside the program, this

corresponds to checking whether the message `Alice.M` can be derived from the intruder knowledge and whether any honest agent playing a role in $\mathcal{R}$ believes that at least one of the other roles in $\mathcal{R}$ is indeed played by i, which we can read as having indeed $i \in \mathcal{R}$. This corresponds to the following assertion, to be added at the end of the program:

```
1   prove ((not(IK |- Alice.M) or
2           (Alice_1.B^1_1 = i) or ... (Alice_1.B^1_m = i) or ...
3           (Alice_n.B^n_1 = i) or ... (Alice_n.B^n_m = i))
```

where $Alice_j$, for $1 \leq j \leq n$, is a role such that $Alice_j \in \mathcal{R}$ and $si(Alice_j) \neq i$, $\{Bob_1, \dots, Bob_m\} \subseteq \mathcal{R}$ is the subset of those roles in $\mathcal{R}$ that are instantiated with i by si and $B\textasciicircum j\_l$, for $1 \leq j \leq n$ and $1 \leq l \leq m$, is the variable referring to the role Bob_l in the specification of the role $Alice_j$.

Example 4. For NSL, assume that we want to verify the confidentiality of the variable `Nb` (contained in the specification of *Bob*) between the roles in the set $\{Alice, Bob\}$. We can express this goal by appending at the end of the program the assertion `prove ((not(IK |- Bob.Nb))or (Bob.A = i))`.   □

3.2.2.3 Integrity. In this case, we assume that two variables (possibly of two different roles) are specified in input as the variables containing the value whose integrity needs to be checked. The check will consist in verifying whether the two variables, at a given point of the session execution, also given in input, evaluate to the same. Let `M` in the role *Alice* and `M'` in the role *Bob* be the two variables; then the corresponding correctness assertion will be `prove(Alice.M = Bob.M')`.

3.2.3 Combining More Sessions.
Now we need to define a program that properly "combines" the programs related to all the sessions in the scenario. The idea is that such a program allows for executing, in the proper order, all the instructions of all the sessions in the scenario; the way in which instructions of different sessions are interleaved will be determined by the value of further input variables, denoted by `X`, which can be seen as choices of the intruder with respect to the flow of the execution. Namely, we start to execute each session sequentially and we get blocked when we encounter the receipt of a message sent by a role that is played by the intruder. When all the sessions are blocked on instructions of that form, the intruder chooses which session has to be reactivated.

In the following, we will see a sequential program as a graph (which can be simply obtained by representing its control flow) on which the algorithm of Sect. 3.3 will be executed. We adapt from [13] some notions concerning programs and program runs. A *program graph* is a finite, rooted, labeled graph (Λ, l_0, Δ) where Λ is a *finite set of program locations*, l_0 is the *initial location* and $\Delta \subseteq \Lambda \times \mathcal{A} \times \Lambda$ is a *set of transitions* labeled by actions from a set $\mathcal{A}$, consisting in the instructions of the program. A *program path* of length k is a sequence of the form $l_0, a_0, l_1, a_1, \dots, l_k$, where each *step* $(l_j, a_j, l_{j+1}) \in \Delta$ for $0 \leq j < k - 1$. The set $\mathbb{D}$ of *data states* is the set of all the maps $V \to D$ from the set V of program variables to the set D of possible data values, i.e., integers (for variables of the form X_i), ground messages (for variables denoting messages) or sets of ground messages (for the special variable IK). The *semantics* $Sem(a)$ *of an action* $a \in \mathcal{A}$ is a subset of $\mathbb{D} \times \mathbb{D}$. We assume an initial data state d_0. A *program run* of length k is a pair (π, σ), where π is a program path $l_0, a_0, l_1, a_1, \ldots, l_k$ and $\sigma = d_0, \ldots, d_k$ is a sequence of data states such that $(d_j, d_{j+1}) \in Sem(a_j)$ for $0 \le j < k$. A *state* is a pair (l, d) such that $l \in \Lambda$ and $d \in \mathbb{D}$.

We have seen in Sects. 3.2.1 and 3.2.2 how to generate the program, and thus the corresponding control flow graph of a single session. The program graph corresponding to a whole scenario can be obtained by composing the graphs of the single sessions. Given a program graph, an *intruder location* is a location of the graph corresponding to the receipt of a message sent from a role played by i. A *block* $\mathcal{B}$ *of a program graph* $\mathcal{G}'$ is a subgraph of $\mathcal{G}'$ such that its initial location is either the initial location of $\mathcal{G}'$ or an intruder location. The *exit locations of a block* $\mathcal{B}$ are the locations of $\mathcal{B}$ with no outgoing edges. Intuitively, we proceed by decomposing a session program graph $\mathcal{G}^i$ into a sequence of blocks starting at each intruder location. The idea is that each such block will occur as a subgraph in the general scenario graph $\mathcal{G}$ (possibly with more than one occurrence). Namely, each path of the resulting graph will contain all the blocks of the scenario just once, and the set of all paths will cover all the possible sequences that respect the order of the single sessions. For instance, given the block structures $(\mathcal{B}_1^1, \mathcal{B}_2^1)$ and $(\mathcal{B}_1^2)$, the resulting graph will contain a path corresponding to the execution of $\mathcal{B}_1^1, \mathcal{B}_2^1, \mathcal{B}_1^2$ in this order, as well as a path for $\mathcal{B}_1^1, \mathcal{B}_1^2, \mathcal{B}_2^1$, as well as a path for $\mathcal{B}_1^2, \mathcal{B}_1^1, \mathcal{B}_2^1$. A simple algorithm for automatically performing this composition has been devised; we omit it due to lack of space.

Example 5. Fig. 3 shows the program graph for the scenario consisting of the session instances si_1 and si_2 such that $si_1(Alice) = a$, $si_1(Bob) = i = si_2(Alice)$ and $si_2(Bob) = b$ for NSL. Note that the set of instructions concerning a block are grouped into a single edge (and the corresponding lines of code in the programs of Example 2 are used to label the edge in the figure). For clarity, the initialization section and the goal assertions are reported on separate edges, though they belong to a larger block. Note also that, for clarity, variable names are subscripted with the number of the session where they occur, e.g., a variable Alice.B occurring in the program of si_2 is renamed as Alice_2.B.   □

3.3   Algorithm for Symbolic Execution and Annotation

In this section, we recall the IntraLA algorithm of [13] and describe how we can calculate interpolants in our case. The algorithm executes symbolically a program graph searching for goal locations, which represent attacks. In the case when we fail to reach a goal, an annotation (i.e., a formula expressing a condition under which no goal can be reached) is produced by using Craig interpolation. Through a backtrack phase, such an annotation is propagated to the other nodes of the graph and can be used to block a later phase of symbolic execution along an uninteresting run, i.e., a run for which the information contained in the annotation allows one to foresee that it will not reach a goal.

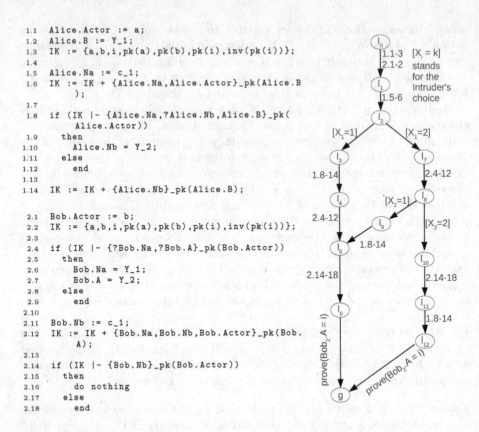

```
1.1    Alice.Actor := a;
1.2    Alice.B := Y_1;
1.3    IK := {a,b,i,pk(a),pk(b),pk(i),inv(pk(i))};
1.4
1.5    Alice.Na := c_1;
1.6    IK := IK + {Alice.Na,Alice.Actor}_pk(Alice.B
       );
1.7
1.8    if (IK |- {Alice.Na,?Alice.Nb,Alice.B}_pk(
       Alice.Actor))
1.9    then
1.10      Alice.Nb = Y_2;
1.11   else
1.12      end
1.13
1.14   IK := IK + {Alice.Nb}_pk(Alice.B);

2.1    Bob.Actor := b;
2.2    IK := {a,b,i,pk(a),pk(b),pk(i),inv(pk(i))};
2.3
2.4    if (IK |- {?Bob.Na,?Bob.A}_pk(Bob.Actor))
2.5    then
2.6      Bob.Na = Y_1;
2.7      Bob.A = Y_2;
2.8    else
2.9      end
2.10
2.11   Bob.Nb := c_1;
2.12   IK := IK + {Bob.Na,Bob.Nb,Bob.Actor}_pk(Bob.
       A);
2.13
2.14   if (IK |- {Bob.Nb}_pk(Bob.Actor))
2.15   then
2.16      do nothing
2.17   else
2.18      end
```

Fig. 3. NSL example: program for session si_1 (top-left), program for session si_2 (bottom-left), control flow graph for the whole scenario (right)

We will use a *two-sorted first-order language with equality*. The first sort is based on the algebra of messages, over which we allow a set of unary predicates $\mathcal{DY}_{IK}^j$ for $1 \leq j \leq n$ with a fixed $n \in \mathbb{N}$, whose meaning will be clarified below. The second sort is based on a signature containing variables (denoted in our examples by Xi) and uninterpreted constants (for which we use integers), and allows no functions and no predicates other than equality. We assume fixed the sets of constants and denote by $\mathcal{L}(\mathcal{V})$ the *set of well-formed formulas* of such a two-sorted first-order language defined over a (also two-sorted) set $\mathcal{V}$ of variables, to be instantiated with the variables and parameters of our programs.

First, we introduce some notions concerning symbolic execution. Let V be the set of program variables (for which, in the following, we will use standard math fonts). A *symbolic data state* is a triple (P, C, E), where P is a (two-sorted) *set of parameters*, i.e., variables not in V, $C \in \mathcal{L}(P)$ is a *constraint over the parameters*, and the *environment* E is a map from the program variables V to terms of the corresponding sort defined over P, with the only exception of the variable IK, which is mapped instead to a set of message terms. We denote by S the *set of symbolic data states*. Given its definition, a symbolic data state s can be characterized by the predicate $\chi(s) = C \wedge (\bigwedge_{v \in V \setminus \{IK\}} (v = E(v))) \wedge (\bigwedge_{M \in E(IK)} \mathcal{DY}^0_{IK}(M))$. Note that the variable IK is treated in a particular way, i.e., we translate the fact that $E(IK) = \mathcal{M}$ for some set $\mathcal{M}$ of parametric messages into a formula expressing that a predicate $\mathcal{DY}^0_{IK}$ holds for the messages in $\mathcal{M}$. A symbolic data state s can be associated to the set $\gamma(s)$ of data states produced by the map E for some valuation of the parameters satisfying the constraint C. We assume a defined initial symbolic data state $\gamma(s_0) = \{d_0\}$. A *symbolic state* is a pair $(l, s) \in \Lambda \times S$. A *symbolic interpreter* SI is a total map from the set $\mathcal{A}$ of actions to $S \times S$ such that for each symbolic data state s and action a, $\cup \gamma(SI(a)(s)) = Sem(a)(\gamma(s))$. Intuitively, SI takes a symbolic data state s and an action a and returns a non-empty set of symbolic data states, which represent the set of states obtained by executing a on s.

The *algorithm state* is a triple (Q, A, G) where Q is the set of *queries*, A is a *(program) annotation* and $G \subseteq \Lambda$ is the set of *goal locations* that have not been reached. A query is a symbolic state. During the execution of the algorithm, the set of queries is used to keep track of which symbolic states still need to be considered, i.e., of those symbolic states whose location has at least one outgoing edge that has not been symbolically executed, and the annotation is a decoration of the graph used to prune the search. Formally, a program annotation is a set of pairs in $(\Lambda \cup \Delta) \times \mathcal{L}(V)$. We will write these pairs in the form $l : \phi$ or $e : \phi$, where l is a location, e is an edge and ϕ is a formula called the *label*. When we have more than one label on a given location, we can read them as a disjunction of conditions: we define $A(l) = \bigvee \{\phi \mid l : \phi \in A\}$. For an edge $e = (l_n, a, l_{n+1})$ the label $e : \phi$ is *justified* in A if starting from the precondition formula ϕ and by executing the action a, the postcondition produced is $A(l_{n+1})$, i.e., when it implies the annotation of l_{n+1} after executing a. In that case, we write $\mathcal{J}(e : \phi, A)$. Let $Out(l)$ be the set of outgoing edges from a location l; the label $l : \phi$ is justified in A when, for all edges $e \in Out(l)$, there exists $e : \psi \in A$ such that ψ is a logical consequence of ϕ. An annotation is justified when all its elements are justified. A justified annotation is inductive and if it is initially true, then it is an inductive invariant. The algorithm maintains the invariant that A is always justified. A query $q = (l, s)$ is *blocked* by a formula ϕ when $s \models \phi$ and we then write $Bloc(q, A(\phi))$. With respect to q, the edge e is blocked when $Bloc(q, A(e))$ and the location l is blocked when $Bloc(q, A(l))$.

The rules of the algorithm IntraLA are given in Fig. 4. First, we initialize the algorithm state to $(\{(l_0, s_0)\}, \emptyset, G_0)$, i.e. the algorithm starts from the initial location, the initial symbolic data state, an empty annotation and a set G_0 of goals to search for, which is given as input.

The *Decide* rule is used to perform symbolic execution. By symbolically executing one program action, it generates a new query from an existing one. It may choose any edge that is not blocked and any symbolic successor state generated by the action a. If the generated query is itself not blocked, it is added to the query set. In the rule, SI is a symbolic interpreter, l_n and s_n are the currently considered location and symbolic data state, respectively, and l_{n+1} and s_{n+1} the location and symbolic data state obtained after executing a. The side conditions

$$\frac{Q, A, G}{Q + (l_{n+1}, s_{n+1}), A, G} \; Decide \qquad \frac{Q, A, G}{Q, A + e : \phi, G} \; Learn \qquad \frac{Q, A, G}{Q - q, A + l_n : \phi, G - l_n} \; Conjoin$$

$$q = (l_n, s_n) \in Q \qquad\qquad q = (l_n, s_n) \in Q \qquad\qquad q = (l_n, s) \in Q$$
$$e = (l_n, a, l_{n+1}) \in \Delta \qquad e = (l_n, a, l_{n+1}) \in \Delta \qquad \neg Bloc(q, A(l_n))$$
$$\neg Bloc(q, A(e)) \qquad\qquad Bloc(q, \phi) \qquad\qquad (\forall e \in Out(l_n).$$
$$s_{n+1} \in SI(a)(s_n) \qquad\qquad \mathcal{J}(e : \phi, A) \qquad\qquad e : \phi_e \in A \land Bloc(q, \phi_e))$$
$$\neg Bloc((l_{n+1}, s_{n+1}), A(l_{n+1})) \qquad\qquad\qquad\qquad \phi = \bigwedge \{\phi_e \mid e \in Out(l_n)\}$$

Fig. 4. Rules of the algorithm IntraLA with corresponding side conditions

of the *Decide* rule are that moving from s_n to s_{n+1}, the first needs to be into the query set and the branch between the two nodes must exist and not be blocked.

During the backtrack phase, two rules are used: *Learn* generates annotations and *Conjoin* merges annotations coming from different branches. If some outgoing edge $e = (l_n, a, l_{n+1})$ is not blocked, but every possible symbolic step along that edge leads to a blocked state, then the rule infers a new label ϕ that blocks the edge, where the formula ϕ can be any formula ϕ that both blocks the current query and is justified. In the following, we will explain how it can be obtained by exploiting the Craig interpolation lemma [7], which states that given two first-order formulas α and β such that $\alpha \land \beta$ is inconsistent, there exists a formula γ (their *interpolant*) such that α implies γ, γ implies $\neg\beta$ and $\gamma \in \mathcal{L}(\alpha) \cap \mathcal{L}(\beta)$.

Let μ be a term, a formula, or a set of terms or of formulas. We write μ' for the result of adding one prime to all the non-logical symbols in μ. Intuitively, the prime is used to refer to the value of a same variable in a later step and it is used in *transition formulas*, i.e., formulas in $\mathcal{L}(V \cup V')$. Since the semantics of an action $Sem(a)$ expresses how we move from a data state to another, we can easily associate to $Sem(a)$ a transition formula. With a slight abuse of notation, in the following, we will use $Sem(a)$ to denote the corresponding transition formula.

In our context, the most interesting case is when the action a is represented by a conditional statement, with a condition of the form $IK \vdash M$ for some message M. The intuitive meaning of the statement $IK \vdash M$ is that the message M can be derived from a set of messages denoted by IK by using the standard Dolev Yao intruder inference power. In our treatment, we fix a value n as the maximum number of inference steps that the intruder can execute in order to derive M. We observe that this is not a serious limitation of our method since several results (e.g., [17]) show that, when the number of sessions is finite, as in our case, it is possible to set an upper bound on the number of inference steps needed. Such a value can be established a-priori by observing the set of messages exchanged in the protocol scenario; we assume such an n to be fixed for the whole scenario. We use formulas of the form $\mathcal{DY}_{IK}^j(M)$, for $0 \le j \le n$, with the intended meaning that M can be derived in j steps of inference by the intruder. In particular, the predicate $\mathcal{DY}_{IK}^0$ is used to represent the initial knowledge IK, before any inference step is performed. Under the assumption on the n mentioned above, the statement $IK \vdash M$ can be expressed as the formula $\mathcal{DY}_{IK}^n(M)$. The formula

$$
\begin{aligned}
\varphi_j = \forall M. \, (&\mathcal{DY}_{IK}^{j+1}(M) \leftrightarrow (\mathcal{DY}_{IK}^j(M) \vee (\exists M'. \, \mathcal{DY}_{IK}^j([M,M']) \vee \mathcal{DY}_{IK}^j([M',M])) \\
&\vee \, (\exists M_1, M_2. \, M = [M_1, M_2] \wedge \mathcal{DY}_{IK}^j(M_1) \wedge \mathcal{DY}_{IK}^j(M_2)) \\
&\vee \, (\exists M_1, M_2. \, M = \{M_1\}_{M_2} \wedge \mathcal{DY}_{IK}^j(M_1) \wedge \mathcal{DY}_{IK}^j(M_2))) \\
&\vee \, (\exists M'. \, \mathcal{DY}_{IK}^j(\{M\}_{M'}) \wedge \mathcal{DY}_{IK}^j(inv(M'))) \vee (\exists M'. \, \mathcal{DY}_{IK}^j(\{M\}_{inv(M')}) \wedge \mathcal{DY}_{IK}^j(M')) ,
\end{aligned}
$$

in which $\leftrightarrow$ denotes the double implication and each quantification has to be intended over the sort of messages, expresses (as a disjunction) all the ways in which a given message can be inferred by the intruder in one step, i.e. by an operation of analysis or construction, thus moving from a knowledge (denoted by the predicate) $\mathcal{DY}_{IK}^j$ to a knowledge (denoted by the predicate) $\mathcal{DY}_{IK}^{j+1}$.

A theory $\mathcal{T}_{Msg}(n)$ over the sort of messages is obtained by enriching classical first-order logic with equality with the axioms φ_j, for $1 \le j < n$, together with additional axioms formalizing that any two distinct ground terms are not equal.

Now let $\alpha = \chi(s_n)$ and $\beta = Sem(a) \wedge \neg A(l_{n+1})'$. We can obtain the formula ϕ we are looking for, in the rule *Learn*, as an interpolant for α and β, possibly by using an interpolating theorem prover. With regard to this, we observe that, in the presence of our finite scenario assumption, when mechanizing such a search, the problem can be simplified by restricting the domain to a finite set of messages.

Finally, the rule *Conjoin* is applied when all the outgoing edges of the location in a query q are blocked. The location in q is labeled with the conjunction of the labels that block the outgoing edges. If the location is a goal, then we remove it from the set of remaining goals. Finally, the query is discarded from Q.

The algorithm terminates when no rules can be applied. In [13], the correctness of the algorithm, with respect to the goal search, is proved: the proof given there applies straightforwardly to the slightly simplified version we have given.

Theorem 1. Let G_0 be the set of goal locations provided in input. If the algorithm terminates with the algorithm state (Q, A, G), then all the locations in $G_0 \setminus G$ are reachable and all the locations in G are unreachable.

The output of our method can be of two types. If no goal has been reached, then we have a proof that no attack can be found, with respect to the security property of interest, in the finite scenario that we are considering. Otherwise, for each goal location that has been found, we can generate a test case, in the form of an attack trace, which can be easily inferred from the information in the symbolic data state corresponding to the last step of execution. We also note that, by a trivial modification of the rule *Conjoin*, we might easily obtain an algorithm that keeps searching for a goal that has already been reached through a different path, thus allowing to extract more attack traces for the same goal.

Example 6. Here we show the execution of the algorithm on the NSL graph of Fig. 3: Fig 5 summarizes the algorithm execution. Note that in the table, we use statements of the form $IK \vdash M$ in the constraint set as an abbreviation

N	Rule	Edge	A	C	E
0	Init	-	∅	∅	∅
1	Decide	(l_0,l_1)	∅	C_0	$E_0 \oplus \{(Alice_1.Actor, a), (Y_1.y_1), (Alice_1.Bob, y_1),$ $(Bob_2.Actor, b),$ $(IK, \{a,b,i, pk(a), pk(b), pk(i), inv(pk(i))\})\}$
2	Decide	(l_1,l_2)	∅	C_1	$E_1 \oplus \{(Alice_1.Na, c_1),$ $(IK, IK_1 \cup \{c_1, a\}_{pk(y_1)})\}$
3	Decide	(l_2,l_3)	∅	$C_2 \cup \{(x_1=1)\}$	$E_2 \oplus \{(X_1, x_1)\}$
4	Decide	(l_3,l_4)	∅	$C_3 \cup \{IK_2 \vdash$ $\{c_1, y_2, y_1\}_{pk(a)}\}$	$E_3 \oplus \{(Alice_1.Nb, y_2),$ $(IK, IK_2 \cup \{y_2\}_{pk(y_1)})\}$
5	Decide	(l_4,l_5)	∅	$C_4 \cup \{IK_4 \vdash$ $\{y_4, y_3\}_{pk(b)}\}$	$E_4 \oplus \{(Y_3, y_3), (Bob_2.A, y_3), (Y_4, y_4), (Bob_2.Na, y_4),$ $(Bob_2.Nb, c_2), (IK, IK_4 \cup \{y_4, c_2, b\}_{pk(y_3)})\}$
6	Decide	(l_5,l_6)	∅	$C_5 \cup \{IK_5 \vdash \{c_2\}_{pk(b)}\}$	E_6
7	Learn	-	$\{(l_6,g): Bob_2.A=i\}$	C_6	E_6
8	Conjoin	(l_6,g)	$A_7 \cup \{l_6: Bob_2.A=i\}$	C_7	E_7
9	Learn	-	$A_8 \cup \{(l_5,l_6): Bob_2.A=i \vee C_V\}$	C_8	E_8
10	Conjoin	(l_5,l_6)	$A_9 \cup \{l_5: Bob_2.A=i \vee C_V\}$	C_9	E_9
11	Decide	(l_2,l_7)	A_{10}	$\{(x_1=2)\}$	$E_2 \oplus \{(X_1, x_1)\}$
12	Decide	(l_7,l_8)	A_{10}	$C_{11} \cup \{IK_2 \vdash$ $\{y_4, y_3\}_{pk(b)}\}$	$E_2 \oplus \{(Y_3, y_3), (Bob_2.A, y_3), (Y_4, y_4), (Bob_2.Na, y_4),$ $(Bob_2.Nb, c_2), (IK, IK_2 \cup \{y_4, c_2, b\}_{pk(y_3)})\}$
13	Decide	(l_8,l_9)	A_{10}	$C_{12} \cup \{(x_2=1)\}$	$E_{12} \oplus \{(X_2, x_2)\}$
14		(l_9,l_5)	A_{10}	C_{13}	E_{13}

In step 9, $C_V \in \mathcal{L}(V)$ is a constraint over V s.t. C_V entails $IK_5 \nvdash \{Bob_2.Nb\}_{pk(Bob_2.Actor)}$

Fig. 5. Execution of the algorithm on the control flow graph for NSL

for the set of constraints over the parameters that make the (translation of the) statement satisfiable. Further, P_i, C_i and E_i denote, respectively, the set of parameters, the set of constraints and the environment at step i of the execution.

After the initialization, symbolic execution steps are performed from query (l_0, s_0) to (l_5, s_6) by using the rule *Decide* (steps 1–6). In step 7, we note that any symbolic execution step through the edge (l_6, g), leads to a blocked query. The algorithm thus creates interpolants and propagates them back to l_5 (steps 7−10), where the symbolic execution restarts, via applications of *Decide*, until step 14. Again, any symbolic step on the query (l_9, s_{13}) along the edge (l_9, l_5) leads to a blocked query, i.e., it generates a symbolic state that entails the annotation $Bob_2.A = i \vee C_V$. This is a concrete example of how the annotation method can improve the search procedure: we can stop following the path of query (l_9, s_{13}) as the annotation ensures we will never reach a goal.

By applying the method to NSPK, instead, we reach the goal with an execution close to the one seen for NSL. In fact, in the corresponding of step 14, we have that the inequality $Bob_2.A \neq i$ does not make the constraint set unsatisfiable. To extract an attack trace, first we consider the values of the x_j parameters contained in the last constraint set, i.e., $\{x_1 = 2, x_2 = 1\}$, which express the order in which the two sessions are interleaved, thus obtaining a symbolic attack trace (Fig. 2, left). We can further instantiate this trace, by using parameter and constant values of the last symbolic data state, thus obtaining the instantiated attack trace (Fig. 2, right). In particular, we note that y_3 is not constrained to be equal to i; this allows the intruder to act as pretending to be the honest agent a in the second session, from which we get the man-in-the-middle-attack.   □

4   Experiments and Results

We have implemented a Java prototype called SPiM (Security Protocol inter-polation Method) based on Z3 [16] and iZ3 [14] for satisfiability checking and interpolant generation, respectively. We use a modified version of the algorithm in [13], where we propagate annotations only if they can be effectively used to stop the execution of some other path (i.e., during the backtracking we only annotate locations and edges that can be reached by some path not visited yet).

In order to show that the method concretely speeds up the validation, we have tested SPiM with and without the interpolation part (consisting of the rules Learn and Conjoin) on NSL and NSPK. The total execution time on a general purpose computer ranges from 8s for NSPK to 83s for NSL. While for NSPK there are no pruned paths and consequently the two versions of the algorithm perform with the same time, on NSL SPiM is 1.5-3.5% (depending on the quality of the computer used) faster when using interpolation. This experiment shows that, even on examples where the annotation method does not prune the search space considerably (in NSL we only save two steps of symbolic execution), the time of validation tends to decrease when using interpolant-based annotations. This is also confirmed by the fact that, as observed during the execution on the NSL example, the average time needed to calculate and propagate an interpolant is 9.1-27.3% lower than the average time used to perform a step of symbolic execution together with the corresponding satisfiability checking.

5   Concluding Remarks

We have presented a method that starts from a formal security protocol specifi-cation and combines Craig interpolation (to prune useless traces so as to avoid a quantifier elimination phase that is usually an expensive task, cf. [13]), symbolic execution and the standard Dolev-Yao intruder model to search for goals, i.e., possible attacks on the protocol. In particular, our method adopts (almost ver-batim) the IntraLA algorithm proposed by McMillan in [13]. Other approaches have similarly benefited from IntraLA, e.g., it has been integrated in the BLAST tool [9], but our results are different from theirs in terms of both the application field and the methodology we have used to perform the analysis. In fact, one of the main differences between our work and [9,13], is the way we construct the control flow graph, in particular to accommodate the fact that security pro-tocols are not sequential programs when we analyze them in the presence of a Dolev-Yao intruder. For this, we have taken inspiration from protocol analysis tools such as the AVANTSSAR Platform [1], from which we have lifted the input specification language and the formalization of the intruder actions.

Given its prototypical nature, some aspects of our method require further work. For instance, the full automation of the generation of control flow graphs and the handling of infinite scenarios will allow us to compare with other security protocol verification tools [1,2], with which we also expect useful interaction.

We are currently working at extending the procedure for translating protocols into sequential programs in order to cover all the constructs of the ASLan++

language, thus enabling the application of our method to more complex security protocols, as well as at giving a formal proof of the correctness of such a translation. We also aim to extend the method with the possibility of expressing protocol goals as LTL properties (like in AVANTSSAR) as we would like to use Craig interpolation not only to prune the search space but also to check which of the possible reachable states can or can not lead to the intended goal.

References

1. Armando, A., et al.: The AVANTSSAR Platform for the Automated Validation of Trust and Security of Service-Oriented Architectures. In *TACAS*, LNCS 7214:267–282. Springer, 2012.
2. Armando, A., et al.: The AVISPA Tool for the Automated Validation of Internet Security Protocols and Applications. In *CAV*, LNCS 3576:281–285. Springer, 2005.
3. Armando, A., Carbone, R., Compagna, L., Cuéllar, J., Tobarra Abad, L.: Formal Analysis of SAML 2.0 Web Browser Single Sign-On: Breaking the SAML-based Single Sign-On for Google Apps. In *FMSE*. ACM, 2008.
4. Armando, A., Pellegrino, G., Carbone, R., Merlo, Balzarotti, D.: From Model-Checking to Automated Testing of Security Protocols: Bridging the Gap. In *TAP*, LNCS 7305:3–18. Springer, 2012.
5. Basin, D., Mödersheim, S., Viganò, L.: OFMC: A symbolic model checker for security protocols. *Int. Journal of Information Security*, 4(3):181–208, 2005.
6. Büchler, M., Oudinet, J., Pretschner, A.: Security mutants for property-based testing. In *TAP*, LNCS 6706:69–77. Springer, 2011.
7. Craig, W.: Three uses of the Herbrand-Gentzen theorem in relating model theory and proof theory. *The Journal of Symbolic Logic*, 22(3):pp. 269–285, 1957.
8. Dolev, D., Yao, A.: On the Security of Public-Key Protocols. *IEEE Transactions on Information Theory*, 2(29), 1983.
9. Henzinger, T. A., Jhala, R., Majumdar, R., McMillan, K. L.: Abstractions from proofs. In *POPL*, pp. 232–244. ACM, 2004.
10. King, J. C.: Symbolic execution and program testing. *CACM*, 19(7):385–394, 1976.
11. Lowe, G.: Breaking and Fixing the Needham-Shroeder Public-Key Protocol Using FDR. In *TACAS*, LNCS 1055:147–166. Springer, 1996.
12. McMillan, K. L.: Applications of Craig Interpolants in Model Checking. In *TACAS*, LNCS 3440:1–12. Springer, 2005.
13. McMillan, K. L.: Lazy annotation for program testing and verification. In *CAV*, LNCS 6174:104–118. Springer, 2010.
14. McMillan, K. L.: Interpolants from Z3 proofs. In *FMCAD*, pp. 19–27, 2011.
15. Mitchell, J. C., Mitchell, M., Stern, U.: Automated analysis of cryptographic protocols using Murphi. In *Security and Privacy*, pp. 141–151. IEEE CS, 1997.
16. De Moura, L., Bjørner, N.: Z3: An efficient SMT solver. In *TACAS*, LNCS 4963:337–340. Springer, 2008.
17. Rusinowitch, M., Turuani, M.: Protocol insecurity with a finite number of sessions and composed keys is NP-complete. *TCS*, 299:451–475, 2003.
18. von Oheimb, D., Mödersheim, S.: ASLan++ — a formal security specification language for distributed systems. In *FMCO*, LNCS 6957:1–22. Springer, 2010.

RDAS: A Symmetric Key Scheme
for Authenticated Query Processing
in Outsourced Databases

Lil María Rodríguez-Henríquez and Debrup Chakraborty

Departamento de Computación, CINVESTAV-IPN
Av. IPN No. 2508, Col. San Pedro Zacatenco, México, D.F. 07360, México
lrodriguez@computacion.cs.cinvestav.mx, debrup@cs.cinvestav.mx

Abstract. Security of outsourced databases is an important problem of current practical interest. In this paper we address the problem of authenticated query processing in outsourced databases. We describe the syntax of a generic scheme for authenticated query processing called RDAS, and provide security definitions for RDAS in line with concrete provable security. Then, we propose a new scheme called RDAS1 which enables a client to ensure both correctness and completeness of the query results obtained from a server. Our solution involves use of bitmap indices and message authentication codes in a novel manner. We prove that RDAS1 is secure relative to our security definition. Finally, we discuss a concrete improvement over RDAS1 (which we call RDAS2) and provide performance data for both RDAS1 and RDAS2 on a real data base.

Keywords: Database security, query authentication, bitmap index, MACs.

1 Introduction

Cloud computing holds the promise of revolutionizing the manner in which enterprises manage, distribute, and share information. The data owner (client) can out-source almost all its information processing tasks to a "cloud". The cloud can be seen as a collection of servers (we shall sometimes refer to it as the server) which caters the data storage, processing and maintenance needs of the client. Needless to say this new concept of computing has already brought significant savings in terms of costs for the data owner.

Among others, an important service provided by a cloud is *Database as a Service (DAS)*. In this service the client delegates the duty of storage and maintenance of his/her data to a third party (an un-trusted server). This model has gained lot of popularity in the recent times. The DAS model allows the client to perform operations like create, modify and retrieve from databases in a remote location [6]. These operations are performed by the server on behalf of the client. However, delegating the duty of storage and maintenance of data to a third party brings in some new security challenges.

R. Accorsi and S. Ranise (Eds.): STM 2013, LNCS 8203, pp. 115–130, 2013.

The two main security goals of cryptography are privacy and authentication. These security issues are relevant to the outsourced data also. The client who keeps the data with an untrusted server has two main concerns. The first one being that the data may be sensitive and the client may not want to reveal the data to the server and the second one is the data whose storage and maintenance has been delegated to the server would be used by the client. The typical usage of the data would be that the client should be able to query the database and the answers to the client's queries would be provided by the server. It is natural for the client to be concerned about a malicious server who does not provide correct answers to the client queries. In this work we are interested in this problem. We aim to devise a scheme in which the client would be able to verify whether the server is responding correctly to its queries.

We consider the scenario where a client delegates a relational data base to an un-trusted server. When the client queries its outsourced data, it expects in return a set of records (query reply) satisfying the query's predicates. As the server is not trusted, so it must be capable of proving the correctness of its responses. We describe the intricacies of the problem with the help of an example. Consider the relational database of employees data shown in Table 1.

Table 1. Relation $R1$ (This relation would serve as a running example)

EmpId	Name	Gender	Level
TRW	Tom	M	L_2
MST	Mary	F	L_1
JOH	John	M	L_2
LCT	Lucy	F	L_1
ASY	Anne	F	L_1
RZT	Rosy	F	L_2

We consider that this relation has been delegated by a client to a server, and the client poses the following query

SELECT $*$ FROM $R1$ WHERE $Gender = $ 'M' OR $Level = $ 'L_2'.

The correct response to this query is the set Res consisting of three tuples

Res $= \{(\text{TRW, Tom, M}, L_2), (\text{JOH, John, M}, L_2), (\text{RZT, Rosy, F}, L_2)\}.$

In answering the query the server can act maliciously in various ways. In the context of authentication we are concerned with two properties of the response namely *correctness* and *completeness*, denote two different malicious activities of the server. We explain these notions with an example below:

1. **Incorrect result:** The server responds with three tuples, but changes the tuple (TRW, Tom, M, L_2), to (TRW, Tom, F, L_2). Moreover, it can be the case that the server responds with Res$\cup\{$(BRW, Bob, M, L_2), i.e., it responds with an extra tuple which is not a part of the original relation.

2. **Incomplete result:** The server may not respond with the complete result, i.e., it can delete some valid results from the response, i.e., instead of responding with Res it responds with Res − {(TRW, Tom, M, L_2)}.

The problem of correctness can be easily handled in the symmetric setting by adding a message authentication code to each tuple. A secure message authentication code is difficult to forge, and thus this property would not allow the server to add fake entries in its response. The completeness problem is more difficult and its solution is achieved through more involved schemes.

The problem of query completeness has been largely addressed by some interesting use of authenticated data structures. The basic idea involved is to store the information already present in the relation in a different form using some special data structures. This redundancy along with some special structural properties of the used data structures help in verifying completeness.

A large part of the literature uses tree based authentication structures like the Merkeley hash tree [8] or its variants. Some notable works in this direction are reported in [3, 5, 7–9, 13, 14, 19]. These techniques involve using a special data structure along with some cryptographic authentication mechanism like hash functions and/or signatures schemes. The tree based structures yield reasonable communication and verification costs. But, in general they require huge storage at server side, moreover the query completeness problem is largely addressed with respect to range queries and such queries may not be relevant in certain scenarios, say in case of databases with discrete attributes which do not have any natural metric relationship among them.

Signature schemes have also been used in a novel manner for solving the problem. One line of research has focussed on aggregated signatures [10–12, 15, 16]. Signature aggregation helps in reducing the communication cost to some extent and in some cases can function with constant extra communication overhead. A related line of research uses chain signatures. If one uses chain signatures as in [11], the use of specialized data structures may no longer be required.

Our Contributions: Though there have been considerable amount of work on authenticated query processing on relational data bases, but it has been acknowledged (for example in [20]) that the problem of query authentication largely remains open. An unified cryptographic treatment of the problem is missing in the literature. In most existing schemes cryptographic objects have been used in an ad-hoc manner, and the security guarantees that the existing schemes provide are not very clear. In this work we initiate a formal cryptographic study of the problem of query authentication in a distinct direction. We propose a new scheme which does not use any specialized data structure to address the completeness problem. Our solution involves usage of bitmap indices for this purpose. Bitmap indices have gained lot of popularity in the current days for their use in accelerated query processing [18], and many commercially available databases like Oracle, IBM DB2, Sybase IQ now implement some form of bitmap index scheme in addition to the more traditional B-tree based schemes. Thus, it may be easy to incorporate a bitmap based scheme in a modern database without significant extra cost. To our knowledge, bitmaps have not been used till date for a security goal. In addition to bitmap indices we use a secure message authentication code (MAC) as the only cryptographic object. We show that by the use of these simple objects one can design a query authentication scheme which allows verification of both correctness and completeness of query results.

In concrete terms in this paper we describe a generic scheme which we call as relational database authentication scheme (RDAS) which can provide the functionality of authenticated query processing in static databases. We define the security goals of RDAS in line with the tradition of concrete provable security. Then we propose a RDAS called RDAS1. RDAS1 is designed using message authentication codes and bitmap indices in a novel manner. RDAS1 is capable of authenticated query processing of simple select queries and select queries involving disjunctions of equality conditions. We point out various directions in which RDAS1 can be modified to incorporate other types of queries. In particular we propose a modification called RDAS2 which is capable of authenticating a larger class of queries. Finally we provide some experimental data on performance of RDAS1 and RDAS2.

2   Preliminaries and Notations

Relations: By $R(A)$ we would denote a relation over a set of attributes A. If $A = \{a_1, a_2, \cdots a_n\}$, we shall sometimes write $R(a_1, a_2, \cdots, a_n)$ instead of $R(A)$. We will assume that each attribute has a set of permitted values, i.e., the domain of the attribute. Given an attribute a, $\mathsf{Dom}(a)$ would represent its domain. We are mainly concerned with attributes whose domains are finite, note that for a static database each attribute always has a finite domain. By cardinality of an attribute we shall mean the cardinality of the domain of the attribute. We will denote the cardinality of an attribute a by $\mathsf{Card}(a) = |\mathsf{Dom}(a)|$.

A tuple t in a relation is a function that associates with each attribute a value in its domain. Specifically if $A = \{a_1, a_2, \cdots a_n\}$ and $R(A)$ be a relation then the jth tuple of relation $R(A)$ would be denoted by t_j^R and for $a_i \in A$ by $t_j^R[a_i]$ we shall denote the value of attribute a_i in the jth tuple in R. For $B \subseteq A$, $t_j^R[B]$ will denote the set of values of the attributes in B in the jth tuple. We shall sometimes omit the subscripts and superscripts from t_j^R and denote the tuple by t if the concerned relation is clear from the context and the tuple number is irrelevant.

Binary Strings: The set of all binary strings would be denoted by $\{0, 1\}^*$, and the set of n bit strings by $\{0, 1\}^n$. For $X_1, X_2 \in \{0, 1\}^*$, by $X_1 || X_2$ we shall mean the concatenation of X_1 and X_2; and $|X_1|$ will denote the length of X_1 in bits. By $\mathsf{bit}_i(X)$ we will denote the ith bit of X. We shall always consider that the domains of all attributes in the relations are subsets of $\{0, 1\}^*$, this would allow us to apply transformations and functions on the values of the tuples without describing explicit encoding schemes.

Bitmaps: Consider a relation $R(a_1, \ldots, a_m)$ with nT many rows. Consider that for each attribute a_i, $\mathsf{Dom}(a_i) = \{v_1^i, v_2^i, \ldots v_{\lambda_i}^i\}$, thus $\mathsf{Card}(a_i) = \lambda_i$ for $1 \leq$

$i \leq m$. We define the bitmap of an attribute a_i corresponding to its value v_j^i in the relation R as $\mathsf{BitMap}_R(a_i, v_j^i) = X$, where X is a binary string, such that $|X| = \mathsf{nT}$ and for $1 \leq k \leq \mathsf{nT}$,

$$\mathsf{bit}_k(X) = \begin{cases} 1 & \text{if } t_k^R[a_i] = v_j^i \\ 0 & \text{otherwise.} \end{cases}$$

Consider the relation $R1$ on the attributes $\{\mathsf{EmpID}, \mathsf{Name}, \mathsf{Gender}, \mathsf{Level}\}$ as shown in Table 1. Here we have $\mathsf{Dom}(\mathsf{Gender}) = \{\mathrm{M}, \mathrm{F}\}$ and $\mathsf{Dom}(\mathsf{Level}) = \{L_1, L_2\}$. Hence we can compute the following bitmaps:

$$\mathsf{BitMap}_{R1}(\mathsf{Gender}, \mathrm{F}) = 010111 \;,\; \mathsf{BitMap}_{R1}(\mathsf{Gender}, \mathrm{M}) = 101000$$
$$\mathsf{BitMap}_{R1}(\mathsf{Level}, L_1) = 010110 \;,\; \mathsf{BitMap}_{R1}(\mathsf{Level}, L_2) = 101001$$

Message Authentication Codes: Message authentication codes provide authentication in the symmetric key setting. It is assumed that the sender and the receiver share a common secret key K. Given a message x, the sender uses K to generate a footprint of the message. This footprint (commonly called a tag) is the message authentication code (MAC) for the message x. The sender transmits the pair $(x; \mathsf{tag})$ to the receiver. The receiver uses K to verify that (x, tag) is a properly generated message-tag pair. Verification is generally performed by regenerating the tag on the message x and comparing the generated tag with the one received. We shall call the algorithm for generating the tag as a MAC. Assuming that the size of the tag is τ bits, we see the tag generation scheme as a function $\mathsf{MAC} : \mathcal{K} \times \mathcal{M} \to \{0,1\}^\tau$, where $\mathcal{K}$ and $\mathcal{M}$ are the key and message spaces respectively. In most cases we shall write $\mathsf{MAC}_K(x)$ instead of $\mathsf{MAC}(K, x)$.

3   Relational Database Authentication Scheme (RDAS): Definitions and Basic Notions

A relational database authentication scheme (RDAS) consists of a tuple of algorithms $(\mathcal{K}, \mathcal{F}, \Phi, \Psi, \mathcal{V})$, which are described in details in the following paragraphs.

$\mathcal{K}$ is the **key generation algorithm** and it selects one (or more) keys from a pre-specified key space and outputs them.

$\mathcal{F}$ is called the **authentication transform**, which takes in a set of relations $\mathcal{R}$ and a set of keys and outputs another set of relations $\mathcal{R}'$ along with some additional data (M_s, M_c). If the set of keys is K, we shall denote this operation as $(\mathcal{R}', M_c, M_s) \leftarrow \mathcal{F}_K(\mathcal{R})$. A client who wants to store the set of relations $\mathcal{R}$ in an un-trusted server, transforms $\mathcal{R}$ to $\mathcal{R}'$ using the authentication transform $\mathcal{F}$ and a set of keys. The transform $\mathcal{F}$ produces some additional data other than the set of relations $\mathcal{R}'$, the additional data consists of two distinct parts M_s and M_c. The set of relations $\mathcal{R}'$ along with M_s are stored in the server and the keys and the data M_c are retained in the client. The key generation algorithm and the authentication transform are executed in the client side.

We call Φ as the **query translator**, it is a transformation which takes in a query for the relations in $\mathcal{R}$ and converts it into a query for relations in $\mathcal{R}'$. For ease of discussion we shall refer a query for $\mathcal{R}$ to be a $\mathcal{R}$-query and a query for $\mathcal{R}'$ to be a $\mathcal{R}'$-query. Thus, given a $\mathcal{R}$-query q, $\Phi(q)$ would be a $\mathcal{R}'$-query. Thus by use of the transform Φ, the client would be able to translate queries meant for $\mathcal{R}$ to queries which can be executed on the transformed relations in $\mathcal{R}'$.

Ψ is the **response procedure**. To execute a query q on $\mathcal{R}$, the client converts the query to $\Phi(q)$ and sends it to the server. The server executes the function Ψ, which takes in the query $\Phi(q)$ and uses $\mathcal{R}'$ and M_s. The output of Ψ is ρ, which we call as the response of the server. The server returns it to the client.

The **verification procedure** is a keyed transform $\mathcal{V}_K$ which runs in the client. It takes as input the query q, a response ρ of the server and M_c and outputs either an answer ans for the query q or outputs a special symbol $\perp$ which signifies reject.

3.1 Correctness and Security

If we fix the set of relations $\mathcal{R}$, then a $\mathcal{R}$-query q when executed in $\mathcal{R}$ would have a fixed answer say $\mathsf{ans}(\mathcal{R}, \mathsf{q})$. Our goal is to transform $\mathcal{R}$ to $\mathcal{R}'$ using a RDAS in such a way that if the query $\Phi(q)$ is sent to the server, then the answer ans should be recoverable from the server response ρ through the procedure $\mathcal{V}$, if the server follows the protocol correctly. On the other hand, if the server is malicious, i.e., it deviates from the protocol and sends a response ρ' distinct from the correct response ρ then the procedure $\mathcal{V}$ should reject the response by outputting $\perp$. In other words, if the answer to a $\mathcal{R}$-query is ans, then after running the protocol, $\mathcal{V}$ will either produce ans or $\perp$, it would not produce an answer ans' distinct from ans.

In the security model, we allow the adversary to choose the primary set of relations $\mathcal{R}$. Given this choice of $\mathcal{R}$, we compute $(\mathcal{R}', M_c, M_s) \leftarrow \mathcal{F}_K(\mathcal{R})$, for a randomly selected set of keys K which is unknown to the adversary. We give $\mathcal{R}'$ and M_s to the adversary. The adversary chooses a $\mathcal{R}$-query q and the challenger provides the adversary with $\Phi(q)$, finally the adversary outputs a response ρ, and we say that the adversary is *successful* if $\mathcal{V}_K(\rho, q, M_c) \notin \{\perp, \mathsf{ans}(\mathcal{R}, \mathsf{q})\}$.

Definition 1. *Let* $\mathsf{Succ}_{\mathcal{A}}$ *be the event that a specific adversary* $\mathcal{A}$ *is successful in the sense as described above. We say that a RDAS is* (ϵ, t)-secure *if for any adversary* $\mathcal{A}$ *which runs for time at most* t, $\Pr[\mathsf{Succ}_{\mathcal{A}}] \leq \epsilon$.

4   RDAS1: A Generic Scheme for Select Queries Involving Arbitrary Disjunctions

We discuss a basic scheme for a secure RDAS which works only if the queries made are single attribute select queries or select queries involving disjunctions of an arbitrary number of equality conditions. We call this scheme as RDAS1.

We describe the scheme assuming that the set of initial relations $\mathcal{R}$ is a singleton set consisting of a single relation $R(B)$, where $B = \{b_1, b_2, \ldots, b_{|B|}\}$ is the set of attributes, and consider $A = \{a_1, \ldots, a_m\} \subseteq B$ to be a set of attributes on which queries are allowed, we shall call A the set of *allowed attributes*. It is possible that $B = A$. The procedure $\mathcal{F}$ converts R into two relations R_α and R_β, i.e, $\mathcal{R}' = \{R_\alpha, R_\beta\}$ and M_s is empty and $M_c = \mathsf{nT}$, where nT is the number of tuples in R. The only cryptographic object used by RDAS1 is a message authentication code $\mathsf{MAC} : \mathcal{K} \times \{0,1\}^* \to \{0,1\}^\tau$, where $\mathcal{K}$ is the key space. In what follows, we shall describe the procedures involved in RDAS1 considering a generic relation $R(B)$, where the set of allowed attributes is $A \subseteq B$. Also we shall throughout consider the relation $R1$ in Table 1 as a concrete example, and for simplicity, for $R1$ we shall consider the set of allowed attributes to be $\{\mathtt{Gender}, \mathtt{level}\}$.

RDAS1.$\mathcal{K}$: The key space for RDAS1 is the same as the key space of the associated message authentication code MAC. The key generation algorithm selects a key K uniformly at random from $\mathcal{K}$.

RDAS1.$\mathcal{F}$: $\mathcal{F}$ produces two relations R_α and R_β by the action of the key. The relation R_α is defined on the set of attributes $B \cup \{\mathtt{Nonce}, \mathtt{Tag}\}$, i.e., R_α has two more attributes than in R. If R contains nT many tuples then R_α also contain the same number of tuples. The procedure for populating the tuples of R_α is depicted in Figure 1. What this procedure does is compute a MAC for each row. The relation R_β contains the attributes $\{\mathtt{Name}, \mathtt{SearchKey}, \mathtt{RowNo}, \mathtt{Tag1}\}$, irrespective of the attributes in relation R. Where $\mathsf{Dom}(\mathtt{Name}) = \{a_1, \ldots, a_m\}$, i.e., the allowed attributes in R. And, $\mathsf{Dom}(\mathtt{SearchKey}) = \mathsf{Dom}(a_1) \cup \mathsf{Dom}(a_1) \cup \cdots \cup \mathsf{Dom}(a_m)$. Let $\Omega = \cup_{i=1}^{m} (\{a_i\} \times \mathsf{Dom}(a_i))$, note that the elements of Ω are ordered pairs of the form (x, y) where $x \in \mathsf{Dom}(\mathtt{Name})$ and $y \in \mathsf{Dom}(\mathtt{SearchKey})$, and $|\Omega| = \sum_{i=1}^{m} \mathsf{Card}(a_i) = N$. Let $\mathcal{L}$ be a list of the elements in Ω in an arbitrary order. If (x, y) be the i-th element in $\mathcal{L}$, then we shall denote x and y by $\mathcal{L}_i^1$ and $\mathcal{L}_i^2$ respectively, where $1 \leq i \leq N$. The way the relation R_β is populated is also shown in Figure 1. This procedure allows the client to store all possible pairs $\mathcal{L}_i^1, \mathcal{L}_i^2$ along with the MAC calculated over this pair concatenated with the respective bitmap and $\mathtt{RowNo}$. Note that the bitmap is not explicitly stored in the relation R_β. The transform $\mathcal{F}$ is executed in the client side, and the resulting relations R_α and R_β are stored in the server.

For a concrete example, if RDAS1.$\mathcal{F}$ has as input the relation $R1$ (see Table 1) and the set of allowed attributes is $\{\mathtt{Gender}, \mathtt{level}\}$, then it would produce as output the relations $R1_\alpha$ and $R1_\beta$ as shown in Table 2. The relation $R1_\alpha$ is almost the same as that of $R1$, except that it has two additional attributes, $\mathtt{Nonce}$ and $\mathtt{Tag}$. The attribute $\mathtt{Nonce}$ just contains the row numbers and is thus unique for each row. The attribute $\mathtt{Tag}$ is the message authentication code computed for a message which is produced by concatenating all the values of the attributes in that tuple.

The relation $R1_\beta$ contains the attributes $\{\mathtt{Name}, \mathtt{SearchKey}, \mathtt{RowNo}, \mathtt{Tag1}\}$, where in this case, $\mathsf{Dom}(\mathtt{Name}) = \{\mathtt{Gender}, \mathtt{Level}\}$, $\mathsf{Dom}(\mathtt{SearchKey}) = \{M, F\} \cup$

Creating R_α	Creating R_β
1. **for** $j = 1$ to nT	1. **for** $j = 1$ to N
2. **for** $i = 1$ to $\|B\|$	2. $t_j^{R_\beta}[\text{Name}] \leftarrow \mathcal{L}_j^1;$
3. $t_j^{R_\alpha}[b_i] \leftarrow t_j^R[b_i];$	3. $t_j^{R_\beta}[\text{SearchKey}] \leftarrow \mathcal{L}_j^2;$
4. **end for**	4. $t_j^{R_\beta}[\text{RowNo}] \leftarrow \text{nT} + j;$
5. $t_j^{R_\alpha}[\text{Nonce}] \leftarrow j;$	5. $L \leftarrow \mathcal{L}_j^1\|\mathcal{L}_j^2\|\text{BitMap}_R(\mathcal{L}_j^1,\mathcal{L}_j^2)\|(\text{nT}+j);$
6. $H \leftarrow t_j^R[b_1]\|\ldots\|t_j^R[b_m]\|j;$	6. $t_j^{R_\beta}[\text{Tag1}] \leftarrow \text{MAC}_K(L);$
7. $t_j^{R_\alpha}[\text{Tag}] \leftarrow \text{MAC}_K(H);$	7. **end for**
8. **end for**	

Fig. 1. Creating R_α and R_β

$\{L_1, L_2\}$. The tuples in $R1_\beta$ are populated according to the procedure as shown in Figure 1, and the specific relation $R1_\beta$ is shown in Table 2.

RDAS1.Φ: The transform Φ, transforms a query meant for the original relation R to a set of queries which are meant to be executed on the relations R_α and R_β which are stored in the server side. As mentioned, the allowed queries for RDAS1 are of the following form:

Q: SELECT * FROM R WHERE $a_1 = v_1$ OR $a_2 = v_2$ OR $\ldots\ldots$ OR $a_l = v_l$

Table 2. Relations $R1_\alpha$ and $R1_\beta$

Relation $R1_\alpha$

EmpId	Name	Gender	Level	Nonce	Tag
TRW	Tom	M	L_2	1	Y_1
MST	Mary	F	L_1	2	Y_2
JOH	John	M	L_2	3	Y_3
LCT	Lucy	F	L_1	4	Y_4
ASY	Anne	F	L_1	5	Y_5
RZT	Rosy	F	L_2	6	Y_6

Relation $R1_\beta$

Name	SearchKey	RowNo	Tag1
Gender	F	7	Y_7'
Gender	M	8	Y_8'
Level	L_1	9	Y_9'
Level	L_2	10	Y_{10}'

The allowed set of queries are thus select queries on arbitrary numbers of disjunctions on different or repeated attributes [1], which includes select queries on a single attribute of the form SELECT * FROM R WHERE $a_i = v$. Given as input a valid query q, $\Phi(q)$ outputs two queries one for the relation R_α (which we call q_α) and the other for R_β (which we call q_β). For the specific query Q, $\Phi(Q)$ will output the following queries:

Q_α: SELECT * FROM R_α WHERE $a_1 = v_1$ OR $a_2 = v_2$ OR $\ldots\ldots$ OR $a_l = v_l$
Q_β: SELECT * FROM R_β WHERE (Name $= a_1$ AND SearchKey $= v_2$) OR $\ldots\ldots$ OR (Name $= a_l$ AND SearchKey $= v_l$)

In the concrete example, consider the following query $Q1$ on the relation $R1$

$Q1$: SELECT * FROM $R1$ WHERE Gender = 'M' OR Level= 'L_2'

---

[1] By a query of disjunction on repeated attributes we mean a query like: SELECT * FROM R WHERE $a_1 = v_1$ OR $a_1 = v_2$ OR $a_2 = v_3$. Here the attribute a_1 is repeated twice.

Applying the transformation $\Phi(Q1)$, the output queries $Q1_\alpha$ and $Q1_\beta$ would be the following:

$Q1_\alpha$: SELECT * FROM $R1_\alpha$ WHERE $Gender =$ 'M' OR $Level =$ 'L_2'
$Q1_\beta$: SELECT * FROM $R1_\beta$ WHERE ($Name =$ 'Gender' AND $Searchkey =$'M') OR ($Name =$ 'Level' AND $Searchkey =$'L_2')

The reason for the specific structure of the q_β queries would be clear from the description of the verification process and the associated example.

RDAS1.Ψ: As discussed, Ψ is the transform executed in the server to generate the response for a set of queries produced by Φ. In RDAS1 the response of the server is constructed just by running the queries specified by Φ on R_α and R_β. We denote the response by $S = (S_\alpha, S_\beta)$ where S_α and S_β corresponds to responses of q_α and q_β respectively. Thus, for the example, the server executes the queries $Q1_\alpha$ and $Q1_\beta$ on $R1_\alpha$ and $R1_\beta$ respectively and thus returns the response $S1 = (S1_\alpha, S1_\beta)$ which is shown in Table 3.

Table 3. Left side: Answer $S1_\alpha$, Right side: Answer $S1_\beta$

Relation $S1_\alpha$

EmpId	Name	Gender	Level	Nonce	Tag
TRW	Tom	M	L_2	1	Y_1
JOH	John	M	L_2	3	Y_3
RZT	Rosy	F	L_2	6	Y_6

Relation $S1_\beta$

Name	SearchKey	RowNo	Tag1
Gender	M	8	Y_8'
Level	L_2	10	Y_{10}'

RDAS1.$\mathcal{V}$: The verification procedure receives as input the response $S = (S_\alpha, S_\beta)$ from the server, the original query and the keys. The response of the server consists of two parts. We denote these two parts as two sets S_α and S_β which are responses to the queries q_α and q_β respectively. Thus, S_α and S_β contains tuples from the relations R_α and R_β respectively.

The transformed queries q_α and q_β are also disjunctions of conditions, for a q_α query the conditions are of the form $a_i = v_i$, where a_i is an attribute and v_i its value, and for a q_β query the conditions are of the form Name $= v$ AND SearchKey $= w$. Thus, for the description below, we consider that C_1^α OR C_2^α OR ... C_l^α is a α query where each C_i^α is an equality condition and C_1^β OR C_2^β OR ... C_l^β is a β query where each C_i^β is a conjunction of two equality conditions. Note that the number of conditions in q_α and q_β would always be the same. Let SaT be a predicate which takes as input a tuple t and a condition C (which can also be a query q) and outputs a 1 if the tuple t satisfies the condition C, otherwise outputs a zero. With these notations defined, we are ready to describe the verification algorithm. The verification algorithm consists of three procedures: α-Verify, makeBitMap and β-Verify. The procedures are shown in Figure 2, and they are applied sequentially in the same order as stated above.

The verification procedure checks for both the correctness and the completeness of the server response against the original query q. Note that the server response consists of two distinct parts S_α and S_β, the S_α part corresponds to

```
α-Verify
1.  for all tuples t ∈ S_α
2.      if SaT(t, q_α) = 0, return ⊥
3.      ta ← MAC_K (t[b_1]|| ... ||t[b_{|B|}]||t[Nonce]);
4.      if ta ≠ t[Tag] , return ⊥;
5.  end for
```

```
makeBitMap
6.  for i ← 1 to l
7.      X_i ← 0^{nT};
8.  end for
9.  for all tuples t ∈ S_α
10.     for i ← 1 to l
11.         if SaT(t, C_i)
12.             j ← t[Nonce];
13.             bit_j(X_i) ← 1;
14.         end if
15.     end for
16. end for
```

```
β-Verify
17. for i ← 1 to l
18.     T[i] ← 0;
19. end for
20. for i ← 1 to l
21.     for all tuples t ∈ S_β
22.         if SaT(C_i^β, t) = 1
23.             T[i] ← T[i] + 1;
24.             LL ← t[Name]||t[SearchKey]||X_i||t[RowNo];
25.             if MAC_K(LL) ≠ t[Tag1] return ⊥;
26.         endif
27.     end for
28. end for
29. for i ← 1 to l
30.     if T[i] ≠ 1 return ⊥;
31. end for
32. return ∏_{(b_1,b_2,...,b_{|B|})} S_α;
```

Fig. 2. The procedures involved in the verification process

the real result of the original query q and the S_β part assists the verification process to verify the completeness of the result in S_α. In the part α-Verify, the verification procedure checks for the correctness of the tuples returned by the server. As in the transformed relation R_α a message authentication code is associated with each tuple of the original relation, hence the α-Verify part of the verification procedure checks whether the contents of the tuples in S_α are not modified. If any of the the tuples in S_α are modified then the computed message authentication code on the tuple will not match the attribute Tag. If the computed value of tag does not match with the attribute Tag for any tuple then the verification process rejects by returning ⊥. Moreover in line 2 it checks whether each tuple in S_α do satisfy the specified query. If the verification process does not terminate in the α-Verify phase then it means that the tuples in S_α are all valid tuples of the relation R_α and they all satisfy the specified query q_α. The other two parts of the verification process checks the completeness of the response.

Corresponding to each condition Name $= v$ AND SearchKey $=$ w in q_β the procedure makeBitMap constructs the corresponding bitmap $\text{BitMap}_{R_\alpha}(v,w)$ using the server response S_α. Note that if the server response S_α is correct then makeBitMap would be able to construct the bitmaps corresponding to each condition in q_β correctly. This is possible due to the specific type of the allowed queries. Recall that an allowed query is formed only by the disjunctions of equality conditions. In the procedure corresponding to the l conditions in q_β, l bitmaps are constructed which are named $X_1, \ldots, X_l$ (See the example later for more explanation).

In the procedure β-Verify the response S_β is verified using the bitmaps $X_1, \ldots, X_l$ constructed before. The procedure β-Verify first verifies whether S_β contains tuples corresponding to each condition in q_β, this is done using the counter $T[i]$, where i runs over the conditions in q_β. Notice, that for every condition C_i^β the server must return only one tuple in S_β. The other parts of the procedure involves in verifying the tags of the tuples against the tag's of the computed bitmaps.

To make the exposition clearer let us consider the same example we have so far considered, i.e., the relation $R1$ the queries $Q1_\alpha$, $Q1_\beta$ and the corresponding server responses of $S1_\alpha$ and $S1_\beta$ (which are shown in Table 3). Given these responses the procedure α-Verify will not terminate, as all the tuples in $S1_\alpha$ do satisfy the conditions in $Q1_\alpha$ and as they are correct responses in the sense that they are just copies of the tuples present in the relation R_α, hence the corresponding message authentication codes will match. Given the responses in $S1_\alpha$, one can compute the bitmaps $\mathsf{BitMap}_{R_\alpha}(\mathtt{Gender}, M)$ and $\mathsf{BitMap}_{R_\alpha}(\mathtt{Level}, L_2)$. To see this, see the response $S1_\alpha$ in Table 3, where it says that the tuples satisfying the condition $\mathtt{Gender}{=}M$ OR $\mathtt{Level}{=}L_2$ are the tuples with the nonce values 1, 3 and 6. Now, as the verification procedure has as input the whole of response $S1_\alpha$, hence it can predict correctly that the rows with the nonce value 1 and 3 satisfies the condition $\mathtt{Gender}{=}M$ and all the tuples in $S1_\alpha$ (i.e., with nonce values 1, 3, 6) satisfies the condition $\mathtt{Level}{=}L_2$. Thus, knowing that the total number of tuples in R_α to be 6, and assuming that server response is complete then the bitmap can be computed as $\mathsf{BitMap}_{R_\alpha}(\mathtt{Gender}, M) = 101000$. Note that the 1st and 3rd bits of this bitmap are only one, as it corresponds to the response in $S1_\alpha$. Similarly one can compute $\mathsf{BitMap}_{R_\alpha}(\mathtt{Level}, L_2) = 101001$. This is precisely what the procedure makeBitMaps would do for the example that we consider. The computation of the individual bitmaps $\mathsf{BitMap}_{R_\alpha}(\mathtt{Gender}, M)$ and $\mathsf{BitMap}_{R_\alpha}(\mathtt{Level}, L_2)$ are possible from $S1_\alpha$ as the $Q1_\alpha$ query is a disjunction of equality conditions, if in the contrary the query was a conjunction of conditions then there would be no way to compute the individual bitmaps in a straightforward way, this explains the reason for the query restriction that we impose.

Once these bitmaps are computed by using the procedure β-Verify one can verify the correctness of the response $S1_\beta$. As one can concatenate corresponding the bitmaps computed by the procedure makeBitMaps with the other attributes of the tuples in S_β and compute the tag using the message authentication code and thus verify if the computed tag matches the attribute Tag1.

The procedure β-Verify basically verifies the correctness of the response S_β, this verification is done by using the bitmaps constructed using the response S_α. The correctness of the response S_β implies the completeness of the response S_α.

4.1 Security of RDAS1

We can distinguish two possibilities for breaking RDAS1: infringe the correctness or violate the completeness of the response for a fixed query. To break the correctness the opponent must make changes in one or more tuples of S_α and still pass the verification process. This implies that the adversary must forge the respective MACs. On the other hand, to violate the completeness, the adversary must change the respective bitmaps in S_β which also implies forging the respective MACs. Now, we introduce this notion in a formal way.

Theorem 1. *Consider an arbitrary adversary $\mathcal{A}$ attacking* RDAS1 *in the sense of definition 1. Let $\mathcal{A}$ choose a relation R with* nT *tuples and the relation be such that the transformed relation R_β contains n' tuples. Then there exist an adversary $\mathcal{B}$ attacking the message authentication code* MAC *such that*

$$\Pr[\mathrm{Succ}_{\mathcal{A}}] \leq \Pr[\mathcal{B} \text{ forges }].$$

Also, B asks at most nT $+ n'$ *queries to its oracle and runs for time $t_{\mathcal{A}} + ($nT $+ n')(c + t_{\mathrm{MAC}})$, where $t_{\mathcal{A}}$ is the running time of $\mathcal{A}$, t_{MAC} is the time for one MAC computation and c is a constant.*

For space limitations we skip the proof, it would be presented in the full version, which would be published in the IACR eprint archive.

4.2 Costs and Overheads

Storage Cost: Given a relation $R(B)$ with nT tuples, let $\mathsf{size}(t_i[b])$ denote the size of the attribute b in the tuple t. Then the total size of R (which we also denote by $\mathsf{size}(R)$) would be given by

$$\mathsf{size}(R) = \sum_{i=1}^{\mathsf{nT}} \sum_{b \in B} \mathsf{size}(t_i[b]).$$

If this relation R is converted into (R_α, R_β) with RDAS1.F, then we would have,

$$\mathsf{size}(R_\alpha) = \mathsf{size}(R) + \sum_{i=1}^{\mathsf{nT}} (\mathsf{size}(t_i[\mathsf{Nonce}]) + \mathsf{size}(t_i[\mathsf{Tag}])),$$

if we assume a tag of constant length of τ bits then we would have

$$\mathsf{size}(R_\alpha) \leq \mathsf{size}(R) + \mathsf{nT}(\lg \mathsf{nT} + \tau).$$

Again considering the set of allowed attributes of R as $A = \{a_1, a_2, \ldots, a_m\}$, and $N = \sum_{i=1}^{m} \mathsf{Card}(a_i)$, we will have

$$\mathsf{size}(R_\beta) = \sum_{i=1}^{N} (\mathsf{size}(t_i[\mathsf{Name}]) + t_i[\mathsf{SearchKey}] + t_i[\mathsf{RowNo}] + \mathsf{size}(t_i[\mathsf{Tag1}])).$$

If we consider s_{Name} and s_{sk} the maximum size of the values of the attributes Name and SearchKey, then we would have

$$\mathsf{size}(R_\beta) \leq N(s_{\mathsf{Name}} + s_{\mathsf{sk}} + \lg(\mathsf{nT} + N) + \tau).$$

The total cost of storage at the server side would be $\text{size}(R_\alpha) + \text{size}(R_\beta)$, and at the client side would be $\lg(n\mathsf{T})$ as in the client we need to store the number of tuples in the original relation.

Communication Cost: Consider the query SELECT * FROM R_α WHERE $a_1 = v_1$ OR $a_2 = v_2$ OR ...... OR $a_l = v_l$, let the number of tuples satisfying the query be num. Let siz be the size of the response in a normal scenario without authentication. Then the maximum size of the server response in case of RDAS1 would be

$$\text{siz}_{\text{RD1}} = \text{siz} + \text{num} \times (\lg n\mathsf{T} + \tau) + l \times (s_{\text{Name}} + s_{\text{sk}} + \lg(n\mathsf{T} + N) + \tau), \quad (1)$$

where the first two terms corresponds to the S_α response and the remaining term counts for the S_β response.

5   Selects Involving Arbitrary Boolean Connectives

Here we propose an extension of RDAS1 which can support queries of the form

$Q:$ SELECT * FROM R WHERE $(a_1 = v_1)$ Δ_1 $(a_2 = v_2)$ Δ_2 ...... Δ_{l-1} $(a_l = v_l)$,

where Δ_is are arbitrary Boolean connectives. An easy solution to this case would be to change RDAS1 to a new protocol RDAS2 along the following lines:

1. The relation R_β produced by RDAS2.$\mathcal{F}$ would contain explicit bitmaps corresponding to the attributes and the values. Specifically, the attributes present in R_β should be {Name, SearchKey, RowNo, bitmap, tag1}. Thus, for creating the relation R_β we need to add a line $t_j^{R_\beta}[\text{bitmap}] \leftarrow \text{BitMap}_R(\mathcal{L}_j^1, \mathcal{L}_j^2)$ after line 5 in the procedure **Creating** R_β in Fig. 1.
2. The query translation procedure and the response procedure for RDAS2 remains same as that of RDAS1.
3. The response procedure also remains the same, i.e., the server just answers the q_α and q_β queries, but as the R_β relation now explicitly contains the bitmaps, hence the bitmaps would also be a part of the query.
4. For the verification procedure in RDAS2 it is not required to create the bitmaps any more, the client verifies the S_α response by the procedure α-Verify in Fig. 2, then it verifies the tags of the individual bitmaps returned in S_β and finally computes the result bitmap using the returned bitmap and checks if the result bitmap matches with the result returned.

We now state the storage and communication costs for RDAS2 following the notations in Section 4.2. The size of R_α in case of RDAS2 would be the same as in RDAS1, the size of R_β would be

$$\text{size}(R_\beta) \leq N(s_{\text{Name}} + s_{\text{sk}} + \lg(n\mathsf{T} + N) + \tau + n\mathsf{T}).$$

The size of a server response in case of RDAS2 would be

$$\mathsf{siz}_{RD2} = \mathsf{siz}_{RD1} + l \times \mathsf{nT} \tag{2}$$

where siz_{RD1} is the size of the response of RDAS1, as given in Eq. (1). In case of RDAS2, though we state that the bitmaps are to be explicitly stored in the relation R_β, but as most commercial data bases uses bitmaps indices for accelerating query processing, hence this may not amount to extra storage in some systems. Moreover bitmaps can be compressed, there has been substantial work on suitable encoding of bitmaps such that their sizes can be reduced and the Boolean operations be applied on the compressed bitmaps [1, 2]. Applying proper encoding of the bitmaps can drastically reduce both storage and communication costs. Details about this would appear in the full version of the paper.

6   Experimental Results

In this section we discuss some experimental results on the performance of RDAS1 and RDAS2. Both RDAS1 and RDAS2 can be implemented with any secure MAC, we chose PMAC instantiated with an AES with 128 bit key (we use the description in [17]). For implementation of AES we use the new Intel dedicated instructions for it.

All results were obtained by testing the implementation in a four-core i5-2400 Intel processor (3.1GHz) machine, with a Ubuntu 12.04.02 LTS operating system. We used PostgreSQL 9.1.9 for our database and used the gcc 4.7.3 compiler.

We used Census-Income data set [4] to test performance of our schemes. This data contains weighted census data extracted from the 1994 and 1995 current population surveys conducted by the U.S. Census Bureau. The number of instances in the data set is 199523. The data contains 42 demographic and employment related variables, the sum of the cardinalities of all the attributes is 103419, and the total size of the dataset size is 99.1 MB.

The experiments were performed using the set of queries presented in Table 4 (a). Table 4 (a) shows the characteristics of the queries in terms of the number of restrictions and the size of the query response, all of them are disjunctions of equality conditions. The last column shows the percentage of the response size in terms of the whole database size. Note that the number of restrictions corresponds to the number of tuples which would be included in a correct and complete S_β response and the response size would be same as the number of tuples in the S_α result. In Table 4 (b) we report the time required for executing the set of queries in Table 4 (a). We report times for normal execution (i.e. without any authentication) and RDAS1 and RDAS2. All reported times are the average of 250 executions of the same query. The response sizes for the queries can be easily computed using equations (1) and (2). For concrete numerical values see the full version.

Table 4. Performance Information

(a) Summary of the different queries used for performance testing

Query Id	Number of Restrictions	Response Size (tuples)	Database Percentage
Q1	10	20115	10
Q2	20	35452	18
Q3	30	92791	46
Q4	40	106065	53
Q5	50	198869	99

(b) Execution times for OR queries. All times are in milliseconds.

Query Id	Normal time	RDAS1 Avg time	RDAS1 Extra Overhead(%)	RDAS2 Avg time	RDAS2 Extra Overhead(%)
Q1	680.93	829.33	21.79	827.06	21.46
Q2	1223.09	1652.09	47.10	1516.33	35.01
Q3	2784.97	4076.28	46.36	3604.09	29.41
Q4	3192.06	4582.93	43.58	4004.43	25.45
Q5	6130.07	10781.05	75.87	9222.51	50.45

7   Conclusion

We presented RDAS a generic framework for authenticated query processing and provided the syntax and security definition of a RDAS. We also provided two concrete constructions RDAS1 and RDAS2 which uses bitmap indices and message authentication codes in a novel way. There are other ways in which RDAS1 and RDAS2 can be improved, for example communication costs can be drastically reduced using aggregate message authentication codes. These possibilities would be discussed in the full version of the paper.

Acknowledgements. The authors acknowledge the support from CONACYT project 166763.

References

1. Chan, C.Y., Ioannidis, Y.E.: Bitmap index design and evaluation. In: Haas, L.M., Tiwary, A. (eds.) SIGMOD Conference, pp. 355–366. ACM Press (1998)
2. Chan, C.Y., Ioannidis, Y.E.: An efficient bitmap encoding scheme for selection queries. In: Delis, A., Faloutsos, C., Ghandeharizadeh, S. (eds.) SIGMOD Conference, pp. 215–226. ACM Press (1999)
3. Devanbu, P.T., Gertz, M., Martel, C.U., Stubblebine, S.G.: Authentic data publication over the internet. Journal of Computer Security 11(3), 291–314 (2003)
4. Frank, A., Asuncion, A.: UCI machine learning repository (2010)
5. Goodrich, M.T., Tamassia, R., Triandopoulos, N.: Super-efficient verification of dynamic outsourced databases. In: Malkin, T. (ed.) CT-RSA 2008. LNCS, vol. 4964, pp. 407–424. Springer, Heidelberg (2008)
6. Hacigümüs, H., Mehrotra, S., Iyer, B.R.: Providing database as a service. In: ICDE, p. 29. IEEE Computer Society (2002)
7. Li, F., Hadjieleftheriou, M., Kollios, G., Reyzin, L.: Dynamic authenticated index structures for outsourced databases. In: Chaudhuri, S., Hristidis, V., Polyzotis, N. (eds.) SIGMOD Conference, pp. 121–132. ACM (2006)

8. Merkle, R.C.: A certified digital signature. In: Brassard, G. (ed.) CRYPTO 1989. LNCS, vol. 435, pp. 218–238. Springer, Heidelberg (1990)
9. Mouratidis, K., Sacharidis, D., Pang, H.: Partially materialized digest scheme: an efficient verification method for outsourced databases. VLDB J. 18(1), 363–381 (2009)
10. Mykletun, E., Narasimha, M., Tsudik, G.: Authentication and integrity in outsourced databases. In: NDSS, The Internet Society (2004)
11. Narasimha, M., Tsudik, G.: DSAC: integrity for outsourced databases with signature aggregation and chaining. In: Herzog, O., Schek, H.-J., Fuhr, N., Chowdhury, A., Teiken, W. (eds.) CIKM, pp. 235–236. ACM (2005)
12. Narasimha, M., Tsudik, G.: Authentication of outsourced databases using signature aggregation and chaining. In: Li Lee, M., Tan, K.-L., Wuwongse, V. (eds.) DASFAA 2006. LNCS, vol. 3882, pp. 420–436. Springer, Heidelberg (2006)
13. Nuckolls, G.: Verified query results from hybrid authentication trees. In: Jajodia, S., Wijesekera, D. (eds.) Data and Applications Security 2005. LNCS, vol. 3654, pp. 84–98. Springer, Heidelberg (2005)
14. Palazzi, B., Pizzonia, M., Pucacco, S.: Query racing: Fast completeness certification of query results. In: Foresti, S., Jajodia, S. (eds.) Data and Applications Security and Privacy XXIV. LNCS, vol. 6166, pp. 177–192. Springer, Heidelberg (2010)
15. Pang, H., Jain, A., Ramamritham, K., Tan, K.-L.: Verifying completeness of relational query results in data publishing. In: Özcan, F. (ed.) SIGMOD Conference, pp. 407–418. ACM (2005)
16. Pang, H., Zhang, J., Mouratidis, K.: Scalable verification for outsourced dynamic databases. PVLDB 2(1), 802–813 (2009)
17. Rogaway, P.: Efficient instantiations of tweakable blockciphers and refinements to modes OCB and PMAC. In: Lee, P.J. (ed.) ASIACRYPT 2004. LNCS, vol. 3329, pp. 16–31. Springer, Heidelberg (2004)
18. Wrembel, R., Koncilia, C.: Data warehouses and OLAP: concepts, architectures, and solutions. Gale virtual reference library. IRM Press (2007)
19. Yang, Y., Papadopoulos, S., Papadias, D., Kollios, G.: Spatial outsourcing for location-based services. In: Alonso, G., Blakeley, J.A., Chen, A.L.P. (eds.) ICDE, pp. 1082–1091. IEEE (2008)
20. Zheng, Q., Xu, S., Ateniese, G.: Efficient query integrity for outsourced dynamic databases. IACR Cryptology ePrint Archive, 2012:493 (2012)

Socio-Technical Study
on the Effect of Trust and Context
When Choosing WiFi Names

Ana Ferreira[1,2], Jean-Louis Huynen[1,2], Vincent Koenig[1,2],
Gabriele Lenzini[2], and Salvador Rivas[1]

[1] Educational Measurement and Applied Cognitive Science
[2] Interdisciplinary Centre for Security Reliability and Trust
Univ. of Luxembourg, Luxembourg (LU)
{firstname.lastname}@uni.lu

Abstract. We study trust and context as factors influencing how people choose wireless network names. Our approach imagines the mindset of a hypothetical attacker whose goal is to ensnare unsuspecting victims into accessing dishonest WiFi access points. For this purpose, we conducted an online survey. We used two separate forms. The first form asked a random group of participants to rate a list of wireless names according to their preferences (some real and others purposely made-up) and afterwards with implied trust in mind. The second form was designed to assess the effect of context and it asked a different set of respondents to rate the same list of wireless names in relation to four different contexts. Our results provide some evidence confirming the idea that trust and context can be exploited by an attacker by purposely, or strategically, naming WiFi access points with reference to trust or within certain contexts. We suggest, in certain cases, possible defence strategies.

1 Introduction

Even "secure" systems can turn out to be vulnerable when attackers target not the system and its security mechanisms but the people interacting with it. In such situations, security is not a purely technical property but rather a socio-technical quality stemming from factors such as people's behaviours with regard to technology and the underline cognitive and psychological factors.

Can we protect systems whose weaknesses lay in the behaviours and minds of users? Likely we can, but not without better understanding how the "user component" works. A few general behavioural and cognitive principles have been identified (e.g., see [1–7]), but socio-technical security is mostly newly evolving research.

While security experts are just starting to explore this new field, hackers already master the art. They usually know the "user component" more deeply than do average security engineers. They also have an advantage: finding one vulnerability is easier than protecting the whole system, which requires finding and fixing all vulnerabilities. However, this duality offers us an interesting perspective: we can take the intruder's viewpoint, plan and assess socio-technical

R. Accorsi and S. Ranise (Eds.): STM 2013, LNCS 8203, pp. 131–143, 2013.

attacks, then change hats and take the security engineering side, this time trying to patch the discovered vulnerabilities.

To illustrate this, we imagine the mind-set of an attacker who intends to set-up a fake WiFi access point and who speculates on the best strategy to name it to "phish" people. A good strategy could be to choose names that relate to trust and/or context.

Trust is a catalyst factor in many indirect/remote interactions as the ones daily happening over the Internet (e.g., [8, 9]). By addressing this element, we are interested in understanding whether people think spontaneously of trust when choosing names or whether instead they need to be hinted before the idea of trust triggers in their mind. If trust is feeble in people's minds, an attacker could easily deviate people's trust onto something that can be controlled, but if it is strong, the attacker could still plan to gain people's trust, as it is usually done, by impersonating the object of trust (cf. Section 4).

Context, at least in this paper, is the physical or the social space where actions and decisions occur (e.g., in a laboratory, at work, at home). By addressing context we are interested in understanding whether this factor has an effect on people's choices of names. If that is true, an attacker can be more effective by contextualising his/her attack or by fooling users to be in a context favourable to him/her. However, this brings new ideas on how to contain these context-exploiting attacks, for example by securing the access to the context (cf. Section 4).

In summary, the aim of this paper is to present a study that investigates the effect that trust and context have on users when choosing wireless network names. Our study relates to decisions that do not require complex probabilities, balancing risks, or evaluating security with respect to goals: in such complex scenarios, user choices are ruled by principles of mental economics [3, 4], out-of-scope here.

1.1   Use-Case Scenario

Our hypothetical use-case scenario consists of a set of wireless network names (SSIDs), various locations, and a user. The user is expected to scan and choose an SSID from a list of names that his/her device detects to get Internet access. This can happen in four different well known locations: the university, a shopping mall (a specific one), the city centre, and a hospital (a specific one).

On the other hand, our scenario imagines an attacker whose intent is to deploy a dishonest WiFi base station. This station's name will appear in the list of available SSIDs that the user can browse from its device. The attacker seeks to maximize the number of victims, so s/he looks for alluring names that inspire security, convenience, or trustworthiness with names such as 'secured_hotspot', or takes advantage of the location to inspire legitimacy with names such as 'wifi_unilu'. Table 1 shows a comprehensive view of the 12 SSIDs used in this study, including those existing and those made up. The SSIDs have been carefully compiled: they may or may not exist in the region where the study was conducted, evoke security or freeness, or be location-specific.

Table 1. Existing/nonexistent wireless names and their grouping in relation to security and context. Security: (G1-existing; G2-nonexistent; G3-nonexistent and related to security; G4-nonexistent and not related to security). Context: (L1-existing and expected in the context; L2-existing and not expected in the context; L3-nonexistent and expected in the context; L4-nonexistent and not expected in the context).

	G1	G2	G3	G4	University				City Center				Shopping				Hospital			
					L1	L2	L3	L4	L1	L2	L3	L4	L1	L2	L3	L4	L1	L2	L3	L4
eduroam																				
uni-visitor																				
uni-student																				
wifi_unilu																				
hotcity																				
Hotel_le_Place_D'Armes																				
Cafe_de_Paris																				
secured_hotspot																				
secure_wifi_BelleEtoile																				
free_wifi_BelleEtoile																				
Maroquinerie_Kirchberg																				
free_AP																				

Research Questions. We intend to answer two research questions about preferences in wireless network names:
(RQ1): *Does thinking about trust affect participants' preferences?* (RQ2): *Does context affect participants' preferences?*

2   The Survey

For reasons of feasibility and ethics we opted for a survey rather than an experimental setup, the latter being e.g., the setup of a "malicious" access point airing different SSIDs. Our survey asks respondents to rate a list of SSIDs according to their preferences while excluding technical aspects such as signal strength or protected access. We also question them about their sense of trust or in relation to specific contexts. Our survey relies on an online questionnaire rather than a paper-pencil version that would have required a large logistical effort to field and to encode, while not offering the same level of convenience to the respondent. The questionnaire was structured into four parts: (1) the socio-demographics part that surveys respondents about their age, gender, education, IT skills and comfort using IT; (2) the "general preferences" part that lists 12 SSIDs the respondents are asked to rate with regard to their general preferences based on a 5 point Likert scale (i.e., 1-Not at all preferred, 2-Not very preferred, 3-Neutral, 4-Preferred, 5-Most preferred), respectively; (3) the "trust" part lists the same 12 SSIDs and asks respondents to rate them with special regard to trust when connecting/avoiding them (i.e., 1-Not at all trusted, 2-Not very trusted, 3-Neutral, 4-Trusted, 5-Highly trusted); (4) the "context" part consists of 4 specific and familiar locations, each of these locations listing the same 12 SSIDs, asking respondents to rate them regarding specific contexts when connecting/avoiding them (same Likert scale as for the general preferences).

Table 2. Sociodemographics for the population of the survey for conditions 1 and 2

Demographics	Condition 1 (n=59)	Condition 2 (n=40)	Total (n=99)
Female	36%	58%	45%
Male	64%	42%	55%
Age (average)	27%	25%	26%
High School	19%	28%	22%
Bachelor Degree	49%	50%	49%
Master Degree	20%	7%	15%
PhD	10%	13%	11%
Very comfortable using IT	69%	73%	70%
Somewhat comfortable using IT	27%	25%	26%
Very good IT skills	34%	23%	29%
Good IT skills	37%	60%	46%
Average IT skills	25%	15%	21%

The instructions provided to the respondents have been translated from English to German and French in order to accommodate the multilingual population of Luxembourg and surrounding areas. The respondents were randomly associated with one of two conditions. Condition 1 is designed to assess the effect of trust by administering the following questionnaire parts to each assigned respondent: socio-demographic → general preference → trust. Condition 2 is designed to assess the effect of context with respondents answering the following parts: socio-demographic → general preference → context. We recruited participants by sending an invitation via email to students and staff from the University of Luxembourg.

Data were collected within a MySql database and exported to a CSV file format. Statistical analyses were done using the R statistical analysis software [10]. The collected data were analysed using basic descriptive statistics, followed by specific analysis of variance tests (t-tests [11] and Wilcoxon rank [12] tests) in order to assess the significant differences between general preferences and the trust condition (cf. condition 1, RQ1) and between general preferences and the context condition (cf. condition 2, RQ2). In order to apply t-tests on data derived from Likert scales, we systematically verified its normal distribution and also employed the Wilcoxon signed-rank test to further support t-test results. We also included open questions (analysed manually) that allowed respondents to provide the rationale for their ratings.

3   Results

A total of 235 participants took part in our study; however our analysis focuses on the 99 completed cases (136 cases have not been fully completed and thus have not been considered for analysis). As shown in Table 2 our sample is rather balanced with regard to gender. On average our respondents are rather young (age 26), mostly highly educated (over 75% have a bachelor degree or higher), very IT literate and highly skilled (75%).

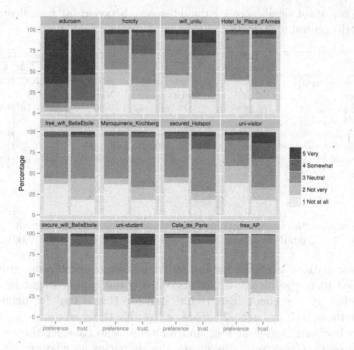

Fig. 1. General preferences vs. trust. in condition 1 for each SSID.

Next, we present the results obtained for conditions 1 and 2. Whenever possible, we proceed by first describing general tendencies as visualized through graphical representations, followed by more specific analyses whose results are presented as tables. Differences between repeated measures have systematically been computed as follows: measure 2 − measure 1. Negative differences suggest than on average measure 1 > measure 2 and positive values suggest measure 2 > measure 1. More precisely, a negative value indicates a decrease in trust/preferences and conversely a positive value suggests an increase in trust/preference. The statistical tests inform us on the significance of these differences.

3.1 Trust

Fig. 1 displays general preference and trust results side-by-side for all 12 SSIDs in condition 1. In general we find a tendency towards higher preference ratings (except for eduroam) when invoking trust. This is illustrated by a systematic change in the extremes of the Likert scores, shown in Fig. 1 (cf. RQ1), change that happens regardless of the name's properties (existing, open, secure, etc.). A large proportion of the respondents report a neutral preference for each of the wireless network names.

Table 3.(a) shows the significant results for the whole sample, indicating that on average the shift from general preferences to trust was towards a more discerning preference (higher positive values).

Table 3. Statistical significance for the differences between: (a) general preferences and trust; (b) general preferences and trust but for groups G1-G4

	Diff. (trust pref.)
Whole sample	0.38**#
Male	0.32*#
≤ 24 years old	0.49**#
> 24 years old	-
≤ Bachelor Degree	0.40*#
> Bachelor Degree	-
≤ Good IT skills	0.50**#

(a)

	Diff. (trust pref. Gx)			
	G1	G2	G3	G4
Whole sample	0.32***###	0.45*	0.47*	0.44*
Males	0.30**###	-	-	-
≤ 24 years old	0.40**##	0.59*	0.70*	0.53*
> 24 years old	0.23*	-	-	-
≤ Bachelor Degree	0.31**##	0.49*	-	0.47*
> Bachelor Degree	0.34*##	-	-	-
≤ Good IT skills	0.40**##	0.59*	0.62*	0.58*

(b)

Legend: For all tables superscripts have the following meaning: t-test result: $^*p < 0.05$; $^{**}p < 0.01$; $^{***}p < 0.001$. Wilcoxon result: $^\#p < 0.05$; $^{\#\#}p < 0.01$; $^{\#\#\#}p < 0.001$.

A similar pattern is shown for the other socio-demographic sub-groups. We also studied more specifically what subgroups of our sample might be particularly affected by this effect. Test results indicate this is true for male participants, for those who are aged 24 years or less, for those who have successfully finished a bachelor degree or less, and for those who consider themselves not very IT literate. Conversely, this means that participants who are not part of these subgroups tend to be more cautious with their ratings in the condition of trust-awareness; our results suggest that age, general education and IT skills contribute to shaping these attitudes.

In addition to the preceding person-centric analysis, we analysed the data more closely under the perspective of wireless network names, allowing us e.g., to better understand whether the formerly described effects apply to all SSIDs or to subsets only. To this end, we grouped wireless network names with regard to our objectives of including them in our study.

Fig. 2 presents the results between general preferences and trust for the four groups G1-G4 (cf. Table 1). Table 3.(b) shows the t-test results for the difference in ratings between general preferences and trust, for each of the 4 groups.

The results suggest a strong and systematic effect of trust for G1, for the entire sample, except those participants who describe themselves to be very IT literate. Regarding fake SSIDs (G2), there is still an effect noticeable both for the entire sample and more specifically for subgroups of lower age, lower education and lower IT literacy. This pattern is almost identical for G3 (fake names related to security) and G4 (fake names not related to security). The effects demonstrated for G2, G3 and G4 require further attention as they especially indicate potentially unsafe user behaviour. It should be noted that participants who think themselves very IT literate do not demonstrate any effect of trust awareness and it might well be that these participants are aware of trust issues already when considering SSIDs.

Table 4 shows the results of the analysis of the open questions. The two most common reasons for participants' preferences are the fact that they use the

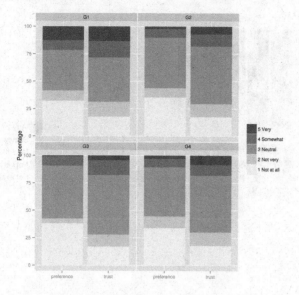

Fig. 2. General preferences vs. trust for groups G1-G4

Table 4. Most common reasons related to general preferences (G) and trust (T) for all choices, choices that change to nonexistent names (CPTUN), or to nonexistent names related to security (CPTSN), and that do not change from general preferences to trust

	All choices (n =53)		CPTUN (n =11)		CPTSN (n =10)		No change (n =18)	
	G	T	G	T	G	T	G	T
Do not use other networks	30	6	4	–	3	–	7	2
Do not know other networks	22	26	2	1	4	1	5	1
Security	13	3	3	1	-	-	2	2
Easy Access	8	-	-	-	-	-	2	-
Trust	3	10	-	3	-	1	-	1

networks or they know them, not necessarily because they consider them trusted or secured.

3.2 Context

Fig. 3 displays the SSID preference ratings for only 4 of the 12 names that show some change throughout the contexts (i.e., University, City Center, Shopping Mall and Hospital) as compared to the general and non-context dependent situation, which is labeled "generic" in the figure.

Table 5 shows the significant results about the effect that context awareness has on respondent's names preference ratings.

In contrast to the findings for condition 1, significant results in the context condition indicate a decrease in preference ratings when respondents are made aware of specific contexts. This applies to the University context where the effect

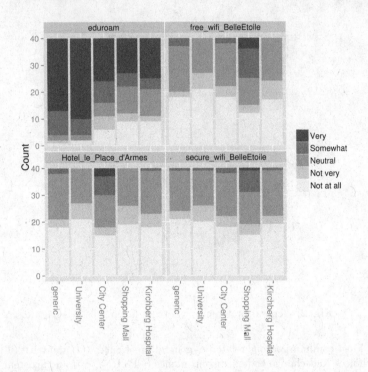

Fig. 3. Selection made for eduroam, Hotel_le_Place_d'Armes, secure_wifi_BelleEtoile and free-wifi_BelleEtoile within the four contexts by all participants of condition 2

is demonstrated for the entire sample of respondents and, only for specific sample groups in the shopping mall and hospital context. The shopping mall indeed seems to demonstrate an effect specifically for female respondents and for those who are more educated. This is also true for the hospital context, the results indicate an effect for respondents aged more than 24 years old. These effects indicate that these respondents may be more aware when choosing a name for those three contexts.

Similar to our analysis for condition 1, we completed our analysis for condition 2 by a specific name grouping, illustrated in Table 1.

Table 5. Statistical significance for the differences between general preferences and the contexts (in this case, there is no statistical significance for the context "city center")

	Difference (Context preference-generic preference)		
	University	Shopping Mall	Hospital
Whole sample	-0.15*♯	-	-
Females	-	-0.23*♯	-0.33*♯
> 24 years old	-	-	-0.27*♯
> bachelor degree	-	-0.32*	-0.37*♯

Fig. 4 compares between general preferences and the four groups (L1-L4) for all the contexts. Participants rate higher the SSIDs for L1 - existing and are expected within the university and the city center while in the other two contexts (e.g., shopping mall and the hospital) participants rate higher the names for L2 - existing but are not expected in that context. The figure also shows a tendency for participants to rate higher nonexistent wireless network names but which may be expected in the context (L3) (e.g., for the university, shopping mall and hospital contexts).

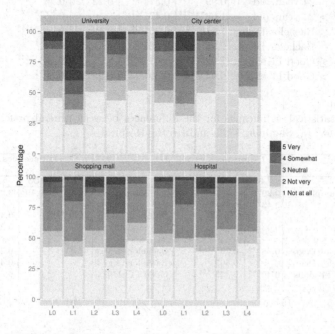

Fig. 4. General preferences in the 4 groups (L1-L4) for all the contexts

Table 6 provides an overview of the effects that the University context has on user's preferences. Group L1 of "existing names and expected in the context", are all affected by the university context in the sense that these names are rated higher, respondents thus being more cautious when context-aware. In contrast, group L2 of "existing names but not expected in the context", have been rated lower when awareness about the context was included, except for male respondents. The "nonexistent and not expected names in the context" (L4) have systematically been rated lower. Finally, the "nonexistent and expected" names (L3) show a weaker effect on the entire sample and higher effects for subgroups of respondents younger than 24 years, with less than a bachelor degree, or proficient with IT.

Table 7.(a) provides an overview of the effects that the shopping mall context has on user's preferences. This context seems to be associated with a less

Table 6. Statistical significance for the differences between general preferences and the context of the University

	Differences (L* − generic)			
	L1	**L2**	**L3**	**L4**
Whole sample	1.00***###	-0.40***###	-0.10#	-0.47***###
Males	0.86***###	-	-	-0.48**###
Females	1.10***###	-0.50***###	-	-0.46***###
≤ 24 years old	0.99***###	-0.37**##	-0.22#	-0.43***###
> 24 years old	1.03***###	-0.47**##	-	-0.55**##
≤ Bachelor Degree	1.01***###	-0.35**##	-0.18#	-0.40***###
> Bachelor Degree	0.95**#	-0.60**#	-	-0.71*#
≤ Good IT skills	1.02***###	-1.41***###	-	-0.46***###
> Good IT skills	0.94***##	-0.39*#	-0.22***#	-0.50*#

Table 7. Statistical significance for the differences between general preferences and the context for: (a) Shopping Mall, and (b) the Hospital

	Differences (L* − generic)	
	L3	**L4**
Whole sample	0.29*	-0.36**###
Male	0.43*#	-0.48***###
Female		
≤ 24 years old	0.43**#	-0.32*#
> 24 years old	-	-0.44**##
≤ Bachelor Degree	0.38**#	-0.30*##
> Bachelor Degree	-	-0.56**#
≤ Good IT skills	0.40**#	-0.43**###

(a)

	Differences (L* − generic)		
	L1	**L3**	**L4**
Whole sample	-	-0.19#	-0.28*#
Males	0.69*	-	-
Females	-0.49***##	-	-0.44***###
≤ 24 years old	-	-	-0.22#
> 24 years old	-	-	-0.40**##
≤ Bachelor Degree	-	-	-0.22#
> Bachelor Degree	-	-	-0.49**#
≤ Good IT skills	-	-	-0.32*##

(b)

pronounced effect on user response patterns as there is no significant difference for groups L1 and L2. However, there is a series of effects indicating a rating increase in subgroup L3 and a general decrease in ratings for L4.

Table 7(b) provides an overview of the effects that the hospital context has on user's preferences. This context is associated with few significant effects. Results for L1 indicate positive ratings for males while the opposite for female respondents. There is also a decrease in ratings for the whole respondent sample in L3. And finally, consistent with results in Table 7(a), L4 names are systematically rated lower, except for male respondents.

Table 8 shows the results for the open questions relating to context. Again, the most common reasons relate to the use and knowledge of the network names, and that they provide easy access. To note that outside the University context, the most common reason states clearly that the place where the participants are, can greatly influence their choices.

Table 8. Most common reasons for general preferences and each context

	General pref.	University	City Centre	Shopping Mall	Hospital
Do not use other networks	34	11	7	3	2
Do not know other networks	15	8	7	-	-
Easy Access	9	7	5	2	3
Security	5	1	3	3	1
Place where I am	-	-	9	10	2

4   Security Discussion

In our scenario the attacker pondered the best strategy for naming his malicious SSID to "hook" the most people to choose it when accessing the Internet. The results of our survey show three main elements that could make our attacker more successful.

Trust. Let us look at Fig. 1. It compares the preferences before and after for the entire sample. Let us focus on the two highest ratings, "very preferred" and "somewhat preferred": when taken together they indicate a positive preference.

For all network names, with the puzzling exception of "eduroam" (commented in the next paragraph) the preference of a network has increased after people have been asked to think about trust. This seems to indicate that an attacker can gain people's trust by suggesting trust in the name, at least if he uses names similar to the ones we use in our study. Fig. 2 shows, in fact, that the increment in preference is almost the same regardless whether the network name exists or not. We therefore conclude that an attacker would be more effective by suggesting or including the word "trust" in the network name itself. If this hypothesis were true, names that hint "trust" should rate better than those suggesting "security" or "freeness"; proving or disproving this claim is left as future work.

We comment now the small drop in trust regarding 'eduroam'. From the analysis of the open answers it emerges that people said to prefer 'eduroam' because they know the network (= have been told to use it); however they said to trust 'eduroam' only indirectly (or better comparatively), that is they do not know whether to trust the other networks. Therefore there is reason to believe that people chose 'eduroam' by habit, which is a known principle of mental economics. It would be interesting to test whether people would still use 'eduroam' (by habit) in contexts outside the University (i.e., the Shopping Mall), where this network has no reason to exist. This would be an attack to implement with little effort.

Context. The discussion about context is less straightforward. Fig. 3 shows that people prefer a network that communicates a context-specific meaning. For example, the made-up 'free_wifi_BelleEtoile' rated higher in the shopping mall context than in general (Belle Etoile is an existing shopping mall, where there is no existing SSID reminding that name). This can appear obvious, but Fig. 4, which shows the results for groups gives more useful insights. In the context "Shopping Mall" the increment is positive for all the made-up networks that refer to it (e.g., cf. Table 7.(a) first row, first column); but in context "University" this does not happen. Here, made-up names referring to the context (group $L3$, which includes 'wifi_unilu' for example) rated less on average (cf. Table 6 first row, third column)[1].

Our sample, mostly students and employees of the university, know better what network is available at the university. They do not expect networks to appear without notice. Thus, the strategy of contextualizing names has less impact at the university, at least for the possible victims who regularly frequent the university, as our population. However, it may work for guests or visitors, who may not be so aware of what access point exists.

In fact, in contexts like the shopping mall, the same strategy of contextualizing made-up names works nicely: those names out-rate the existing ones. An attacker targeting public places can thus increase odds by including the context in the name of a dishonest base station. Conferences, for example, are sites where such an attack could work very well.

What could be a recommendation to prevent such kinds of attacks? One suggestion, which could be tested for efficacy, would be to advertise the names of legitimate networks, for example by deploying stickers informing visitors about the legitimate access points. (An attacker can do the same, but this requires him to work and expose himself more). Another defence consists in avoiding to leave unused names which are related to the context. For example, a hotel should re-name SSID with the hotel's name. Such simple action is usually disregarded: it is common to see WiFi with the name of the router (e.g., 'linksys01') or with that of the network provider (e.g., 'Numericable_6A85').

5   Conclusion and Future Work

In this paper we tested a few hypothesis about how people are biased to choose WiFi access point names when we offer them a pool of names among which there are names of real WiFi networks, names that remind security and trust and names that relate with the current location (context).

Our result shows that, in familiar contexts, adding security or freeness in the names does not bias user's preferences; however, in unfamiliar contexts the choice of even expert people is biased towards names reminding the context. These results devise sever socio-technical attacks that can be easily launched by interfering with user's knowledge of the context. To contain those attacks we have suggested a few simple socio-technical defences. Testing whether these are effective in preventing people from falling victims of attacks was not in the scope of this paper, but needs to be proved and will be done as future work.

The study carried on in this paper has some limitations. We did not have a larger and more diversified population, as we had permission to broadcast our survey only within the university. The small sample size did not allow for more

---

[1] We got a similar despite weaker result for the context "Hospital" but with a different explanation. The contextualized name 'maroquinerie_Kirchberg' is ambiguous because Kirchberg is also the name of a large zone of the city where the hospital and many other offices stand, while Maroquinerie is out-of-context.

complex multivariate statistical analyses and we had less participants for condition 2 of the survey, as they had to fill more information. Also, not many participants filled the open questions. In addition to the experiment we plan to do, we would like to improve our survey and include more effective ways to characterize the participants (e.g., student - area of study, not student - area of work or research) so that we can identify specific characteristics that may help us better understand their different behaviours. We think it would also be useful to analyse in more detail each wireless network name separately and verify its statistical significance. It may be that one or two names have more meaning than others and can in themselves be used to improve or mitigate socio-technical attacks.

We would have liked to set up attacks with real WiFi access points in real places; however launching such actions and harvesting the data for the analysis requires an authorization from an ethical committee and a compliance with our legal framework, assurances that were not ready for this paper. We plan it as future work.

Acknowledgments. We thank E. François for helping with the on-line questionnaire and K. Weinerth and S. Doublet for the translations. This research is supported by FNR Luxembourg, project I2R-APS-PFN-11STAS.

References

1. Borgida, E., Nisbett, R.E.: The Differential Impact of Abstract vs. Concrete Information on Decisions. J. of Applied Social Phychology, 258–271 (1977)
2. Tversky, A., Kahneman, D.: Rational Choice and The Framining of Decisions. J. Business 59, 251–278 (1986)
3. Anderson, R.: Information Security Economics - and Beyond. In: van der Meyden, R., van der Torre, L. (eds.) DEON 2008. LNCS (LNAI), vol. 5076, p. 49. Springer, Heidelberg (2008)
4. Adams, A., Sasse, A.: Users Are Not the Enemy. Comm. ACM 42, 40–46 (1999)
5. West, R.: The Psychology of Security. Communication of the ACM 51(4), 34–38 (2008)
6. Dhamija, R., Tygar, J.D., Hearst, M.: Why phishing works. In: Proceedings of the SIGCHI Conference on Human Factors in Computing Systems, CHI 2006, pp. 581–590. ACM, New York (2006)
7. Sunshine, J., Egelman, S., Almuhimedi, H., Atri, N., Cranor, L.F.: Crying wolf: An empirical study of SSL warning effectiveness. In: Proc. of USENIX 2009 (2009)
8. Gambetta, D.: Can We Trust Trust? In: Gambetta, D. (ed.) Trust: Making and Breaking Cooperative Relatioins, ch. 13, pp. 213–237. Basil Blackwell (2000)
9. Castelfranchi, C., Falcone, R.: Trust Theory: A Socio-Cognitive and Computational Model. Wiley (2010)
10. R Development Core Team, R: A Language and Environment for Statistical Computing, R Foundation for Statistical Computing, Vienna, Austria (2008), http://www.R-project.org, ISBN 3-900051-07-0
11. Lehmann, E.L.: 'Student' and small-sample theory. Statistical Science 14, 418–426 (1999)
12. Wilcoxon, F.: Individual comparisons by ranking methods. Biometrics Bulletin 1(6), 80–83 (1945)

Probabilistic Cost Enforcement of Security Policies

Yannis Mallios[1], Lujo Bauer[1], Dilsun Kaynar[1],
Fabio Martinelli[2], and Charles Morisset[3]

[1] Carnegie Mellon University, Pittsburgh, PA, USA
[2] Istituto di Informatica e Telematica, National Research Council, Pisa, Italy
[3] Newcastle University, Newcastle, UK

Abstract. This paper presents a formal framework for run-time enforcement mechanisms, or monitors, based on probabilistic input/output automata [3,4], which allows for the modeling of complex and interactive systems. We associate with each trace of a monitored system (i.e., a monitor interposed between a system and an environment) a probability and a real number that represents the cost that the actions appearing on the trace incur on the monitored system. This allows us to calculate the probabilistic (expected) cost of the monitor and the monitored system, which we use to classify monitors, not only in the typical sense, e.g., as sound and transparent [17], but also at a more fine-grained level, e.g., as cost-optimal or cost-efficient. We show how a cost-optimal monitor can be built using information about cost and the probabilistic future behavior of the system and the environment, showing how deeper knowledge of a system can lead to construction of more efficient security mechanisms.

1 Introduction

A common approach to enforcing security policies on untrusted software is run-time monitoring. Run-time monitors, e.g., firewalls and intrusion detection systems, observe the execution of untrusted applications or systems, e.g., web browsers and operating systems, and ensure that their behavior adheres to a security policy.

Given the ubiquity of run-time monitors and the negative impact they have on the overall security of the system if they fail to operate correctly, it is important to have a good understanding of their behavior and strong guarantees about their correctness. Such guarantees can be achieved through the use of formal reasoning.

Schneider introduced security automata [22], an automata-based framework to formally model and reason about run-time enforcement of security policies. Several extensions have been proposed to investigate different definitions of and requirements for enforcement, such as soundness, transparency, and effectiveness (e.g., [17]). A common observation is that once requirements for enforcement are set more than one implementation of a monitor might be able to fulfill them.

Two examples of common run-time enforcement mechanisms are transport layer proxies and TCP scrubbers [18]. Both of these convert ambiguous TCP flows to unambiguous ones, thereby preventing attacks that seek to avoid detection by network intrusion detection systems (NIDS). Transport layer proxies interpose between a client and a server and create two connections: one between the client and the proxy, and one

R. Accorsi and S. Ranise (Eds.): STM 2013, LNCS 8203, pp. 144–159, 2013.
© Springer-Verlag Berlin Heidelberg 2013

between the proxy and the server. TCP scrubbers leave the bulk of the TCP processing to the end points: they maintain the current state of the connection and a copy of packets sent by the external host but not acknowledged by the internal receiver. Fig. 1 (adapted from [18]) depicts the differences between the two mechanisms in a specific scenario.

Although both mechanisms correctly enforce the same high-level "no ambiguity" policy, the proxy requires twice the amount of buffering as the scrubber, which suggests that the proxy is more costly (in terms of computational resources).

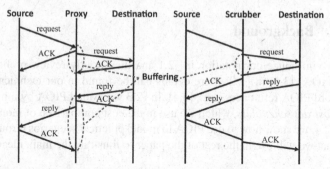

Fig. 1. TCP transport layer proxies and scrubbers. The circled portions represent the amount of time that data is buffered.

Recent work has started looking at cost as a metric to classify and compare such monitors. Drabik et al. introduced a framework that calculated the overall cost of enforcement based on costs assigned to the enforcement actions performed by the monitor [10]; this framework can be used to calculate and compare the cost of different monitors' implementations. This framework provides means to reason about cost-aware enforcement, but its enforcement model does not capture interactions between the target and its environment, including the monitor; recent work has shown that capturing such interactions can be valuable [19]. In addition, in practice the cost of running an application may depend on the ordering of its actions, which may in turn depend on the scheduling strategy. Finally, one might also wish to ensure that a monitor enforces a cost policy, which defines which costs are acceptable; practical cost policies can depend on a probabilistic model of the system's behavior, e.g., take into account the likelihood of particular events. For example, a security policy that describes how to protect a system against different attacks might depend on the probability that these attacks, e.g., a DDOS attack or insider attack, will occur against that particular system.

The main contribution of this paper is a formal framework that enables us to (1) model monitors that interact with probabilistic targets and environments (i.e., targets and environments whose behavior we can characterize probabilistically), (2) check whether such monitors enforce a given security policy, and (3) calculate and compare their cost of enforcement. More precisely:

1. Our framework is based on probabilistic I/O automata [3,4]. This allows us to reason about partially ordered events in distributed and concurrent systems, and the probabilities of events and sequences of events.
2. We extend probabilistic I/O automata with *abstract schedulers* to allow fair comparison of systems where a policy is enforced on a target by different monitors.
3. We define cost security policies and cost enforcement, richer notions of (boolean) security policies and enforcement [22]. Cost security policies assign a cost to each

trace, allowing richer classification of traces than just as bad or good. We also show how to encode boolean security policies as cost security policies.

4. Finally, we show how to use our framework to compare monitors' implementations and we identify the sufficient conditions for constructing cost-optimal monitors.

2 Background

We introduce our notation in §2.1 and then briefly review probabilistic I/O automata (PIOA) [3,4] in §2.2; more details can be found in our technical report [20] or standard PIOA references, e.g., [3,4]. In §2.3 we extend PIOA by introducing the notion of *abstract schedulers*, which we use in the cost comparison of monitors in §5. Finally, in §2.4, we show how to use PIOA to model practical scenarios through a running example that we will use in the rest of the paper to illustrate the main ideas of our framework.

2.1 Preliminaries

A σ-field over a set X is a set $\mathcal{F} \subseteq 2^X$ that contains the empty set and is closed under complement and countable union. A pair $(X, \mathcal{F})$ where $\mathcal{F}$ is a σ-field over X, is called a *measurable space*. A measure on a measurable space $(X, \mathcal{F})$ is a function $\mu : \mathcal{F} \to [0, \infty]$ that is countably additive: for each countable family $\{X_i\}_i$ of pairwise disjoint elements of $\mathcal{F}$, $\mu(\cup_i X_i) = \Sigma_i \mu(X_i)$.

A *probability measure* on $(X, \mathcal{F})$ is a measure on $(X, \mathcal{F})$ such that $\mu(X) = 1$. A *sub-probability measure* on $(X, \mathcal{F})$ is a measure on $(X, \mathcal{F})$ such that $\mu(X) \leq 1$. We use $\mathsf{Disc}(X)$ and $\mathsf{SubDisc}(X)$ to denote, respectively, the set of discrete probability measures and discrete sub-probability measures on X. If μ is a probability measure then use $\mathsf{supp}(\mu)$ to denote the set of elements that have non-zero measure. We let $\delta(x)$ denote the discrete probability measure that assigns probability 1 to $\{x\}$.

A *signed measure* on $(X, \mathcal{F})$ is a function $\nu : \mathcal{F} \to [-\infty, \infty]$ such that: (1) $\nu(\emptyset) = 0$, (2) ν assumes at most one of the values $\pm\infty$, and (3) for each countable family $\{X_i\}_i$ of pairwise disjoint elements of $\mathcal{F}$, $\nu(\cup_i X_i) = \Sigma_i \mu(X_i)$ with the sum converging absolutely if $\nu(\cup_i X_i)$ is finite.

Given two discrete measures μ_1, μ_2 we denote by $\mu_1 \times \mu_2$ the *product measure*, such that $\mu_1 \times \mu_2(x, y) = \mu_1(x) \cdot \mu_2(y)$ (i.e., component-wise multiplication).

A function $f : X \to Y$ is said to be measurable from $(X, \mathcal{F}_X) \to (Y, \mathcal{F}_Y)$ if the inverse image of each element of $\mathcal{F}_Y$ is an element of $\mathcal{F}_X$. Given measurable f from $(X, \mathcal{F}_X) \to (Y, \mathcal{F}_Y)$ and a measure μ on $(X, \mathcal{F}_X)$, the function $f(\mu)$ defined on $\mathcal{F}_Y$ by $f(\mu)(C) = \mu(f^{-1}(C))$ for each $C \in Y$ is a measure on $(Y, \mathcal{F}_Y)$ and is called the *image measure* of μ under f. If $\mathcal{F}_X = 2^X$, $\mathcal{F}_Y = 2^Y$, and μ is a sub-probability measure, then the image measure $f(\mu)$ is a sub-probability satisfying $f(\mu)(Y) = \mu(X)$.

2.2 Probabilistic I/O Automata

An *action signature* S is a triple of three disjoint sets of actions: *input*, *output*, and *internal* actions (denoted as $input(S)$, $output(S)$, and $internal(S)$). The *external* actions

$extern(S)=input(S) \cup output(S)$ model the interaction of the automaton with the environment. Given a signature S we write $acts(S)$ for the set of all actions contained in the signature, i.e., $acts(S) = input(S) \cup output(S) \cup internal(S)$.

A probabilistic I/O automaton (PIOA) P is a tuple $(sig(P), Q(P), \bar{q}_P, R(P))$, where: (1) $sig(P)$ is an action signature; (2) $Q(P)$ is a (possibly infinite) set of *states*; (3) $\bar{q}_P$ is a *start state*, with $\bar{q}_P \in Q(P)$; and (4) $R(P) \subseteq Q(P) \times acts(P) \times \mathsf{Disc}(Q(P))$ is a transition relation, where $\mathsf{Disc}(Q(P))$ is the set of discrete probability measures on $Q(P)$.

Given a PIOA P, we write $acts(P)$ for $acts(sig(P))$. We assume that P satisfies the following conditions: (i) *Input enabling:* For every state $q \in Q(P)$ and input action $\alpha \in input(P)$, α is enabled[1] in q; and (ii) *Transition determinism:* For every state $q \in Q(P)$ and action $\alpha \in acts(P)$, there is at most one $\mu \in \mathsf{Disc}(Q(P))$ such that $(q, \alpha, \mu) \in R(P)$. If there exists exactly one such μ, it is denoted by $\mu_{q,\alpha}$, and we write $\mathsf{tran}_{q,\alpha}$ for the transition $(q, \alpha, \mu_{q,\alpha})$.

A *non-probabilistic execution* e of P is either a finite sequence, $q_0, a_1, q_1, a_2, \ldots, a_r, q_r$, or an infinite sequence $q_0, a_1, q_1, a_2, \ldots, a_r, q_r, \ldots$ of alternating states and actions such that: (1) $q_0 = \bar{q}_P$, and (2) for every non-final i, there is a transition $(q_i, a_{i+1}, \mu) \in R(P)$ with $q_{i+1} \in \mathsf{supp}(\mu)$.

We write $\mathsf{fstate}(e)$ for q_0, and, if e is finite, we write $\mathsf{lstate}(e)$ for the last state of e. The *trace* of an execution e, written $\mathsf{trace}(e)$, is the restriction of e to the set of external actions of P. We say that t is a *trace* of P if there is an execution e of P such that $\mathsf{trace}(e) = t$. We use $\mathsf{execs}(P)$ and $\mathsf{traces}(P)$ (resp., $\mathsf{execs}^*(P)$ and $\mathsf{traces}^*(P)$) to denote the set of all (resp., all finite) executions and traces of an PIO automaton P.

The symbol λ denotes the empty sequence. We write $e_1; e_2$ for the concatenation of two executions the first of which has finite length and $\mathsf{lstate}(e_1) = \mathsf{fstate}(e_2)$. When σ_1 is a finite prefix of σ_2, we write $\sigma_1 \preceq \sigma_2$, and, if a strict finite prefix, $\sigma_1 \prec \sigma_2$.

An automaton that models a complex system can be constructed by *composing* automata that model the system's components. When composing automata P_i, where $i \in I$ and I is finite, their signatures are called *compatible* if their output actions are disjoint and the internal actions of each automaton are disjoint with all actions of the other automata. When the signatures are compatible we say that the corresponding automata are compatible too. The composition $P = \prod_{i \in I} P_i$ of a set of compatible automata $\{P_i : i \in I\}$ is defined as:

1. $sig(P) = \prod_{i \in I} sig(P_i) = \Big(output(P) = \cup_{i \in I} output(P_i),\ internal(P) = \cup_{i \in I} internal(P_i),\ input(P) = \cup_{i \in I} input(P_i) - \cup_{j \in I} output(P_j) \Big)$;
2. $Q(P) = \prod_{i \in I} Q(P_i)$;
3. $\bar{q}_P = \prod_{i \in I} \bar{q}_{P_i}$;
4. $R(P)$ is equal to the set of triples $(q, a, \prod_{i \in I} \mu_i)$ such that:
   (a) a is enabled in some $q_i \in q$, $i \in I$ and
   (b) for all $i \in I$ if $a \in acts(P_i)$ then $(q_i, a, \mu_i) \in R(P_i)$, otherwise $\mu_i = \delta(q_i)$.

Nondeterministic choices in P are resolved using a *scheduler*. A *scheduler* for P is a function $\sigma : \mathsf{execs}^*(P) \to \mathsf{SubDisc}(R(P))$ s.t., if $(q, a, \mu) \in \mathsf{supp}(\sigma(e))$ then $q =$

---

[1] If a PIOA P has a transition $(q, \alpha, \mu) \in R(P)$ then we say that action α is *enabled* in state q.

lstate(e). Thus, σ decides (probabilistically) which transition (if any) to take after each finite execution e. Since this decision is a discrete sub-probability measure, it may be the case that σ chooses to *halt* after e with non-zero probability: $1 - \sigma(e)(R(P)) > 0$.

A scheduler σ together with a finite execution e *generates* a measure $\epsilon_{\sigma,e}$ on the σ-field $\mathcal{F}_P$ generated by cones of executions, where the cone $C_{e'}$ of a finite execution e' is the set of executions that have e' as prefix. The construction of the σ-field is standard [3,4]. The measure of a cone $\epsilon_{\sigma,e}(C_{e'})$ is defined recursively as:

1. 0, if $e' \npreceq e$ and $e \npreceq e'$;
2. 1, if $e' \preceq e$;
3. $\epsilon_{\sigma,e}(C_{e''})\mu_{\sigma(e'')}(a,q)$, if e' is of the form $e''\,a\,q$, $e \preceq e''$. Here, $\mu_{\sigma(e'')}(a,q)$ is defined to be $\sigma(e'')(\text{tran}_{\text{lstate}(e''),a})\mu_{\text{lstate}(e''),a}(q)$, that is, the probability that $\sigma(e'')$ chooses a transition labeled by a and that the new state is q.

Given a probability measure ϵ on $\mathcal{F}_P$, we define the *trace distribution* of ϵ, denoted tdist(ϵ) to be the image measure of ϵ under trace, i.e., for each cone of traces C_t, trace(ϵ)(C_t) = $\epsilon(\text{trace}^{-1}(C_t))$. We denote by tdists($P$) the set of trace distributions of (probabilistic executions of) P.

2.3   Abstract Schedulers

In this section we introduce abstract schedulers, a novel extension of PIOA and one of the contributions of this paper. Abstract schedulers are used in the cost comparison of monitors (§5). Given a signature S, an *abstract scheduler* τ for S is a function $\tau : (extern(S))^* \to \text{SubDisc}(extern(S))$. τ decides (probabilistically) which action appears after each finite trace[2] t. Note that an abstract scheduler τ assigns probabilities to all possible (finite) traces over the given signature.

An abstract scheduler τ together with a finite trace t *generate* a measure $\zeta_{\tau,t}$ on the σ-field $\mathcal{F}_{P_T}$ generated by cones of traces, where the cone $C_{t'}$ of a finite trace t' is the set of traces that have t' as prefix. The measure of a cone $\zeta_{\tau,t}(C_{t'})$ is defined recursively as:

1. 0, if $t' \npreceq t$ and $t \npreceq t'$;
2. 1, if $t' \preceq t$;
3. $\zeta_{\tau,t}(C_{t''})\tau(t'')(\{a\})$, if t' is of the form $t''; a$, $t \preceq t''$.

Standard measure theoretic arguments ensure that $\zeta_{\tau,t}$ is well defined and a probability measure.

Refining abstract schedulers. Abstract schedulers give us (sub-)probabilities for all possible traces over a given signature. However, a given PIOA P might exhibit only a subset of all those possible traces. Thus, we would like to have a way to *refine* an abstract scheduler τ to a scheduler σ that corresponds to the particular PIOA P and is "similar" to τ w.r.t. assigning probabilities. This similarity can be made more precise

---

[2] Note that the term "trace" is overloaded: it refers to either the result of applying the function trace to an execution e or to a sequence of external actions. It will be clear from the context to which of the two cases we refer each time.

as follows. First, if an abstract scheduler τ assigns a zero probability to a trace t, then this means that t cannot happen (e.g., the system stops due to overheating). Thus, even if t is a trace that P can exhibit, we would like σ to assign it a zero probability. Second, assume we have a trace t that can be extended with actions a, b, or c, and an abstract scheduler τ that assigns a non-zero probability to all traces $t; X$, with $X \in \{a, b, c\}$ and $\tau(t)(X) = 1$, i.e., τ does not allow for the system to stop after t. If $t; a$ is a trace that P can exhibit, we would like σ to assign it the same probability as τ. However, if P cannot exhibit that trace, σ should assign it a zero probability. But then σ would be a sub-probability measure, i.e., it would allow for P to halt, whereas τ does not. To solve this problem, we proportionally re-distribute the probabilities that τ assigns to the traces that P can exhibit. These two cases are formalized as follows.

Given an *abstract scheduler* τ over a signature S, and a PIOA P with $sig(P) = S$, we define the *refinement* function $\mathsf{refn}(\tau, P) = \tau'$, where $\tau' : (extern(S))^* \to \mathsf{SubDisc}(extern(S))$, i.e., a function that maps an abstract scheduler and a PIOA to another abstract scheduler, as follows:
Let $t = t'; a \in (extern(S))^*$ in

- if $t \notin \mathsf{traces}(P)$ or $\tau(t')(\{a\}) = 0$, then $\tau'(t')(\{a\}) = 0$;
- otherwise, $\tau'(t')(\{a\}) = \dfrac{\tau(t')(\{a\})}{\big(\tau(t')(A)\big) + \big(1 - \tau(t')(extern(S))\big)}$,
  where $A = \{x \in extern(S) \mid t'; x \in \mathsf{traces}(P)\}$.

Given an abstract scheduler τ and a PIOA P, standard measure theoretic arguments ensure that if τ together with a finite trace t generate a probability measure $\zeta_{\tau,t}$ on the σ-field $\mathcal{F}_{P_T}$ generated by cones of traces, so does the abstract scheduler $\mathsf{refn}(\tau, P)$, i.e., it generates a probability measure $\zeta'_{\mathsf{refn}(\tau,P),t}$ on the σ-field $\mathcal{F}_{P_T}$.

We now formalize the relationship between schedulers and abstract schedulers. Given an abstract scheduler τ over a signature S, and a PIOA P with $sig(P) = S$, a scheduler σ is *derivable* from τ iff σ is a scheduler for P such that for all executions $e \in \mathsf{execs}(P)$ the trace distributions of $\epsilon_{\sigma,e}$ are equal to the probability measures of $\mathsf{trace}(e)$ assigned by the refinement of τ on P, i.e., for all executions $e, e'' \in \mathsf{execs}(P)$, $\mathsf{tdist}(\epsilon_{\sigma,e})(C_{e''}) = \zeta'_{\mathsf{refn}(\tau,P),\mathsf{trace}(e)}(C_{\mathsf{trace}(e'')})$.

2.4 Running Example Modeled Using PIOA

To illustrate how our framework can be used to model enforcement scenarios we will consider a running example of a file server S, illustrated in Fig. 2a.

Clients (C_1 through C_n in the figure) can request to open or close a particular file. The server responds to the requests by returning a file descriptor or an acknowledgment that the file was closed successfully. Given a security policy P stating that at most one client at a time can access a particular file, a monitor is interposed between the clients and the server to enforce P (Fig. 2b). The monitor has the ability to *deny* access to a file requested by a client.

We now show how to model the running example using PIOA. Each client C_i requests to open a file x through an $open_i(x)$ output action. Once the client receives a file descriptor through an $fd_i(x)$ input action, it requests to close the file through an $close_i(x)$ action. When it receives an acknowledgment that the file was closed, it stops

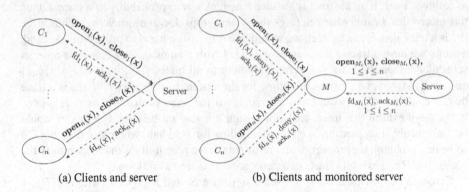

| (a) Clients and server | (b) Clients and monitored server |

Fig. 2. Diagrams of interposing a monitor between clients and server

requesting access to the file. If, however, the client is denied access to the file, it probabilistically chooses between requesting the file again and permanently discontinuing requesting the file.

A state diagram of C_i is shown in Fig. 3.[3] The ellipse represents the communication interface of the automaton and the circles the automaton's states. Inputs are depicted as arrows entering the automaton, and we only show the effect of the action, i.e., the automaton's end state. Each output action is depicted with two arrows: (1) a straight arrows between states, to depict the precondition and effect on states; and (2) a dashed arrow to show that action becomes visible outside the automaton. The server S implements a stack of size one: it replies with a

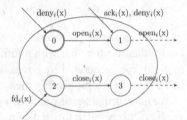

Fig. 3. Client PIOA state transition diagram

file descriptor or an acknowledgment of closing a file for the latest request. This means that if a scheduler allows two requests to arrive before the server is given a chance to reply, then the first request is ignored and the last request is served.

To further illustrate some of the capabilities of our framework we introduce two example types of monitor:

- M_{DENY} always denies access to a file that is already open;
- M_{PROB} uses probabilistic information about future requests to make decisions. More precisely, a client i is always granted a request to open a file that is available. Otherwise, if the file is unavailable, i.e., a client j has already opened it, the monitor checks whether (1) after force-closing the file for j, j will ask to re-open the file with probability less than 0.5; and (2) after denying access to i, i will re-ask with probability greater than 0.5. If both hold, the monitor gives access to i; otherwise it denies access.

---

[3] Pseudocode and additional state diagrams for clients and the server can be found in our technical report [20].

Signature: Input: $open_i(x)$, $close_i(x)$,
$fd_{M_i}(x)$, $ack_{M_i}(x)$,
where x is a filename
Output: $open_{M_i}(x)$, $close_{M_i}(x)$,
$fd_i(x)$, $ack_i(x)$, $deny_i(x)$,
where x is a filename

States: p: list (of triples) of requests
from clients to monitor
q: list (of triples) of responses
from monitor to clients
r: list (of pairs) of active
connections

Start States: $p = q = r = nil$

Transitions: $open_i(x)$
Effect: $p := p@[\langle op, i, x \rangle]$
$close_i(x)$
Effect: $p := p@[\langle cl, i, x \rangle]$
$fd_{M_i}(x)$
Effect: $q := q@[\langle fd, M_i, x \rangle]$

$ack_{M_i}(x)$
Effect: $q := q@[\langle ack, M_i, x \rangle]$
$open_{M_i}(x)$
Precondition: $p = \langle op, i, x \rangle :: p'$
$\wedge \nexists \langle x, j \rangle \in r, j \neq i$
Effect: $p := p'$
$r := r@[\langle x, i \rangle]$
$close_{M_i}(x)$
Precondition: $p = \langle cl, i, x \rangle :: p'$
Effect: $p := p'$
$r := r \setminus [\langle x, i \rangle]$
$fd_i(x)$
Precondition: $q = \langle fd, M_i, x \rangle :: q'$
Effect: $q := q'$
$ack_i(x)$
Precondition: $q = \langle ack, M_i, x \rangle :: q'$
Effect: $q := q'$
$deny_i(x)$
Precondition: $p = \langle op, i, x \rangle :: p'$
$\wedge \exists \langle x, j \rangle \in r, j \neq i$
Effect: $p := p'$

Fig. 4. M_{DENY} PIOA definition

The pseudocode[4] for M_{DENY} is depicted in Fig. 4. The pseudocode for M_{PROB} is similar and can be found in our technical report [20], along with additional details about the structure of the monitors.

Let us now consider the composed system $\Pi = C_1 \times \ldots \times C_n \times M \times S$. The states of the composed system will be $n + 2-$ tuples of the form $q_\Pi = \langle q_{C_1}, \ldots, q_{C_n}; q_M, q_S \rangle$. An example execution for M_{DENY} is: $e_{M_{DENY}} = q_{\Pi_0}\ open_1(x)\ q_{\Pi_1}\ open_{M_1}(x)\ q_{\Pi_2}$ $fd_{M_1}(x)\ q_{\Pi_3}\ fd_1(x)\ q_{\Pi_4}\ open_2(x)\ q_{\Pi_5}\ deny_2(x)\ q_{\Pi_6}\ open_2(x)\ q_{\Pi_7}\ deny_2(x)\ q_{\Pi_8}$. The trace of $e_{M_{DENY}}$ is: $t_{M_{DENY}} = \text{trace}(e_{M_{DENY}}) = open_1(x)\ open_{M_1}(x)\ fd_{M_1}(x)$ $fd_1(x)\ open_2(x)\ deny_2(x)\ open_2(x)\ deny_2(x)$.

In $t_{M_{DENY}}$ client C_1 asks to open file x and is given access, after which client C_2 asks to open the same file and is denied access by the monitor.

Let us consider the scheduler σ that schedules transitions based on the following high-level pattern: $\left([C_1, \ldots, C_n];\ M^*;\ S;\ M^* \right)^\infty$. This pattern says that σ chooses equiprobably one of the clients to execute some transition, and then, deterministically, the monitor gets a chance to execute as many actions as it needs, then the server responds with one transition, and finally the monitor gets again the chance to do as much work as it needs. This pattern repeats finitely or infinitely many times.

Let us assume that σ chooses each client to take a turn with probability $P(C_i) = \frac{1}{n}$. Then the probability of $e_{M_{DENY}}$ is given by the measure $\epsilon_{\sigma, \bar{q}}$ on the cone of executions that have $e_{M_{DENY}}$ as prefix, i.e., $\epsilon_{\sigma, \bar{q}}(C_{e_{M_{DENY}}})$. It is easy to calculate that $\epsilon_{\sigma, \bar{q}}(C_{e_{M_{DENY}}}) = \frac{0.1}{n^2}$. Similarly, we can calculate the probabilities of $t_{M_{DENY}}$ (more details can be found in our technical report [20]).

---

[4] We use the precondition pseudocode style that is typical in I/O automata papers (e.g., [3,4]).

3   Probabilistic Cost of Automata

In this section we develop the framework to reason about the cost of an automaton P.

A cost function assigns a real number to every trace over a signature S, i.e., every possible sequence of external actions of S. More formally, a *cost function* is a signed measure cost on the σ-field $\mathcal{F}_{P_T}$ generated by cones of traces, i.e., cost : $\mathcal{F}_{P_T} \to [-\infty, \infty]$, where P_T are the traces of an automaton P with signature S that generates all possible traces of its signature. Remember that a cone C_t of a finite trace t is the set of traces that have t as prefix. Thus, there is a one-to-one correspondence between traces and the cones they infer. Although traces are the subject of our analysis, cones are their (sound) mathematical representation.

We calculate the expected cost of a trace, called *probabilistic cost*, by multiplying the probability of the trace with its cost. More formally, given a scheduler σ and a cost function cost, the *probabilistic cost of a cone of a trace* C_t is defined as $\mathrm{pcost}_\sigma(C_t) = (\epsilon_{\sigma,\bar{q}}(\mathrm{trace}^{-1})(C_t))\mathrm{cost}(C_t)$.

Probabilistic costs of traces can be used to assign expected costs to automata: the probabilistic (i.e., expected) cost of an automaton is the set of probabilistic costs of its traces. However, it is often useful for the cost to be a single value, rather than a set. For example, we might want to build a monitor that does not allow a system to overheat, i.e., it never goes above a threshold temperature. In this case the cost of an automaton (e.g., the composition of the monitor automaton with the system automaton) could be the maximal cost of all traces. Similarly, we might want to build a monitor that "cools down" a system, i.e., lowers a system's temperature below a threshold, infinitely often. Here we could assign the cost of an automaton to be the minimal cost that appears infinitely often in its (infinite) set of traces, and check whether that value is smaller than the threshold. It is clear that it can be beneficial to abstract the function that maps sets of probabilistic costs of traces to single numbers. We formalize this as follows.

Given a scheduler σ and a cost function cost, the *probabilistic cost of a PIOA P* is defined as $\mathrm{pcost}_\sigma^{\mathbb{F}}(P) = \mathbb{F}_{t \in \mathrm{traces}(P)}(\mathrm{pcost}_\sigma(C_t))$. Note that the definition is parametric in the function $\mathbb{F}$. As an example, consider the infinite set $v = \{v_0, v_1, \ldots\}$, where each v_i is the probabilistic cost of some trace of P (ranging over a finite set of possible costs); then, $\mathbb{F}$ could be (following definitions of Chatterjee et al. [6]): (1) $\mathrm{Sup}(v) = sup\{v_n \mid n \geq 0\}$, or (2) $\mathrm{LimInf}(v) = liminf_{n \to \infty} v_n = lim_{n \to \infty} inf\{v_i \mid i \geq n\}$. Sup chooses the maximal number that appears in v (e.g., the maximal temperature that a system can reach). LimInf chooses the minimal number that appears infinitely often in v (e.g., the temperature that the system goes down to infinitely often).

If $\mathrm{cost}_\sigma(C_t) \geq 0$ for some trace t, then we call $\mathrm{cost}(C_t)$ the *value of* t. If $\mathrm{cost}(C_t) \leq 0$, then the absolute value of $\mathrm{cost}_\sigma(C_t)$ is the *cost of* t. We define similarly the probabilistic value and cost of a trace t and a PIOA P.

Note that cost carries value/cost information. For example, if we were to assign values to actions r_1 and r_2, e.g., 2 and 5 respectively, then cost can assign different values to their interleavings that might not clearly relate to the values of the actions, e.g., $\mathrm{cost}(r_1; r_2) = 0$ and $\mathrm{cost}(r_2; r_1) = 20$.

In our technical report we show how one can define the cost of a system given cost functions for its components [20]: such an approach can be used to embed the framework of Drabik et al. [10] in ours, showing that our framework is at least as expressive.

4 Cost Security Policy Enforcement

In this section we define security policies and what it means for a monitor to enforce a security policy on a system.

Cost security policies. A monitor M is a PIOA. A monitor mediates the communication between system components S_i which are also PIOA. Thus, the the output actions of each S_i are inputs to the monitor, and the monitor has corresponding outputs that it forwards to the other components. More formally, given an index set I and a set of components $\{S_i\}$, $i \in I$, we assume that $acts(S_i) \cap acts(S_j) = \emptyset$, for all $i, j \in I$, $i \neq j$. Our goal is to model and reason about the external behavior of the monitored system. Thus, we also assume that $internal(S_i) = \emptyset$, for all $i \in I$. Since the system components S_i are compatible, we will refer to their composition $\Pi_{i \in I} S_i$ as system S. A monitored system is the PIOA that results from composing M with S.[5]

The cost function defined in §3 describes the impact of a monitor on a system. A cost function is not necessarily bound to a specific security policy, which allows for the analysis of the same monitor against different policies. In practice, a monitor's purpose is to ensure that some policy is respected by the monitored system. In the running example, the monitor's role is to ensure that a file is not simultaneously open by two clients. Furthermore, since each *deny* action comes with a cost, it is desirable for the cost of monitoring to be limited. This motivates the need to define a cost security policy.

Given a (monitored) system P, a *cost security policy* over $sig(P)$ is a cost function, i.e., a signed measure Pol on the σ−field $\mathcal{F}_{P_T}$ generated by cones of traces that range over $sig(P)$, i.e., $\text{Pol} : \mathcal{F}_{P_T} \to [-\infty, \infty]$. When we talk about the signature, actions, etc. of Pol, we refer to the signature, actions, etc. of P. Cost security policies associate a cost with each trace. For instance, if a trace t corresponds to a particular enforcement interaction between a monitor and a client, then $\text{Pol}(C_t) = 10$ could describe that such enforcement (i.e., t) is allowed only if its cost is less than 10. Our definition of policies extends that of security properties [22]: security properties are predicates, i.e., binary functions, on sets of traces, whereas we focus on policies that are functions whose range is the real numbers (as opposed to $\{0, 1\}$). We leave the investigation of enforcement for securities policies defined as sets of sets of traces (e.g., [22,8,19]) for future work.

Given a cost security policy Pol and a scheduler σ the *probabilistic cost security policy* pPol_σ under σ is defined as $\text{pPol}_\sigma(C_t) = \left(\epsilon_{\sigma,\bar{q}}(\text{trace}^{-1})(C_t)\right)\text{Pol}(C_t)$.

Cost security policy enforcement. Given a scheduler σ, a cost function cost, a policy Pol, a monitor M, and a system S (compatible with M), we say that M $n-enforces_{\leq}$ (resp., $n-enforces_{\geq}$) Pol on S under σ and cost if and only if the probabilistic cost of the monitored system differs by at most n from the probabilistic cost that the policy assigns to the traces of the monitored system, i.e.,:

$$\left(\text{pcost}_\sigma^{\mathbb{F}}(M \times S)\right) - \left(\mathbb{F}_{t \in \text{traces}(M \times S)}\text{pPol}_\sigma(C_t)\right) \leq n \text{ (resp., } \geq n\text{), i.e.,}$$

$$\left(\mathbb{F}_{t \in \text{traces}(M \times S)}\text{pcost}_\sigma(C_t)\right) - \left(\mathbb{F}_{t \in \text{traces}(M \times S)}\text{pPol}_\sigma(C_t)\right) \leq n \text{ (resp., } \geq n\text{).}$$

---

[5] By assumption, M and S are compatible. In scenarios where this is not the case, one can use renaming to make the automata compatible [19,3,4].

We say that a monitor M *enforces$_\leq$* (resp., *enforces$_\geq$*) a security policy P on a system S under a scheduler σ and a cost function cost if and only if M $0-$enforces$_\leq$ (resp., $0-$enforces$_\geq$) P on S under σ.

The definition of enforcement says that a monitor M enforces a policy Pol on a system S if the probabilistic cost of the monitored system under some scheduler σ and cost function cost is less (resp. greater) than or equal to the cost that the policy assigns to the behaviors that the monitored system can exhibit. We define enforcement using two comparison operators because different scenarios might assign different semantics to the meaning of enforcement: One might use a monitor to maximize the value of a monitored system with respect to some base value, e.g., in our running example, we may want to give access to as many unique clients as possible since the server is making extra money by delivering advertisements to them; thus, the monitor has motive to give priority to every new request for accessing a file. In other cases, one might use a monitor to minimize the cost of the monitored system with respect to some allowed cost, e.g., we might want to minimize the state that the monitor and the server keep to provide access to files, in which case caching might be cost-prohibitive. Without loss of generality in this paper we focus on $\leq$; similar results hold for $\geq$.

Enforcement is defined with respect to a global function $\mathbb{F}$. $\mathbb{F}$ transforms the costs of all traces of a monitored system to a single value. As described in §3, this value could represent the maximum value of all traces, their average, sum, etc. Thus, $\mathbb{F}$ can model situations where an individual trace might have cost that is cost-prohibited by the policy (e.g., overheating temporarily), but the monitored system as a whole is still within the acceptable range (i.e., before and after the overheating the system cools down enough).

In the previous instantiation of our running example, there might exist some trace t where $\mathrm{cost}(t) > \mathrm{Pol}(t) > -\infty$, typically when a client keeps asking for a file that is denied. Although this would intuitively mean that the cost security policy is not respected for that particular trace, it might be the case that M enforces Pol, as long as Pol is globally respected, which could happen, e.g., if the probability of t is small enough. This illustrates a strength of our framework: we can allow for some local deviations, as long as they do not impact the global properties, i.e., overall expected behavior, of the system. If we wish to constrain each traces, we can define *local enforcement*, which requires that the cost of *each trace* of the monitored system is below (or above) a certain threshold, as opposed to enforcement which requires that the value of some function computed over *all traces* of the monitored system is below (or above) a certain threshold. Note that local enforcement can be expressed through a function $\mathbb{F}$ that universally quantifies the cost difference from the threshold over all traces of the monitored system. Local enforcement could be useful, for example, to ensure that a system *never* overheats even momentarily, whereas enforcement would be useful if we want to have probabilistic guarantees of the system; e.g., we accept a 0.001% probability that the system will become unavailable due to overheating.

A question a security designer might have to face is whether it is possible, given a boolean security policy that describes what should not happen and a cost policy that describes the maximal/minimal allowed cost, to build a monitor that satisfies both. This problem can help illuminate a common cost/security tradeoff: the more secure a mechanism is, the more costly it usually is.

There is a close relationship between boolean security policies (e.g., [22]) and cost security policies: given a boolean security policy there exists a cost security policy such that if the cost security policy is n−enforceable then the boolean security policy is enforceable as well (and vice versa). Specifically, given a boolean security policy P, we write Pol_P for the function such that $\mathsf{pPol}_P(C_t) = 0$ if $P(t)$ holds, and $-\infty$ otherwise. Given a predicate P, if we instantiate function $\mathbb{F}$ with the function that returns the least element of a set and function cost with the function that maps every (trace) cone to 0, and if M 0−enforces$_\leq$ Pol_P, then any trace belongs to P. In other words, our framework is a generalization of the traditional enforcement model.

In the other direction, since cost security policies are more expressive than boolean security policies, we need to pick a bound that will serve as a threshold to classify traces as acceptable or not. Given a probabilistic cost security policy pPol, a cost function cost, a scheduler σ and a bound $n \in \mathbb{R}$, we say that a trace t *satisfies* $\mathsf{Pol}_{\mathsf{cost},n,\sigma}$, and write $\mathsf{Pol}_{\mathsf{cost},n,\sigma}(t)$ if and only if $\mathsf{pPol}(C_t) \geq \mathsf{pcost}_\sigma(C_t) - n$.

Expressing cost security policies as boolean security policies allows one to embed in our framework a notion of sound enforcement [17]: a monitor is a sound enforcer for a system S and security policy P if the behavior of the monitored system obeys P. As described above, one encodes P in our framework as Pol_P, which returns $-\infty$ if a trace violates P and 0 otherwise. Sound enforcement can be expressed as 0−enforcement$_\leq$ using a global function $\mathbb{F}_P$ that assigns $-\infty$ to the cost of the automaton composition that represents the monitored system if some trace has cost $-\infty$, and 0 otherwise. Specifically, if a monitor soundly enforces P on a system, all its traces will belong to P and Pol_P will map them all to 0, which when applied to $\mathbb{F}_P$, will result in a global cost of 0. If the monitor is not sound, then the global cost will be $-\infty$. Thus, a monitor soundly enforces a boolean security policy P if and only if the monitor 0−enforces$_\leq$ the cost security policy Pol_P under $\mathbb{F}_P$ and $\mathsf{cost}(\_) = 0$.

A notion of transparency is often used to define practically useful policy enforcement (e.g., [17]). Due to space constraints, we discuss this in our technical report [20].

5   Cost Comparison

Given a system S, a function $\mathbb{F}$, a scheduler σ and a monitor M, $\mathsf{pcost}_\sigma^{\mathbb{F}}(M)$ and $\mathsf{pcost}_\sigma^{\mathbb{F}}(M \times S)$ are values in $[-\infty, \infty]$, and as such provide a way to compare monitors.

To meaningfully compare monitors, we need to fix the variables on which the cost of a monitor depends, i.e., functions $\mathbb{F}$ and cost, and the scheduler σ. Difficulties arise when trying to fix a scheduler for two different monitors (and thus monitored systems), even if they are defined over the same signature. States of the monitors, and thus their executions, will be syntactically different and we cannot directly define a single scheduler for both. Moreover, since schedulers assign probabilities to specific PIOA and their transitions, one scheduler cannot be defined for two different monitors.

To overcome this difficulty we rely on the abstract schedulers introduced in §2.3. Namely, to compare two monitored systems we use a single abstract scheduler which we then refine into schedulers for each monitored system.[6]

---

[6] An abstract scheduler τ also provides a meaningful way to compare monitors with different signatures: calculate the union S of the signatures of the two monitors and (1) use a τ with

Abstract schedulers allow us to "fairly" compare two monitors, but additional constraints are needed to eliminate impractical corner cases. To this end we introduce *fair abstract schedulers*. An abstract scheduler τ over the signature of a class of monitored targets $\mathcal{M} \times \mathcal{S}$ is *fair* (w.r.t. comparing monitors) if and only if (1) the monitors get a chance to respond to targets' actions infinitely often (i.e., the monitors are not starved), and (2) for every trace t of a monitored target, every extension t' of t by a monitor's actions, i.e., $t' = t; a$ with $a \in extern(M)$, is assigned the same probability by τ.

Constraint (1) ensures that a fair abstract scheduler will not starve the monitor, i.e., the monitor will always eventually be given a chance to enforce the policy. Constraint (2) ensures that the abstract scheduler is not biased towards a specific monitoring strategy. For example, an unfair scheduler could assign zero probability to arbitrary monitoring actions (e.g., the scheduler "stops" insertion monitors [16]) and non-zero probability to monitors that output "valid" target actions verbatim (i.e., the scheduler allows suppression monitors [16]). Such a scheduler would be unlikely to be helpful in performing a realistic comparison of the costs of enforcement of an insertion and a suppression monitor. There might be scenarios where such schedulers are appropriate[7], but in this paper we pursue only the equiprobable scenario.

Given a system S, a function $\mathbb{F}$, a function pcost, two monitors M_1 and M_2 with $sig(M_1) = sig(M_2)$, an abstract scheduler τ over $sig(M_1 \times S)$, and two schedulers σ_1 (for $M_1 \times S$) and σ_2 (for $M_2 \times S$) derivable from τ, we say that M_2 is less costly than a monitor M_1 and write $M_2 \leq M_1$, if and only if $\mathrm{pcost}_{\sigma_2}^{\mathbb{F}}(M_2 \times S) \leq \mathrm{pcost}_{\sigma_1}^{\mathbb{F}}(M_1 \times S)$. Note that in the particular case where $\mathrm{pcost}_{\sigma}^{\mathbb{F}}$ corresponds to the expected cost of all the traces in $M \times S$, the ordering relation $\leq$ roughly corresponds to the notion of "globally more-efficient" of [10]. A monitor M is *cost optimal* for a system S if and only if for all monitors M' with $sig(M) = sig(M')$, $M \leq M'$.

The next theorem formalizes the intuition that a monitor that exploits knowledge about the scheduler and the cost function should be more cost efficient than monitors that do not. The theorem shows that such knowledge can be exploited to build a cost optimal monitor. Note that in the theorem the cost function and scheduler are universally quantified, i.e., the monitor is cost optimal for any abstract scheduler and cost function.

Theorem 1. *Given an abstract scheduler τ and a function $\mathbb{F}$ that is monotone[8] and continuous (i.e., it preserves limits), there is a cost-optimal monitor that optimizes its transitions based on a scheduler σ (derived from τ) and cost function* cost[9].

Thm. 1 provides a generic description of the conditions sufficient for constructing a cost-optimal monitor. In the constructive proof of Thm. 1 we build a monitor that keeps

---

signature S, and (2) extend each monitor's signature to S. This is useful when comparing monitors of different capabilities, e.g., a truncation and an insertion monitor [16], where the insertion monitor might exhibit additional actions, e.g., logging.

[7] This is a similar situation with having various definitions for fairness [15].

[8] Given two sets of real numbers $X, Y \in 2^{\mathbb{R}}$ we write $X \sqsubseteq Y$ if and only $\forall x \in X : \exists y \in Y : x \leq y$. We write $x \sqsubseteq y$ for $\{x\} \sqsubseteq \{y\}$, i.e., $x \sqsubseteq y \Leftrightarrow x \leq y$. We say that a function $f : 2^{\mathbb{R}} \to \mathbb{R}$ that is *monotone* if and only if it is monotone under the ordering $\sqsubseteq$, i.e., if $X \sqsubseteq Y$ then $f(X) \sqsubseteq f(Y)$.

[9] Proofs can be found in our technical report [20].

at its state the past execution, and at each state the next transition taken by the monitor minimizes the expected cost of the trace using σ and cost in its calculation.

Running example. Typically, when a monitor modifies the behavior of the system some cost is incurred (e.g., the usability of the system decreases, computational resources are consumed). For instance, in the running example, one way monitors can modify the behavior of the system is by denying an access to a client. If we assume that each deny action incurs a cost of 1, then we can define a function cost_D that associates with each trace the cost n, where n is the number of denies that appear in the trace.

Moreover, let us assume that (1) $\mathbb{F}$ is Sup, and (2) the abstract scheduler τ follows the pattern $\left([C_1, \ldots, C_n]; \ M^*; \ S; \ M^*\right)^{\infty}$ as described in §2.4. Assuming we have two clients C_1 and C_2, our monitored system is $\Pi = C_1 \times C_2 \times M \times S$. If M is M_{DENY}, then we refine τ to the scheduler $\sigma_{M_{DENY}}$; dually, the scheduler for M_{PROB} will be $\sigma_{M_{PROB}}$. The probabilistic cost of the monitored system with M_{DENY} is $\sup_{t \in \text{traces}(\Pi_{M_{DENY}})} (\text{pcost}_{\sigma_{M_{DENY}}}(C_t))$, and similarly for M_{PROB}.

We first observe that with such a cost function, the maximal (i.e., best) reachable cost is 0, meaning that no deny action is returned. It follows that the cost-optimal monitor never denies any action, and, clearly, this monitor does not generally respect the requirement that at most one client at a time should have access to a particular file.

Second, we observe that if we assume that C_1 and C_2 ask for a file after a denied request with probability p_1 and p_2 respectively, with $p_1 < p_2$, then C_1 is less likely to ask again for a file which has been denied. In this case, it is better to deny an access to C_1 rather than to C_2, in order to limit the number of deny actions. Hence, with such a system, we have $M_{PROB} \leq M_{DENY}$.

Finally, observe that the last result is sound only under the assumption that schedulers $\sigma_{M_{DENY}}$ and $\sigma_{M_{PROB}}$ are compatible with τ. If that was not the case, then $\sigma_{M_{DENY}}$ could starve C_2 (or $\sigma_{M_{PROB}}$ could starve C_1). This would give M_{DENY} an unfair advantage over M_{PROB}, and we would have as a result that $M_{DENY} \leq M_{PROB}$. Such unfair comparisons are ruled out by requiring schedulers to be compatible.

6 Related Work

The first model of run-time monitors, *security automata*, was based on Büchi Automata [22]. Security automata observe individual executions of an untrusted application and halt the application if the execution is about to become invalid. Since then, several similar models have extended or refined the class of enforceable policies based on the enforcement and computational powers of monitors (e.g., [12,14,11]).

Recent work has revised these models or adopted alternate ones to more conveniently reason about applications, the interaction between applications and monitors, and enforcement in distributed systems. This includes Martinelli and Matteucci's model of run-time monitors based on CCS [21], Gay et al.'s *service automata* based on CSP for enforcing security requirements in distributed systems [13], Basin et al.'s language, based on CSP and Object-Z (OZ), for specifying security automata [1], and Mallios et al.'s I/O automata-based model for reasoning about incomplete mediation and knowledge the monitor might have about the target [19]. Although these models are richer and orthogonal revisions to security automata and related computational and operational extensions, they maintain the same view of (enforceable) security policies: binary predicates over sets of executions. In this paper we take a richer view assigning costs and probabilities to traces and define cost-security policies and cost-enforcement, which, as shown in §4, is a strict extension of binary-based security policies and enforcement.

Drábik et al. introduce the notion of calculating the cost of an enforcement mechanism [10], based on a relatively simple enforcement model that does not include input/output actions or a detailed calculation of the execution probabilities. To some extent, the notion of cost security policy defines a threshold characterizing the maximal/minimal cost reachable, while taking the probability of reaching this threshold into account. Such a notion of threshold is also used by Cheng et al., where accesses are associated with a level of risk, and decisions are made according to some predefined risk thresholds, without detailing how such policies can be enforced at runtime [7]. In the context of runtime enforcement, Bielova and Massacci propose to apply a distance metrics to capture the similarity between traces [2], and we could consider the cost required to obtain one trace from another as a distance metrics.

An important aspect of this work is to consider that a property might not be locally respected, i.e., for a particular execution, as long as the property holds globally. This possibility is also considered by Drabik et al., who quantify the tradeoff correctness/transparency for non-safety boolean properties [9]. Caravagna et al. introduce the notion of lazy controllers, which use a probabilistic modeling of the system in order to minimize the number of times when a system must be controlled, without considering input/output interactions between the target and the environment as we do [5].

7   Conclusion

We have introduced a formal framework based on probabilistic I/O automata to model and reason about interactive run-time monitors. In our framework we can formally reason about probabilistic knowledge monitors have about their environment and combine it with cost information to minimize the overall cost of the monitored system. We have used this framework to (1) calculate *expected costs of monitors* (§3), (2) define *cost security policies* and *cost enforcement*, richer notions of traditional definitions of security policies and enforcement [22] (§4), and (3) order monitors according to their expected cost and show how to build an optimal one (§5).

Acknowledgments. This work was supported in part by NSF grant CNS-0917047 and by EU FP7 projects NESSoS and SESAMO.

References

1. Basin, D., Olderog, E.-R., Sevinc, P.E.: Specifying and analyzing security automata using CSP-OZ. In: Proceedings ACM Symposium on Information, Computer and Communications Security (ASIACCS), pp. 70–81 (2007)
2. Bielova, N., Massacci, F.: Predictability of enforcement. In: Erlingsson, Ú., Wieringa, R., Zannone, N. (eds.) ESSoS 2011. LNCS, vol. 6542, pp. 73–86. Springer, Heidelberg (2011)

3. Canetti, R., Cheung, L., Kaynar, D., Liskov, M., Lynch, N., Pereira, O., Segala, R.: Task-structured probabilistic I/O automata. Technical Report MIT-CSAIL-TR-2006-060 (2006)
4. Canetti, R., Cheung, L., Kaynar, D., Liskov, M., Lynch, N., Pereira, O., Segala, R.: Task-structured probabilistic i/o automata. In: Proceedings of 8th International Workshop on Discrete Event Systems, pp. 207–214 (2006)
5. Caravagna, G., Costa, G., Pardini, G.: Lazy security controllers. In: Jøsang, A., Samarati, P., Petrocchi, M. (eds.) STM 2012. LNCS, vol. 7783, pp. 33–48. Springer, Heidelberg (2013)
6. Chatterjee, K., Doyen, L., Henzinger, T.A.: Quantitative languages. In: Kaminski, M., Martini, S. (eds.) CSL 2008. LNCS, vol. 5213, pp. 385–400. Springer, Heidelberg (2008)
7. Cheng, P.-C., Rohatgi, P., Keser, C., Karger, P.A., Wagner, G.M., Reninger, A.S.: Fuzzy multi-level security: An experiment on quantified risk-adaptive access control. In: Proceedings of the 2007 IEEE Symposium on Security and Privacy, pp. 222–230 (2007)
8. Clarkson, M.R., Schneider, F.B.: Hyperproperties. J. Comput. Secur. 18(6), 1157–1210 (2010)
9. Drábik, P., Martinelli, F., Morisset, C.: A quantitative approach for inexact enforcement of security policies. In: Gollmann, D., Freiling, F.C. (eds.) ISC 2012. LNCS, vol. 7483, pp. 306–321. Springer, Heidelberg (2012)
10. Drábik, P., Martinelli, F., Morisset, C.: Cost-aware runtime enforcement of security policies. In: Jøsang, A., Samarati, P., Petrocchi, M. (eds.) STM 2012. LNCS, vol. 7783, pp. 1–16. Springer, Heidelberg (2013)
11. Falcone, Y., Fernandez, J.-C., Mounier, L.: What can you verify and enforce at runtime? Intl. Jrnl. Software Tools for Tech. Transfer (STTT) 14(3), 349–382 (2012)
12. Fong, P.W.: Access control by tracking shallow execution history. In: Proceedings of the 2004 IEEE Symposium on Security and Privacy, pp. 43–55 (2004)
13. Gay, R., Mantel, H., Sprick, B.: Service automata. In: Barthe, G., Datta, A., Etalle, S. (eds.) FAST 2011. LNCS, vol. 7140, pp. 148–163. Springer, Heidelberg (2012)
14. Hamlen, K.W., Morrisett, G., Schneider, F.B.: Computability classes for enforcement mechanisms. ACM Trans. Program. Lang. Syst. 28(1), 175–205 (2006)
15. Kwiatkowska, M.: Survey of fairness notions. Information and Software Technology 31(7), 371–386 (1989)
16. Ligatti, J., Bauer, L., Walker, D.: Edit automata: Enforcement mechanisms for run-time security policies. International Journal of Information Security 4(1-2), 2–16 (2005)
17. Ligatti, J., Bauer, L., Walker, D.: Run-time enforcement of nonsafety policies. ACM Transactions on Information and System Security 12(3), 1–41 (2009)
18. Malan, G.R., Watson, D., Jahanian, F., Howell, P.: Transport and application protocol scrubbing. In: Proceedings of INFOCOM 2000, pp. 1381–1390 (2000)
19. Mallios, Y., Bauer, L., Kaynar, D., Ligatti, J.: Enforcing more with less: Formalizing target-aware run-time monitors. In: Jøsang, A., Samarati, P., Petrocchi, M. (eds.) STM 2012. LNCS, vol. 7783, pp. 17–32. Springer, Heidelberg (2013)
20. Mallios, Y., Bauer, L., Kaynar, D., Martinelli, F., Morisset, C.: Probabilistic cost enforcement of security policies. Technical Report CMU-CyLab-13-006, CyLab, Carnegie Mellon University (2013)
21. Martinelli, F., Matteucci, I.: Through modeling to synthesis of security automata. Electron. Notes Theor. Comput. Sci. 179, 31–46 (2007)
22. Schneider, F.B.: Enforceable security policies. ACM Trans. Inf. Syst. Secur. 3, 30–50 (2000)

Selective Disclosure
in Datalog-Based Trust Management

Nik Sultana[1], Moritz Y. Becker[2], and Markulf Kohlweiss[2]

[1] Cambridge University
[2] Microsoft Research, Cambridge

Abstract Credential-based and policy-based access control, also called
trust management, is an elegant solution for access control in open decentralised systems. Existing solutions support very expressive policy
languages, but suffer from usability and privacy issues. We present a
light extension of Datalog-based trust management that supports both
legacy authentication mechanisms and anonymous credentials. We mo-
tivate our design decisions and demonstrate the effectiveness of our language through a prototype implementation.

1 Introduction

One of the fundamental assumptions of access control for traditional, centralised systems, is that authorisation must be preceded by identity authentication
[1,2]. This assumes a closed world, in which all legitimate users of the system are
known. It is often said that these assumptions do not hold in open, decentralised
IT systems such as the Internet, where strangers may legitimately access resources from a service [3]. Credential-based and policy-based access control, also
called *trust management*, is an elegant solution for access control in such systems [4,5]. In this approach, authorisation is based on public-key credentials that
prove possession of properties such as age, nationality, or group membership. Authority over these properties may be delegated to third parties, and the precise
requirements and conditions for access, as well as the information conveyed by
the credentials themselves, are expressed in a high-level machine-readable policy
language.

The most serious concern of trust management is its lack of privacy management.[1] If anything, trust management, with its emphasis on combining trust
information from multiple identity providers, is arguably more privacy invasive
than existing authentication mechanisms, such as passwords and identity certificates. In traditional trust management, credentials are atomic objects, and one
cannot choose what to disclose during a transaction. As a result, users will often
disclose more information than strictly necessary.

Mostly independently of trust management, the cryptographic community
challenged the traditional approach of identity-based authorisation preceded by

---

[1] This weakness is shared by the more general concept of public-key infrastructures [6],
of which trust management is an instance.

R. Accorsi and S. Ranise (Eds.): STM 2013, LNCS 8203, pp. 160–175, 2013.
© Springer-Verlag Berlin Heidelberg 2013

authentication, through the concept of *anonymous credentials* [7,8]. Their motivation lay in the need to minimise the leakage of personal information when using public-key certificates. Anonymous credentials allow for efficient proofs of credential ownership, i.e., of rights or certified attributes. This is achieved in a way that avoids disclosure of unnecessary information, such as attributes which are irrelevant to the access request. Moreover, the use of anonymous credentials is untraceable — a proof of credential ownership is unlinkable (except possibly via its disclosed attributes) to the issuing transaction trace, or to other proof traces of credential ownership. The integration of authorisation with authentication also affects secure session-key establishment. Traditional PKI-based key exchange and password-based key exchange [9] generate matching keys for valid identity certificates or matching passwords respectively — they abort or produce non-matching keys otherwise. Recently, this has been extended to much more expressive access-control policies [10,11], however, without considering a high-level policy language.

There is a striking complementarity between trust management and anonymous credentials. While trust management is hindered by privacy concerns, a weakness of anonymous credentials is their barebone cryptography, and the integration challenge this poses [12,13]. Somewhat independently, researchers from both the trust-management and trust-negotiation communities, and the cryptography community, designed two policy language proposals, ATNL [14] and CARL [15], aiming to overcome these weaknesses. We revisit these two approaches, and focus on a small feature subset; we support anonymous clients, which is a core feature of CARL, but only mentioned as a possible extension in ATNL. We implicitly rely on HTTPS and the web browser's certificate management as the main client-side policy. Unlike ATNL we do not support trust negotiation, but we do support a weak form of policy hiding [16]. More precisely, we provide annotations which can be used to hide constants in the service's policy (e.g., passwords).

Contributions. We specify a policy language (§3.1) for specifying the service-side access control policy as well as the policy's disclosure requirements relating to the user's credentials. The language is a light extension of Datalog (§3.1). It also provides an abstraction for credentials that encompasses both digitally signed credentials as well as unsigned data items. Using Datalog is advantageous because it is well-studied and has a well-understood semantics, and by staying close to Datalog our language is more interoperable and extensible with other policy language research. Our extension supports both anonymous scenarios, as well as scenarios in which an identifier for the user is revealed and linked to prior sessions of the user. Similarly we support both scenarios with cryptographic credentials and legacy scenarios in which users authenticate purely through their knowledge of secret constants in the service's policy (e.g., passwords).

In addition to the language, we specify a service-side mechanism (§3.1), based on logical abduction [17], for extracting credential requirements. Abduction is a well-understood form of logical inference. Intuitively, it involves finding hypotheses which, taken together, can lead to a specific conclusion being deduced.

In our setting, abduction refers to the process of finding which combinations of credentials suffice to satisfy the access control policy for a specific request.

We implemented a prototype which includes both service and client components. The service-side component includes an API intended to assist in developing and maintaining web applications, by programmatically generating web interfaces from the service's policy. The client component consists of a browser plug-in which manages credentials, and interacts with the service, under the user's supervision.

Our prototype also implements a protocol (§3.2) based on logic resolution, zero-knowledge proofs, and secure two-party computation, for checking if a set of credentials satisfy given credential requirements. The requirements may specify (signed or unsigned) service secrets (such as a password, or a stored credit card number, or a memorable date). The protocol ensures that the information leaked to either party (about the service's requirement and the user's attempt to satisfy it) depends only on the policy and the available cryptographic mechanisms, and not on artifacts of the language and the protocol flow. Advanced cryptography can restrict leakage to the absolute minimum required by the policy. For backward-compatibility our protocol gracefully degrades to the strongest mechanism supported by both the client and the server – in the worst-case, this consists of simple web-form posts protected by server-authenticating HTTPS.

2 Background

Trust Management. We start by outlining some trust-management scenarios and their formalisation in Datalog. We label scenarios to facilitate reference in later sections.

Our first scenario, DISCOUNT, is based on an example used by Camenisch et al. [15] in the description of their CARL system, encoded in our syntax as follows:

can_discount() :–
        x.**StudentID**$(\ldots, [year], \ldots)$,
        EducationBoard.**UniversityID**$(x, \ldots)$,
        PittsbghTheater.**DiscountCred**$(\ldots, expDate)$,
        $expDate > $ today() .

In this scenario, an anonymous user qualifies for a discount if she is a student at an EducationBoard-accredited university, and if they possess a (non-expired) discount credential from PittsbghTheater. Our syntax is based on Datalog, which is described in more detail in §3.1. Here we give a quick outline of its presentation. We use typefaces to distinguish types of information. Constants are shown in monospace, variables in *italics*, and predicate and function names in sans. An atom consists of a predicate applied to terms (formed out of constants and variables). Predicates shown in **bold sans** denote credentials. The prefix parameter of credential predicates denotes the issuer of the credential, e.g. PittsbghTheater. Any of an atom's parameters may be decorated by square or angular brackets; these indicate the *disclosure mode* (§3.1) of that parameter—for instance, square brackets around a parameter encode the requirement for the user to reveal the parameter's value to the service. Principals are identified with their public keys (which is encoded as a constant). As a result, we write `Alice` or Alice interchangeably. The satisfaction of the policy shown above would entail the disclosure of the *year* value (from the user's **StudentID** credential) to the service. On the other hand, the service does not learn the precise value of *expDate*—the service only learns that *expDate* is in the future.

The above scenario uses delegation or certificate chains. Current state of the art anonymous credential systems do not support hiding public keys, and therefore do not allow users to hide their university in this scenario. Our language is technology-neutral—as is that by Camenisch et al [15]. New cryptographic schemes may hide more information, while legacy technologies, such as X.509, are traceable and have to reveal all.

In scenario BOOKING, user `Alice` wishes to purchase flight tickets using `SmartAir`'s web service. As seen from her side, after picking a flight she is led to a web page showing her different options for payment, for identification at the airport, for collecting air-miles using a frequent flier program, and for redeeming discount vouchers. `SmartAir`'s policy includes:

$$id() :-$$
$$isId([idn], [sur], [dob], [nat], [exp]),$$
$$exp - curTime() \geq 6 \text{ months.}$$
$$isId(idn, sur, dob, nat, exp) :-$$
$$x.\textbf{ePassport}(idn, sur, dob, nat, exp, biomData),$$
$$isEPassportIssuer(x).$$
$$isId(idn, sur, dob, nat, exp) :-$$
$$x.\textbf{passport}(idn, sur, dob, nat, exp).$$

The access request id() succeeds if the user is identifiable to the system. A user is identifiable if she can present a passport, of which there are two kinds. The first is an **ePassport** credential. Such a credential needs to be signed by a suitable issuer (to whom authority is delegated). The above policy does not require the disclosure of biometric data (*biomData*) from **ePassport** when the user makes the access request id().

Alternatively, the user could present a **passport** credential, which is self-asserted—that is, the user instantiates x herself. Self-asserting is comparable to the currently pervasive method, where people type information into web forms, and provide no other proof of ownership (in addition to presenting the passport at the gate, in this setting). We use this device to make our system backward-compatible, by allowing website designers to continue to support, or offer a transition from, unauthenticated form-based input. If the rules of the policy can be satisfied by self-asserted credentials, then the input to these credentials can be drawn from a form that is generated from the policy itself. A service can benefit from our system even if most of their clients do not install the plug-in, as the same mechanism for synchronising the policy with the user-interface can be used. Once the form is posted to the service it will check if the policy is satisfied by the user's input, and grant access accordingly.

In scenario MANAGE we assume that Alice has successfully booked a flight from SmartAir in the past, and now wishes to manage her flight (e.g., specify her dietary requirements). The relevant portion of SmartAir's policy is shown next.

$$\text{manageFlights}(email) :-$$
$$\text{storedIdNum}(email, idn),$$
$$\text{isId}(\langle idn \rangle, sur, dob, nat, exp).$$

The angular brackets surrounding idn stipulate a *service secret*. This snippet expresses that if a user possesses some identification credential which is linked to an email address (supplied by the user when purchasing a flight) and if that user knows the credential's idn, then she may manage that flight. In the case of **passport** this credential would be self-asserted.

Anonymous Credentials. The privacy-friendly extension of trust management relies on anonymous credentials, also called private-key certificates, minimum disclosure tokens or minimum disclosure credentials [18,19]. Conceptually an anonymous credential is a zero-knowledge proof of knowledge (and thus possession) of a conventional cryptographic credential, i.e. of a public-key certificate. Efficient instantiations of anonymous credentials make use of zero-knowledge proofs of knowledge (ZKPK) of discrete logarithm relations [20,21] and dedicated protocols for proving knowledge of signatures [22].

For instance, using the notation of Camenisch et al [23] for DISCOUNT, let σ_1, σ_2, σ_3 denote the signatures by PittsbghU, EducationBoard and PittsbghTheater certifying the relevant credential attributes. Let Vrf denote the predicate corresponding to the verification algorithm, which given a public key, a signature, and a list of messages, verifies the validity of these signatures. In cryptographic notation we write

$$\exists \sigma_1, \sigma_2, \sigma_3, \ldots, expDate.$$
$$\text{Vrf}(\text{PittsbghU}, \sigma_1, (\text{StudentID}, \ldots, 2012, \ldots)) \land$$
$$\text{Vrf}(\text{EducationBoard}, \sigma_2, (\text{UniversityID}, \text{PittsbghU}, \ldots)) \land$$
$$\text{Vrf}(\text{PittsbghTheater}, \sigma_3, (\text{DiscountCred}, \ldots, expDate)) \land$$
$$expDate > \text{today}()$$

for the proof goal related to student and discount credentials. Multiple proofs by the same user are unlinkable, as the signatures themselves are hidden by the ZKPK. Note also the inclusion of the predicate names, StudentID and DiscountCred, among the messages for distinguishing different types of credentials by the same issuer. Moreover, only these labels, the issuer public keys, and the student's matriculation year (2012) are explicitly revealed to the service (since the other parameters are bound by the $\exists$-quantifier).

Strictly speaking, revealing σ_2 would not affect traceability much if PittsbghU is already revealed. Novel cryptographic techniques [24], however, allow hiding

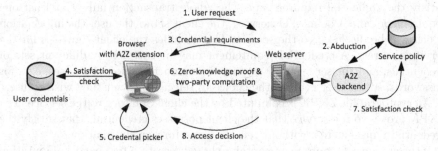

Fig. 1. Architectural overview

the intermediary public keys in certification chains, albeit at some performance costs.

3   A2Z

We describe our policy language with a focus on strong cryptographic privacy protection. We call our system A2Z both for its backward compatibility and for its prototype which combines attribute-based credentials (ABC) with secure two-party computation (2PC) and zero-knowledge proofs of knowledge (ZKPK).

Architecture.   Our system's architecture is sketched in Fig. 1, and the flow between components is described next.

1. The user submits an access request to the service, typically via her web browser.

2. The web application itself is policy-neutral, except for a mapping from the request to one or more corresponding query predicates. This mapping is used to invoke the A2Z backend, which runs *abductive queries* against the service's local access policy. Both the query predicates and the policy are written in Datalog. Intuitively, the result of an abductive query is a formula that describes the minimal sets of missing credentials that would make the query true if the credentials were added to the policy.

3. The credential requirements, i.e., the abductive answers, are employed in two related tasks. First, they are enriched with presentational guidance provided by website developers to build a service specific user interface stub. Second, they are serialised to XML and sent back to the user's browser. For legacy clients without the plug-in, the answers are filtered for self-asserted credentials and the interface is already fully functional; thus steps 4-7 are skipped.

4. The A2Z browser plug-in recognises the incoming credential requirements, deserialises them, and runs them as *deductive queries* against the user's set of credentials. User credentials are Datalog assertions that may be unsigned, self-signed, or signed by third parties. The answer of a deductive query is a (possibly empty) set of Datalog proof trees. The root (or the conclusion) of each proof tree is the original query (i.e., a credential requirement), and the leaves are user credentials. Resolution [25] is the sole rule in this proof calculus.

5. At this point, the client knows whether the user's credentials can in principle satisfy the credential requirements. The whole transaction fails if at least one requirement cannot be met. Otherwise, the client shows the user the information which will be disclosed to the service. This includes the client's guesses for the service's secrets. A credential requirement may be satisfied by different sets of credentials, and the service may restrict the number of allowed guesses, e.g., for passwords, so the user is given the choice to select which set they wish to use.

6. A cryptographic ZKPK is computed by the client and sent to the service. The ZKPK proves to the service that the client possesses credentials that satisfy the credential requirements, without revealing any further information.

If the credential requirement contains shared secrets, a two-party computation (2PC) could be carried out to establish if the deductive answers selected by the client match the ones expected by the service. The protocol ensures that the client's guess is not leaked to the service, and the service only learns whether the match succeeds. The ZKPK guarantees that the guesses made by the user in the 2PC are consistent with her credentials.

7. The service verifies the integrity of the client's ZKPK and the outcome of the 2PC and checks it against the original credential requirements.

8. If all satisfaction checks succeed, the service grants the user access to the requested resource. The information revealed by the ZKPK may also be used for further processing.

3.1   Computing Credential Requirements

We now elaborate Steps 1 – 3 from Fig. 1.

Datalog. We use Datalog [26] as a common language for expressing both the policy of a service, as well as user credentials.

A Datalog *atom*, ranged over by P, has the form $\mathsf{p}(\overrightarrow{e})$, where p is a predicate name and the *parameters* $\overrightarrow{e}$ are a sequence of variables x and constants C matching the arity and type of p. We fix a subset of predicate names called *constraint predicate names*; an atom constructed from such a predicate name is a *constraint*. We also fix a unary relation $\vdash$ on ground (i.e., variable-free) constraints [27], e.g. $\vdash 1 < 2$.

A Datalog *clause* γ is either a non-constraint atom, or a *rule* of the form $P :\!- P_1 \wedge \ldots \wedge P_n$, for some $n \geq 1$, where $P_1, \ldots, P_n$ are atoms, and P is a non-constraint atom. The atom P is called the *head*, and the conjunction of atoms $P_1 \wedge \ldots \wedge P_n$ is called the *body* of the clause. The turnstile ":–" can be read as "if". A Datalog *program* Π is a finite set of clauses.

Definition 1. *A program Π entails a ground atom P (we write $\Pi \vdash P$) if either $P \in \Pi$, or P is a constraint and $\vdash P$ holds, or there exists a ground instance $P_0 :\!- P_1 \wedge \ldots \wedge P_n$ of some rule $\gamma \in \Pi$, such that $P = P_0$ and $\Pi \vdash P_i$, for all $i \in \{1, \ldots, n\}$.*

A *query* is a formula φ over atoms, possibly involving conjunction ($\wedge$), disjunction ($\vee$), and existential quantification ($\exists$). Variables occurring in a query are *free* if they are not bound by an existential quantifier. A query is *closed* if it does not contain any free variables. We extend the entailment relation to queries in the standard way. For instance, the query $\exists x.\, \mathbf{a}(x, [y], z_1, \langle z_2 \rangle)$ is satisfied by any instance of credential $\mathbf{a}$ where the third and fourth parameters are the constants z_1 and z_2 respectively. Operationally, the first parameter is kept private by the client, and the second parameter is revealed to the service.

Definition 2. *The* answers $\mathsf{ans}_\Pi(\varphi)$ *of a (possibly non-closed) query* φ, *with respect to program* Π, *is a set of variable substitutions* θ *such that* $\Pi \vdash \varphi\theta$. *Furthermore, whenever* $\Pi \vdash \varphi\theta'$ *for some substitution* θ', *there exists* $\theta \in \mathsf{ans}_\Pi(\varphi)$ *such that* $\varphi\theta = \varphi\theta'$.

Definition 3. *The* abductive answers $\mathsf{abd}_\Pi(\varphi)$ *of a closed query* φ *with respect to a program* Π *is a set of closed formulas* ρ *of the form* $\exists \overrightarrow{x}.\, P_1 \wedge \ldots \wedge P_n$ *such that the following hold:*

1. $\Pi \cup \{P_1, \ldots, P_n\}\theta \vdash \varphi$, *for all substitutions* θ *that ground* $\overrightarrow{x}$.
2. *If* $\Pi \cup \overrightarrow{P} \vdash \varphi$ *for some finite set of ground atoms* $\overrightarrow{P}$, *then there exists a formula* $\exists \overrightarrow{x}.\, P_1 \wedge \ldots \wedge P_n$ *in* $\mathsf{abd}_\Pi(\varphi)$, *and a substitution* θ *such that* $\{P_1, \ldots, P_n\}\theta \subseteq \overrightarrow{P}$.

For both ans and abd, there are algorithms [28] that compute the *minimal* answer sets, i.e., only the most general substitutions for ans, and the smallest formulas for abd.

Policies and Credentials. We fix a subset of predicate names, called *credential predicate names*. To distinguish them from ordinary predicate names for the purpose of this paper, we write credential predicate names in **bold**. All credential predicate names have an arity of at least 1, and the first parameter identifies the *issuer*. Intuitively, this is the principal (identified by a public key) who vouches for an atomic statement. We write $e.\mathbf{p}(\overrightarrow{e})$ as syntactic sugar for $\mathbf{p}(e, \overrightarrow{e})$.

A *policy rule* is a Datalog clause, and a *policy* is a Datalog program. A *credential* is a Datalog clause involving only credential predicate names. The *issuer* of the credential is the issuer of its head, and is required to be ground. On the abstract level of the policy language, there is no distinction between policy rules and credentials, other than the restriction on predicate names occurring in credentials. On the implementation level, though, credentials are signed with the issuer's private key, and can be verified with the issuer's public key. Policy rules, on the other hand, need not be signed, even if their heads involve credential predicates.

An *access request* to a service is expressed as a ground atom P (*cf.* Step 1, Fig. 1).

Definition 4. *Let* Π *be a service's policy. Its* credential requirements $\mathsf{credReq}_\Pi(P)$ *for access request* P *is defined as* $\{\rho \in \mathsf{abd}_\Pi(P) \mid \rho \text{ only involves credential predicates and constraints }\}$. *A set* Γ *of credentials satisfies* $\mathsf{credReq}_\Pi(P)$, *iff there exists* $\rho \in \mathsf{credReq}_\Pi(P)$ *such that* $\Gamma \vdash \rho$.

Intuitively, the credential requirements specify which combinations of credentials a user needs to possess in order for the access request to be granted. More precisely, it specifies the credential sets that, if added to Π, would be sufficient for proving P (*cf.* Step 2, Fig. 1). This is formalised by the following proposition.

Proposition 1. *Let Π be a policy, Γ a set of credentials, and P an access request. Γ satisfies* $\mathsf{credReq}_\Pi(P)$ *iff* $\Pi \cup \Gamma \vdash P$.

Disclosure Modes. Our policies specify not just the credentials required for access, but also the disclosure requirements for the credentials' parameters. This is expressed by means of tags placed on the parameters of atoms which occur in credential requirements. These tags are called *disclosure modes*, of which there are three:

1. An unadorned parameter e denotes no service-side disclosure requirements for this parameter. If e is a constant, it is transmitted to the user in plaintext. If it is a variable, the user may hide the actual value of this parameter using a zero-knowledge proof.
2. If x is a variable, then $[x]$ denotes a parameter that must be *revealed*, i.e., the user is required to disclose the corresponding constant value in the credential.
3. If C is a constant, then $\langle C \rangle$ denotes a parameter that is a *service secret*, i.e., a value (such as a passcode or a stored credit card number) that the service does not wish to disclose to the user unless the user can guess the value.

Recall that the credential requirements are computed dynamically from the policy for a specific access request. The disclosure modes within the credential requirements are computed from the policy during the same process. To ease integration with existing Datalog processing tools, we encode the disclosure modes as extra predicate parameters. Every "normal" predicate parameter, apart from the issuer, is associated with a disclosure mode parameter in the same predicate. The disclosure mode parameter can take the values reveal and secret, or it can be a variable—this encodes a "don't care" disclosure mode, which in practice means that the user can keep the corresponding value private. For instance, the adorned atom $S.\mathbf{p}(\langle 123 \rangle, 4, x, [y])$ is encoded as $S.\mathbf{p}(123, \mathsf{secret}, 4, dm_1, x, dm_2, y, \mathsf{reveal})$. This encoding allows the disclosure modes to be propagated automatically during the abduction process.

We also slightly modify the specification of $\mathsf{credReq}$ such that for all $\rho \in \mathsf{credReq}_\Pi(P)$, reveal-variables $[x]$ in ρ are not existentially quantified; i.e., they remain free in ρ. Furthermore, secret parameters $\langle C \rangle$ in ρ are implemented as fresh, mutually distinct, variables. As a result, when the user's client application receives ρ, it knows which variables are secret parameters, but it cannot infer the original secret value. As we shall see later, ρ will be used by the client as a Datalog query, so the answers of ρ will provide ground instantiations of all reveal and secret parameters.

Example 1. Consider the following policy fragment of `PittsbghTheater`, adapted from DISCOUNT:

> free_entry() :– PittsbghU.**StudentID**($name$, [$course$], ...),
> PittsbghTheater.**Receipt**($name$, $\langle code \rangle$, $date$, ...),
> Winning($code$),
> today() − $date \leq$ days(7) .
> Winning(1234).

This policy captures a scheme run by `PittsbghTheater` to allow a `PittsbghU` student to attend a show for free if (i) that student has already attended a show at `PittsbghTheater` during the last week (and possesses a receipt for it), (ii) the receipt is linked to the student's ID credential via the student's name, (iii) the student's receipt contains a specific (winning) code value (which the service does not want to reveal to the client), and (iv) the student is willing to reveal their degree programme to the service. The credential requirements for the access request free_entry() is the singleton set containing the formula

$$\exists\, date, name.\ \texttt{PittsbghU}.\textbf{StudentID}(name, [course], ...) \land$$
$$\texttt{PittsbghTheater}.\textbf{Receipt}(name, \langle 1234 \rangle, date, ...) \land$$
$$\texttt{today}() - date \leq \texttt{days}(7)$$

In the credential requirements sent to the client, '1234' is blanked out.

Sending Credential Requirements to the Client. In the simplest case, upon receiving the user's access request P, the service computes $\mathsf{credReq}_\Pi(P)$ and sends it to the client (Step 3, Fig. 1), which then computes the credential sets that satisfy the credential requirements, and presents them to the user to choose from.

In scenarios where $\mathsf{credReq}_\Pi(P)$ is large, or if there are many ways for satisfying each ρ using the user's credentials, then the interactive credential picking process (Step 6, Fig. 1) will be unwieldy since various combinations of credentials will be displayed to the user.

Example 2. Let $\mathsf{credReq}_\Pi(P)$ be the set $\{\rho_1, \rho_2\}$, where $\rho_1 := \exists x.\, \mathbf{a}(x, [y]) \land \mathbf{b}([z])$ and $\rho_2 := \exists x.\, \mathbf{b}(x) \land \mathbf{b}([y]) \land x \neq y$. Recall that multiple requirements $\rho \in \mathsf{credReq}_\Pi(P)$ are interpreted as a big disjunction—in this example, the user can derive P using their credentials Γ iff $\Gamma \vdash \rho_1 \lor \rho_2$.

Now let Γ be the following collection

$$\{\mathbf{a}(1,2),\ \mathbf{a}(2,3),\ \mathbf{b}(1),\ \mathbf{b}(2),\ \mathbf{b}(3),\ \mathbf{b}(4)\}$$

Then the user will have to pick among 14 choices: 2×4 for ρ_1, and $\binom{4}{2}$ for ρ_2.

To make the selection less unwieldy, we can ask the user to "preselect" which $\rho \in \mathsf{credReq}_\Pi(P)$ they aim to satisfy. To support this, the service could dynamically generate a web form from $\mathsf{credReq}_\Pi(P)$ that displays the disjunction of different requirements ρ in a human-readable format, and lets the user pick exactly one ρ

to satisfy. In our implementation, credential atoms in the policy are annotated with meta-information (such as descriptive strings) that is carried along during the abduction process. In this way, the code that produces the web form can be kept completely policy-agnostic. Fig. 2(a) shows an example screenshot of such a form.

3.2   Satisfaction Check and Credential Picker

We now elaborate Steps 4 – 5 in Fig. 1. In addition to the credential requirements, a service may also push additional credentials to the user. Such credentials are usually used for delegation of authority by the service. Let Γ be the set consisting of the user's credentials in union with the pushed policy rules from the service.

For each $\rho \in \mathsf{credReq}_\Pi(P)$, the client computes an answer set $\Theta_\rho = \mathsf{ans}_\Gamma(\rho)$ (Step 4, Fig. 1). (User credentials do not contain disclosure modes, and the computation of ans ignores the disclosure modes in ρ.) Note that every $\theta \in \Theta_\rho$ is a substitution that grounds precisely the reveal and secret variables in ρ. (Unadorned variables are implicitly $\exists$-bound since they are kept private to the client.)

Example 3. Continuing from Example 1, imagine that Alice, a student, turns up at the theatre with the following credentials:

$$\mathrm{cr}_1 = \mathtt{PittsbghU}.\textbf{StudentID}(\mathtt{Alice}, \mathtt{CS}, \dots).$$
$$\mathrm{cr}_2 = \mathtt{PittsbghTheater}.\textbf{Receipt}(\mathtt{Alice}, 9876, 12/12, \dots).$$
$$\mathrm{cr}_3 = \mathtt{PittsbghTheater}.\textbf{Receipt}(\mathtt{Alice}, 1234, 13/12, \dots).$$

Assuming that the date-interval constraint is satisfied, then following the local satisfaction check we find that the singleton credential requirement seen earlier can be satisfied in two ways:

$$\{(\mathit{code} \mapsto 9876, \mathit{course} \mapsto \mathtt{CS}), (\mathit{code} \mapsto 1234, \mathit{course} \mapsto \mathtt{CS})\}$$

Now the user is asked to pick an answer θ from $\bigcup_\rho \Theta_\rho$ to disclose to the service (Step 6, Fig. 1). The challenge here is to provide a user-friendly interface that graphically represents the disclosure concisely and yet informatively. One option would be to display each combination of ρ and θ (where $\rho \in \mathsf{credReq}_\Pi(P)$ and $\theta \in \Theta_\rho$) as a row of cards. Each card corresponds to an atom in ρ, containing fields with friendly descriptors of the issuer, the predicate name, and the other parameters of the atom (with variables instantiated by θ). Visual cues (e.g. colours or typographic markup) could be used to distinguish hidden (i.e., existentially quantified) values from revealed parameters and service secrets.

For each such row of cards, the representation can be switched to an advanced view, which additionally displays all credentials involved in proving $\rho\theta$, and again uses markup to show precisely what is, and what is not, disclosed to the service. This is useful because, as we shall see below, not only $\rho\theta$ is disclosed to the service, but, depending on the employed technology, so will the issuers and the basic structure of the credentials involved.

The user can then pick one answer and consent to disclosure. Continuing from Example 3, Alice's choice of credentials must include cr_1 (from which '*course* = CS' is disclosed to the service), and additionally either cr_2, or cr_3. Only the latter will lead to a successful match for *code*.

3.3 Verification of User Credentials

We now turn to Steps 6 – 8 in Fig. 1. The user needs to convince the service that her guesses in θ were correct and that she possesses credentials that let her derive $\rho\theta$, where $\rho \in \mathsf{credReq}_\Pi(P)$. If the user were unconcerned about privacy, the client could just send a subset of the user's credentials $\Gamma' \subseteq \Gamma$, such that $\Gamma' \vdash \rho\theta$, to the service, together with the proof conclusion $\rho\theta$ itself.

However, this solution would disclose more credential information to the service than necessary. To see how to minimise the amount of information disclosed, first consider the set $\Gamma' \subseteq \Gamma$ of credentials involved in proving $\rho\theta$, i.e., $\Gamma' \vdash \rho\theta$. Note that we can uniformly and injectively rename constants and predicate names $\overrightarrow{e}$ in Γ' to fresh variables $\overrightarrow{f}$.[2] This renaming is restricted to constants and predicate names which do not occur in $\rho\theta$. This produces an "obfuscated" set of Datalog clauses $\Gamma^{\maltese} = \Gamma'[\overrightarrow{f}/\overrightarrow{e}]$. Since the renaming is injective, $\Gamma^{\maltese} \vdash \rho\theta$ holds.

Now the client sends descriptions of $\Gamma^{\maltese}$, ρ and θ to the service, together with a ZKPK that $\Gamma^{\maltese}$ is an obfuscation of valid credentials that the user possesses. More precisely, the proof states that there exist constants and predicate names $\overrightarrow{e}$, such that the user possesses signed credentials for $\Gamma^{\maltese}[\overrightarrow{e}/\overrightarrow{f}]$. In order to be able to construct a zero-knowledge proof of knowledge (ZKPK) of such statements, we also require that the renaming leaves all issuer constants occurring in Γ' intact.

When issuing cryptographic credentials, issuers serialise the Datalog clauses in Γ to tuples,[3] to encode them using anonymous credential techniques [22,24]. Users can then use standard ZKPK techniques to produce a proof [29,30]. The service then proceeds to check that the following conditions hold:

1. $\rho \in \mathsf{credReq}_\Pi(P)$. (Ensuring that the user's proof conclusion corresponds to a credential requirement.)
2. For all `reveal`-variables $[x]$ in ρ, $\theta(x)$ is a constant. (Ensuring that `reveal` parameters are indeed revealed.)
3. For all `secret`-variables $\langle C\rangle$ in ρ, $\theta(\langle C\rangle) = C$. (Ensuring that the service secrets are matched by the user.)
4. $\Gamma^{\maltese} \vdash \rho\theta$ (Ensuring that the obfuscated credentials are sufficient for proving the conclusion.)
5. The zero-knowledge proof is valid and indeed proves that the user possesses credentials that can be renamed to $\Gamma^{\maltese}$.

If all these checks succeed, the service is convinced that the user possesses valid credentials that satisfy the credential requirements (including the disclosure re-

---

[2] Recall that in the credential signatures, predicate names are encoded as constants.

[3] For instance, $\mathtt{A.p}(x) \mathbin{:-} \mathtt{B.q}(x,3), \mathtt{C.r}(x)$ could be encoded as a tuple $(\mathtt{p}, \mathtt{A}, x, -, \mathtt{q}, \mathtt{B}, x, 3, -, \mathtt{r}, \mathtt{C}, x)$ signed by $\mathtt{A}$, which can also be easily decoded back into a Datalog clause.

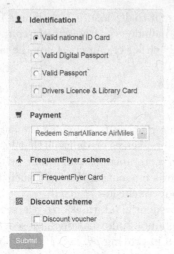

(a) Form synthesised automatically from the underlying policy, using the presentational guidance written into the web application.

(b) Mocked-up credential picker for scenario MANAGE. The fields are coloured depending on their disclosure mode. In this case only the Course and ID Number are revealed, and the mark-up indicates that the latter is a service secret (described in §3.1).

Fig. 2. User interface

quirements). The service does not learn anything more about the user's credentials apart from what is leaked by $\Gamma^{\varkappa}$ – essentially, the number of rules, the length of the rule bodies and the arities of the predicates (and even these could be hidden by padding), the issuer public keys, and the constraints between variables, constants and predicate names. To protect the clients, she can match her guesses against the server's secrets using a secure two-party computation protocol (2PC), such as the protocol by Kissner et al. [31]. Instead of revealing θ in the clear she can verifiably encrypt its values [32] such that they are only revealed in case of a match.

4   Related Work

Several policy languages for enabling the use of zero-knowledge proofs and anonymous credentials have been proposed. One of the most closely-related languages to our own, is the *card-based access-control requirements language* (CARL) [15]. This also inspired the work by Ardagna et al. [12], who extended existing open technologies (rather than produce a new language as in CARL). Also based on CARL is the work by Camenisch et al [33] on the ABC4Trust project, who give a sweeping description of a comprehensive language framework. Other related work includes that by Ardagna et al [34], who employ a sophisticated system of weighting attribute values by their sensitivity.

Another closely related work is the *attribute-based trust negotiation language* (ATNL) [14] for *automated trust negotiation* (ATN) between parties unfamiliar with one another. ATNL is based on the RT family of languages, which are based on Datalog. ATNL's more fine-grained regard of credential information helps mitigate avoidable failures in ATN. That is, instead of entire credentials, only attributes, or proofs (of attributes, or of credentials) need be revealed during negotiation. Other protocols, employed by ATNL and described by Frikken at al [16], allow more hiding of policy information than our system, but this comes at an increased complexity cost. Instead of using abductive inference, Lee et al [35] describe a method which casts the problem as pattern-matching.

Both CARL and ATNL support advanced cryptographic features which we currently do not. ATNL specifies a much more sophisticated protocol than ours— we rely on the human user to decide whether to submit credentials to the service. We contend that our approach offers an appealing mix of privacy features and pragmatism. For instance, our approach focuses on browser-based usage and makes it clearer how to support legacy authentication and authorisation methods, by providing the means to extract Web content (e.g., forms) from access policies. We argued that this allows services to support traditional, as well as more privacy-aware end-user technologies, within the same framework.

5 Conclusion

Datalog-based languages are simple to understand and use, and this makes them appealing. We have made a small extension to Datalog to interpret annotations related to disclosure; these annotations restrict the disclosure of information from the server to the client, and vice versa. We also found it useful to use the access policy as the basis of the user interface; this also ensures that the UI is consistent with the policy. Furthermore, should the client not have the browser plug-in installed, the system degrades gracefully: the server could produce a form-based interface for the user to fill out (simulating self-asserted credentials), instead of relying on the plug-in to carry out the cryptographic protocols. Should the user have the plug-in, the authentication and authorisation steps are fully-automated, and the user will be informed (prior to disclosure) about which information is being protected. The actual cryptographic protocols used in implementations of the architecture can vary, and the degree of disclosure of data will vary accordingly. In future work we would like to experiment with different cryptographic technologies in addition to the basic support implemented in our prototype. This includes tighter integration with secure session establishment and server authentication. We would also like to experiment with improving the usability of the prototype, including at the server end, and look for ways to improve integration with existing technologies, and facilitate deployment.

Acknowledgements. We thank Jason MacKay, Zhenqin Chuo, George Danezis, Cédric Fournet for tool support and feedback, and the anonymous reviewers for their comments.

References

1. Lampson, B.W.: Protection. Operating Systems Review 8(1), 18–24 (1974)
2. Miller, M., Yee, K.P., Shapiro, J., Inc, C.: Capability Myths Demolished. Technical report, Johns Hopkins University Systems Research Laboratory (2003)
3. Lee, A.J., Winslett, M., Basney, J., Welch, V.: The Traust Authorization Service. ACM Trans. Inf. Syst. Secur. 11(1) (2008)
4. Blaze, M., Feigenbaum, J., Keromytis, A.D.: The Role of Trust Management in Distributed Systems Security. In: Vitek, J. (ed.) Secure Internet Programming. LNCS, vol. 1603, pp. 185–210. Springer, Heidelberg (1999)
5. di Vimercati, S.D.C., Foresti, S., Jajodia, S., Paraboschi, S., Psaila, G., Samarati, P.: Integrating trust management and access control in data-intensive Web applications. TWEB 6(2), 6 (2012)
6. Brands, S.: Rethinking Public Key Infrastructures and Digital Certificates. MIT Press (2000)
7. Chaum, D.: Security Without Identification: Transaction Systems to Make Big Brother obsolete. Communications of the ACM 28(10), 1030–1044 (1985)
8. Camenisch, J.L., Lysyanskaya, A.: An Efficient System for Non-transferable Anonymous Credentials with Optional Anonymity Revocation. In: Pfitzmann, B. (ed.) EUROCRYPT 2001. LNCS, vol. 2045, pp. 93–118. Springer, Heidelberg (2001)
9. Bellovin, S.M., Merritt, M.: Augmented Encrypted Key Exchange: A Password-Based Protocol Secure against Dictionary Attacks and Password File Compromise. In: Denning, D.E., Pyle, R., Ganesan, R., Sandhu, R.S., Ashby, V. (eds.) ACM Conference on Computer and Communications Security, pp. 244–250. ACM (1993)
10. Camenisch, J., Casati, N., Gross, T., Shoup, V.: Credential Authenticated Identification and Key Exchange. In: Rabin, T. (ed.) CRYPTO 2010. LNCS, vol. 6223, pp. 255–276. Springer, Heidelberg (2010)
11. Blazy, O., Chevalier, C., Pointcheval, D., Vergnaud, D.: Efficient UC-Secure Authenticated Key-Exchange for Algebraic Languages. IACR Cryptology ePrint Archive 2012, 284 (2012)
12. Ardagna, C.A., Camenisch, J., Kohlweiss, M., Leenes, R., Neven, G., Priem, B., Samarati, P., Sommer, D., Verdicchio, M.: Exploiting cryptography for privacy-enhanced access control: A result of the PRIME Project. Journal of Computer Security 18(1), 123–160 (2010)
13. PrimeLife Project (2012), http://www.primelife.eu/ (accessed in December 2012)
14. Li, J., Li, N., Winsborough, W.: Automated trust negotiation using cryptographic credentials. In: Proceedings of the 12th ACM conference on Computer and Communications Security, pp. 46–57. ACM (2005)
15. Camenisch, J., Mödersheim, S., Neven, G., Preiss, F.S., Sommer, D.: A card requirements language enabling privacy-preserving access control. In: Joshi, J.B.D., Carminati, B. (eds.) SACMAT, pp. 119–128. ACM (2010)
16. Frikken, K.B., Li, J., Atallah, M.J.: Trust Negotiation with Hidden Credentials, Hidden Policies, and Policy Cycles. In: NDSS. The Internet Society (2006)
17. Peirce, C.S.: Abduction and Induction. In: Buchler, J. (ed.) Philosophical Writings of Peirce. Dover Publications, Oxford (1955)
18. Belenkiy, M., Camenisch, J., Chase, M., Kohlweiss, M., Lysyanskaya, A., Shacham, H.: Randomizable Proofs and Delegatable Anonymous Credentials. In: Halevi, S. (ed.) CRYPTO 2009. LNCS, vol. 5677, pp. 108–125. Springer, Heidelberg (2009)

19. Bichsel, P., Camenisch, J., Groß, T., Shoup, V.: Anonymous credentials on a standard Java card. In: Al-Shaer, E., Jha, S., Keromytis, A.D. (eds.) ACM Conference on Computer and Communications Security, pp. 600–610. ACM (2009)
20. Schnorr, C.: Efficient Signature Generation for Smart Cards. Journal of Cryptology 4(3), 239–252 (1991)
21. Chaum, D., Pedersen, T.P.: Wallet databases with observers. In: Brickell, E.F. (ed.) CRYPTO 1992. LNCS, vol. 740, pp. 89–105. Springer, Heidelberg (1993)
22. Camenisch, J.L., Lysyanskaya, A.: A Signature Scheme with Efficient Protocols. In: Cimato, S., Galdi, C., Persiano, G. (eds.) SCN 2002. LNCS, vol. 2576, pp. 268–289. Springer, Heidelberg (2003)
23. Camenisch, J., Krenn, S., Shoup, V.: A Framework for Practical Universally Composable Zero-Knowledge Protocols. In: Lee, D.H., Wang, X. (eds.) ASIACRYPT 2011. LNCS, vol. 7073, pp. 449–467. Springer, Heidelberg (2011)
24. Abe, M., Fuchsbauer, G., Groth, J., Haralambiev, K., Ohkubo, M.: Structure-Preserving Signatures and Commitments to Group Elements. In: Rabin, T. (ed.) CRYPTO 2010. LNCS, vol. 6223, pp. 209–236. Springer, Heidelberg (2010)
25. Robinson, J.: A machine-oriented logic based on the resolution principle. Journal of the ACM (JACM) 12(1), 23–41 (1965)
26. Ceri, S., Gottlob, G., Tanca, L.: What You Always Wanted to Know About Datalog (And Never Dared to Ask). IEEE Transactions on Knowledge and Data Engineering 1(1), 146–166 (1989)
27. Li, N., Mitchell, J.C.: DATALOG with Constraints: A Foundation for Trust Management Languages. In: Dahl, V. (ed.) PADL 2003. LNCS, vol. 2562, pp. 58–73. Springer, Heidelberg (2002)
28. Becker, M.Y., Nanz, S.: The role of abduction in declarative authorization policies. In: Hudak, P., Warren, D.S. (eds.) PADL 2008. LNCS, vol. 4902, pp. 84–99. Springer, Heidelberg (2008)
29. Camenisch, J., Kiayias, A., Yung, M.: On the Portability of Generalized Schnorr Proofs. In: Joux, A. (ed.) EUROCRYPT 2009. LNCS, vol. 5479, pp. 425–442. Springer, Heidelberg (2009)
30. Groth, J., Sahai, A.: Efficient Non-interactive Proof Systems for Bilinear Groups. In: Smart, N.P. (ed.) EUROCRYPT 2008. LNCS, vol. 4965, pp. 415–432. Springer, Heidelberg (2008)
31. Kissner, L., Song, D.: Privacy-Preserving Set Operations. In: Shoup, V. (ed.) CRYPTO 2005. LNCS, vol. 3621, pp. 241–257. Springer, Heidelberg (2005)
32. Camenisch, J.L., Damgård, I.B.: Verifiable encryption, group encryption, and their applications to separable group signatures and signature sharing schemes. In: Okamoto, T. (ed.) ASIACRYPT 2000. LNCS, vol. 1976, pp. 331–345. Springer, Heidelberg (2000)
33. Camenisch, J., Dubovitskaya, M., Lehmann, A., Neven, G., Paquin, C., Preiss, F.-S.: Concepts and Languages for Privacy-Preserving Attribute-Based Authentication. In: Fischer-Hübner, S., de Leeuw, E., Mitchell, C. (eds.) IDMAN 2013. IFIP AICT, vol. 396, pp. 34–52. Springer, Heidelberg (2013)
34. Ardagna, C.A., di Vimercati, S.D.C., Foresti, S., Paraboschi, S., Samarati, P.: Minimising disclosure of client information in credential-based interactions. IJIPSI 1(2/3), 205–233 (2012)
35. Lee, A.J., Winslett, M.: Towards an efficient and language-agnostic compliance checker for trust negotiation systems. In: Proceedings of the 2008 ACM Symposium on Information, Computer and Communications Security, pp. 228–239. ACM (2008)

Towards a Detective Approach to Business Process-Centered Resilience

Thomas Koslowski and Christian Zimmermann

University of Freiburg, Germany
{koslowski,zimmermann}@iig.uni-freiburg.de

Abstract. Protection of today's interconnected and complex information infrastructures is of high priority. Traditionally, protection means robustness: preventively identify the threats to business processes and propose countermeasures within the context of a risk analysis. This, however, only covers known risks having punctual effects upon the IT infrastructure. In contrast, the notion of *resilience*, as a refinement of trustworthiness, is getting attention both in academia and within organizations as a denominator to move beyond survival and even prosper in the face of adverse conditions. This paper reports on ongoing work towards the development of PREDEC, a detective framework to realize resilience in the context of business processes. Specifically, it firstly motivates the need for operational resilience and corresponding tool support at the level of processes. Secondly, it sketches the operation and building blocks of PREDEC, which currently employs process mining techniques to analyze process event logs to assess systems' resilience. Finally, it describes the intended evaluation steps to be undertaken once PREDEC is completely implemented.

Keywords: Operational Resilience, Automated Detection, Process Intelligence, Resilient BPM.

1 Introduction

The intensive use of densely interconnected and complex IT-systems incurs risks with increasingly severe disruptive effects. Today, most decision makers, either public administrators or private organizations, have come to understand that protection of information systems is of high priority. But the expanding landscape of emerging risks illustrates the borderless and unpredictable nature of risk and uncovers the limits of traditional risk management practices and theories in the face of highly interconnected systems: *new emerging risks* or *new surprises* lack a priori indication of occurrence, they exhibit the potential to "cascade" through time and space at different speeds and their relation between origin, evolution and final consequence are frequently ill-understood [14,25]. But just because some systems are complex does not mean they are unmanageable or impossible to govern. However, managing them requires different methods and rests on other assumptions than classical risk and security management.

R. Accorsi and S. Ranise (Eds.): STM 2013, LNCS 8203, pp. 176–190, 2013.
© Springer-Verlag Berlin Heidelberg 2013

Where we had come to expect predictability and consistency, we now must accept the necessity of dealing with the consequences of uncertainty [30].

Against this background, the notion of resilience is getting attention as a denominator to move beyond survival and even prosper in the face of challenging conditions [25,29]. Resilience is an emergent property associated with an organization's capacity to continue its mission despite disruption through mindfulness [41], resourceful agility and recoverability, e.g., [15,25]. Therefore, resilience is a combination of technical design features, such as fault-tolerance and dependability [9], with organizational features such as mindfulness, training and decentralized decision making [8,41].

Today, enterprise systems and information infrastructures increasingly build upon processes. Generally speaking, processes are structured specifications of personnel and business data usage that run (at least) semi-automated in a business process management (BPM) system. Examples of systems building upon processes can be found in very different domains and range from, e.g., organizations' supply chains, banking backbone infrastructure to parts of critical infrastructure such as smart grids or nuclear power plants. The advantage of process-orientation is the decoupling of infrastructure and organizational workflows as a means to enhance enterprises' overall performance and effectiveness.

The current state of the art at the intersection of business processes management and resilience approaches the high-level design of resilient information systems [8], the satisfiability of workflows [11,39], change propagation [18] and incident response [23]. However, there are no approaches and technical frameworks that put processes in a "resilience loop" which also encompasses adaption.

In this paper, we report on ongoing work towards PREDEC, a detective framework to assert the resilience of business process-based information technology infrastructures. According to the BPM lifecycle, the analysis of processes can happen at design time *(a priori)*, at runtime and offline *(a posteriori)* [2] (compare Figure 2). While the first two timepoints allow for preventive mechanisms to avoid violations, a posteriori methods based on the analysis of event logs are detective. Casting them into the context of resilience, preventive methods are in place to allow for robustness (resistance against incidents) whereas detective approaches serve as an input for business process redesign and, if in large scale, re-engineering. However, extensive literature review in the field of risk-aware BPM reveals that current approaches focus on the design-time phase, while concepts and artifacts with focus on runtime and offline analysis are rare [26,36]. The ultimate goal of PREDEC is to enable organizations to automatically identify and assess the interdependence of assets and processes. In order to extract the interdependencies we employ process mining techniques developed by [2,37]. Additionally, we employ techniques as developed by, e.g., [38] to elicit sociometric data from event logs in order to build social networks of the subjects involved in process executions. In that, we aim at augmenting the assessment of interdependence of assets and processes with a social network perspective.

Paper structure. The next section describes our research context and design. We highlight the increasing attention paid to resilience management as a complementary approach to process-oriented security and risk management in detail. In that, we provide a brief overview of existing work on resilience in IS research with an emphasis on resilient BPM. By screening prior research, we show that there is a lack of research on (semi-automatic) BPM resilience tools. In Section 3, we present our approach to automated business process resilience detection based on event log data. We introduce the components of our approach and the requirements they have to meet in order to allow for elicitation of structures from event logs and resilience detection on these structures. In Section 4, we discuss our findings and provide an overview on our ongoing and future work. Finally, we summarize our work in Section 5.

2 Research Context and Design

Although resilience is widely recognized in related disciplines such as Computer Science [42], Contingencies and Crisis Management [12], or Safety Engineering [25], there is an apparent incongruity between the level of interest paid by business managers and the attention that organizational and IS scholars have given to resilience. Today, only a limited number of IS resilience research exists [32]. This research gap is surprising, since resilience is often said to be a combination of social or organizational and technical qualities and therefore a research topic well suited for IS research. Hence, we provide a brief overview of existing work on resilience in IS research in order to derive key concepts as a foundation to gather requirements for our proposed resilience detection framework.

Based on a literature review, we developed a resilience management cycle [32] (depicted in Figure 1) for automated support for resilient BPM according to the well-established BPM lifecycle. The cycle contains four phases adapted primarily from [8] and [15], beginning with (i) *Detection* in order to identify failures, potential weaknesses and exceptional process executions. (ii) The purpose of *Diagnosis and Evaluation* is to collect and assess vulnerabilities, and consequently to determine a set of intervention types. (iii) The next stage covers *Treatment and Recovery*, including the actual selection and implementation of supportive actions and automatic corrections. (iv) Finally, the phase of *Escalation and Institutionalization* guarantees enrichment or revision of the current knowledge base, and aims to establish and facilitate an organization-wide resilience culture.

In accordance with the resilient management cycle, it is natural to focus on the detection stage first. Hence, in order to detect operational resilience, we aim to automatically identify failures (cause a loss of acceptable service [31]), exceptional process executions [25], and potential weaknesses (such as interdependencies and bottlenecks [43,41]) by means of forensic techniques. Before we describe the PREDEC framework and its modules, we first review current research and identify several research gaps to formulate our research agenda.

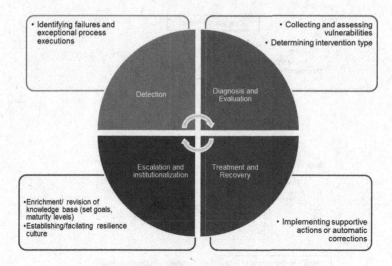

Fig. 1. The Resilience Management Cycle

2.1   Status Quo and Shortcomings

The majority of recent work on IS resilience and related research remains on a
pure conceptual level. For example, a recent literature review on IS resilience has
been carried out by [32], proposing an IS research agenda on resilience and resilience management. Through a comprehensive collection and evaluation of relevant literature, the authors identified and consolidated a myriad of limitations
and research gaps: Resilience is rarely acknowledged in theoretical discussions of
IS domains, which results in a lack of understanding of antecedents, principles
and outcomes of IS resilience. The current state of art is dominated by conceptual or anecdotal contributions. This results not only in a lack of empirical
work to validate IS resilience, but also in the lack of systematic resilience requirements for either IS design or methodological approaches. Moreover, current
attempts to operationalize IS resilience are still on a very immature stage and
impede both empirical evaluation of current research work as well as the actual
implementation and validation of techniques and IS artifacts to make resilience
operational. Finally, the paper discusses the integration of resilience and BPM
[32]: Although the management of risks in BPM has been well recognized in the
past few years, the link between resilience and BPM is largely neglected so far,
leading to an absence of frameworks and approaches.

Interestingly, current literature reviews on so-called risk-aware BPM by [26]
or [36] show, that the vast majority of contributions concentrate on design-time
risk-management in BPM systems, while approaches at run-time and the exploitation of process-related log files a posteriori are largely neglected. But as
highlighted in the previous section, resilience focuses on run-time and a pos-
tiori analytics in order to manage consequences of risks, as also illustrated in
Figure 2.

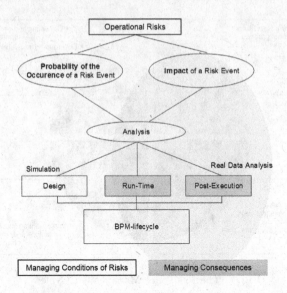

Fig. 2. The Resilience Management Cycle

Recent frameworks for resilient BPM such as [8] tend to state very abstract implementation suggestions. For example, [8] and [15] provide a set of fundamental requirements for supporting resilient BPM. While these works capture basic requirements for resilient IS design, they lack empirical validation, concrete implementation guidelines, as well as artifacts to support the implementation of resilience in IS. Thus, concrete measures are mostly missing, leading to inefficient or even misleading resilience strategies. Effective and cost-efficient tools that could be used for the (semi-)automated detection of BPM resilience are missing. Furthermore, existing methods provide decision makers with limited intuitive support-tools at high personnel costs and, thus, fail to assist them in enhancing and maintaining resilience of BPM.

2.2   Research Questions and Objectives

We pursue to address these essential, yet open, issues by providing a new approach to supporting decision makers in automatically detecting the occurrence of hazards, and therefore addressing the sensitivity and resilience of information infrastructures.

RQ1: **Requirements for Detection of Resilience Measures in Event Log Data:** What are fundamental requirements for resilient BPM? How can they be translated into measures in order to provide decision makers with a resilience detection service based on analysis of event logs?

RQ2: **Assessing Suitability of Process Mining Techniques for Resilience Detection:** How can event logs be used to detect hazards' occurrence and resilience levels of business processes and associated resources and activities?

RQ3: **(Semi-) Automated Resilience Detection:** What and how much log-data has to be depicted for resilience detection and how must the data be displayed to decision makers in order to support them in making better decisions according to their corporate requirements?

In order to answer these research questions we attempt to make the following contributions. We aim at: (i) Combining and systematizing the related but still disconnected fields of IS resilience and process-orientation. The development of a BPM resilience cycle corresponds with the BPM lifecycle and enables and proposes how to build and enhance resilient BPM. (ii) Providing event log specifications to enable process-centric resilience detection. The requirements and measures developed serve as basis for eliciting and subsequently assessing structural characteristics of information infrastructures. (iii) Making a major step beyond the state of the art by introducing a methodology that allows for a (semi-)automated conformance check based on resilient BPM principles. (iv) Providing decision makers with a comprehensive methodology for analyzing and diagnosing the resilience of information infrastructures and thereby generating meaningful insights and evidences in an intuitive and economic manner. These contributions serve as groundwork for supporting subsequent steps of the resilience management cycle, such as escalation and institutionalization. (v) Rendering the tedious work of manually combing the knowledge from best practice guidelines with the actual infrastructure obsolete. (vi) Enabling the objective detection of vulnerabilities on executed processes instead of intended process models. (vii) Setting the ground for subsequent phases on the BPM resilience cycle, such as diagnosis and evaluation, treatment and recovery, as well as escalation and institutionalization.

3 Process Resilience Detection

In the following, we introduce PREDEC, a process-oriented framework for information infrastructure resilience. In Section 3.1 we introduce the PREDEC framework and its components. In Section 3.2, we provide a detailed description of PREDEC's components and analyze the requirements of these components, introduce process-oriented resilience measures and further elaborate PREDEC's underlying mechanisms.

3.1 The PREDEC Framework

The PREDEC framework constitutes a process-oriented and a posteriori approach to determining information infrastructure resilience. As depicted in Figure 3, BPM systems' event logs build the fundament of process resilience detection with PREDEC. On these event logs, elicitation techniques building upon, e.g., process mining [6] or complex event processing [17] are applicable in order to elicit processes' control and information flow data as well as sociometric data. These techniques allow for elicitation of control flows, i.e., process models [37], data flows, i.e., the indirect flows of information between actors in a process [3] and sociometric data, i.e., social structures of subjects performing processes' activities [38]. Based on resilience-oriented analysis of this information, insight can be gained into the resilience of an organization's interdependent processes.

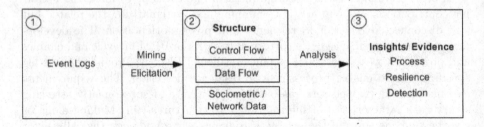

Fig. 3. Overview of the PreDec framework

In the following, we examine the PREDEC's components and analyze the requirements they must meet in order to effectively and precisely provide for resilience detection.

3.2   Components and Requirements

In order to effectively and precisely provide for resilience detection, the components of the PREDEC must meet the following requirements.

Event Logs. The requirements for event logs regard both their structure (i.e. *what* to log), quality (i.e. *how good* to log) and their integrity (i.e. *how* to log). The following addresses these requirements accordingly and indicates the corresponding mechanisms necessary to achieve a sufficient level of assurance for PREDEC.

Figure 4 depicts the minimal set of fields to be logged per entry in order to provide a basis for elicitation. Each event in the business process management system corresponds to an activity of a business process triggered during its run. Hence, the `CaseID` records the business process run in which an `Activity` has taken place. The timestamp captures the `StartPoint` and the `Endpoint` of an activity. The organizational perspective is captured by the `Originator` of the activity (subject or role that triggers the event) and its `OrganizationalUnit`. Finally, the data perspective records the `Input` and the `Output` fields of the particular activity. Of course, for the latter, only the type of data serving as input (or produced as output) is recorded; the actual fields are not recorded. Although this information altogether amount to only a few fields, this is sufficient to feed

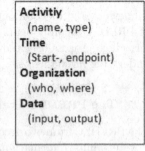

Fig. 4. Entry structure

powerful elicitation mechanisms based upon, e.g., process mining [6] or complex event processing [17]. Hence, this provides a sufficient basis for PREDEC.

As for the quality, Aalst [37, Chap. 4.2] provides five maturity levels for event logs, ranging from worst (Level 1) to best (Level 5). PREDEC requires logs with at least Level 3, which encompass, e.g., tables in ERP systems, event logs in CRM systems and transactions logs of DBM systems. This is because, at this level, information can be correlated and organized in a way that allows the compilation of logs exhibiting the structure in Fig. 4. Logs exhibiting a higher maturity level are already recorded using this structure (Level 4) or are grounded upon semantic annotations and ontologies explaining the meaning of each activity in the enterprise context.

Turning to the integrity, to provide a reliable log basis for detection, the events must faithfully record the activity of the system. In particular, it should be impossible, say, for an attacker to hide its traces or manipulate the logs so that false-positives (detection of resilience-relevant incidents that did not happen) and false-negatives (overlooking resilience-relevant incidents) arise. To achieve this, secure logging mechanisms [1] must be in place to provide (a) tamper evidence and, in some situations, (b) confidentiality of event logs.

While the requirements for event logs regarding elicitation of control and data flow are well examined, requirements for event logs regarding elicitation of sociometric data have become subject to research only recently. In order to elicit sociometric data, i.e., social network graphs, from event logs, these event logs must reflect relations between subjects executing processes' activities. As shown by [38], elicitation of these relations from event logs structured as described above is feasible. Hence, provided event logs meet the requirements stated above, they provide a sufficient basis for elicitation of sociometric data for PREDEC.

Elicitation Techniques. The elicitation techniques envisaged for the realization of the PREDEC framework build upon process mining [6,38]. In particular, when using these techniques, there is a trade-off between the following quality criteria [37, Chap. 5.1] (see [5] for details):

- *Fitness*: the elicited structures (e.g. process model or social network graph) should allow for the behavior seen in the event log.
- *Precision*: the elicited structures should *not* allow for behavior completely unrelated to what was seen in the event log.
- *Generalization*: the elicited structures should generalize the example behavior seen in the event log.
- *Simplicity*: the elicited structures should be as simple as possible.

Technical approaches for the PREDEC framework must seek a balance between good fitness and precision, thereby minimizing the number of false-positives and false-negatives arising from measurement errors. A structure having good fitness is able to replay most of the traces in the event log. Precision is related to the notions of *underfitting* in data mining: a structure having poor precision is underfitting (i.e. it allows for behavior that is very different from what is in the log). Tackling this trade-off is one of the key challenges in process mining.

Resilience Measures. Recent studies on resilience emphasize the integration of organizational and technological views, as well the integration of related, but usually disjointed activities of IS security, business continuity and IT operations [7,15]. According to the CMU-CERT Resilience Management Model [15], an operational resilience requirement is defined as a constraint that an organization places on the productive capability of assets to ensure viability when charged into business processes. These requirements provide the foundation for how to enhance the resilience of assets and related processes. They embody organizational objectives, risk appetite and tolerance, critical success factors, and operational constraints [15]. Moreover, [8] propose fundamental requirements for resilient BPM: They support (i) various levels of severity, ranging from simple failures of key resources to catastrophic accidents; (ii) the coexistence of stable processes with unstable changes in the operating environment; (iii) the dynamic construction and update of situation awareness; (iv) assistance for knowledge representation and management, a fundamental drive to decision-making [20]; (v) flexible operations and unplanned tasks whenever necessary; (vi) the opportunity to experiment with and learn from the novel, innovative and challenging situations that emerge from hazards; and finally (vii) the transition from emergency to normal operations.

In line with the resilience management cycle introduced in Section 2, we focus on the detection phase. The purpose of this phase is to collect, record, and distribute information about the operational resilience of BPM on a timely basis. Effective resilience detection provides essential information about changes/deviations [25,31], such as hazard occurrence and exceptional process executions, but also potential weaknesses, such as high utilization at the margin of resources' or processes' capacity. Data collection, logging, and measurement are at the heart of resilience detection: they address the organization's competencies for identifying, collecting, logging, and disseminating information needed to ensure that operational resilience management processes are performed consistently and within acceptable tolerances [15]. This requires an effective measurement and analysis process that transforms operational resilience objectives and requirements into visible measures. Measures need to express the gap between intended process-goals and actual process-goals. Works on BPM re-engineering [10,24,43] and risk-aware [10], and resilient BPM in particular [15], provide a solid basis for measures for the attempted resilience detection framework. However, deriving meaningful measures for resilience detection requires the alignment with organizational goals and missions [15]. As these objectives need to be interpreted and tailored for a specific organization, we use the well-established objective-driven approach suggested by [7]. The rationale behind it is to assure that resilient measures for extraction and detection have a direct link with operational goals and therefore impact the resilience of diverse organizational missions.

Although we expect variations in appropriate measures due to the unique characteristics of different organizations, we attempt to derive well-established high-level resilience measures suggested by recent work. To date, we have collected almost 50 candidates of resilience measures from the literature or expert interviews. Due to space limitations, we briefly describe a selection of resilience measure examples capturing characteristics such as capacity, time, and interdependence (depicted in Table 1). For example, capacity represents upper bounds or thresholds on resources and processes for reliable function. It is well acknowledged that a system's resilience decreases when capacity is exceeded [12,25]. As recoverability is imperative for resilience, we aim to integrate time-based measures such as *response time* (time span until reacting on customer query) [43], or *lay time* (time, in which a process stagnates and no handling is possible).

Table 1. Examples of (BPM) Resilience Measures

Measure	Definition	Type	Source
Bottlenecks	An activity with lower capacity determines process capacity	Capacity	[43]
Staff Workload	Utilization rate of employees involved in a process (partial aspect of resource utilization rate)	Capacity	[24]
Throughput	Number of transactions and requests which could be processed simultaneously	Capacity	[10]
Organizational Interfaces	Interaction between internal departments	Inter-dependence	[10]
Response Time	Time span until reacting on customer query	Time	[43]
Lay Time	Time, in which a process stagnates and no handling is possible	Time	[24]

Based on log-data, generated from business process model executions, and the resilience requirements derived from operational resilience objectives, resilience measures are automatically generated. As input we use event-log data introduced in the previous paragraph. With the help of the elicitation techniques for business processes and associated resources different susceptibility values are extracted and assigned, either quantitatively (e.g., transactions per hour, number of activities executed in parallel, total number of activities) or qualitative (e.g., High, Medium, and Low). With this input data at hand for each resource, a business process-wide resilience value is calculated. While similar approaches such for instance business process importance determination [19] do not incorporate dynamic aspects such as duration of activities and recovery times. But the integration of time-factors is said to be a crucial determinant of business process resilience [15,28].

Analysis Techniques. Automatic calculation of resilience measures based on event logs requires application of appropriate analysis techniques to be applied on the structures elicited from the event logs.

Process mining provides a basis upon which control flow and data flow information can be gained from the log files. Specifically, processes can be reconstructed using process discovery techniques. These techniques reconstruct the control flow, i.e. the structure of the process, possibly extracting time information regarding the duration of tasks. Process discovery approaches usually build a Petri net' model of the process. These approaches can be classified as [5]:

- Abstraction-based algorithms. These algorithms construct a model based on ordering relations (preceding/-succeeding) amongst process activities.
- Heuristic-based algorithms. In contrast to abstraction-based algorithms, heuristic methods additionally consider the frequency of ordering relations. This allows the discovery of models that describe the most common behavior recorded in an event log.
- Search-based algorithms. Abstracting from local properties like ordering relations, genetic algorithms mimic the process of evolution.
- Region-based algorithms. Based on a behavioral process specification (language or state-space), the aim of this group of algorithms is to construct a Petri net with corresponding behavior.

Further, commercial process mining suites (e.g. Disco) often make use of fuzzy mining methods for the description of process behavior. Instead of focusing on the detection of the process structure in the sense of OR or AND structures, they only view activity transitions and their frequency within the process log.

The analysis of these structures, which is partly automated, can be used to visualize, for example, bottlenecks and throughput.

Conformance checking can be used to detect deviations between the expected process behavior and the actual behavior encoded in the event logs [4]. These techniques carry on a trace-based analysis and can be used to determine, e.g., the time needed for each execution and the number of different executions.

The bulk of work on process mining focuses on analyzing the control flow of the process. Recent works also deal with data flows or, more generally, resources used in the process [5]. Data flows can be used to identify potential leaks or key resources in the enterprise, as well as monitor their continuous consumption. Similarly, staff workload and work transfer can be asserted by inspecting the corresponding traces.

These techniques can be merged with techniques to analyze sociometric data. Techniques to analyze sociometric data, i.e., social networks, build on the techniques of social network analysis. Social network analysis refers to the collection of methods, techniques and tools aiming at the analysis of social networks. These are based on the methods and techniques of graph theory and have been subject to research for decades, e.g., by [34,40]. The suitability of social network detection and analysis in order to discover information flows within organizations has been subject to extensive research. Discovery of social network by analysis of e-mail interaction has been examined by, e.g., [22,33]. Diesner et al. examine organizational crises from a social network analysis perspective based on analysis of communication flow via e-mail [16]. In [21], Fischbach et al. present an approach to discover social networks from employees' interactions by tracking these interactions via wearable sensors. Van der Aalst and Song introduced an approach to discover social networks from event logs [38].

However, while the suitability of network analysis techniques for resilience detection has been addressed, e.g., in the fields of social-ecological systems [27] or computer networks [35], the implications of social structures with regard to the resilience of business processes have not been considered by research yet.

In order to constitute suitable tools to support resilience detection in process-centered information infrastructures, the techniques of social network analysis have to be able to assess subjects' positions within the social network with respect to actual process executions and resilience measures. The social network analysis techniques for resilience detection envisaged for the realization of PREDEC build on centrality measures and measures based on co-workership and event types, e.g., [38]. Calculation of resilience measures such as, e.g., capacity measures or interdependence measures, such as *Organizational Interfaces* (cf. Table 1), can be supported by social network analysis techniques. For example, betweenness analyses of social networks can support detection of *bottlenecks* while social network analysis metrics custom crafted for social networks elicited from event logs, such as *handover of work metrics* [38], can support calculation of interdependence measures. Hence, techniques of social network analysis are well suited for enhancing resilience detection with PREDEC. Moreover, social network analysis results can lucidly be visualized by tools like, e.g., [13], in order to provide decision makers with intuitive insight into resilience measures.

4   Envisaged Evaluation and Ongoing Work

Mindfulness, an organization's capability to perceive cues, interpret them, and respond appropriately [14,28], is crucial to maintain and enhance resilient operation. Ongoing research aims at elaborating the conception and implementation of intuitive user interfaces based on process mining techniques in order to evaluate the effectiveness of PREDEC in real business cases. Specifically, the current efforts address the following.

Firstly, the design of an automated process resilience detector (PREDEC) as an a posteriori checking module to complement and support established risk-aware BPM architectures, such as those mentioned in [20]. In contrast to those approaches with emphasis on design-time analysis to calculate operational risks based on (either subjective or historical) threat probabilities (focus on the cause of events) [36], the a posteriori resilience approach will focus on the business processes' interdependencies and potential to cascade, so-called ripple effect [28]. The detection service addresses further questions, such as: (i) Do the actual process models correspond with the intended concepts?; (ii) Does the observed system behavior meet requirements of the respective compliance or security standard?; and (iii) Can we derive further information about the dynamic system behavior (e.g. recovery time, rate of degradation)? In order to extract the interdependencies and dynamics, we will employ mining techniques for conformance checking [4] as well as process discovery [6,5], which were well-tested in the context of audits.

Secondly, an instantiation of PREDEC will allow us an evaluation in collaboration with practitioners.

As we highlighted in this paper, detecting process resilience effectively assumes the existence of meaningful measures to capture organizational goals and missions. For actual implementation and evaluation in practice, we need to calibrate our high-level set of measurements to fulfill specific requirements and goals of different organizations. A further step for implementing and evaluating PREDEC anticipates the inspection of the PREDEC requirements (such as expert interviews), using heuristic evaluations according to guidlines and checklists, e.g., [15] and Cognitive Walkthroughs using typical task scenarios. The advanced efforts on pre-testing should identify decision makers' acceptance and applicability of the proposed methodologies. To ensure that the PREDEC in fact meets the needs of a broad range of companies, we will evaluate the research results at one small-sized and one large-sized company in Germany.

5   Summary

The traditional understanding of trust amounts to building large information systems that are robust, i.e., they avert failures by mitigating the corresponding risk associated to the execution of business processes. This paper reported on ongoing work towards a process-oriented framework for information infrastructure resilience. The key premise behind PREDEC framework is that in merging robustness and resilience, one can provide for trustworthier information systems that not only prevent incidents, but that, upon an incident, fault or attack, can also bounce back to a stable state and even improve their design. In this setting, we presented a resilience management cycle, introduced the main research questions and schematically sketched the PREDEC and its building blocks.

Clearly, this is just initial work and there is a lot of work ahead. Besides the realization of PREDEC and the ongoing work listed in the previous section, in future we plan to consider the question of how resilience management can be integrated into business process management. On the more technical side, we intend to examine whether and the extent to which other approaches to handling events – e.g. complex event processing and event prediction – provide a more suitable basis for PREDEC.

References

1. Accorsi, R.: Safe-keeping digital evidence with secure logging protocols: State of the art and challenges. In: Goebel, O., Ehlert, R., Frings, S., Günther, D., Morgenstern, H., Schadt, D. (eds.) Proceedings the IEEE Conference on Incident Management and Forensics, pp. 94–110. IEEE Computer Society (2009)
2. Accorsi, R.: Sicherheit im prozessmanagement. digma Zeitschrift für Datenrecht und Informationssicherheit (2013)
3. Accorsi, R., Lehmann, A.: Automatic information flow analysis of business process models. In: Barros, A., Gal, A., Kindler, E. (eds.) BPM 2012. LNCS, vol. 7481, pp. 172–187. Springer, Heidelberg (2012)

4. Accorsi, R., Stocker, T.: On the exploitation of process mining for security audits: the conformance checking case. In: Ossowski, S., Lecca, P. (eds.) SAC, pp. 1709–1716. ACM (2012)
5. Accorsi, R., Stocker, T., Müller, G.: On the exploitation of process mining for security audits: the process discovery case. In: Proceedings of the ACM Symposium on Applied Computing, pp. 1462–1468. ACM (2013)
6. Accorsi, R., Ullrich, M., van der Aalst, W.M.P.: Process mining. Informatik Spektrum 35(5), 354–359 (2012)
7. Allen, J.H., Curtis, P.D., Gates, L.P.: Using defined processes as a context for resilience measures (2011)
8. Antunes, P., Mourão, H.: Resilient business process management: Framework and services. Expert Syst. Appl. 38(2), 1241–1254 (2011)
9. Avizienis, A., Laprie, J.-C., Randell, B., Landwehr, C.: Basic concepts and taxonomy of dependable and secure computing. IEEE Trans. Dependable Secur. Comput. 1(1), 11–33 (2004)
10. Balasubramanian, S., Gupta, M.: Structural metrics for goal based business process design and evaluation. Business Process Management Journal 11(6), 680–694 (2005)
11. Basin, D.A., Burri, S.J., Karjoth, G.: Optimal workflow-aware authorizations. In: ACM Symposium on Access Control Models and Technologies, pp. 93–102. ACM (2012)
12. Boin, A., McConnell, A.: Preparing for critical infrastructure breakdowns: The limits of crisis management and the need for resilience. Journal of Contingencies & Crisis Management 15(1), 50–59 (2007)
13. Borgatti, S.P., Everett, M.G., Freeman, L.C.: UCINET for windows: Software for social network analysis. In: Analytic Technologies, Harvard (2002)
14. Butler, B.S., Gray, P.H.: Reliability, mindfulness, and information systems. MIS Quarterly 30(2), 211–224 (2006)
15. Caralli, R.A., Allen, J.H., Curtis, P.D., Young, L.R.: Cert resilience management model, version 1.0 (2010)
16. Diesner, J., Frantz, T.L., Carley, K.M.: Communication networks from the enron email corpus "It's always about the people. enron is no different". Computational & Mathematical Organization Theory 11(3), 201–228 (2005)
17. Etzion, O.: Complex event processing. In: Liu, L., Özsu, M.T. (eds.) Encyclopedia of Database Systems, pp. 412–413. Springer, Heidelberg (2009)
18. Fdhila, W., Rinderle-Ma, S., Reichert, M.: Change propagation in collaborative processes scenarios. In: CollaborateCom, pp. 452–461. IEEE (2012)
19. Fenz, S., Ekelhart, A., Neubauer, T.: Business process-based resource importance determination. In: Dayal, U., Eder, J., Koehler, J., Reijers, H.A. (eds.) BPM 2009. LNCS, vol. 5701, pp. 113–127. Springer, Heidelberg (2009)
20. Fenz, S., Neubauer, T., Accorsi, R., Koslowski, T.: FORISK: Formalizing information security risk and compliance management. In: Annual IEEE/IFIP International Conference on Dependable Systems and Networks (2013)
21. Fischbach, D.K., Gloor, D.P.A., Schoder, P.D.D.: Analysis of informal communication networks - a case study. Business & Information Systems Engineering 1(2), 140–149 (2009)
22. Fisher, D., Dourish, P.: Social and temporal structures in everyday collaboration. In: Proceedings of the SIGCHI Conference on Human Factors in Computing Systems, CHI 2004, pp. 551–558. ACM, New York (2004)
23. Freiling, F.C., Schwittay, B.: A common process model for incident response and computer forensics. In: IMF, pp. 19–40 (2007)

24. Harrington, H.J.: Business process improvement: The breakthrough strategy for total quality, productivity, and competitiveness. McGraw-Hill, New York (1991)
25. Hollnagel, E., Woods, D.D., Leveson, N. (eds.): Resilience engineering: Concepts and precepts. Ashgate, Aldershot and England and and Burlington and VT (2006)
26. Jakoubi, S., Tjoa, S., Goluch, G., Quirchmayr, G.: A survey of scientific approaches considering the integration of security and risk aspects into business process management. In: DEXA Proceedings of the 20th International Workshop on Database and Expert Systems Application, pp. 127–132.
27. Janssen, M.A., Bodin, O., Anderies, J.M., Elmqvist, T., Ernstson, H., McAllister, R.R., Olsson, P., Ryan, P.: Toward a network perspective of the study of resilience in social-ecological systems. Ecology and Society 11(1), 15 (2006)
28. Koslowski, T.G., Geoghegan, W., Longstaff, P.H.: Organizational resilience: A review and reconceptualization. In: Barr, P., Rothaermel, F. (eds.) 33rd Annual International Conference of the Strategic Management Society, Atlanta, VA, September 28-October 1 (2013)
29. Longstaff, P.H., Koslowski, T.G., Geoghegan, W.: Translating resilience: A framework to enhance communication and implementation. In: 5th International Symposium on Resilience Engineering, Soesterberg, Netherlands, June 25-27 (2013)
30. McCann, J.E., Selsky, J.W.: Mastering turbulence: The essential capabilities of agile and resilient individuals, teams, and organizations, 1st edn. Jossey-Bass, San Franciso (2012)
31. Meyer, J.F.: Model-based evaluation of system resilience. In: Annual IEEE/IFIP International Conference on Dependable Systems and Networks (2013)
32. Müller, G., Koslowski, T.G., Accorsi, R.: Resilience - a new research field in business information systems? In: Proceedings of the 16th International Conference on Business Information Systems. Springer, Heidelberg (2013)
33. Ogata, H., Yano, Y., Furugori, N., Jin, Q.: Computer supported social networking for augmenting cooperation. Computer Supported Cooperative Work (CSCW) 10(2), 189–209 (2001)
34. Scott, J.: Social network analysis. Sage, Newbury Park (1991)
35. Sterbenz, J., Cetinkaya, E., Hameed, M., Jabbar, A., Rohrer, J.: Modelling and analysis of network resilience. In: 2011 Third International Conference on Communication Systems and Networks (COMSNETS), pp. 1–10 (2011)
36. Suriadi, S., Weiss, B., Winkelmann, A., ter Hofstede, A., Wynn, M., Ouyang, C., Adams, M., Conforti, R., Fidge, C., La Rosa, M., et al.: Current research in risk-aware business process management-overview, comparison, and gap analysis. QUT ePrints, 50606 (2012)
37. van der Aalst, W.: Process Mining - Discovery, Conformance and Enhancement of Business Processes. Springer (2011)
38. van der Aalst, W.M.P., Reijers, H.A., Song, M.: Discovering social networks from event logs. Comput. Supported Coop. Work 14(6), 549–593 (2005)
39. Wang, Q., Li, N.: Satisfiability and resiliency in workflow authorization systems. ACM Trans. Inf. Syst. Secur. 13(4), 40 (2010)
40. Wasserman, S., Faust, K.: Social Network Analysis: Methods and Applications (Structural Analysis in the Social Sciences). Cambridge University Press (1994)
41. Weick, K.E., Sutcliffe, K.M.: Managing the unexpected: Resilient performance in an age of uncertainty, 2nd edn. Jossey-Bass, San Francisco (2007)
42. Wolter, K.: Resilience assessment and evaluation of computing systems. Springer, Berlin, London (2012)
43. Yen, V.C.: An integrated model for business process measurement. Business Process Management Journal 15(6), 865–875 (2009)

IF-Net: A Meta-Model for Security-Oriented Process Specification

Thomas Stocker and Frank Böhr

University of Freiburg, Germany
{stocker,boehr}@iig.uni-freiburg.de

Abstract. In this paper we propose a new Petri net-based meta-model for the specification of workflows. While existing approaches for workflow modeling typically address the consistency of process models, there is no de-facto standard for models which also comprise security-related aspects. Besides basic workflow properties such as executing subjects and transition guards, the proposed IF-Net approach allows net parts to be annotated with security levels in a way that information flow control mechanisms can be applied. By introducing distinguishable token types, IF-Net allows the modeling of both, the control- and data-flow of a workflow in an intuitive way. Altogether IF-Net allows the specification of workflows in a detailed way and provides a basis for the formal verification of security properties on these specifications.

1 Introduction

Over 70% of all business processes deployed today are automated and rely on workflow management systems for their execution [10]. The mapping of business processes into workflows (i.e. excecutable specifications of business processes) and their automated execution allows their flexible adoption to business changes and easier integration of external resources. Economic advantages arise due to efficient information exchange between business partners, higher flexibility of workflows and lower infrastructure cost [2].

However, the benefits of automated, flexible processes are accompanied by a significant risk with respect to the adherence to security, privacy and regulatory compliance requirements [21,20]. Organizations building upon process automation must ensure that these requirements are not violated, or that violations are at least detected. This is particularly challenging for the confidentiality of data, which is a security requirement of utmost relevance for companies' operation, e.g. in e-banking and telecommunications.

Current state of the art for modeling security properties for business processes encompass formal languages for model-driven development, such as UMLsec [15], and industrial specification languages equipped with annotations for the secure realization of processes at the level of services and infrastructure, e.g. SecureBPMN [7] and other extensions [31]. Further, while Petri net-based formalisms to reason about the consistency of business processes are well-accepted

R. Accorsi and S. Ranise (Eds.): STM 2013, LNCS 8203, pp. 191–206, 2013.
© Springer-Verlag Berlin Heidelberg 2013

in the literature [25,26,3], there are no approaches that allow the comprehensive modeling of processes for security reasoning.

This paper presents IF-Net, a Petri net-based formalism to modeling security aspects of business processes. Specifically, IF-Net subsumes and extends the previous proposals based upon Petri nets. It allows net parts to be annotated with security levels in a way a subsequent information flow analysis can be applied. By introducing distinguishable token types, IF-Net allows modeling both the control- and data-flow of a process in an expressive manner.

This paper provides the following contributions:

- It defines IF-Net, a novel meta-model for the formal specification of processes considering both functional and non-functional aspects in form of security requirements.
- It illustrates the usage of IF-Nets in case studies.
- It points to the realization of IF-Net. Currently, there is a comprehensively tested Java-implementation of all concepts. It is available at the open-source platform Sourceforge (`http://sourceforge.net/projects/sepiaframework`).

The ultimate goal in the development of IF-Net is to provide an expressive formalism and, correspondingly, automated tool support for the design-time identification of noncompliance with security, privacy and regulatory requirements. This paper, focusing on confidentiality, addresses the detection of violations caused by structural vulnerabilities in business processes, as well as dataflows that violate the designated authorization policies.

Overall, IF-Net is merely a first step towards the achievement of this goal. Ongoing work designs automated translations of literate BPMN specifications into IF-Net models following the approach of Lohmann et al. [19] and uses the probabilistic model-checking tool PRISM [18] to check IF-Net models. The further version of this paper will describe this progress, as well as report on a case study.

Paper structure. The rest of the paper is organized as follows: In section 2 we give an overview of related work. Section 3 contains mathematical preliminaries for the definition of IF-Nets in section 4. Section 5 presents use cases for the proposed meta-model.

2   Related Work

Process calculi such as Communicating Sequential Processes (CSP), Calculus of Communicating Systems (CCS) and Algebra of Communicating Processes (ACP) are a common way in computer science in formally defining the behavior of net systems (processes), especially in terms of parallel composition and communication. In the context of modeling and reasoning about workflows, π-calculus seemed to be a promising candidate, but its suitability is controversial[23,27]. The main criticism is that while it is able to capture most of the relevant control flow aspects of a workflow, there are examples showing that for some (relatively simple) constructs, it is not straightforward to provide a correct π-calculus formula [28]. Generally, over the last year, we observed a trend away from event-based techniques over to state-based techniques, such as Petri nets [22], for modeling workflows. Petri nets allow formal specification, and are capable of encoding a processes' state explicitly [28].

While there are works generally showing how different aspects of workflows (e.g. control flow and timing) can be modeled with Petri nets [3], one of the first attempts of introducing a tailored Petri net dialect for the specification and analysis of business processes was the definition of the WF-net meta-model [25,30]. To ensure the definition of models that make sense from a business perspective, it puts some restrictions on the shape of Petri nets. Considering the class of *safe* Petri nets, it e.g. requires nets to be connected and to contain explicit start and end places. To extend the scope of workflow related analysis based on Petri nets, WF-nets have been extended by the WFD-net meta-model which additionally considers data elements (attributes) together with usage modes (read, write, destroy) which are annotated to Petri net transitions [24]. The possibility of assigning guards to transitions in such high-level Petri nets [13] allows to model preconditions on attribute values for activity execution. In comparison to WF-net, WFD-net models can be used to detect data flow errors in workflow models, such as *missing data*. However, high level Petri nets do not necessarily produce the desired results for some special cases (advanced synchronization, modeling cancellation patterns) [29]. The workflow language YAWL [12] tries to solve these problems by introducing additional features e.g. for multiple instances. These approaches solely focus on the consistency of process models and do not take security-related properties into account.

Works applying Petri net theory for the specification of workflows together with specific security properties and their subsequent analysis can be categorized by the security property they consider. For the verification of mandatory access control constraints, Jian et al. use a colored Petri net dialect to specify the security model with the help of security classes and access constraints [14]. Rakkay et al. showed that role based access control requirements can also be specified and analyzed on basis of Colored Petri nets [11]. In addition to traditional access control, Katt et al. proposed a method applying Colored Petri nets for Usage Control policy specification [16]. Considering integrity requirements, Zhang et al. propose a Petri net based approach to verify the Strict Integrity Policy proposed by Biba [5]. Using a set of integrity levels, they analyze the coverability graph of the Petri net to find policy violations. Atluri et al. use Petri nets to model Chinese Wall security policies in workflows [4,32]. These policies relate to confidentiality and integrity and tackle conflict of interest issues.

There are also applications in the area of information flow control, which allows to reason about structural process vulnerabilities allowing (hidden) information flow [8]. Seminal work in this direction includes the approach of Knorr for the specification and verification of multilevel security requirements [17] and the work of Frau et al. showing the capabilities of Structural Non-Interference [9].

However, there is no common meta-model for the specification of workflows and information flow properties. Accorsi and Lehmann considered Petri nets with security labels, assigning confidentiality levels to transitions and data attributes and clearances to subjects [1]. The method works on safe Petri nets with only one token type. The consideration of data flows is rather complicated, as it has to be implicitly encoded in the structure of the net, e.g. by introducing special transitions modeling the execution of a transition with a specific data usage.

Further meta models which are not based on Petri nets exist. UMLsec is an extension of UML that allows to express security relevant information within UML diagrams [15]. It focuses on system specifications, not on workflows analysis. SecureBMPN is a design-time modeling approach and focuses on run-time enforcement of security requirements for business process-driven systems [6]. It is based on BPMN and does not provide a formal definition of the modeling elements which is important for automated analysis.

With IF-Net we present a Petri net dialect which allows, in comparison with other Petri net dialects, a more intuitive way of modeling data flow with the help of colored tokens which stand for data attributes. Additionally IF-Net allows to define business processes in a formal way, comprising the control flow (order of activities) and data flow together with security related properties. Thereby it provides a basis for powerful low-level security analysis in terms of information flow control, which is capable of reasoning about security properties related to the control- and data-flow of a business process. Providing a model which allows to analyze this kind of properties with respect to workfows is the main purpose of IF-Net. Similar to WF-net it defines soundness criteria to distinguish valid net specifications (e.g. connectedness, liveness).

3   Preliminaries

This section provides mathematical preliminaries, and introduces Colored Workflow Nets, a Colored Petri net dialect tailored for workflow modeling which is the basis of the proposed IF-Net meta-model.

3.1   Multiset

A multiset of set S is defined as a function $S_M : S \to \mathbb{N}_0$ which returns the cardinality of each element in the multiset. The set of all multisets of S is denoted by S^+. For convenience we introduce the multiset notation $m = [e_1^{k_{e_1}}, \cdots, e_n^{k_{e_n}}]$ with $m(e_i) = k_{e_i}, \forall i \in \{1 \cdots n\}$ and zero otherwise. The support of a multiset S_M is defined as: $\text{supp}(S_M) = \{s \in S \mid S_M(s) > 0\}$. A relation $\leq$ is defined between two multisets S' and S'' in the following way: $S'_M \leq S''_M \Leftrightarrow \forall_{s \in S} S'(s) \leq S''(s)$.

3.2   Colored Petri Net (CPN)

A CPN is a 7-tuple $(P, T, F, I, O, C, \mathcal{C})$ and extends classical Petri nets by distinguishable token types. The type of a token is defined by its color, where $\mathcal{C}$ is the set of possible token colors.

P, T, F: P is the set of places, T is the set of transitions (and $P \cap T = \emptyset$). $F \subseteq (P \times T) \cup (T \times P)$ is called the flow relation.

I, O: The input and output functions are used to specify the number and kind of tokens which hare consumed/produced when transitions fire. I is the input function and defined as $I : (P \times T) \cap F \rightarrow C^+$. O is the output function and defined as $O : (T \times P) \cap F \rightarrow C^+$. I and O have to fulfill the following two conditions:

- $\forall (t, p) \in (T \times P) \cap F : O(t, p) \not\equiv 0$
- $\forall (p, t) \in (P \times T) \cap F : I(p, t) \not\equiv 0$

These conditions make sure that the Petri net does not contain ineffective relations, i.e. connections between transitions and places which do not transport any tokens. For convenience we introduce the following notation for the produced and consumed token colors of transitions:

- **Consumed tokens**
  $N_c : T \rightarrow \mathcal{P}(\mathcal{C})$
  $N_c(t) = \bigcup_{i \in \bullet t} (\text{supp} I(i, t))$
  $N_c|_{\mathcal{C}_c}(t) = N_c(t) \setminus \{\text{black}\}$

- **Produced tokens**
  $N_p : T \rightarrow \mathcal{P}(\mathcal{C})$
  $N_p(t) = \bigcup_{o \in t\bullet} (\text{supp} O(t, o))$
  $N_p|_{\mathcal{C}_c}(t) = N_p(t) \setminus \{\text{black}\}$

C: C defines the color capacity of a place with $C : P \times \mathcal{C} \rightarrow \mathbb{N}_0 \cup \infty$. The overall capacity of a place p is defined as $\zeta(p) = \sum_{c \in \mathcal{C}} C(p, c)$.

Marking: A marking M is defined as a function $M : P \rightarrow C^+$. M defines the state of a CPN in terms of the number and kind of tokens in all net places. A relation $\leq$ is defined between two markings M' and M'' in the following way: $M' \leq M'' \Leftrightarrow \forall_{p \in P} : M'(p) \leq M''(p)$. We use (CPN, M_0) to denote a CPN with an initial state M_0.

Enabled: A transition $t \in T$ is defined to be enabled in a CPN N with marking M (which is denoted by $(N, M)[t\rangle$) iff:

- $\forall_{p \in \bullet t} : I(p, t) \leq M(p)$
  (enough tokens in input places)
- $\forall_{p \in t\bullet} \forall_{c \in \mathcal{C}} : M(p)(c) + O(p, t)(c) \leq C(p, c)$
  (enough space in output places)

Firing: An enabled transition $t \in T$ can fire in marking M leading to marking M' denoted by $M \xrightarrow{t} M'$ where M' is:

- $\forall_{p \in \bullet t} : M'(p) = M(p) - I(p, t)$
- $\forall_{p \in t\bullet} : M'(p) = M(p) + O(t, p)$
- $\forall_{p \in P \setminus \{\bullet t \cup t\bullet\}} : M'(p) = M(p)$

With respect to business processes, firing a transition relates to executing a task within the process.

k-Bounded CPN: A CPN (N, M) is k-bounded iff $[N, M\rangle$ is finite i.e.:
$\forall_{M' \in [N,M\rangle} \forall_{p \in P} : \sum_{c \in C} M'(p)(c) \leq k$

Bounded CPN: A CPN is bounded iff $\exists_{k \in \mathbb{N}}$: CPN is k-bounded .

3.3 Colored Capacity Petri Net (CCPN)

A CCPN is a CPN where the following condition holds: $\forall_{p \in P} : \zeta(p) \in \mathbb{N}$.

Remark on Boundedness: The capacity of the place with the highest capacity defines an upper bound for the maximum possible amount of tokens in a place. A CCPN is hence k-bounded where $k \leq \max_{p \in P}(\zeta(p))$.

3.4 Colored Workflow Net

A Colored Workflow Net (CWN) is a bounded CPN which additionally satisfies the following properties:

- $\mathcal{C} = \mathcal{C}_c \uplus \{black\}$ [1]
- $\{p \in P | {}^\bullet p = \emptyset\} = \{i\}$ (There is one input place.)
- $\{p \in P | p^\bullet = \emptyset\} = \{o\}$ (There is one output place.)
- $\overline{(N, m_0)} = (P, T \cup \bar{t}, F \cup \{(o, \bar{t}), (\bar{t}, i)\})$ is strongly connected.
- $\sum_{p \in P} m_0(p)(black) = 1$ and $m_0(i)(black) = 1$
  The initial marking has exactly one black token and this token is in place i.

Control Flow Dependency

- $\forall_{t \in T} \exists_{p \in {}^\bullet t} : supp(I(p, t)) \cap \{black\} \neq \emptyset$
  Black token must be consumed.
- $\forall_{t \in T} \exists_{p \in t^\bullet} : supp(O(p, t)) \cap \{black\} \neq \emptyset$
  Black token must be produced.

Soundness: Soundness of CWNs is closely related to the soundness of WFnets [25,30]. A CWN is sound if it satisfies the following properties:

- $\forall m \in [N, m_0\rangle \exists m' \in [N, m\rangle : m'(o)(black) > 0$
  Option to complete, i.e. the process can enter an end state.
- $\forall m \in [N, m_0\rangle : m(o)(black) > 0 \Rightarrow \sum_{p \in P \backslash o} m(p)(black) = 0$
  Proper completion, i.e. there are no remaining control flow tokens when reaching the end state.
- $\forall t \in T : \exists m \in [N, m_0\rangle : (N, m)[t\rangle$
  No dead transitions, i.e. every process activity can be executed in at least one path.

---

[1] The token color black is used to model tokens which represent the control flow. All further token colors (which are contained in $\mathcal{C}_c$) represent data items. Tokens with the same color represent references to the same data item i.e. two red tokens represent the same information which can be accessed via two references.

4   IF-Net

IF-Net builds upon CWN and adds security-specific concepts. To distinguish between classified and unclassified elements, IF-Net splits the process into two logical security domains (*high* for secret, *low* for public). In terms of information flow control, a process is considered secure when no possible execution trace allows information to flow from the *high* domain to the *low* domain (i.e. the domains do not interfere). Non-Interference is a strong and very restrictive notion of security which can consider the confidentiality of both data elements and transitions. Since many relevant security properties (e.g. the Bell-LaPaduala model) and also multi-level security policies can be mapped onto non-interference properties, the consideration of only two security domains is not a real restriction of IF-Net (see Sec. 5). The support of information flow concepts makes it possible to analyze IF-Net specifications with respect to explicit information flows due to direct access operations, but also to hidden information transmission.

An IF-Net is a 10-tuple $(P, T_R, T_D, F, C, I, O, A, AC, \mathfrak{G})$ where $(P, T_R \uplus T_D, F, C, I, O)$ is a sound CWN. Besides regular transitions $(t_R \in T_R)$ there are declassification transitions $(t_D \in T_D)$ used to downgrade classified information to lower security levels.

IF-Net properties and elements are defined as follows:

Analysis Context (AC): The analysis context of an IF-Net is a tuple (L, E, U) where the labeling (L) defines classification and clearance levels for net transitions and data elements and the subject function $(E : T \to U)$ connects IF-Net transitions with subjects. U is the set of all possible subjects. The labeling L is a 3-tuple $L = (S_T, S_U, S_C)$:

- **Classification**: $S_T \to \{high, low\}$ assigns to each transition $t \in T$ whether it is classified as *high* or *low*. The information whether a transition fired or not is not allowed to be known to subjects with clearance *low* if the transition is classified as *high*.
- **Clearance**: $S_U \to \{high, low\}$ assigns to each subject $u \in U$ whether it belongs to the *high* domain or to the *low* domain.
- **Token label**: $S_C : C_c \to \{high, low\}$ assigns to each token color (except black) whether it is classified as *high* or *low*.

Access Function: $A : T_R \times C_c \to \mathcal{P}(\mathcal{M}_A)$ is a function which defines for each regular transition $t \in T_R$ and each token color $c \in C_c$ how the transition accesses the information represented by tokens of color c. Valid access modes are defined as $\mathcal{M}_A = \{read, write, delete, create\}$. A transition can either access existing information (read) or modify existing information (write). A transition can further on produce new information (create) or remove existing information (delete). The following conditions must be fulfilled by the access function in a IF-Net:

- $|A(t,c) \cap \{create, delete\}| \leq 1$
  Information is created or deleted but not both.
- $\forall_{t \in T} \forall_{c \in C_c}$: create $\in A(t,c) \Rightarrow \forall_{p \in \bullet t} : I(p,t)(c) = 0 \land \exists_{p \in t\bullet} : O(t,p)(c) > 0$
  Created information is only produced and not consumed, i.e. c is not in the input bag of t but in the output bag.
- $\forall_{t \in T} \forall_{c \in C_c}$: delete $\in A(t,c) \Rightarrow \forall_{p \in t\bullet} : O(t,p)(c) = 0 \land \exists_{p \in \bullet t} : I(p,t)(c) > 0$
  Deleted information is only consumed but not produced, i.e. c is in the input bag of t but not in the output bag.
- $\forall_{t \in T} \forall_{c \in C_c} : A(t,c) \cap \{delete, create\} = \emptyset \Rightarrow \exists_{p \in \bullet t} : I(p,t)(c) > 0 \land \exists_{p \in t\bullet} : O(p,t)(c) > 0$
  Information which is neither created nor deleted (just processed) is consumed and produced, i.e. c is in the input bag of t and in the output bag.

The functions for produced and consumed token colors of transitions are extended in a natural way to cover access modes:

- **Consumed tokens**
  $N_c^{M_A} : T \times \mathcal{P}(M_A) \to \mathcal{P}(C)$
  $N_c^{M_A}(t,M) = \{c \in N_c(t) \,|\, A(t,c) \supseteq M\}$
  $N_c^{M_A}(t,M)|_\gamma(t) = N_c^{M_A}(t,M) \cap \gamma$
  where γ is an arbitrary set.

- **Produced tokens**
  $N_p^{M_A} : T \times \mathcal{P}(M_A) \to \mathcal{P}(C)$
  $N_p^{M_A}(t,M) = \{c \in N_p(t) \,|\, A(t,c) \supseteq M\}$
  $N_p^{M_A}(t,M)|_\gamma(t) = N_p^{M_A}(t,M) \cap \gamma$
  where γ is an arbitrary set.

Transition Guards: A transition guard is a pair of a predicate name and one token color $(p_g, c) \in P_g \times C_c$ where P_g is the set of all predicate names. Predicates define abstract conditions on data items used during process execution and evaluate to true or false. The function $G : T \to \mathcal{P}(P_g \times C_c)$ assigns to each transition a set of transition guards. The set of all transition guards of the IF-Net is denoted by $\mathcal{G}$ and the pair of those guards with the function is written as $\mathfrak{G} = (\mathcal{G}, G)$.

Enabled: Due to the extended IF-Net structure with respect to transition guards, the necessary conditions for regular transitions $t_R \in T_R$ to be enabled are extended by the requirement that all guards of t_R must evaluate to true.

Declassification Transitions: Transitions $t \in T_D$ are used for declassification i.e. to allow information flow from the *high* to the *low* domain. In a business process, this can happen, when classified information is removed from a document, before it is published or handed to a user with lower clearance. All transitions in T_D additionally fulfill the following conditions:

- There is exactly one input place and one output place:
$\forall_{t_D \in T_D} : \bullet t = \{i_{t_D}\}$ and $t^{\bullet} = \{o_{t_D}\}$
- Declassification transition must be effective, i.e. consume at least one colored token:
$\forall_{t_D \in T_D} : N_c|_{c_c} \neq \emptyset$
- The set of consumed colors and produced colors (without control flow tokens) have no elemets in common. A declassified data item is thus considered to be a new copy of the original data item where some information might be changed.
$N_c(t_D)|_{c_c} \cap N_p(t_D)|_{c_c} = \emptyset$
- The token colors produced by declassification transitions are neither created by any regular transition with access mode "create" nor produced by any other declassification transition:
$$\forall_{t_D \in T_D} : N_p(t_D)|_{c_c} \cap \left(\bigcup_{t \in T_R} N_p^{\{create\}}(t) \cup \bigcup_{t \in T_D \setminus \{t_D\}} N_p(t) \right) = \emptyset$$
- There exists a bijective function $DF_{t_D} : N_c(t_D)|_{c_c} \leftrightarrow N_p(t_D)|_{c_c}$ for each $t_D \in T_D$ that assigns each input token color a unique output token color which represents the declassified information. For each input token color the transition produces exactly the same amount of tokens of corresponding output token color according to function DF.
$$\forall_{t_D \in T_D} \forall_{c \in N_c(t_D)|_{c_c}} : O(o_{t_D}, t_D)(DF_{t_D}(c)) = I(i_{t_D}, t_D)(c)$$
- Produced tokens of declassification transitions are classified *low*:
$\forall_{t_D \in T_D} \forall_{c \in N_P(t_D)|_{c_c}} : S_C(c) = low$
- Declassification transitions are classified *high*:
$\forall_{t_D \in T_D} : S_T(t_D) = high$

Relationship of Token Label, Clearance, Classification and Subjects:
To ensure consistent IF-Net definitions with respect to security levels of transitions, subjects and data items, the following conditions must hold:

- $\nexists_{t \in T} : S_U(E(t)) = low \wedge S_T(t) = high$
Subjects with *low* clearance can not be assigned to transitions which are classified as *high*.
- $\forall_{c \in C_c} \forall_{t \in T_R} : create \in A(t, c) \Rightarrow S_C(c) = S_U(E(t))$
The label of created tokens equals the classification of the subject executing the corresponding transition.

5   Use Cases

IF-Net is not only capable of capturing the shape of a process, but also security related properties. To illustrate the benefit of IF-Net for security analysis, we consider two different use-cases and show for both how the considered process can be modeled in terms of IF-Net with respect to specific security requirements.

Both use-cases consider the process in Fig. 1. The process handles requests of suppliers for details of a prototype construction plan. In order to receive required

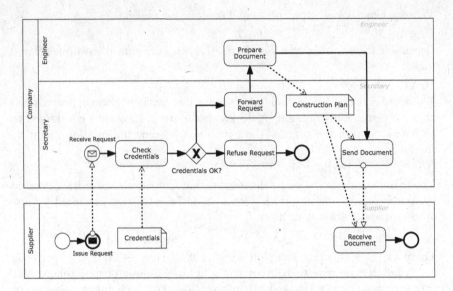

Fig. 1. BPMN specification for the "document request" process

construction details, the supplier issues a request for a specific document. After the secretary checked the permission of the supplier to request plan details, she either refuses the request or forwards it to an engineer who prepares the plan for the supplier. Eventually, the secretary sends the construction plan to the supplier.

5.1   Confidentiality of Data Elements

A recurring security requirement in this process is that no confidential information flows to unauthorized subjects. The BPMN specification in Figure 1 contains the *credentials* a supplier sends with a request to prove he possesses the right to request construction plan details and the *construction plan* itself. Generally, the data perspective of a process can be much more complex than reflected by corresponding specifications which typically concentrate on the different process activities and the order in which they are executed. In this case, the specification abstracted from the *document ID* which is also contained in the request and identifies the concrete construction plan for which details are requested.

Assuming a role-based access control model (RBAC), permissions for system objects are assigned according to roles in the process and activities which are executed by these roles. Here, we assume that for each activity, the data elements it processes together with access modalities (*read*, *write*, ...) are known and subjects inherit permissions on data elements on basis of permissions of their roles to execute these activities. The data elements *document ID* and *credentials* are read by the secretary. In case of a forward, *document ID* is again read by the engineer who reads and modifies the *construction plan* which is finally read by the supplier.

The *construction plan* is the only confidential element which has to be protected from unauthorized access. Although suppliers have to get some knowledge on the construction plan in order to provide best fitting parts, this document might contain some information on new technologies, design aspects or other forms of know-how the production company wants to protect. The basic requirement is that only engineers are allowed to access construction plans.

The model in Figure 2 shows the corresponding IF-Net for the process with respect to this setting. Data elements are modeled with colored tokens, the access modalities *create* and *write* are annotated as abbreviation *cw*. Note that these modalities relate to operations performed on the modeled data elements and not on the corresponding Petri net tokens. When data elements are simply forwarded, there is no annotated access modality. Because construction plans of prototypes may contain classified information, which should not be visible for suppliers, the engineer generates a declassified version of the construction plan in a separate step. This operation results in the generation of a new token (orange), which is passed to the supplier in the step "Send Document" by the secretary.

To check the confidentiality of data elements, the net is *labeled* in a way that it encodes the security requirements. For the classified data element "original document", the corresponding token (yellow) gets level *high*, as well as all subjects which are authorized to obtain information about the token (only the engineer) and all transitions that are allowed to handle this information (transition "Get Document" and the declassification transition). The complete labeling is given by:

activities	data elements	subjects
Issue Request{low}	*credentials{low}*	*Supplier{low}*
Receive Request{low}	*document ID{low}*	*Secretary{low}*
Refuse Request{low}	*original document{high}*	*Engineer{high}*
Forward Request{low}	*declassified document{low}*	
Get Document{high}		
Remove Information{high}		
Send Document{low}		
Receive Document{low}		

IF-Nets with encoded security requirements can be used as input for information flow analysis which checks if there are possible process execution paths that allow flows from *high* to *low*. In this example, there are no such information flows, because of the declassification transition. This nicely illustrates the benefit of declassification transitions in cases where flows from *high* to *low* are required for regular processing. Without declassification, reasoning can be inconvenient, since there is no way to specify downgraded information. Note that each data element requires a separate labeling.

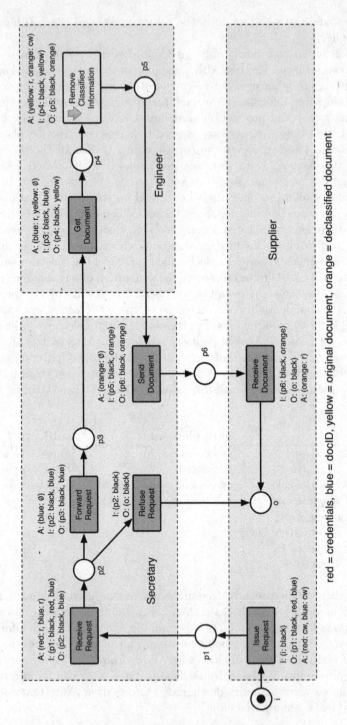

Fig. 2. Example of an IF-Net model

The consideration of only two security levels is not a restriction for confidentiality checks of data elements. Irrespective of the type of access control model (RBAC, Hierarchical RBAC, Access Control List), process activities and subjects can be partitioned in two parts for each considered data element: those with access permission (*high*) and those without access permission (*low*).

In addition to the confidentiality of data elements, information flow-oriented security analysis also allows to reason about the confidentiality of process activities. This is relevant in settings where the execution of high-confidential activities (or more general internal procedures) should be hidden from specific users or user groups. After an unsuccessful login at a system e.g., the information whether the username was invalid or the password is a valuable information that can be used by attackers to identify account names. To check the confidentiality of a process activity, the IF-Net has to be *relabeled*, i.e. the *high*/*low* information has to be adjusted according to the permission of users to know about the execution of the activity. For further reading on confidentiality of process activities with respect to information flow analysis, we refer to [1].

5.2 Multilevel Security

In multilevel security, system objects are categorized in levels that stand for different security domains. Clearances to access objects with specific security levels are used to allow subjects to access objects of specific levels. Typically, security levels are organized in a lattice which describes the relation between security levels (partial order). To access an object of level l_1, a subject has to have a clearance to access objects of level $l_2 \geq l_1$.

Assuming a security lattice *unclassified* $\leq$ *confidential* $\leq$ *secret*, the classification of process objects and clearance of subjects (roles) is given as follows:

classifications		clearances	
credentials	*unclassified*	engineer	*confidential*
document ID	*unclassified*	secretary	*unclassified*
construction plan	*confidential*	supplier	*unclassified*

The information about access modalities (*read, write, ...*) can be used to reason about the conformance of the process to confidentiality policies like Bell-LaPadula. This policy requires that there is no *read up*, i.e. no subjects get information on objects at higher levels they have permission and no *write down*, i.e. subjects on higher levels put information in objects where also subjects with lower clearance have access to. Although a lattice of security domains may have more than two entries, such policies can be verified using an approach with only two levels *high*/*low*. For this the lattice has to be partitioned and the process has to be labeled multiple times. Here, the first partition would be {*unclassified*}, {*confidential, secret*} whereas {*unclassified*} stands for *low* and {*confidential, secret*} stands for *high*.

Again, the labeling ensures, that the process encodes the security requirement. Subjects/roles and data elements have to be labeled accordingly. For the first partition, the labeling is the same as in the previous use case. If there is no partition for which illicit flows are detected, the security domains are properly separated and the process definition fulfills the multilevel security requirement.

Note that security domains can also stand for integrity classes. In this case, integrity policies like BiBa can be verified analogously.

6   Conclusion

This paper presents IF-Net, a novel meta-model for the formal specification of business processes. Based on a Colored Petri net dialect with distinguishable token types, it explicitly models data elements with token colors and adopts workflow-specific properties from CWNs. The feature of enriching control- and data-flow specifications with security-related aspects provides a basis for automated and formally founded security analysis of business processes. Specifically, it supports information flow control by providing appropriate modeling capabilities. By allowing explicit declassification with the help of downgrading transitions, it provides a flexible way of making information flow analysis applicable for practical process analysis purposes. The presented IF-Net approach was implemented in the SEPIA-framework and published on the open-source platform Sourceforge to foster further improvement/extension and to allow other researchers to perform experiments and case-studies.

While the focus of this paper was on the expressiveness of IF-Net, future work will consider analysis mechanisms on basis of IF-Nets and the mapping of information flow properties to business requirements such as Separation of Duty, Binding of Duty, Chinese wall and Conflict of Interest. Currently we are experimenting with the adaption of structural net patterns that capture specific security properties, such as hidden information transmission along the control flow of a process [7] to the IF-Net formalism, which originally have been defined on classical Petri nets. Moreover, we are defining special IF-Net patterns that can encode the aforementioned business requirements. For the verification of security properties based on IF-Net specifications, we are considering state-of-the-art Model Checking approaches and tools like PRISM [18].

References

1. Accorsi, R., Lehmann, A.: Automatic Information Flow Analysis of Business Process Models. In: Barros, A., Gal, A., Kindler, E. (eds.) BPM 2012. LNCS, vol. 7481, pp. 172–187. Springer, Heidelberg (2012)
2. Accorsi, R., Lowis, L., Sato, Y.: Automated certification for compliant cloud-based business processes. Business & Information Systems Engineering 3(3), 145–154 (2011)
3. Adam, N., Atluri, V., Huang, W.: Modeling and analysis of workflows using petri nets. Journal of Intelligent Information Systems 10, 131–158 (1998)
4. Atluri, V., Chun, S., Mazzoleni, P.: A Chinese Wall Security Model for Decentralized Workflow Systems. In: Computer and Communications Security, CCS 2001, pp. 48–57 (2001)

5. Biba, K.: Integrity considerations for secure computer systems. Technical report, MITRE Corporation (1977)
6. Brucker, A.D., Hang, I., Lückemeyer, G., Ruparel, R.: SecureBPMN: modeling and enforcing access control requirements in business processes. In: Proceedings of the 17th ACM Symposium on Access Control Models and Technologies, SACMAT 2012, pp. 123–126. ACM (2012)
7. Busi, N., Gorrieri, R.: Structural non-interference in elementary and trace nets. Mathematical Structures in Computer Science 19, 1065–1090 (2009)
8. Denning, D.E., Denning, P.J.: Certification of Pograms for Secure Information Flow. Communications of the ACM 20, 504–513 (1977)
9. Frau, S., Gorrieri, R., Ferigato, C.: Petri Net Security Checker: Structural Non-Interference at Work. In: Degano, P., Guttman, J., Martinelli, F. (eds.) FAST 2008. LNCS, vol. 5491, pp. 210–225. Springer, Heidelberg (2009)
10. Harmon, P., Wolf, C.: Business process trends. Technical report (2010), http://www.pbtrends.com
11. Rakkay, H., Boucheneb, H.: Security analysis of role based access control models using colored petri nets and cPNtools. In: Gavrilova, M.L., Tan, C.J.K., Moreno, E.D. (eds.) Transactions on Computational Science IV. LNCS, vol. 5430, pp. 149–176. Springer, Heidelberg (2009)
12. ter Hofstede, A.H.M.: Yawl: Yet Another Workflow Language. Information Systems 30, 245–275 (2005)
13. Jensen, K.: Coloured Petri Nets: Basic Concepts, Analysis Methods and Practical Use. EATCS Series, vol. 1. Springer (2003)
14. Jiang, Y., Lin, C., Yin, H., Tan, Z.: Security analysis of mandatory access control model. In: IEEE International Conference on Systems, Man and Cybernetics, pp. 5013–5018 (2004)
15. Jürjens, J.: UMLsec: Extending UML for secure systems development. In: Jézéquel, J.-M., Hussmann, H., Cook, S. (eds.) UML 2002. LNCS, vol. 2460, pp. 412–425. Springer, Heidelberg (2002)
16. Katt, B., Hafner, M., Zhang, X.: A usage control policy specification with petri nets. In: Collaborative Computing: Networking, Applications and Worksharing, pp. 1–8 (2009)
17. Knorr, K.: Multilevel Security and Information Flow in Petri Net Workflows. Technical report, Telecommunication Systems - Modeling and Analysis, Special Session on Security Aspects of Telecommunication Systems (2001)
18. Kwiatkowska, M., Norman, G., Parker, D.: PRISM 4.0: Verification of probabilistic real-time systems. In: Gopalakrishnan, G., Qadeer, S. (eds.) CAV 2011. LNCS, vol. 6806, pp. 585–591. Springer, Heidelberg (2011)
19. Lohmann, N., Verbeek, E., Dijkman, R.: Petri net transformations for business processes – A survey. In: Jensen, K., van der Aalst, W.M.P. (eds.) Transactions on Petri Nets and Other Models of Concurrency II. LNCS, vol. 5460, pp. 46–63. Springer, Heidelberg (2009)
20. Lowis, L., Accorsi, R.: Finding vulnerabilities in SOA-based business processes. IEEE Transactions on Service Computing 4(3), 230–242 (2011)
21. Müller, G., Accorsi, R.: Why are business processes not secure? In: Festschrift for Prof. Johannes Buchmann. LNCS. Springer (to appear)
22. Murata, T.: Petri nets: Properties, analysis and applications. Proceedings of the IEEE 77, 541–580 (1989)
23. Smith, H., Fingar, P.: Workflow is just a Pi-process (2004)

24. Trčka, N., van der Aalst, W.M.P., Sidorova, N.: Data-flow anti-patterns: Discovering data-flow errors in workflows. In: van Eck, P., Gordijn, J., Wieringa, R. (eds.) CAiSE 2009. LNCS, vol. 5565, pp. 425–439. Springer, Heidelberg (2009)

25. van der Aalst, W.M.P.: The Application of Petri Nets to Workflow Management. Journal of Circuits, Systems, and Computers 8, 21–66 (1998), http://www.fairdene.com/picalculus/workflow-is-just-a-pi-process.pdf

26. van der Aalst, W.M.P.: Workflow Verification: Finding Control-Flow Errors Using Petri-Net-Based Techniques. In: van der Aalst, W.M.P., Desel, J., Oberweis, A. (eds.) Business Process Management. LNCS, vol. 1806, pp. 161–183. Springer, Heidelberg (2000)

27. van der Aalst, W.M.P.: Why workflow is NOT just a Pi-process (2004)

28. van der Aalst, W.M.P.: Pi calculus versus petri nets: Let us eat "humble pie" rather than further inflate the "pi hype". BPTrends 5, 1–11 (2005)

29. van der Aalst, W.M.P., ter Hofstede, A.H.M.: Workflow patterns: On the expressive power of (petri-net-based) workflow languages. In: Workshop on Practical Use of Coloured Petri Nets and the CPN Tools, pp. 1–20. Technical Report DAIMI PB-560 (2002), http://www.bptrends.com/publicationfiles/02-04%20ART%20WhyworkflowisNOTjustaPi%20-%20Aalst1.pdf

30. van der Aalst, W.M.P., Weijters, T., Maruster, L.: Workflow Mining: Discovering Process Models from Event Logs. IEEE Trans. Knowl. Data Eng. 16, 1128–1142 (2004)

31. von Stackelberg, S., Böhm, K., Bracht, M.: Embedding 'break the glass' into business process models. In: Meersman, R., Panetto, H., Dillon, T., Rinderle-Ma, S., Dadam, P., Zhou, X., Pearson, S., Ferscha, A., Bergamaschi, S., Cruz, I.F. (eds.) OTM 2012, Part I. LNCS, vol. 7565, pp. 455–464. Springer, Heidelberg (2012)

32. Zhang, Z., Hong, F., Liao, J.: Modeling chinese wall policy using colored petri nets. In: Computer and Information Technology, CIT 2006, p. 162 (2006)

Authenticity Control of Relational Databases by Means of Lossless Watermarking Based on Circular Histogram Modulation

Javier Franco-Contreras[1,3], Gouenou Coatrieux[1,3], Nora Cuppens-Boulahia[2,3], Fréderic Cuppens[2,3], and Christian Roux[1,3]

[1] Institut Mines-TELECOM, TELECOM Bretagne, Inserm U1101,
Brest, 29238 France
{javier.francocontreras,gouenou.coatrieux}@telecom-bretagne.eu
[2] Institut Mines-TELECOM, TELECOM Bretagne, UMR CNRS 3192 Lab-STICC
Cesson Sévigné 35576 France
[3] Université européenne de Bretagne, France

Abstract. In this paper, we adapt the reversible watermarking modulation originally proposed by De Vleeschouwer *et al.* for images to the protection of relational databases. Message embedding is achieved by modulating the relative angular position of the circular histogram center of mass of one numerical attribute. It is fragile and can be used for database authentication. Beyond the application framework, we theoretically evaluate the performance of our scheme in terms of distortion and capacity. We further experimentally verify these theoretical limits within the framework of one medical database of more than one million of inpatient hospital stay records. We show that under the central limit theorem assumptions, experimental results fit theory.

1 Introduction

Supported by the development of efficient data-mining tools, but not only, databases take nowadays an important place in decision making processes and are consequently more and more shared or remotely accessed. At the same time, this ease of manipulation may endanger data. They can be redistributed or modified without permission. Notice that the number of reported data leaks and frauds each year is not negligible, even in sensitive domains such as healthcare [1]. Several security mechanisms have already been deployed for relational databases protection, but most of them, like access control and encryption, protect the data before granting the access. Similarly, shared with the data, digital signatures allow us to verify data integrity. Once access is bypassed or ancillary security attributes removed, data are no longer protected.

Watermarking can advantageously complete the previous solutions. It is a kind of "*a posteriori*" protection which consists in the "imperceptible" embedding of a message, like some security attributes (e.g. digital signature, authenticity code), into a multimedia host document (e.g. image or database) based on the principle

R. Accorsi and S. Ranise (Eds.): STM 2013, LNCS 8203, pp. 207–222, 2013.
© Springer-Verlag Berlin Heidelberg 2013

of controlled distortion. Basically, it modifies or alters host data so as to encode the message. Resulting distortions, i.e. differences between original host data and their watermarked version, correspond to the watermark. By definition, the watermark should be transparent to the user and independent from the data storage format. Thus, watermarking allows the normal use and access to data while keeping them protected. Since the seminal work of Agrawal *et al.* in 2002 [2], several database watermarking methods have been proposed [3–5]. Among them, we can distinguish two main classes: i) "robust" methods, commonly employed in copyright or fingerprinting/traitor tracing frameworks [6, 7], where the embedded message should survive database modifications being innocent or malevolent; ii) "fragile" methods that introduce a watermark which will not survive data modifications and are mostly devoted to database authentication [8–10]. Herein, we are interested in fragile watermarking.

Whatever the above methods, their authors assume some data distortion (e.g. modification of attributes' values [3] or of tuples' order [8]) can be carried out for message insertion without perturbing any *a posteriori* uses of data. In order to better take into account watermark imperceptibility, most recent schemes consider distortion constraints. For instance, in [3] the embedding process does not modify numerical attributes for which data quality conditions, measured in terms of mean square error, are not respected. Shehab *et al.* additionally consider attribute statistics constraints (e.g. mean, stan) on attribute values and statistics (e.g. mean, standard deviation) and adapt the watermark amplitude by means of optimization techniques [5]. In [4] and [11] Gross-Amblard and Lafaye *et al.* look at preserving the response to a priori known queries of aggregation, and modulate pairs of tuples in consequence.

Another whole set of methods is based on the modulation of the order of tuples within a relation [8, 9, 12]. As they do not modify attributes' values, they are named "distortion-free". However, such a technique makes the watermark dependent on the way the database is stored, inducing constrains on the database management system, while limiting the application range this family of methods can be used for.

One last category of methods refers to reversible or lossless watermarking. The reversibility property allows the recovery of the original data from their watermarked version by inverting watermarking modifications. It becomes then possible: i) to let access to the watermarked data (unless the watermark interferes with database post-uses); ii) to come back to the original data for the watermark update or when databases post-process requires it. Until now, existing reversible approaches have been derived from lossless image watermarking. This is why they mostly work on numerical attributes rather than on categorical attributes, with the exception of [13].

Regarding numerical attributes, Zhang *et al.* [14] apply the well known histogram shifting modulation. Working on the difference between consecutive pre-ordered tuples, they right shift bins next to the histogram maximum of one digit (in the real value range [1,9]) so as to create an empty bin. In order to embed one bit, samples associated to the histogram maximum are shifted to the gap (bit value '1') or left unchanged ('0'). The capacity of this method directly depends on the probability distribution of the considered digit. In case of a flat histogram, i.e. a uniform distribution, the capacity is null (there is no maximum). As shown by the authors, except for the most significant digits, all the other have a uniform probability density . As a consequence, achieving an acceptable capacity may induce a high database distortion. Another approach proposed by Chang et al. [15] consider the use of a support vector machine (SVM) classifier. One SVM is trained with a set of tuples selected so as to obtain a classification function $f(V)$ used by next to predict the values of one numerical attribute. Then, they apply difference expansion modulation for message embedding. Basically, they "expand" the differences between original and predicted values adding one virtual Least Significant Bit that is used for embedding message bits. The distortion magnitude is unpredictable and as underlined by its authors, it can be high in some cases.

In this work, we present a novel lossless fragile watermarking method which modulates numerical attributes of relational database. It is based on the circular histogram modulation which has been originally proposed by De Vleeschouwer et al. [16] for images. Our method does not depend on the storing structure of the database. It alters the angle between the centers of mass of circular histograms associated to groups of values of one numerical attribute of the relation. As we will demonstrate, this angle follows a zero-mean normal distribution, resulting in a high capacity for a low introduced distortion. At the same time, because the modification made to attribute's values is constant, we can predict the corresponding database distortion. Compared to the above schemes, based on the properties of the numerical attributes exploited for embedding, our scheme solution can be parameterized by the user according to his or her capacity and distortion needs.

The rest of this paper is organized as follows. In Section 2 we present the main steps of a common chain of database watermarking before introducing our reversible fragile scheme in Section 3. In Section 4, we theoretically evaluate the capacity and distortion performance of our scheme. We then empirically verify these theoretical limits in Section 5 by means of experiments conducted on one real medical database of patient stay records.

2   Database Watermarking

By definition, a database DB is composed of a finite set of relations $\{R_i\}_{i=1,...,N_R}$. From here on and for sake of simplicity, we will consider one database based on one single relation constituted of N unordered tuples $\{t_u\}_{u=1,...,N}$, each of M attributes $\{A_1, A_2, \ldots, A_M\}$. The attribute A_n takes its values within an attribute domain and $t_u.A_n$ refers to the value of the nth attribute of the uth tuple. Each tuple is uniquely identified by either one attribute or a set of attributes, we call its primary key $t_u.PK$.

Most database watermarking schemes work according to the procedure depicted in figure 1. It relies on two main stages: message embedding and message

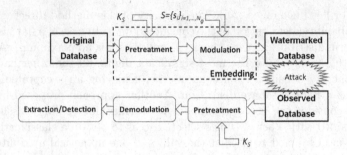

Fig. 1. A common database watermarking chain

detection/extraction. As shown, the embedding stage includes a pretreatment process, the objective of which is to make the watermark insertion/reading independent of the way database is stored. It consists in a "tuple grouping operation" which output is a set of N_g non-intersecting groups of tuples $\{G^i\}_{i=1,...,N_g}$.

The usual strategy for determining the group number of one tuple relies on a cryptographic hash function applied to its primary key $t_u.PK$, concatenated with a secret watermarking key K_S as exposed in (1) where '|' represents the concatenation operator) [3] [5]. The use of a cryptographic hash function, such as the Secure Hash Algorithm (SHA), ensures the secure and equal distribution of tuples into groups.

$$n_u = H(K_S|t_u.PK)modN_g \qquad (1)$$

By next, one bit or symbol of the message is embedded per group by modulating the values of one or several attributes accordingly the retained watermarking modulation. Thus, with N_g groups, one may expect inserting a message that corresponds to a sequence of N_g symbols $S = \{s_i\}_{i=1,...,N_g}$.

Watermark extraction works in a similar way. Tuples are first reorganized in N_g groups. From each group, one message symbol is detected or/and extracted depending on the exploited modulation. Unless tuple primary keys are not modified, the knowledge of the watermarking key ensures synchronization between embedding and reading stages.

3   Proposed Scheme

In [16], De Vleeschouwer *et al.* propose to divide a grayscale image into blocks of pixels, each equally divided into two sub-blocks. The histograms of both sub-blocks are then mapped onto a circle. In order to embed one bit in a block, the relative angle between the two circular histograms' center of mass is modulated. Depending on the bit value to embed in a block, this operation results in shifting of $\pm\Delta$ the pixel gray values of one pixel sub-block and of $\mp\Delta$ those of the other. In this work, we apply this modulation in order to embed one symbol s_i of the watermark (or equivalently of the message) in one group of tuples G^i.

Let us consider one group of tuples G^i and A_n be the numerical attribute selected for embedding. G^i is equally divided in two sub-groups of tuples $G^{A,i}$ and $G^{B,i}$, following the same strategy depicted in Sect. 2. More clearly, the subgroup membership $n_{u_{sg}}$ of one tuple is given by:

$$n_{u_{sg}} = \begin{cases} G^{A,i} \text{ if } H(K_S|t_u.PK)mod2 = 0 \\ G^{B,i} \text{ if } H(K_S|t_u.PK)mod2 = 1 \end{cases} \qquad (2)$$

Once $G^{A,i}$ and $G^{B,i}$ constituted, the histograms of the attribute A_n in each of them are calculated and mapped onto a circle. Then, and as illustrated in Fig.2(a), the histogram center of mass $C^{A,i}$ (resp. $C^{B,i}$) of the sub-group $G^{A,i}$ (resp. $G^{B,i}$) and its associated vector $V^{A,i}$ (resp. $V^{B,i}$) are calculated. To do so, let us assume the attribute domain of A_n corresponds to the integer range $[0,L\text{-}1]$. The module and phase of $V^{A,i}$ (resp. $V^{B,i}$) can be calculated from its Cartesian coordinates given by:

$$\begin{aligned} X &= \tfrac{1}{M} \sum_{l=0}^{L-1} n_l \cos(\tfrac{2\pi l}{L}) \\ Y &= \tfrac{1}{M} \sum_{l=0}^{L-1} n_l \sin(\tfrac{2\pi l}{L}) \\ M &= \sum_{l=0}^{L-1} n_l \end{aligned} \qquad (3)$$

where n_l is the cardinality of the circular histogram class l of $G^{A,i}$ (i.e. when A_n takes the integer value l). As a consequence, the module of $V^{A,i}$ equals $R = \sqrt{X^2 + Y^2}$ and its phase, we also call mean direction μ, is given by:

$$\mu = \begin{cases} \arctan(Y/X) \text{ if } X > 0 \\ \tfrac{\pi}{2} \text{ if } X = 0, Y > 0 \\ -\tfrac{\pi}{2} \text{ if } X = 0, Y < 0 \\ \pi + \arctan(Y/X) \text{ else} \end{cases} \qquad \cdot(4)$$

Let us now consider the embedding of a sequence of bits into the database, i.e. inserting the symbol $s = \{0/1\}$ in G^i. As in [16], we modulate the relative angle $\beta_i = (\widehat{V^{A,i}, V^{B,i}}) \simeq 0$ between $V^{A,i}$ and $V^{B,i}$. β^i is changed into its watermarked version β_i^W by rotating the circular histograms of $G^{A,i}$ and $G^{B,i}$ in opposite directions respectively with an angle step α as follows (see Fig.2(b)):

$$\beta_i^W = \begin{cases} \beta_i - 2\alpha \text{ if } s = 0 \ (\beta_i^W < 0) \\ \beta_i + 2\alpha \text{ if } s = 1 \ (\beta_i^W > 0) \end{cases} \qquad (5)$$

In our example, the angle step α is given by:

$$\alpha = \left| \frac{2\pi\Delta}{L} \right| \qquad (6)$$

where Δ corresponds to the shift amplitude of the histogram (see Fig. 2(b)). We will explain in Section 3.1 how this angular modification affects the linear histogram of the attribute.

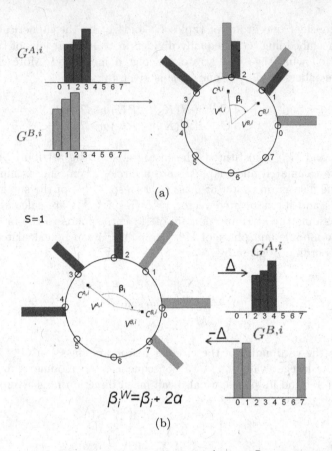

Fig. 2. a) Histogram mapping of each sub-group G^A and G^B onto a circle. The angle between vectors pointing centers of mass is modulated in order to embed one message symbol s. b) Embedding of s=1 correspond to a rotation of the circular histograms of $G^{A,i}$ and $G^{B,i}$ in opposite directions with an angle step α so as to modify the sign of β_i. This is equivalent to the addition of $-\Delta$ to the attribute values in $G^{B,i}$ and Δ to those of $G^{A,i}$.

At the reading stage, based on the above rules, the sign of β_i^{W} indicates the embedded symbol value as well as the rotation direction for inverting the insertion process and recovering the original value of β_i.

However, at this point, not all of the groups can convey one symbol of message. In fact and from a more general point of view, we propose to distinguish three classes of groups. In the case $|\beta_i| < 2\alpha$ one can insert $s = 0$ or $s = 1$, as it is possible to swap the position of $V^{A,i}$ and $V^{B,i}$. We refer these groups as "carrier-groups". We also identify two other kinds of groups: "non-carrier groups" and "overflowed groups". They have to be considered separately and handled specifically so as to make the scheme fully reversible. Non-carrier groups are those for which the angle distortion α is not big enough to make change the sign of β_i (see Fig.3(a)). In order not confusing such non-carriers with carriers at the reading stage, they are modified in the following way (see Fig.3(a)):

$$\beta_i^{\mathrm{W}} = \begin{cases} \beta_i + 2\alpha \text{ if } \beta_i > 0 \\ \beta_i - 2\alpha \text{ if } \beta_i < 0 \end{cases} \tag{7}$$

This process results in increasing the angle $\widehat{V^{A,i}, V^{B,i}}$. They are identified at the reading stage with watermarked angle values such as $|\beta_i^{\mathrm{W}}| > 4\alpha$ and easily differentiated from carriers, which belong to the range $[-4\alpha, 4\alpha]$. Thus the reader just has to add or subtract α based on (7) so as to restore these watermarked non-carrier groups.

"Overflow-groups" are groups for which an "angle overflow" occurs if modified. Basically and as illustrated in Fig. 3(b), one overflow-group is a non-carrier group which angle $|\beta_i|$ exceeds $\pi - 2\alpha$. If it is modified according to rules given in (7), an undesired sign change will occur when turning β_i into β_i^{W} inducing in error the watermark reader. Indeed, this latter will not restore properly the original angle β_i by inverting (7). For instance, if $\beta_i > \pi - 2\alpha$ and $\beta_i > 0$ (see Fig. 3(b)) then adding 2α will lead to $\beta_i^{\mathrm{W}} < 0$. On its side the reader will thus restore the group subtracting 2α instead of -2α. The solution we adopt so as to manage these problematic groups and to make the modulation reversible is the following one. At the embedding stage, these groups are not modified and we inform the reader by means of an overhead inserted along with the message. This will avoid the reader confusing overflow groups with non-carriers. The overhead corresponds to a vector of bits O_v stating that watermarked groups such as $\beta_i^{\mathrm{W}} > \pi - 2\alpha$ or $\beta_i^{\mathrm{W}} < -(\pi - 2\alpha)$ are overflow-groups (unmodified) or non-carrier groups. If $O_v(k) = 1$ then the kth group such as $\beta_i^{\mathrm{W}} > \pi - 2\alpha$ or $\beta_i^{\mathrm{W}} < -(\pi - 2\alpha)$ is a non-carrier group; otherwise it is an overflow-group.

Performance of the above method in terms of capacity depends on the number of carrier-groups and of the size of the overhead i.e. number overflow-groups. We will see in Sect. 4 that this capacity rely in part on the statistical properties of the numerical attribute exploited for message embedding and also on the number of tuples per group.

3.1 Linear Histogram Modification

β_i rotations can be performed in different ways in the linear domain, i.e on the attribute values. We propose two different strategies depending on the probability distribution of the numerical attribute A_n. Both are equivalent from the perspective of β_i but they allow us to minimize the database distortion.

In the case of numerical attributes of probability distribution centered on its domain range and concentrated around it, we propose to modify groups by adding Δ to the values in $G^{A,i}$ and $-\Delta$ to those in $G^{B,i}$ in order to modify the angle β_i of 2α (inversely for a modification of -2α). The idea is to distribute the

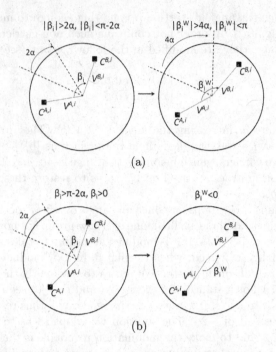

(a)

(b)

Fig. 3. Problematic groups: Non-carrier groups and overflow groups (black squares represent circular histogram centers of mass). a) Non-carrier groups are such $|\beta_i| > 2\alpha$ (*on the left*); they are watermarked applying (7) (*on the right*). b) Overflow groups are such as $|\beta_i^W| > \pi - 2\alpha$. In the given example $\beta_i^W > \pi - 2\alpha$ (*on the left*); if modified the reader will identify $\beta_i^W < 0$ and will not properly invert (7); it will subtract 2α to β_i^W instead of -2α (*on the right*).

distortion onto both groups instead of one and to limit the number of attributes values jumps between attribute domain range extremities (as example a jump from the value 0 to 7 in Fig. 2(b)). For an attribute range $[0, L - 1]$, these jumps represent a modification of $|L - \Delta|$ to the corresponding attribute value.

If now the attribute has its probability density concentrated around one of its domain range extremities, let us say the lower one for example, one must avoid shifting to the left its histogram. Indeed, this will increase jump occurrences and maximize the database distortion. Thus, instead of modifying attribute's values in both $G^{A,i}$ and $G^{B,i}$, we propose to use one of them only, selected according to the sought final sign of β_i, and to shift its attributes values in the opposite direction of the lower domain range by adding them 2Δ. In this way, values in the lower extremity of the domain are never flipped, resulting in a significant reduction of introduced distortion compared to previous strategy. Nevertheless, this second strategy presents a disadvantage as the mean value of the attribute distribution is increased of Δ.

4 Theoretical Performance

In this section we first theoretically evaluate the capacity of our scheme and then its distortion. Both depend on the statistical distribution of β_i, the shift amplitude Δ and obviously of the attribute distribution.

4.1 Capacity Performance

By definition, capacity directly depends on the number of carrier groups, i.e. those for which $|\beta_i| < 2\alpha$ (see Sect. 3 and Fig. 4). In fact, the number of carriers defines the global capacity of our scheme and it can be established from the probability density function (p.d.f) of β_i. p.d.f which can be computed whatever the numerical attribute. To do so, let us first recall that β_i is associated to the group of tuples G^i and that it corresponds to the angle between the centers of mass of two circular histograms of the same attribute A_n in two tuple subgroups $G^{A,i}$ and $G^{B,i}$. Because each histogram represents the distribution of A_n, we can refer to some results issued from circular statistics, a sub-discipline of statistics that deals with data measured by angles or vectors [17, 18].

As a preliminary statement, let us consider the circular data distribution of one attribute θ (i.e. its histogram mapped onto a circle). This can be seen as the p.d.f $f(\theta)$ of a discrete random variable θ which takes L values around the circle, in the finite set $\{\frac{2\pi l}{L}\}_{l=0,...,L-1}$. The mean direction μ of θ, which in fact corresponds to the phase of the vector associated to the center of mass of θ circular histogram, can be estimated based on a finite number of θ samples. Based on the Law of large numbers and with the help of the central limit theorem, it was shown by Fisher and Lewis [19] that for any circular data distribution $f(\theta)$, the distribution of the mean direction estimator approaches a normal distribution centered on the real mean direction of the circular data distribution.

Let us now consider β_i. When we modulate it, we in fact modulate the angle between two mean directions $\mu^{A,i}$ and $\mu^{B,i}$ of two circular histograms attached to the same attribute A_n in a group G^i. Indeed, $\mu^{A,i}$ (resp. $\mu^{B,i}$) calculated on the sub-group $G^{A,i}$ (resp. $G^{B,i}$) can be seen as the estimator of the mean direction of the attribute A_n (i.e. $\theta = A_n$ in the above) using a number of samples or tuples $\frac{N}{2N_g}$, where N and N_g are the number of tuples in the database and the number of groups respectively.

As a consequence, we can state that both $\mu^{A,i}$ and $\mu^{B,i}$ follow a normal distribution. Because the difference between two normally distributed random variables is also a normally distributed random variable, our angle $\beta_i = \mu^{A,i} - \mu^{B,i}$ follows a centered normal distribution $\mathcal{N}(0, \sigma_{\beta_i}^2)$ of variance $\sigma_{\beta_i}^2$.

Based on this statement, the probability a group of tuples is a carrier-group for a given angle shift α (see Sect. 3) is defined as:

$$\mathbb{P}_{\text{carrier}} = \Phi(\frac{2\alpha}{\sigma_{\beta_i}}) - \Phi(-\frac{2\alpha}{\sigma_{\beta_i}}) \tag{8}$$

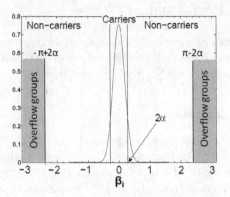

Fig. 4. β_i distribution

where Φ is the cumulative distribution function for a normal distribution:

$$\Phi(\frac{2\alpha}{\sigma_{\beta_i}}) = \frac{1}{\sigma_{\beta_i}\sqrt{2\pi}} \int_{-\infty}^{2\alpha} e^{\frac{-t^2}{2\sigma^2_{\beta_i}}} \, dt \tag{9}$$

being t an auxiliary random variable. As common convention, we take $\Phi(-\infty) = 0$ and $\Phi(\infty) = 1$.

In practice, considering one numerical attribute A_n, a database of N tuples and N_g groups, one just has to estimate $\sigma^2_{\beta_i}$ to establish the global capacity limit of our fragile scheme. To do so, let us first estimate the variance of the mean directions $\mu^{A,i}$ and $\mu^{B,i}$ as in [20], we have

$$\sigma^2_{\mu^{A,i}} = \sigma^2_{\mu^{B,i}} = \frac{\sigma^2_s}{\frac{N}{2N_g}R^2} \tag{10}$$

where: R corresponds to the module of the center of mass vector (i.e. $V^{A,i}$, see Sect. 3) and σ^2_s is defined as[20]:

$$\sigma^2_s = \sum_{l=0}^{L-1} sin^2(\frac{2\pi l}{L})f(\frac{2\pi l}{L}) \tag{11}$$

where values $\{\frac{2\pi l}{L}\}_{l=0,...,L-1}$ are the bins of the circular histogram attached to the attribute A_n and $f(\frac{2\pi l}{L})$ their corresponding probabilities. Again, as β_i results from the difference of two normally distributed random variables $\mu_{A,i}$ and $\mu_{B,i}$, its variance is:

$$\sigma^2_{\beta_i} = \frac{2\sigma^2_s}{\frac{N}{2N_g}R^2} \tag{12}$$

Notice that the above normal distribution assumption of β_i is verified when $\frac{N}{2N_g} \geq 30$ (see [21] for further details).

The carrier probability can then be derived from (8), and the global capacity of our scheme C_T one may expect is given by

$$C_T = N_g \cdot \mathbb{P}_{\text{carrier}} \tag{13}$$

Once the global capacity C_T is known, one must subtract to it the number of bits used for encoding the overhead, i.e. $|O_v|$ bits. This latter is directly linked to the probability β_i belongs to the range $[-\pi, -\pi + 4\alpha] \bigcup [\pi - 4\alpha, \pi]$. We recall that the overhead is a vector which components indicate by '0' or '1' whether a watermarked angle β_i^W in the range $[-\pi, -\pi + 2\alpha] \bigcup [\pi - 2\alpha, \pi]$ has been shifted or not (see end of Section 3). $|O_v|$ is upper bounded such as:

$$|O_v| \leq N_g \cdot \mathbb{P}_{[-\pi, -\pi+4\alpha] \bigcup [\pi-4\alpha, \pi]} = N_g \cdot \mathbb{P}_{\text{ofw}} \tag{14}$$

Where

$$\mathbb{P}_{\text{ofw}} = \left[\Phi(\frac{\pi}{\sigma_{\beta_i}}) - \Phi(\frac{\pi - 4\alpha}{\sigma_{\beta_i}}) \right] + \left[\Phi(-\frac{(\pi - 4\alpha)}{\sigma_{\beta_i}}) - \Phi(-\frac{\pi}{\sigma_{\beta_i}}) \right] \tag{15}$$

Finally, the length of the message one may expect to embed is also upper bounded

$$C \leq C_T - |O_v| \tag{16}$$

From these results, we can conclude that, for a fixed value of α, the embedding capacity directly depends on the attribute's statistics. By extension, any uniformly distributed attribute will not be watermarkable as $\sigma_{\beta_i}^2$ will tend to ∞ (see (12)) and the capacity to 0 (see (8)).

4.2   Introduced Distortion

Let us consider the mean square error (MSE) as data distortion measure. As presented in Sect. 3, depending on the attribute p.d.f., we propose two linear histogram modification strategies in order to modulate β_i. If both do not modify overflow groups, they do not introduce the same distortion into other groups. In the first strategy, values are in majority shifted of $|\Delta|$. In case of jump between the attribute domain range extremities, this shift becomes $|L - \Delta|$. Based on the fact that tuples are uniformly and equally distributed into N_g groups, we can assume that each of them contains the same number of "jumped" values. As a consequence, the MSE is calculated as:

$$MSE = (1 - \mathbb{P}_{\text{ofw}}) \cdot [(\frac{\mathbb{P}_{\text{lim}}}{2})((L - \Delta)^2 + \Delta^2) + (1 - \mathbb{P}_{\text{lim}})\Delta^2] \tag{17}$$

where $\mathbb{P}_{\text{lim}} = \mathbb{P}_{\text{up}} + \mathbb{P}_{\text{low}}$ and $\mathbb{P}_{\text{up}}$ and $\mathbb{P}_{\text{low}}$ correspond to the probabilities one attribute value falls in the high and low attribute domain ranges that are subject to "jump", respectively. Given the probability distribution of the attribute A_n, one can see as a discrete random variable, the probability that A_n takes a value V is $f(V) = \mathbb{P}(A_n = V)$, then we have

$$\mathbb{P}_{\text{up}} = \sum_{V=L-1-\Delta}^{L-1} f(V) \quad \mathbb{P}_{\text{low}} = \sum_{V=0}^{\Delta} f(V) \tag{18}$$

As shown, our method's distortion directly depends on the value of Δ and on the attribute distribution. The number of elements at the extremities of the attribute domain has a high impact and so does the domain length itself, i.e. L in the above.

For the second strategy, only values in one subgroup $G^{A,i}$ (resp. $G^{B,i}$) are modified of 2Δ so as to modulate β_i. This results in a MSE given by

$$MSE = \frac{(1 - \mathbb{P}_{\text{ofw}}) \cdot [(\mathbb{P}_{\text{up}})(L - 2\Delta)^2 + (1 - \mathbb{P}_{\text{up}})(2\Delta)^2]}{2} \qquad (19)$$

The next Section shows the effectiveness of this strategy in the case of attributes whose probability distribution is not centered over the domain range.

5   Results

In this section, we present some experimental results in terms of capacity and distortion applying our method onto one real database. As we will see, they fit the above theoretical performance.

5.1   Dataset and Watermarking Scheme Parametrization

Our test database is constituted of one relation of about one million tuples issued from one real medical database containing pieces of information related to inpatient stays in French hospitals. In this table, each tuple associates fifteen attributes like the hospital identifier (*id_hospital*), the patient stay identifier (*id_stay*), the patient age (*age*), the stay duration (*dur_stay*) and several other data useful for statistical analysis of hospital activities. In order to constitute the groups and subgroups of tuples (see Sect.2), the attributes *id_hospital* and *id_stay* were concatenated and considered as the primary key. Two numerical attributes were considered for message embedding: patient age (*age*) and stay duration (*dur_stay*). Notice also that results are given in average after 30 random simulations with the same parameterization but with different tuples.

5.2   Capacity Results

Herein, interest is given to the influence of the attribute shift amplitude Δ over the final capacity. We recall that the angle shift α of β_i depends on Δ (see (6)). As illustrated in Fig. 5, where the attribute *age* is used for embedding with a fixed number of groups $N_g = 5000$ and an attribute shift amplitude Δ varying in the range $[1, 5]$, capacity increases along with Δ and verifies the theoretical limit we define in Sect. 4. Obviously, one must also consider that the attribute distortion increases along with the capacity (see also Sect. 5.3. In a second experiment, we looked at evaluating the capacity according to the attribute statistical moments. To do so, attributes *age* and *dur_stay* were watermarked with the same values of Δ while considering a varying number of groups such as $N_g \in 1000, 3000, 5000, 10000$. Notice that the more important the number of

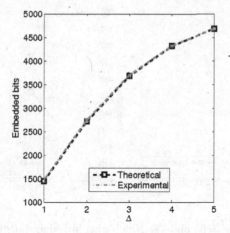

Fig. 5. Achieved *Age* capacity for different shift amplitude Δ taking $N_g = 5000$ groups

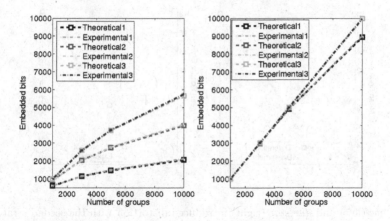

Fig. 6. *Age* (left) and *dur_stay* (right) capacity results considering a fixed shift amplitude and for different size of groups

groups, the smaller is the number of tuples per groups. Again, and as depicted in Fig.6, obtained capacities fit the theoretical limit we defined in Sect. 4.1. Given results confirm that the capacity depends on the properties of the attributes considered for embedding and especially of its standard deviation (see Sect. 4). We can insert more data within the attribute *dur_stay* which is of smaller variance.

5.3 Distortion Results

As presented in Sect. 4.2, the distortion depends on the attribute distribution, the shift amplitude Δ as well as on the linear histogram modulation strategy used. In order to verify this dependence, attributes *age* and *dur_stay* were watermarked

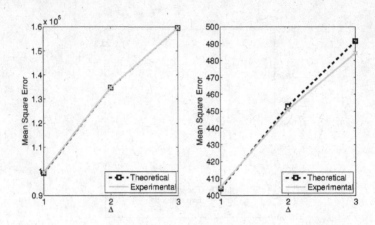

Fig. 7. *age* (left) and *dur_stay* (right) introduced distortion

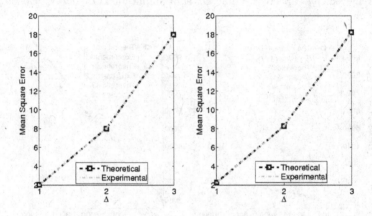

Fig. 8. *age* (left) and *dur_stay* (right) introduced distortion with the second strategy

with the same values of Δ in the range $[1, 3]$ while considering a number of groups $N_g = 10000$. For both attributes, in accordance to Fig. 7, experimental results fit the theoretical values given in Sect. 4.2. This confirms that global distortion stands not only on Δ, but also on the attribute domain and its probability distribution. However, it remains predictable as all these parameters can be calculated before the embedding process.

Regarding the linear histogram modification, the two previous attributes were also watermarked using the second strategy we propose. Results are depicted in Fig. 8. As we can see, in both cases distortion is highly reduced. Indeed, these attributes have their distributions concentrated the lower extremity of their attribute domain.

6   Conclusion

In this paper, we have proposed a fragile lossless relational database watermarking scheme which makes use of circular histogram modulation. It can be used for verifying the integrity of the database embedding for example a digital signature of the database within itself. According to the probability distribution of the numerical attribute selected for watermarking, two possible modulations have been proposed. In addition, we theoretically established and verified experimentally the performance of our method in terms of capacity. These results allow the user to select the more appropriate parameters and modulation of our scheme under application constraints established in terms of capacity and distortion.

References

1. McNickle, M.: Top 10 data security breaches in 2012 in Healthcare Finance News (accessed April 17, 2013)
2. Agrawal, R., Kiernan, J.: watermarking relational databases. In: VLDB 2002: Proceedings of the 28th International Conference on Very Large Database, ch.15, pp. 155–166. Morgan Kaufmann, San Francisco (2002)
3. Sion, R., Atallah, M., Prabhakar, S.: Rights protection for relational data. IEEE Trans. on Knowledge and Data Engineering 16(12), 1509–1525 (2004)
4. Gross-Amblard, D.: Query-preserving watermarking of relational databases and xml documents. ACM Trans. Database Syst. 36, 3:1–3:24 (2011)
5. Shehab, M., Bertino, E., Ghafoor, A.: Watermarking relational databases using optimization-based techniques. IEEE Trans. on Knowledge and Data Engineering 20, 116–129 (2008)
6. Li, Y., Swarup, V., Jajodia, S.: Fingerprinting relational databases: schemes and specialties. IEEE Trans. on Dependable and Secure Computing 2(1), 34–45 (2005)
7. Guo, F., Wang, J., Li, D.: Fingerprinting relational databases. In: Proceedings of the 2006 ACM Symposium on Applied Computing, SAC 2006. ACM, New York (2006)
8. Li, Y., Guo, H., Jajodia, S.: Tamper detection and localization for categorical data using fragile watermarks. In: Proceedings of the 4th ACM workshop on Digital Rights Management, DRM 2004, pp. 73–82. ACM, New York (2004)
9. Kamel, I., Kamel, K.: Toward protecting the integrity of relational databases. In: 2011 World Congress on Internet Security (WorldCIS), pp. 258–261. IEEE (February 2011)
10. Guo, J.: Fragile watermarking scheme for tamper detection of relational database. In: 2011 International Conference on Computer and Management (CAMAN), pp. 1–4 (May 2011)
11. Lafaye, J., Gross-Amblard, D., Constantin, C., Guerrouani, M.: Watermill: An optimized fingerprinting system for databases under constraints. IEEE Trans. on Knowledge and Data Engineering 20, 532–546 (2008)
12. Bhattacharya, S., Cortesi, A.: A distortion free watermark framework for relational databases. In: Shishkov, B., Cordeiro, J., Ranchordas, A. (eds.) ICSOFT (2), pp. 229–234. INSTICC Press (2009)
13. Coatrieux, G., Chazard, E., Beuscart, R., Roux, C.: Lossless watermarking of categorical attributes for verifying medical data base integrity. In: 2011 Annual International Conference of the IEEE Engineering in Medicine and Biology Society, EMBC, pp. 8195–8198. IEEE (2011)

14. Zhang, Y., Niu, X., Yang, B.: Reversible watermarking for relational database authentication. Journal of Computers 17(2) (July 2006)
15. Chang, J.N., Wu, H.C.: Reversible fragile database watermarking technology using difference expansion based on svr prediction. In: Proceedings of the 2012 International Symposium on Computer, Consumer and Control, IS3C 2012, pp. 690–693. IEEE Computer Society, Washington, DC (2012)
16. De Vleeschouwer, C., Delaigle, J.F., Macq, B.: Circular interpretation of bijective transformations in lossless watermarking for media asset management. IEEE Trans. on Multimedia 5(1), 97–105 (2003)
17. Mardia, K.V., Jupp, P.E.: Directional statistics. Wiley Series in Probability and Statistics. Wiley, Chichester (1999)
18. Fisher, N.I.: Statistical Analysis of Circular Data. Cambridge University Press (1993)
19. Fisher, N.I., Lewis, T.: Estimating the common mean direction of several circular or spherical distributions with differing dispersions. Biometrika 70(2), 333–341 (1983)
20. McKilliam, R.G.: Lattice theory, circular statistics and polynomial phase signals. PhD thesis, University of Queensland, Australia (2010)
21. Berenson, M., Krehbiel, T., Levine, D.: Basic Business Statistics: Concepts and Applications. Prentice-Hall (2012)

Weighted-Sum Fragile Watermarking in the Karhunen-Loève Domain

Marco Botta[1], Davide Cavagnino[1], and Victor Pomponiu[2]

[1] Dipartimento di Informatica, Università degli Studi di Torino
Corso Svizzera 185, 10149 Torino, Italy
{marco.botta,davide.cavagnino}@unito.it
[2] Department of Radiology, University of Pittsburgh
3362 Fifth Avenue, Pittsburgh, 15213, PA, USA
vpomponiu@acm.org

Abstract. In this paper we present a simple and elegant technique for fragile image watermarking inthe Karhunen-Loève transform (KLT) domain with the objective of content integrity. The proposed method inserts a binary watermark into some KLT coefficients defined using a secret key image. The coefficients are modified according to a rule based on a weighted-modulo sum. The KLT is applied to contiguous blocks of the host image and a Genetic Algorithm (GA) is used to modify the pixel values in such a way that the resulting blocks contain the watermark. Given that the KLT space of insertion of the watermark is kept secret, the security of the method is strong. We experimentally demonstrate that the algorithm achieves an excellent sensitivity even to small modifications of the watermarked image.

Keywords: information hiding, fragile watermarking, genetic algorithms, Karhunen-Loève Transform, tamper localization.

1 Introduction

Digital watermarking, which aims to insert a signal (called watermark) into a digital object, has a rich history beginning in the mid-80s [1]. Since then, many different algorithms have been proposed and we will review some of them in the following.

Depending on the objective to be obtained, digital watermarks may be classified as robust or fragile. Robust watermarks are devised to be resistant to survive processing operations that attempt their removal (maintaining a good quality of the digital object); the classical application of robust watermarks is copyright protection. On the other hand, the main challenge of fragile watermarking is to identify if modifications to the digital object have been performed. This task becomes particularly difficult when the digital object undergoes minimal content alterations. There is also a set of algorithms, called semi-fragile, whose watermark characteristic is to survive mild common signal processing operations but to be removed by stronger alterations. Typical watermarking applications are track of origin, copyright protection, content integrity protection and authentication.

R. Accorsi and S. Ranise (Eds.): STM 2013, LNCS 8203, pp. 223–234, 2013.

In this paper we are mainly concerned with fragile watermarking, whose main properties should be:

- the ability to detect and localize the modified regions of the digital object;
- the characteristic of being imperceptible (during the normal use of the digital object);
- the resistance to attacks aimed at modifying the object without being detected.

Presently, there is a growing trend to enrich the fragile watermarks with a new requirement, namely self-recovery [2]. Simply, it implies the capacity of the watermark to recover the damaged areas of the digital content to its original state.

Generally, the watermark can be directly inserted into the values of the object (like pixels for an image, or audio samples for a sound) or into the coefficients of some transformed domain (like the Fourier transform domain or the discrete cosine transform (DCT) domain). A very complete description of digital watermarking can be found in [1].

In this work we present a fragile watermarking algorithm that can be applied to grayscale bitmap imagesfor effective and efficient content integrity protection. This work is complementary and largely enhances the algorithm presented in [3], by implementing a more accurate function to store the watermark bits into the Karhunen-Loève transform coefficients; this function is derived from the work by Lin et al. [4]. Even though the techniques used here are not novel per se, their combined use to improve performances and detection ability is. It is worth to point out that our approach can yield better quality watermarked images in comparison to state-of-the-art techniques.

The paper is organized as follows: the next section recalls some works having a content on the same topics, then the Karhunen-Loève transform is briefly introduced in Section 3, whilst in Section 4 the main characteristics of Genetic Algorithms are presented. Then, the proposed watermark insertion and verification algorithms are described in Section 5. Experimental results are reported in Section 6 and a discussion is presented in Section 7. The final section draws some conclusions on the method and the improvements shown.

2   Related Works

As many other works make use of the Karhunen-Loève transform and Genetic Algorithms (GAs), we review some of them, along with some fragile watermarking algorithms developed for image authentication and content integrity.

We first present algorithms for fragile watermarking, then conclude this section with some algorithms for robust watermarking.

[5] presents an algorithm that can be applied to color and gray-scale images authentication. A binary watermark (typically an image) is embedded one bit per pixel. A secret binary LookUp Table (a function of three LUTs for color images) is applied to each pixel and the resulting value is compared with the watermark bit to be stored in the pixel: in case of differing values, the pixel is slightly modified, with the lowest distortion, so that the result from the LUT equals the watermark bit. The possible error introduced by the pixel modification is diffused to the nearest pixels

that have not yet been processed: this procedure is performed in such a way as to maintain unaltered the average intensity of each color channel. The authentication applies the LUT (or LUTs) to the pixels extracting the stored watermark and compares it with the original: in case of differences a tampering is detected.

The image authentication algorithm proposed in [6] inserts a fragile watermark in the z-transform zeroes computed from blocks of the image. In detail, rows of 1×N pixels are considered as a signal which is z-transformed; then, the real negative zero in the z-plane is modified according to the watermark bit to be inserted, and the new zeroes are inversely transformed in pixel values (to be rounded). The verification performs the same process by extracting the bits from the real negative zeroes of the z-transform of the pixel blocks and compares them with the original watermark bits.

In [7] the fragile watermarking method is based on Singular Value Decomposition (SVD). The image is divided into square blocks that are SVD transformed after a Least Significant Bit (LSB) substitution of the pixel values. Then, the computed singular values are used, along with the watermark, to modify once more the pixels' LSBs producing the watermarked blocks. The secret parameters of the method are the watermark and the keys used for LSB substitution and permutation. The paper also proposes the application to color images inserting the watermark into the R, G and B channels.

[8] proposes the use of chaotic maps for image authentication and tamper detection. The image is firstly scrambled with an Arnold cat map, then the watermark is XOR-ed with a chaotic sequence (generated from a secret key) and the result is substituted to the LSB plane of the scrambled image. Then, the watermarked image is obtained from another application of an Arnold cat map that de-scrambles the pixels into their original positions. The method resists to attacks like copy and paste, collage and text addition.

The algorithm by Lin et al. [4] divides the image into blocks and uses a weighted sum of pixel values to embed n authentication bits in every block by modifying one pixel by +1 or −1 gray level. We note that the watermark to be embedded is transformed using a secret key in an attempt to increase the security of the method.

The KLT is used in [9] to insert a watermark into a host image divided into blocks: every block is KLT transformed and the obtained coefficients are modified according to unitary matrices defined by the secret watermark. Then, the inverse transform is applied to obtain the marked image. The verification of the originality of an image requires both the original image and the watermark.

In [10] different intelligent optimization algorithms (IOA), among which GAs, are compared in the application of a fragile watermarking method based on DCT. The watermark bits are inserted into the LSB of DCT coefficients. The IOAs are used to compensate for the rounding errors when transforming from the real coefficients space to the integer pixel domain, addressing a problem similar to the one explained in [3].

Also Botta et al. [3] apply a GA to compensate for pixel rounding errors when inserting a fragile watermark in some selected KLT coefficients of image blocks. In that paper, the KLT is used for the security of the method to create a secret embedding space, and one bit is inserted in every chosen coefficient. Differently, in the present paper, the watermark bits are distributed among a set of selected coefficients with an embedding rule derived from [4], which allows for improved image quality.

The following papers present algorithms for the robust watermarking of images and are relevant here because they either use KLT or GAs.

Barni et al. [11]employ the KLT to de-correlate the RGB color bands in the development of a robust watermarking algorithm. The watermark is embedded in the Discrete Fourier Transform coefficients of the new bands, also taking into account the characteristics of the Human Visual System. To reduce the error rate at the detection side, the authors apply the Neyman-Pearson criterion to compute the threshold used in the comparison with a likelihood function.

In [12] a robust image watermarking scheme is developed using the SVD. The singular values are used to detect the complexity of the considered blocks and to choose only those with more complexity. The binary watermark is inserted by modifying two components of one of the SVD vectors, using a threshold to have robustness. To balance between image quality and resistance to attacks aimed at removing the watermark, a GA is used to tune the threshold values for every block. The reported results show a good resistance to attacks.

Also [13] presents a work aimed at robust watermarking of images. The approach uses a cooperative co-evolutionary GA (CCGA) to select a viable wavelet packet basis; this basis is again used by a CCGA to choose the wavelet sub-bands employed to compute the coefficients for watermark embedding. The authors show that the method has a good robustness against some image processing attacks producing images at an acceptable quality.

3   The Karhunen-Loève Transform

A linear transformation is a function that maps a vector x from one space to a vector y into another space, by means of a transformation kernel defined by a matrix A (which is also a basis for the first space). The transformation may be written as $y=Ax$, and the inverse transformation as $x=A^{-1}y$. Depending on the kernel, various linear transformations may be defined: the most widely known are the Fourier transform, the discrete cosine transform (used in the JPEG standard), the Walsh transform and the Hadamard transform. All these transformations have the characteristic that when the size of the vector is defined, then the kernel is fixed.

A linear transformation that does not have a fixed kernel is the Karhunen-Loève transform (KLT) [14]. The kernel of this transformation is computed from a set of (column) vectors with the following procedure:

- the average vector $m = E\{x\}$ is computed;
- the covariance matrix C is then derived: $C = E\{(x-m)(x-m)'\}$;
- the eigenvectors of C are computed, and are arranged as rows in the kernel matrix A by non-increasing value of their associated eigenvalues.

To perform the KLT of a vector z it is sufficient to apply the following formula:

$$y = A\,(z-m) \tag{1}$$

The components of y are called coefficients of the transform, and the position of each coefficient is called order of the coefficient. The space in which y is expressed is called transformed domain or frequency domain. From y it is possible to obtain z using the inverse KLT:

$$z = A^{-1}\,y + m \tag{2}$$

Dividing an image into contiguous non-overlapping blocks of the same size, and considering them as vectors, a KLT kernel can be derived from any image.

4   Genetic Algorithms

A Genetic Algorithm (GA) is a computing paradigm that simulates the biological evolution of individuals towards an "optimum" according to some criteria. When the solution to a problem may be coded as a set of parameters, then different realizations of these parameters form a population of individuals that are evolved as a biological species according to *genetic operators*.

To find an optimal solution to a problem, a GA is initialized with a randomly generated population (having a pre-defined size) of individuals. Then, for a limited number of generations, or epochs, the individuals are mated and mutated to generate new individuals. Each of them is evaluated according to a fitness function that expresses the quality of the solution it is coding.

In each epoch a number of individuals from the population are selected for reproduction: many methods may be used in this selection process, we used the tournament selection where pairs of individuals are chosen and the ones with best fitness are considered for reproduction. To reproduce individuals a crossover operator is applied with probability p_c: it exchanges a randomly chosen subset of parameters between the mated individuals and produces two new offsprings. Every new offspring has a probability p_m of having one of its parameters randomly modified: this operation is called mutation and aims at widening the exploration of the solution's space.

Afterwards, the new individuals are evaluated according to the fitness function, and inserted into the population: again, several strategies can be used to implement this step, such as partial or total replacement of the old population, tournament selection, etc. If a termination criterion is met, then the evolution stops, otherwise a new epoch is started.

Typical termination criterions are:
- maximum number of generations reached: the best individual found so far is returned;
- the fitness of the best individual in the population does not improve for a certain number of generations: this individual is returned.

5   The Proposed Algorithm

The method we propose (called Weighted-Sum KLT, or WS-KLT) can be applied to any image I_h in bitmap format and generates an image containing a fragile watermark. The watermark is computed from features extracted from the host image I_h and a secret key image I_k. The secret key image defines the hidden KLT space in which the watermark (a bit string) is inserted.

The full watermarking algorithm consists of five modules, that we will briefly describe in the following, focusing more on the insertion step which is the core of the whole procedure.

In the following we assume that I_h has size $N{\times}M$, and we divide it into contiguous non-overlapping blocks (called sub-images) of size $n{\times}n$. We assume, for simplicity of discussion, that N and M are multiples of n.

Module 1: basis images generation

The first module generates the basis images from the key image. The basis is computed by dividing I_k into contiguous non-overlapping blocks of size $n{\times}n$ and considering the set of blocks as a random field of vectors from which a Karhunen-Loève basis is computed as previously presented. This module must be executed only once for every key image used.

Module 2: watermark generation

The second module generates the watermark. The binary watermark is obtained from a fixed set O_k of (four) pixels of I_k: the values of the pixels in O_k are used as indexes to pixels of I_h creating a set P_h; the pixels in P_h are, in turn, used as indexes to pixels of I_k, obtaining a set P_k; in this way the watermark is made dependent on both the host image and the key image, to prevent copy-and-paste and transplantation attacks [15]; the values of the set of pixels P_k are used as seeds to a cryptographic hash function like SHA-3 (i.e. the Keccak algorithm [16]), which is called a sufficient number of times to create a watermark W of the required length.

This is a very simple mechanism, that can be made as complex as desired. Anyway, the security of this method depends on the security of the key image: if an attacker knows the secret image, then any more complex selection procedure would not help.

To let the verifier compute the same watermark, the pixels of I_h used in this step will not be modified by the insertion algorithm: anyway we suggest to keep this set small (e.g. two or four pixels). If an attacker modifies any one of the pixels in P_h, the watermark generated by the verification procedure is quite likely to be different from the one inserted, and therefore the image will be found tampered in almost every block.

This procedure must be executed for every host image that must be protected with a fragile watermark.

Module 3: watermark insertion

This module is the core of the procedure: I_h is divided into contiguous non-overlapping blocks (sub-images) of size $n{\times}n$ and s watermark bits are inserted into each such blocks: thus the watermark length is $s \times N \times M/n^2$. In particular, each portion of s bits of the watermark is inserted into a group of $u=2^{s-1}$ $(u \leq n^2)$ KLT coefficients extracted from the sub-image. The orders of the used coefficients constitute a set that must be defined prior to the use of the algorithm, and must be made available for the verification step (but does not need to be kept secret). It should be pointed out that, in principle, the orders could be different in every sub-image, but, for simplicity, we chose coefficients of the same order for all sub-images.

The insertion of the watermark bits into the sub-image is made according to a procedure inspired by Lin et al.'s paper [4], but more flexible; first of all, the s bits of the watermark are considered as binary digits expressing a number L in the range [0, 2^s-1]; then the procedure computes a weighted sum of the selected coefficients c_1, c_2, ..., c_u according to the following equation:

$$L' = (\sum_{i=1}^{u} i \times [c_i]) \bmod 2^s$$ (3)

where $[c_i]$ denotes the integer part of c_i.

If $L'=L$ then the coefficients c_1, c_2, ..., c_u already contain the watermark and nothing needs to be done; however, when $L' \neq L$, the KLT coefficients need to be changed. Since these coefficients are a function of the sub-image pixels (computed as in equation (1)), we use a genetic algorithm (GA) in order to find the almost optimal modifications to the pixels of the sub-image that allow for the watermark bits to be correctly extracted from the KLT coefficients. The use of the correct number u of coefficients according to Lin et al.'s algorithm allows for the GA to modify the pixels in order to change, in principle, only one KLT coefficient; anyway, the GA may change as many coefficients as it needs to obtain the best value for the fitness function.

The GA evolves a population of individuals that are vectors of $n \times n$ pixel intensity modifications of typically ±1 or ±2 gray levels (but mostly are 0). The GA usually runs for a maximum number of generations, but it can be terminated as soon as a viable solution is found. The individual fitness function guides the GA towards the better solutions, and takes into account the distortion of the modified sub-image w.r.t. the original one.

Let us consider a sub-image S_i. The steps involved in the insertion of the watermark bits encoded as a number L are the followings:
1. apply a modification (represented by a GA individual) to the pixels of S_i and obtain S_i^m;
2. compute the KLT coefficients form S_i^m and then compute the weighted sum (3) from the chosen coefficients obtaining L';
3. if $L=L'$ and the distortion is low then stop and proceed to the next sub-image;
4. else go to step 1.

The GA searches for an individual that produces low distortion w.r.t. the original sub-image and allows for the watermark bits to be correctly recovered. When all the sub-images are processed with the previous algorithm, then the watermark has been completely embedded into the image.

Module 4: watermark extraction

Watermark extraction is used by both the insertion module (in the GA fitness function that checks if the sub-image is effectively storing the watermark bits) and the verification module, and needs the key image to derive the KLT basis.

Given a watermarked image, this is firstly divided into sub-images of size $n \times n$. From every such sub-image the watermark bits are extracted from the selected KLT coefficients according to formula (3). The concatenation of the watermark bits of every sub-image makes a bit string which is the extracted watermark W^e.

Module 5: tamper detection/verification

To detect possible image tampering, the extracted watermark W^e is compared with the watermark W that should be contained (the latter may be computed according to the steps in module 2): differing bit values in the same position will indicate a tampered sub-image because an alteration should have modified the pixels and consequently the KLT coefficients.

6   Experimental Results

In order to assess the resulting quality of images watermarked with WS-KLT, we report the average *PSNR* (Peak Signal-to-Noise Ratio) and *SSIM* (Structural Similarity index [17], which measures the degradation and the quality of the resulting image in a way similar to a human evaluation; its value is between −1 and +1, where the largest value means that two images are identical, i.e. no distortion)values along with standard deviations computed over a database of 1000 gray-scale real images taken from [18] (the images are 256 gray levels, i.e. 8 bpp, bitmaps of size 256×256 pixels) by inserting a watermark of 8 bits per block of 8×8 pixels. In this study, we mainly focused on the analysis of the watermarking algorithm properties, and set the GA parameters to default values (population size=100, p_m=0.04, p_c=0.9, terminate if best individual fitness is stable for the last 10 generations).

For comparison, we report the performances of other algorithms [3], [4], [5], [6], [7] and [8] computed by running on the same set of 1000 images an implementation of these watermarking schemes; being the set of images quite large, it is possible to consider the given values representative of the performances of these methods.

Table 1. Quality assessment of different fragile watermarking schemes

Watemarking scheme	PSNR (dB)	SSIM
Yeung and Mintzer [5]	46.06 ± 0.30	0.992
Ho et al. [6]	35.64 ± 1.84	0.898
Rawat and Raman [8]	51.14 ± 0.01	0.997
Oktavia and Lee [7]	51.14 ± 0.01	0.997
Lin et al. [4]	58.06 ± 13.96	0.999
Botta et al.[3]	53.12 ± 0.14	0.998
WS-KLT	**60.02 ± 0.06**	**0.999**

The comparison carried out in Table 1 shows that WS-KLT outperforms all of these schemes in terms of quality, both *PSNR* and *SSIM*. However, it should be pointed out that Lin et al.'s algorithm has a very high standard deviation, meaning that for some images its *PSNR* is higher than WS-KLT, while for others it is very poor. We think this is due to a conceptual problem in Lin et al.'s algorithm, for which we suggested a revision in [19]. Furthermore, it is worth to mention that the number of watermark bits depends on the method and varies a lot from one to another: [5], [7] and [8] embed one bit per pixel, while [3], [6] and WS-KLT embed 8 bits in a block of 64 pixels, and [4] embeds 8 bits in a block of 128 pixels.

7   Discussion

By inserting the watermark into a transformed space instead of the pixel space, WS-KLT is more flexible than the method proposed in [4]. As a matter of fact, in Lin et al. [4] the number of watermark bits per block is strongly related to the size of the block: in order to insert s bits into a block, the size of the block must be 2^{s-1} pixels. In WS-KLT, instead, in a block of 2^{s-1} coefficients we can insert up to 2^{s-1} watermark bits (one bit per coefficient) without varying the size of the block.

The method is quite simple: let the size of a block be 64 (2^6) coefficients. For $s < 7$, we just select 2^{s-1} coefficients, and use them to compute the weighted sum in expression (3). For $s = 7$, we use all the 64 coefficients. For $s > 7$, we need a bit of arithmetic. We can split the KLT coefficients into two (or more) disjoint groups and store different portions of the watermark in each group. As an example, let $s=12$, and split the 64 KLT coefficients into 2 groups u_1 and u_2 of $2^5 = 32$ KLT coefficients each so that we can store $s_1 = 6$ bits in u_1 and $s_2 = 6$ bits in u_2, 12 watermark bits as requested, in a block of only 64 coefficients. In principle, we could create 64 groups of 1 coefficient each, and insert a single watermark bit in each group, so arriving to 64 watermark bits in total in a block. Obviously, the GA has to do a lot of work to guarantee that every group of coefficients stores the correct bits. The resulting quality of the image is only slightly affected, but the localization capability of the method remains the same whatever number of watermark bits are inserted. As a comparison, by inserting a watermark of 12288 bits into 1000 images of 256×256 pixels with Lin et al.'s algorithm (block size 2^5), we obtain a *PSNR* of 48.84±12.8 dB, while with WS-KLT we obtain 57.41±0.06 dB.

7.1   Tamper Detection Ability

As Lin et al.'s algorithm uses a smaller block size(2^5 pixels), it has a better tampering localization ability than WS-KLT in this case. Anyway, it should be pointed out that a design flaw of Lin et al.'s algorithm allows an attacker to successfully tamper an image in such a way that it always goes undetected (simply change by +2 the first pixel in a block and by −1 the second one).

The detection ability of WS-KLT depends on the number of coefficients used to compute the weighted-modulo sum and on how they are influenced by a tampering of the image block. In fact, changing the value of a single pixel in a block may change the value of more than one of the selected coefficients, but being the coefficient space secret, an attacker cannot anticipate if the tampering will go undetected or not.

In order to check the detection ability of WS-KLT, we performed a sensitivity analysis by modifying a single pixel in a block of ±1 (and then ±2) gray levels, and checking if the tamper is detected. Then, we repeated this process for every pixel in a block, for every block in an image and computed the percentage of tampered blocks actually recognized by WS-KLT. It results that WS-KLT detects ~83% tampered blocks for ±1 pixel value modifications and ~97% for ±2 pixel value modifications. These experiments were aimed at evaluating the detection performance of the algorithm when just one single pixel is altered. This should be considered as the bottom line of performances of any detection algorithm. All typical attacks (such as global image processing, e.g. lossy compression, brightness/contrast adjustment, and local manipulations, e.g. object deletion, replacement, etc.) are likely to alter more than 1 pixel of the image and then the detection performance is more likely to be higher in these cases. For example, we tested the capability of the developed algorithm in detecting changes made by JPEG lossy compression (one of the most common image processing tasks) at various quality levels (85, 90, 95, 100). In all cases, using either JPEG or the new JPEG2000 standards, we got 99.998% tampered blocks.

To improve these percentages, one can either insert a larger number of watermark bits per block (but slightly degrading the image quality) or use a larger number of coefficients. The former is generally used to reduce the probability $(1/2^s)$ that a single random block replacement goes undetected. Actually, the latter can be easily done, and even all coefficients in a block can be used to compute the weighted-modulo sum independently of the number of watermark bits to be inserted. In this case, the detection ability increases to 99.49% for ±1 pixel value modifications, with $s=8$ bits per block (of 64 pixels).

8   Conclusions

In this paper, we presented an elegant algorithm for the fragile watermarking of images in bitmap format by extending our previous work with a recently proposed insertion function. The presentedmethod inserts a binary watermark into some coefficients of a KLT space defined with a secret key image. Given that the watermark and the space of insertion depend on a secret key (image), the security of the method is strong: an attacker is not able to compute the watermark bits nor to determine the coefficient values containing the watermark, unless (s)he spots the secret image. When the key shared for the authentication should be transmitted with a low bandwidth requirement (e.g., for real time applications) or when the space for the key storage is an issue (e.g. smartcard applications), a key image generated from a secret random seed (in place of a real image) may be used.

The proposed algorithm (WS-KLT) has a higher sensitivity to pixel tampering, a higher *PSNR* (see Table 1) and lower computation times (16.11±0.3s) w.r.t. the algorithm we proposed in [3] (~56% for ±1 pixel value modifications, ~83% for ±2 pixel value modifications, 53.12 ± 0.14dB, 45.8±1.2s, respectively). We showed that the method has excellent performance (*PSNR* > 60 dB) in comparison to other techniques. The only issue is the computation time of the algorithm: on average, it takes 16.1 seconds to insert a watermark, w.r.t. less than 1 second for [4]. Anyway, the watermark verification process takes only 0.065 seconds on average and allows for real time processing of the watermarked images. Moreover, the verification process time scales linearly with the image size.

Two important directions for further research are reducing the computational time taken by our technique and extending the algorithm to color images represented in various formats.

Acknowledgements. We thank Prof. A.E.Werbrouck for his comments which helped improve the readability of the paper.

References

1. Cox, I.J., Miller, M.L., Bloom, J.A., Fridrich, J., Kalker, T.: Digital Watermarking and Steganography, 2nd edn. Morgan Kaufmann Publishers Inc., San Francisco (2008)
2. He, H., Chen, F., Tai, H.-M., Kalker, T., Zhang, J.: Performance Analysis of a Block-Neighborhood-Based Self-Recovery Fragile Watermarking Scheme. IEEE Transactions on Information Forensics and Security 7(1), 185–196 (2012)
3. Botta, M., Cavagnino, D., Pomponiu, V.: KL-F: Karhunen-Loève Based Fragile Watermarking. In: 5th International Conference on Network and System Security, NSS 2011, pp. 65–72 (2011)
4. Lin, P.-Y., Lee, J.-S., Chang, C.-C.: Protecting the content integrity of digital imagery with fidelity preservation. ACM Trans. Multimedia Comp. Commun. and Appl. 7(3), 15:1–15:20, Article 15 (August 2011)
5. Yeung, M.M., Mintzer, F.: An invisible watermarking technique for image verification. In: Proc. of International Conference on Image Processing, vol. 2, pp. 680–683 (1997)
6. Ho, A.T.S., Zhu, X.-Z., Shen, J., Marziliano, P.: Fragile watermarking based on encoding of the zeroes of the z-transform. IEEE Transactions on Information Forensics and Security 3(3), 567–569 (2008)
7. Oktavia, V., Lee, W.-H.: A Fragile Watermarking Technique for Image Authentication Using Singular Value Decomposition. In: Aizawa, K., Nakamura, Y., Satoh, S. (eds.) PCM 2004. LNCS, vol. 3332, pp. 42–49. Springer, Heidelberg (2005)
8. Rawat, S., Raman, B.: A chaotic system based fragile watermarking scheme for image tamper detection. AEU-International Journal of Electronics and Communications 65, 840–847 (2011)
9. Dafas, P., Stathaki, T.: Digital image watermarking using block-based Karhunen-Loeve transform. In: Proceedings of the 3rd IEEE International Symposium on Image and Signal Processing and Analysis, pp. 1072–1075 (2003)
10. Aslantas, V., Ozer, S., Ozturk, S.: Improving the performance of DCT-based fragile watermarking using intelligent optimization algorithms. Optics Communications 282(14), 2806–2817 (2009)
11. Barni, M., Bartolini, F., De Rosa, A., Piva, A.: Color image watermarking in the Karhunen-Loeve transform domain. Journal of Electronic Imaging 11(1), 87–95 (2002)

12. Lai, C.-C., Yeh, C.-H., Ko, C.-H., Chiang, C.-Y.: Image Watermarking Scheme Using Genetic Algorithm. In: Proc. of Sixth International Conference on Genetic and Evolutionary Computing (ICGEC), pp. 476–479 (2012)
13. Chen, Y.-H., Huang, H.-C.: Robust Image Watermarking Based on Coevolutionary Genetic Algorithm. In: Proc. of Sixth International Conference on Genetic and Evolutionary Computing (ICGEC), pp. 484–487 (2012)
14. Gonzalez, R.C., Wintz, P.: Digital Image Processing, 2nd edn. Addison-Wesley Publishing Company (1987)
15. Barreto, P.S.L.M., Kim, H.Y., Rijmen, V.: Toward secure publickeyblockwise fragile authentication watermarking. In: IEE Proceedings - Vision, Image and Signal Processing 2002, vol. 148(2), pp. 57–62 (2002)
16. The Keccak sponge function family (2012), http://keccak.noekeon.org/
17. Wang, Z., Bovik, A.C.: Mean squared error: love it or leave it? A new look at signal fidelity measures. IEEE Signal Processing Magazine 26(1), 98–117 (2009)
18. Li, L.-J., Wang, G., Li, F.-F.: OPTIMOL: automatic Object Picture collecTion via Incremental Model Learning. In: IEEE Conference on Computer Vision and Pattern Recognition, pp. 1–8 (2008)
19. Botta, M., Cavagnino, D., Pomponiu, V.: 'Protecting the Content Integrity of Digital Imagery with Fidelity Preservation': an improved version. Submitted to ACM Transactions on Multimedia Computing Communications and Applications (2013)

Author Index